THE INVENTION
OF AFRICA

African Systems of Thought

General Editors
Charles S. Bird
Ivan Karp

Contributing Editors
Thomas O. Beidelman
James Fernandez
Luc de Heusch
John Middleton
Roy Willis

THE INVENTION
OF AFRICA

Gnosis, Philosophy, and the
Order of Knowledge

V. Y. MUDIMBE

INDIANA UNIVERSITY PRESS
Bloomington and Indianapolis

JAMES CURREY
London

This book is a publication of

James Currey Ltd
73 Botley Rd
Oxford
OX2 OBS

and

Indiana University Press
601 North Morton Street
Bloomington, Indiana 47404-3797 USA

http://iupress.indiana.edu

Telephone orders   800-842-6796
Fax orders   812-855-7931
Orders by e-mail   iuporder@indiana.edu

Library of Congress Cataloging-in-Publication Data

Mudimbe, V. Y., date
The invention of Africa.
(African systems of thought)
Bibliography: p.
Includes index.
1. Philosophy, African. 2. Knowledge, Theory of.
I. Title. II. Series.
B5310.M84   1988   199'.6   87-45324
ISBN 978-0-253-33126-7
ISBN 978-0-253-20468-4 (pbk.)

12   13   14   12   11   10

British Library Cataloguing in Publication Data
Mudimbe, V. Y., date
The invention of Africa : gnosis, philosophy,
and the order of knowledge.—(African systems of thought).
1. African philosophy
I. Title II. Series
199'.6
ISBN 978-0-85255-203-2 (paper)

To the memory of James S. Coleman

Mors ipsa beatior inde est, quod per
cruciamina leti via panditur ardua iustis, et ad
astra doloribus itur.

—Prudentius, *Hymnus Circa Exequias
Defuncti*

CONTENTS

CONTENTS

INTRODUCTION

This book evolved accidentally, as a result of an invitation to prepare a survey of African philosophy. Strictly speaking, the notion of African philosophy refers to contributions of Africans practicing philosophy within the defined framework of the discipline and its historical tradition (Horton, 1976; Hountondji, 1977). It is only metaphorically, or, at best, from a historicist perspective, that one would extend the notion of philosophy to African traditional systems of thought, considering them as dynamic processes in which concrete experiences are integrated into an order of concepts and discourses (Ladrière, 1979:14–15). I have thus preferred to speak of African *gnosis*. J. Fabian used the notion of *gnosis* in his analysis of a charismatic movement (1969). In this book, the wider frame seems better suited to the range of problems addressed, all of which are based on a preliminary question: to what extent can one speak of an African knowledge, and in what sense? Etymologically, *gnosis* is related to *gnosko*, which in the ancient Greek means "to know."

Specifically, *gnosis* means seeking to know, inquiry, methods of knowing, investigation, and even acquaintance with someone. Often the word is used in a more specialized sense, that of higher and esoteric knowledge, and thus it refers to a structured, common, and conventional knowledge, but one strictly under the control of specific procedures for its use as well as transmission. *Gnosis* is, consequently, different from *doxa* or opinion, and, on the other hand, cannot be confused with *episteme*, understood as both science and general intellectual configuration.

The title is thus a methodological tool: it embraces the question of what is and what is not African philosophy and also orients the debate in another direction by focusing on conditions of possibility of philosophy as part of the larger body of knowledge on Africa called "Africanism." I use this central notion of conditions of possibility in accordance with a recent tradition in which Michel Foucault could, for example, define his own intellectual ambition in terms of its dependence on alterations that Jean Hyppolite introduced into Hegelian philosophy (Foucault, 1982:235–37). What the notion of conditions of possibility indicates is that discourses have not only sociohistorical origins but also epistemological contexts. It is the latter which make them possible and which can also account for them in an essential way.

I shall be dealing with discourses on African societies, cultures, and peoples as signs of something else. I would like to interrogate their modalities, significance, or strategies as a means of understanding the type of knowledge which is being proposed. In fact, I do not address the classical issues of African anthropology or history, the results of which might or might not mirror an objective African reality. Rather I am looking *upstream* of the results, precisely at what makes them possible, before accepting them as commentary on revelation, or restitution, of an African experience.

The book attempts, therefore, a sort of archaeology of African *gnosis* as a system of knowledge in which major philosophical questions recently have arisen: first, concerning the form, the content, and the style of "Africanizing" knowledge; second, concerning the status of traditional systems of thought and their possible relation to the normative genre of knowledge. From the first chapters, which interrogate Western images of Africa, through the chapters analyzing the power of anthropologists, missionaries, and ideologists, to the last, on philosophy, I am directly concerned with the processes of transformation of types of knowledge.

This orientation has two consequences: on the one hand, an apparent attenuation of the originality of African contributions and, on the other, an overemphasis upon external procedures, such as anthropological or religious influences. The fact of the matter is that, until now, Western interpreters as well as African analysts have been using categories and conceptual systems which depend on a Western epistemological order. Even in the most explicitly "Afrocentric" descriptions, models of analysis explicitly or implicitly, knowingly or unknowingly, refer to the same order. Does this mean that African *Weltanschauungen* and African traditional systems of thought are unthinkable and cannot be made explicit within the framework of their own rationality? My own claim is that thus far the ways in which they have been evaluated and the means used to explain them relate to theories and methods whose constraints, rules, and systems of operation suppose a non-African epistemological locus. From this viewpoint the claim of some African philosophers such as O. Bimwenyi (1981a) and F. Eboussi-Boulaga (1981) that they represent an epistemological hiatus should be taken seriously. What does this mean for the field of African studies? To what extent can their perspectives modify the fact of a silent dependence on a Western *episteme*? Would it then be possible to renew the notion of tradition from, let us say, a radical *dispersion* of African cultures?

These are the most important issues in the debate on African philosophy. They oblige me to clarify immediately my position about representatives of African *gnosis*. Who is speaking about it? Who has the right and the credentials to produce it, describe it, comment upon it, or at least present opinions about it? No one takes offense if an anthropologist is questioned. But strangely enough, Africanists—and among them anthropologists—have decided to separate the "real" African from the westernized African and to rely strictly upon the first. Rejecting this myth of the "man in the bush," J. Jahn chose to "turn to those Africans who have their own opinion and who will determine the future of Africa: those, in other words, of whom it is said that they are trying to revive the African tradition" (Jahn, 1961:16). Yet, Jahn's decision seems exaggerated. I would prefer a wider authority: intellectuals' discourses as a critical library and, if I could, the experience of rejected forms of wisdom which are not part of the structures of political power and scientific knowledge.

In sum, rather than simply accept the authority of qualified representatives of African cultures, I would like to study the theme of the foundations of discourse about Africa. It is obvious that in such a subjective work I cannot claim to offer an exhaustive report analyzing all present tendencies or encompassing all within its frame. This book is only a critical synthesis of the complex questions about knowledge and power in and on Africa.

The presuppositions and hypotheses outlined above indicate a range of theoretical alternatives that I have been working on for the last fifteen years. If, from *L'Autre face du royaume* (1973) to *L'Odeur du père* (1982b) and this contribution, my general view has somewhat changed, I believe that my major thesis has remained the same with respect to the analogical form of the social sciences and the history of Africanist discourse. These disciplines do not provide a real comprehension of the *Weltanschauungen* studied. Yet one can also say that it is in these very discourses that African worlds have been established as realities for knowledge. And today Africans themselves read, challenge, rewrite these discourses as a way of explicating and defining their culture, history, and being. It is obvious that since its inception Africanism has been producing its own motives as well as its objects, and fundamentally commenting upon its own being, while systematically promoting a *gnosis*. From this *gnosis* ultimately arose both African discourses on otherness and ideologies of alterity of which négritude, black personality, and African philosophy might be considered to be the best established in the present-day intellectual history of Africa.

Some of my critics (e.g., Mpoyi-Bwatu, 1983; N'Zembele, 1983; Willame, 1976) have aggressively urged me to draw political implications from my conclusions. Others, such as Mouralis (1981, 1984a), have instead thought my project, that of dealing with taboo themes, overly ambitious. I only hope that some people would agree that the task of bringing philosophy to some of its own limits and metaphors in social science, and that of questioning philosophy's ambiguous contacts with unphilosophical discourses, justify my commitment not to philosophy, nor to an *invented Africa,* but to what it essentially means to be an African and a philosopher today. I am grateful to L. Kaumba whose phenomenological study of the significance of identity in my literary work (Kaumba, 1986) forced me to reevaluate the implications of my theses about the Same and the Other in philosophical anthropology. Yet his critique meets my fundamental beliefs: identity and alterity are always given to others, assumed by an I- or a We-subject, structured in multiple individual histories, and, at any rate, expressed or silenced according to personal desires vis-à-vis an *episteme*.

This also implies that from a methodological viewpoint I think, as Foucault put it, that "discourse in general and scientific discourse in particular, is so complex a reality that we not only can but should approach it at different levels and with different methods" (1973: xiv). For this essay I have chosen an archaeological perspective that allows me to address the issue of the progressive constitution of an African order of knowledge. However, for reasons having to do with the bizarre nature of some of the sources used— mainly the anthropological ones—I have preferred not to distinguish the epistemological level of knowledge from the archaeological level of knowledge.

I am deeply indebted to the Joint Committee on African Studies of the Social Science Research Council in conjunction with the American Council of Learned Societies. They invited me to write this study and gave me the necessary facilities. A briefer and slightly different form of chapters three and five was published by the *African Studies Review* in 1985.

The bibliography at the end reveals my intellectual debt to many works and scholars. In this bibliography I present books I have indeed used. I did not think it important to include such authors as Aristotle, Descartes, Diderot, Rousseau, or Voltaire to whom I sometimes refer. In the same manner, it did not seem useful to include a number of narratives and texts by explorers, colonial theorists, and popes. They generally express a normative *doxa* and its submission to an *episteme*. As such, they reveal the development of anthropological and philosophical theories. As to non-English books I quote, I have often—but not always—consulted the originals, even when the existing translations were excellent. Yet apart from stated exceptions, I generally make reference to English versions when available. If an English edition is not mentioned in the bibliography, the translation is my own.

I must express explicitly my gratitude to some friends and colleagues without whom this book would, perhaps, not have been written, or certainly not yet finished: Elizabeth Boyi for her encouragement; Christie Agawu for her editorial assistance; Kofi Agawu, Paul Riesman, and Ivan Karp for their critical evaluations. I am particularly grateful to Arnd Bohm, Walter Michener, David Newbury, and Mildred Mortimer, whose patient reading of the entire manuscript and critical comments helped me clarify many points and translate my Gallic style into the English language. I extend my gratitude to Haverford College and in particular to Robert Stevens, Robert Gavin, Jr., Wyatt MacGaffey, and Judy Young for their support and generosity. Finally I have to express my special thanks to Shirley Averill for her useful suggestions, the typing of many drafts of the manuscript, and her unfailing patience. Roberta L. Diehl and Janet Rabinowitch, my editors, deserve grateful acknowledgment for their advice, support, and efficiency. Needless to say, the ideas, hypotheses, and interpretations put forth in this book are completely my responsibility.

THE INVENTION
OF AFRICA

I

DISCOURSE OF POWER AND KNOWLEDGE OF OTHERNESS

Colonizing Structure and Marginality

> Lord have pity on us! . . . *"The human race?"*
> Phyllis exclaimed, stressing the second word
> in her astonishment. "That's what it says
> here," Jinn assured her. "Don't start off by
> interrupting me."
>
> P. BOULLE, *Planet of the Apes.*

The scramble for Africa, and the most active period of colonization, lasted less than a century. These events, which involved the greater part of the African continent, occurred between the late nineteenth and the mid-twentieth centuries. Although in African history the colonial experience represents but a brief moment from the perspective of today, this moment is still charged and controversial, since, to say the least, it signified a new historical form and the possibility of radically new types of discourses on African traditions and cultures. One might think that this new historical form has meant, from its origins, the negation of two contradictory myths; namely, the "Hobbesian picture of a pre-European Africa, in which there was no account of Time; no Arts; no Letters; no Society; and which is worst of all, continued fear, and danger of violent death"; and "the Rousseauian picture of an African golden age of perfect liberty, equality and fraternity" (Hodgkin, 1957:174–75).

Although generalizations are of course dangerous, *colonialism* and *colonization* basically mean organization, arrangement. The two words derive from the latin word *colĕre,* meaning to cultivate or to design. Indeed the historical colonial experience does not and obviously cannot reflect the peaceful connotations of these words. But it can be admitted that the colonists (those settling a region), as well as the colonialists (those exploiting a territory by dominating a local majority) have all tended to organize and transform non-European areas into fundamentally European constructs.

I would suggest that in looking at this process, it is possible to use three main keys to account for the modulations and methods representative of colonial organization: the procedures of acquiring, distributing, and exploiting lands in colonies; the policies of domesticating natives; and the manner of managing ancient organizations and implementing new modes of production. Thus, three complementary hypotheses and actions emerge: the domination of physical space, the reformation of *natives'* minds, and the integration of local economic histories into the Western perspective. These complementary projects constitute what might be called the colonizing structure, which completely embraces the physical, human, and spiritual aspects of the colonizing experience (see, e.g., Christopher, 1984: 27–87). This structure clearly also indicates the projected metamorphosis envisioned, at great intellectual cost, by ideological and theoretical texts, which from the last quarter of the nineteenth century to the 1950s have proposed programs for "regenerating" the African space and its inhabitants.

A. Césaire thinks that

> the great historical tragedy of Africa has been not so much that it was too late in making contact with the rest of the world, as the manner in which that contact was brought about; that Europe began to propagate at a time when it had fallen into the hands of the most unscrupulous financiers and captains of industry. (Césaire, 1972:23)

He refers to the second part of the nineteenth century, emphasizing the coexistence of "imperialist" ideology, economic and political processes for extending control over African space, and capitalist institutions which ultimately led to dependence and underdevelopment (see also Mazrui, 1974). In a recent book, D. K. Fieldhouse writes that "only a dogmatist would attempt to state categorically that colonialism was either totally inconsistent with economic development in the dependencies or, alternatively, that it was the best possible medium for stimulating their growth. Colonialism was not sufficiently consistent over time to justify any such sweeping assertions, nor were its objectives sufficiently coherent to achieve any particular result" (1981:103). Thus colonialism has been some kind of historical accident, a "largely unplanned and, as it turned out, transient phase in the evolving relationship between more and less developed parts of the world" (1981:49). This accident, on the whole, according to this view, was not the worst thing that could have happened to the black continent.

Essentially, the argument is not new. It has a history that goes back to the debate of the early decades of this century. In his book, *Imperialism: A Study*, J. A. Hobson linked the scramble for Africa to capitalism and capitalist search for higher profits from colonial conquests. For J. A. Schumpeter, in 1919, colonialism as well as its cause, imperialism, did not obey logic. It was "non-rational and irrational purely instinctual inclinations toward war and conquest" that guided "objectless tendencies toward forcible expansion, without definite, utilitarian limits" (Schumpeter, 1951:83). Against the Leninist theme of *Imperialism, the Highest Stage of Capitalism* (1917), he stated that "a purely capitalist world offers no fertile soil to imperialist impulses . . . capitalism is by nature anti-imperialist" (1951:96). And in a voluminous document full of statistics, *The Balance Sheets of Imperialism* (1936), Grover Clark demonstrated that colonialism was not only economically irrational but also ruinous for the colonial powers.

On the opposite side, at the risk of being labeled dogmatists, Marxist interpreters accept the essentials of Lenin's thesis. The contention of neo-Marxists such as Samir Amin, Paul Baran, André Gunder-Frank, and Immanuel Wallerstein is that if colonialism was inconsistent with economic development, it was at least, since its inception, quite consistent with its own economic interests and objectives.

Accordingly, colonialism should have produced a body of knowledge on the means of exploiting dependencies (Rodney, 1981). It should also have produced a kind of empirical technique for implementing structural distortions by positing four main political propositions: first, priority given to the industrial revolution over the agricultural revolution; second, the simultaneous promotion of all branches of industry with a preferential approach to heavy industry; third, emphasis on tertiary and service activities; fourth, preference for exports to the detriment of the total economic system (Amin, 1973). The outcome of these policies was the process of underdevelopment initiated everywhere colonialism occurred. This process can be summed up in three points: First, the capitalist world system is such that parts of the system always develop at the expense of other parts, either by trade or by the transfer of surpluses. Second, the underdevelopment of dependencies is not only an absence of development, but also an organizational structure created under colonialism by bringing non-Western territory into the capitalist world. Third, despite their economic potential, dependencies lack the structural capacity for autonomy and sustained growth, since their economic fate is largely determined by the developed countries (Amin, 1974; Gunder-Frank, 1969; Wallerstein, 1979). From this last contention, some theorists have quickly hypothesized that if Japan has escaped the predicament of underdevelopment, it is because it is the only non-Western country to have escaped colonialism (Bigo, 1974:32, 60).

It seems impossible to make any statement about colonialism without being a dogmatist, particularly where economic organization and growth are concerned. Different as they are in form and intention, the Marxist and peripheral theories have nevertheless the same focus: overseas territory, totally reorganized and submitted to a Western model (Mommsen, 1983). The first theory considers colonial imperialism as a calculated and inevitable culmination of capitalism. If the latter discounts the planned aspect of colonialism, it still assumes the phenomenon to be a consequence of European industrialization and development, somehow bound to expand overseas. Whatever theory one accepts, the application remains the same, leading inevitably to what I have called the colonizing structure responsible for producing marginal societies, cultures, and human beings (Emmanuel, 1969; Bairoch, 1971). Therefore, for the purpose of clarity further on, let me make clear the dichotomy that this structure creates and which is a sign of what I. Sachs calls "europeocentrism." It is a model which

> dominates our thought and given its projection on the world scale by the expansion of capitalism and the colonial phenomenon, it marks contemporary culture imposing itself as a strongly conditioning model for some and forced deculturation for others. (Sachs, 1971:22; quoted by Bigo, 1974:23, n.3)

Because of the colonializing structure, a dichotomizing system has emerged, and with it a great number of current paradigmatic oppositions have developed: traditional versus modern; oral versus written and printed; agrarian and customary communities versus urban and industrialized civilization; subsistence economies versus highly productive economies. In Africa a great deal of attention is generally given to the evolution implied and promised by the passage from the former paradigms to the latter (Mudimbe, 1980). This presupposed jump from one extremity (underdevelopment) to the other (development) is in fact misleading. By emphasizing the formulation of techniques of economic change, the model tends to neglect a structural mode inherited from colonialism. Between the two extremes there is an intermediate, a diffused space in which social and economic events define the extent of marginality (Bigo, 1974:20; Shaw, 1985:33–36). At the economic level, for example, if the relatively low productivity of traditional processes of production (formerly adapted to the then-existing markets and range of trade and exchanges) has been disrupted by a new division of labor which depends upon international markets, then transformation has meant a progressive destruction of traditional realms of agriculture and crafts (Meillassoux, 1975:115). As a second example, one could regard the social disintegration of African societies and the growing urban proletariat as results of a destabilization of customary organizations by an incoherent establishment of new social arrangements and institutions (Turnbull, 1962; Memmi, 1966; Mair, 1975). Finally, if at the cultural and religious levels, through schools, churches, press, and audio-visual media the colonializing enterprise diffused new attitudes which were contradictory and richly complex models in terms of culture, spiritual values, and their transmission, it also broke the culturally unified and religiously integrated schema of most African traditions (Bimwenyi, 1981a). From that moment on the forms and formulations of the colonial culture and its aims were somehow the means of trivializing the whole traditional mode of life and its spiritual framework. The potential and necessary transformations meant that the mere presence of this new culture was a reason for the rejection of unadapted persons and confused minds.

Marginality designates the intermediate space between the so-called African tradition and the projected modernity of colonialism. It is apparently an urbanized space in which, as S. Amin noted, "vestiges of the past, especially the survival of structures that are still living realities (tribal ties, for example), often continue to hide the new structures (ties based on class, or on groups defined by their position in the capitalist system)" (1974:377). This space reveals not so much that new imperatives could achieve a jump into modernity, as the fact that despair gives this intermediate space its precarious pertinence and, simultaneously, its dangerous importance. As P. Bigo put it recently:

> The young nations rightly fear seeing their original world swallowed up in the whirlpools of industrial society and disappear forever, somewhat like animal species we try with difficulty and often in vain to protect against the invasion of technical man. (Bigo, 1974:23)

> There is no doubt that direct or indirect colonialism always provokes in the countries that experience it cultural constraint, a contamination the more profound as it is hidden. Lifestyles and modes of thinking of the dominant nations tend to impose themselves on the dominated nations. Morever, they are accepted, even sought after. Models spring up, alienating factors for the people who adopt them. (Bigo, 1974:24)

At any rate, this intermediary space could be viewed as the major signifier of underdevelopment. It reveals the strong tension between a modernity that often is an illusion of development, and a tradition that sometimes reflects a poor image of a mythical past. It also unveils the empirical evidence of this tension by showing concrete examples of developmental failures such as demographic imbalance, extraordinarily high birth rates, progressive disintegration of the classic family structure, illiteracy, severe social and economic disparities, dictatorial regimes functioning under the cathartic name of democracy, the breakdown of religious traditions, the constitution of syncretic churches, etc. (Bairoch, 1971; Bigo, 1974).

In general, troubled by such confusion, social scientists prefer to plead for a reassessment of programs of modernization. No doubt many theories are still to be proposed and plans to be made. Yet one may already understand that this marginal space has been a great problem since the beginning of the colonializing experience; rather than being a step in the imagined "evolutionary process," it has been the locus of paradoxes that called into question the modalities and implications of modernization in Africa.

Discursive Formations and Otherness

> It is certain that the learned Antelle, without being a misanthrope, was not interested at all

in human beings. He would often declare that
he did not expect much from them anymore . . .

P. BOULLE, *Planet of the Apes.*

The colonializing structure, even in its most extreme manifestations—such
as the crisis of South Africa (see, e.g., Seidman, 1985)—might not be the
only explanation for Africa's present-day marginality. Perhaps this marginality could, more essentially, be understood from the perspective of wider
hypotheses about the classification of beings and societies. It would be too
easy to state that this condition, at least theoretically, has been a consequence
of anthropological discourses. Since Turgot (who in the 1750s first classified
languages and cultures according to "whether the peoples [are] hunters,
shepherds, or husbandmen" [1913–1923, 1:172] and ultimately defined an
ascending path from savagery to commercial societies), non-Western marginality has been a sign both of a possible absolute beginning and of a
primitive foundation of conventional history. Rather than retracing an already too well-known evolutionary hallucination (Duchet, 1971; Hodgen,
1971), let us take a different angle by examining both the issues derived from
a fifteenth-century painting and the allocation of an "African object" to
nineteenth-century anthropology.

Commenting upon *Las Meninas* of Velasquez, M. Foucault writes: "the
painter is standing a little back from his canvas. He is glancing at his model;
perhaps he is considering whether to add some finishing touch, though it is
also possible that the first stroke has not yet been made . . ." (1973:3). The
painter is at one side of the canvas working or meditating on how to depict
his models. Once the painting is finished, it becomes both a given and a
reflection of what made it possible. And Foucault thinks that the order of *Las
Meninas* seems to be an example of "a representation [which] undertakes to
represent itself . . . in all its elements, with its images, the eyes to which it is
offered, the faces it makes visible, the gestures that call it into being." Yet in
the amazing complexity of this painting there is remarkable absence: "the
person it resembles and the person in whose eyes it is only a resemblance"
(Foucault, 1973:16).

Now let us consider Hans Burgkmair's painting *Exotic Tribe.* Is the
painter sitting back contemplating his exotic models? How many? It is not
even certain that a model is present in the room where Burgkmair is thinking
about ways of subsuming particular versions of human beings. The year is
1508. Dürer is still alive. Burgkmair is by then a respected master of the new
school of Augsburg he has founded. He would like to please the Fuggers and
Welsers and has agreed to illustrate Bartolomäus Springer's book on his
travels overseas (Kunst, 1967). He has carefully read Springer's diary, has
probably studied some clumsy pencil or pen-and-ink sketches, and has
decided to draw six pictures of "primitives."

The first picture of the series seems to represent a family. Let us imagine the painter at work. He has just read Springer's description of his voyage, and, possibly on the basis of some sketches, he is trying to create an image of blacks in "Gennea." Perhaps he has decided to use a model, presumably white but strongly built. The painter is staring at the pale body, imagining schemes to transform it into a black entity. The model has become a mirror through which the painter evaluates how the norms of similitude and his own creativity would impart both a human identity and a racial difference to his canvas. Perhaps the artist is already at work. Yet he has to stop regularly, walk around the model, leave the luminous space before the window, and retire into a discreet corner. His gaze addresses a point which is a question: how to superimpose the African characteristics described in Springer's narrative onto the norms of the Italian *contrapposto*? If he succeeds, the painting should be, in its originality, a celebration and a reminder of the natural link connecting human beings and, at the same time, an indication of racial or cultural differences. It should bear witness to the truth of similitudes, analogies, and possibly even the violence of antipathy. At any rate, Kunst notes that

> The nude African depicted from behind conforms to the classical rule of contraposto expressed in the compensatory balance of symmetrical parts of the body in movement: one shoulder leaning on one leg and the other, raised above the free leg. One guesses that this nude man was copied from a classic model to which the artist gave characteristics, jewelry and swords, of an exotic people still strongly attached to nature. (Kunst, 1967:19–20)

It is easy to dismiss my concern about similitude in this particular creative process. Am I not projecting a twentieth-century perspective onto the pictorial techniques of the early sixteenth century? The structure of figures is there in the first small painting, treated in a typical way. The fuss about similitude might just be, after all, only a contemporary hypothesis about the process of establishing links between beings and things from our present viewpoint. Yet it is possible to look for issues stemming from Burgkmair's representation. In effect, we can describe his artistic filiation and his dependence upon the classic ideals of the Renaissance (Kunst, 1967:20). We can also compare the principles of his technique with those apparent in some contemporary works directly or indirectly dealing with black figures, such as Erasmus Grasser's *Moor Dancers* (1480), Hieronymus Bosch's *Garden of Delights* (1500), *Katleen the Moor Woman* (1521) by Albrecht Dürer, and at the very end of the century, Cornelisz van Haarlem's *Batseba* (1594). Speculating about or analyzing the contrasts between white and black figures in these paintings, one could certainly search for a vision which refers to historically conventional explanations—for example, the sense of the characteristics and "the idea of design, that is to say, of expression by means of the pure disposition of contours and masses, and by the perfection and ordering of linear rhythm" (Fry, 1940:165). The complex play of colors in harmony and opposition, the order of shades between the white and the black, are obviously based on such intellectual and conscious references. But does not our understanding of the colorful economies of canvases refer, in a very insistent manner, to invisible traces?

The contrasts between black and white tell a story which probably duplicates a silent but powerful epistemological configuration. *Ex hypothesi* it might simply be a similitude interplay: "*Convenientia, aemulatio, analogy,* and *sympathy* tell us how the world must fold upon itself, duplicate itself, reflect itself, or form a chain with itself so that things can resemble one another. They tell us what the paths of similitude are and the directions they take; but not where it is, how one sees it, or by what mark it may be recognized" (Foucault, 1973:23–24).

Let us return to Burgkmair's finished painting. The three black figures—a boy, a man, a seated woman with a baby pressed to her breast—have the right proportions to one another and to the wider context. All are naked and have either bracelets around their arms or a string around their necks, clear signs that they belong to a "savage" universe (Kunst, 1967:20). The little boy is dancing, his oversized head turned toward the sky. At the center of the canvas, the man, presented in clear, strong lines, is staring at a faraway horizon, brandishing an arrow with his left hand and holding two other arrows in his right hand. He incarnates power, not only because he occupies the central place in the painting, but also because he is the most well-defined signifier in this scene. He is the locus defining the relationship between the boy at his left and the woman at his right, depicted with both a touch of hieratic sense and a slightly instinctual force. At the right, the woman with the baby is seated on a trunk. She seems to be staring pensively at the pelvic area of the man. The curves of her body are canonically executed.

The whole picture, in its simplicity and in the balanced rhythms of its lines, seems a truly charming and decorative painting. Yet what it really expresses is a discursive order. The structure of the figures, as well as the meaning of the nude bodies, proclaim the virtues of resemblances: in order to designate Springer's blacks, the painter has represented blackened whites. This was not rare during the sixteenth and the seventeenth centuries, as a great number of the drawings of the period reveal. That is the case for example, of the fifth picture in Filippo Pigafetta's 1591 edition of his *Relatione del Reame di Congo,* representing three Italianized African women, and that of the African king in the frontispiece of J. Ogilby's 1670 book on Africa. What is important in Burgkmair's painting, as well as in similar drawings, is their double representation.

The first, whose objective is to assimilate exotic bodies into sixteenth-century Italian painting methodology, reduces and neutralizes all differences into the sameness signified by the *white* norm, which, let us keep in mind, is more religious history than a simple cultural tradition. In concrete language this reference meant a "biblical solution to the problem of cultural differences [which] was regarded by most men as the best that reason and faith could propose" (Hodgen, 1971:254); that is, the same origin for all human beings, followed by geographical diffusion and racial and cultural diversification. And it was believed that the Bible stipulated that the African could only be the slave of his brethren.

There is another level, a more discreet one. It establishes a second representation that unites through similitude and eventually articulates distinctions and separations, thus classifying types of identities. Briefly, I can say that in Burgkmair's painting there are two representational activities: on the one hand, signs of an epistemological order which, silently but imperatively, indicate the processes of integrating and differentiating figures within the normative sameness; on the other hand, the excellence of an exotic picture that creates a cultural distance, thanks to an accumulation of accidental differences, namely, nakedness, blackness, curly hair, bracelets, and strings of pearls.

In their arrangements, these differences are pertinent signs. Because of the fundamental order which they reveal, and to which they bear witness, the virtues of resemblance erase physical and cultural variations, while maintaining and positing surface differences as meaningful of human complexity. Diego Velasquez's *Juan de Pareja* (1648) still actualizes this integrating reference, whereas major paintings such as Peter Paul Rubens's *Study of Four Blacks' Heads* (1620), Rembrandt's *Two Negroes* (1697), and Hyacinthe Rigaud's *Young Black* (1697) explicitly express and relate to another order. A new epistemological foundation was then functioning in the West. Theories of diversification of beings, as well as classificatory tables, explain the origins of constructing taxonomies and their objectives (Foucault, 1973:125–65). The framework of Linnaeus's *Systema Naturae* (1735) is just one of the paradigmatic classifications of species and varieties of *Homo Sapiens (europaeus, asiaticus, americanus, afer)* distinguished according to physical and temperamental characteristics (Count, 1950:355). It would be too easy to link it, *upstream,* to discursive formations about the great chain of beings and its hierarchy, and, *downstream,* first to Blumenbach's craniology and, second, to the general anti-African bias of the philosophical and scientific literature of the eighteenth and nineteenth centuries (Lyons, 1975:24–85).

Two very different discursive formations—the discovery of African art and the constitution of the object of African Studies, that is, the "invention" of Africanism as a scientific discipline—can illustrate the differentiating efficiency of such general classifying devices as pattern of reality, designation, arrangement, structure, and character. I have already suggested that resemblance has been pushed out of Rubens's, Rembrandt's, and Rigaud's perceptions of blacks. What is there, given in detailed description, might be considered as a naming and an analysis of an alterity and refers to a new epistemological ordering: a theory of understanding and looking at signs in terms of "the arrangement of identities and differences into ordered tables" (Foucault, 1973:72).

Portuguese sailors brought to Europe the first *feitiços,* African objects supposedly having mysterious powers, in the late fifteenth century. One finds them mostly in well-organized curio cabinets, along with Indian tomahawks or arrows, Egyptian artifacts, and Siamese drums. Some interpreters do consider them to be signs of a state of barbarism (Hodgen, 1971:162–203). Yet one can firmly state that more frequently they are seen as simple curiosities brought back in accordance with the tenth task of the traveler-observer in the table of Varenius's *Geographia generalis* (1650): to consider "famous Men, Artificers, and Inventions of the Natives of all countries" (Hodgen, 1971:167–68). On the whole, these objects are culturally neutral. Because of their shapes and styles, sometimes a bit terrifying, they account for the mysterious diversity of the Same (Bal, 1963:67). It is not until the eighteenth century that, as strange and "ugly" artifacts, they really enter into the frame of African art.

The black continent was still on the maps a *terra incognita,* but its peoples and their material productions were more familiar to travelers, students of the human species, merchants, and European states. From the beginning of the eighteenth century, there had been a tremendous increase in the slave trade and a profitable trans-Atlantic economy which involved most of the Western countries. In West Africa, Dahomey was a powerful commercial partner of European traders. The Ashanti empire expanded, dominating the Akans and the Oyo kingdom further to the east and increasing its power as it grew. Freed slaves and impoverished Africans were settled by European-sponsored organizations in present-day Sierra Leone. On the east coast, in 1729, Africans expelled the Portuguese from their fortresses in the northern region of Mozambique; and down south, in 1770, there was the first war between Dutch immigrants and Bantus. Two years later, James Bruce, traveling from North to Central Africa, reached the source of the White Nile in the very year that Chief Justice Mansfield declared in England that slavery was against the law (Verger, 1968).

In this atmosphere of intense and violent exchanges, *feitiços* became symbols of African art. They were viewed as primitive, simple, childish, and nonsensical. Mary H. Kingsley, at the beginning of this century, summed it up with an axiomatic evaluation: "The African has never made an even fourteenth-rate piece of cloth or pottery" (Kingsley, 1965:669). It seems to me that "a process of aesthetization" (Baudrillard, 1972) took place from the eighteenth century onward. What is called savage or primitive art covers a wide range of objects introduced by the contact between African and European during the intensified slave trade into the classifying frame of the eighteenth century. These objects, which perhaps are not art at all in their "native context," become art by being given simultaneously an aesthetic character and a potentiality for producing and reproducing other artistic forms. Taken in their initial function and significance, might they have created a radical *mise en perspective* of the Western culture wedded to classifications (Baudrillard, 1972)? That is precisely an impossibility. Arts are based on criteria, and it is difficult to imagine that these standards can emerge from outside the "power-knowledge" field of a given culture, a field which, at a historical period, establishes its artistic bible. Therefore it is obvious that fetishes and other "primitive" pieces of art are wonderful because their structure, character, and arrangement demand a designation (Laude, 1979; Wassing, 1969). They are "savage" in terms of the evolutionary chain of being and culture, which establishes a correspondence between advancement in the civilizing process and artistic creativity, as well as intellectual achievements.

At this point, paradoxically, it is a celebration of the African craftsmanship which confirms my analysis. Admiring the beauty of a "Negro sculpture," the late R. Fry was puzzled:

> It is curious that a people who produced such great artists did not produce also a culture in our sense of the word. This shows that two factors are necessary to produce the cultures which distinguish civilised peoples. There must be, of course, the creative artist, but there must also be the power of conscious critical appreciation and comparison. (Fry, 1940:90–91)

Fry is, I am afraid, utterly wrong. The two factors do not and cannot explicate types of cultures. They only constitute a basis for the production of art and its possible modifications over time (see Laude, 1979; Delange, 1967). They cannot completely account for the internal patterns of cultures. At any rate, it is the "power-knowledge" of an epistemological field which makes possible a domineering or humbled culture. From this perspective, the point that Fry makes immediately after has great sense: "It is likely enough that the Negro artist, although capable of . . . profound imaginative understanding of form, would accept our cheapest illusionist art with humble enthusiasm" (1940:91).

My thesis is confirmed, almost *ad absurdum*, by B. Jules-Rosette's study of contemporary African tourist art. She defines this art as an "art produced locally for consumption by outsiders" (1984:9) and strongly insists on the paradoxical interaction between its origin and its destination, that is, its production and its consumption:

> Although the concept of the tourist art system emphasizes how artists and their audiences perceive images and convert them into economic commodities, it does not neglect the expressive components of the interaction. Within the system, both images and actual objects constitute sources of exchange between producers and consumers. Although artists have a definite impression of the tourist audience, consumers often have little direct contact with the artists. (Jules-Rosette, 1984:10)

This concept of tourist art implies, in principle, a critique of the classical understanding of art. It also explicitly means a relativization of what the author calls "assumptions about the manner and quality of tourist art productions"; namely, its mass production character, the relative inexperience of present-day craftspeople, the collectivization in the artistic production, and the dominance of consumer demand over artistic creativity.

A limpid argument upholds the thesis of the study. Tourist art is both a symbolic and an economic exchange. This can be understood, according to Jules-Rosette, by reference to three models: First, the traditional African arts that have ceremonial and social significance may and do become objects produced primarily for external trade. Second, there are, in the very being of tourist art, signs of a major tension existing between "folk culture" and *"haute culture."* Or, as Jules-Rosette puts it: "Folk culture is implicitly contrasted with something else—*haute culture* . . . There is an inherent tension and asymmetry between the ideals of high culture and the profit motives and new reproductive technologies that sustain the growth of the market of popular cultures" (1984:23). As to the horizons of this artistic production, Jules-Rosette insists on the fact of Western reading of African creativity and its propositions for innovations in African workshops.

> The international tourist art market depends upon the Western demand for "exotic" souvenir and gift items and the assumption that they should be procured abroad. The artists and craftspeople utilize this demand as a stimulus for creating new ideas and technologies to meet the needs of the expanding market. (Jules-Rosette, 1984:192)

African tourist art and its contradictions (is it an art? in which sense and according to what kind of aesthetic grid?) are just an *ad vallem* consequence of the process which, during the slave trade period, classified African artifacts according to the grid of Western thought and imagination, in which alterity is a negative category of the Same. It is significant that a great number of European representations of Africans, or more generally of the continent, demonstrated this ordering of otherness. For example, Andreas Schulter's painting, *Africa* (1700), is structured upon a complex relation between a nude black woman and a frightening lion standing protectively behind her voluptuous body. The *African Allegory* (1765) of Cesare Ripa's *Iconologia* (t. IV, fol. 164) is a biblical and scientific text. The continent's name is linked etymologically to Afer, Abraham's son, yet in contrast the continent's peculiarity is presented with powerful symbols: the black color of a horned woman, a monstrous animal with a human face surrounded by serpents and bizarre birds. The African has become not only the Other who is everyone else except me, but rather the key which, in its abnormal differences, specifies the identity of the Same. G. B. Tiepolo's *Africa* (1750–1753), Delacroix's *Algerian Women* (1834), and a multitude of other paintings can be read for their implications: traces of something else whisper, slips of color reveal the meanings, and treads of a secret stair indicate the magnitude of a new order.

These representations are contemporary with the Enlightenment discussions on such axiomatic propositions as "men are born unequal" and such questions as "the place of the savage in the chain of being" (Duchet, 1971; Hodgen, 1971). In the following years, the sagas of exploration begin with J.

Bruce's expedition into Ethiopia in 1770 and Mungo Park's journey to the river Niger in 1795. The novel text which emerges from these expeditions is not fundamentally original (see, e.g., Hammond and Jablow, 1977). It reveals characteristics already well circumscribed and established. The distinction between "savage Negro" and "civil Mohometan," and the commentaries on the Africans' indolence, their unbridled passions, and their cruelty or mental retardation were already there. They formed part of the series of oppositions and of the levels of classification of humans demanded by the logic of the chain of being and the stages of progress and social development. Explorers just brought new proofs which could explicate "African inferiority." Since Africans could produce nothing of value; the technique of Yoruba statuary must have come from Egyptians; Benin art must be a Portuguese creation; the architectural achievement of Zimbabwe was due to Arab technicians; and Hausa and Buganda statecraft were inventions of white invaders (Davidson, 1959; Lugard, 1905; Randall-MacIver, 1906; Sanders, 1969; Mallows, 1984).

This tendency appears in other fields as well. Two French botanists, A. Chevalier in 1938 and R. Portères in the 1950s, suggested that the African continent could have been a very early locus of plant domestication (see e.g., Portères, 1950 and 1962). On the basis of linguistic data, the anthropologist G. P. Murdock expounded a similar proposition and postulated a "Sudanic complex of crops" (Murdock, 1959). These hypotheses were dismissed, and today "by far the most popular view of the origins of cereal-crop agriculture in sub-Saharan Africa is that it was the product of human migration or some form of culture diffusion or stimulus deriving from south-west Asia" (Desmond Clark and Brandt, 1984:11; see also Reed, 1977).

Here is a last illustration. The work of M. Griaule and his disciples in Dogon country has demonstrated the complexity of Dogon astronomical knowledge and its symbolism (e.g., Griaule, 1948, 1952; Griaule and Dieterlen, 1965, 1976; Dieterlen, 1941; Heusch, 1985). Carl Sagan, professor of astronomy at Cornell University, assumed the task of checking the validity of Dogon cosmology. Sagan begins by noting his surprise: "In contrast to almost all prescientific societies, the Dogon hold that the planets as well as the Earth rotate about their axes and revolve about the Sun . . ." (Sagan, 1983:81). Strangely enough, rather than using Griaule and his disciples' documentation, Sagan exploits a certain Temple, who summarized Griaule's discoveries: "The Dogon go further. They hold that Jupiter has four satellites and that Saturn is encircled by a ring . . . Unlike every astronomer before Kepler, the Dogon are said to depict the planets moving correctly in elliptical, not circular orbits" (1983:82). Most amazing for Sagan seems to be the following:

[The Dogons] contend that [Sirius] has a dark and invisible companion star which orbits Sirius . . . once every fifty years. They state that the companion star is very small and very heavy, made of a special metal called "Sagala" which is not found on Earth. The remarkable fact is that the visible star does have an extraordinary dark companion, Sirius B which orbits it in an elliptical orbit once each 50.04 ± 0.09 years. Sirius B is the first example of a white dwarf star discovered by modern astrophysics. Its matter is in a state called "relativistically degenerate," which does not exist on Earth, and since the electrons are not bound to the nuclei in such degenerate matter, it can properly be described as metallic. (Sagan, 1983:83)

How can we explain the Dogons' astronomical knowledge? Sagan has a hypothesis: "I picture a Gallic visitor to the Dogon people . . . He may have been a diplomat, an explorer, an adventurer or an early anthropologist . . ." (1983:87). This man has read, or perhaps still has, a copy of Sir Arthur Stanley Eddington's book, *The Nature of the Physical World,* published in 1928, in which the density of white dwarf stars is discussed.

> The conversation turns to astronomical lore. Sirius is the brightest star in the sky. The Dogon regale the visitor with their Sirius mythology. Then, smiling politely, expectantly, they inquire of their visitor what *his* Sirius myth might be . . . The white dwarf companion of Sirius being a current astronomical sensation, the traveler exchanges a spectacular myth for a routine one. After he leaves, his account is remembered, retold and eventually incorporated into the corpus of Dogon mythology . . . When Marcel Griaule makes mythological inquiries in the 1930s and 1940s, he has his own European Sirius myth played back to him. (Sagan, 1983:88)

All this is sheer speculation. Had Sagan carefully consulted knowledgeable sources (e.g., Griaule, 1948; Dieterlen, 1971; Griaule and Dieterlen, 1965) he would not have confused facts and symbolic levels in order to make his point about a beautiful "full-cycle return of a myth." Let us note three facts. First, the orbiting cycle of Sirius B is analogized and reflected in the celebration of the *sigui,* a ritual introduced by a mythical ancestor of the Dogons, Dyongu Seru. It is celebrated every sixty years; a symbolic period that integrates the fifty years of the revolution of Sirius B (for Dogons, the "star of the *fonio*") plus ten years which makes the ritual agree with the old Mandé system of numeration by sixty and with its esoteric symbols (Dieterlen, 1971:2–3). The last *sigui* ritual took place in 1967 and was filmed by J. Rouch and G. Dieterlen and released under the title *La Caverne de Bongo* (1969, 35 mm. in color). The preceding *sigui* performance was in 1907, and before that in 1847. "The rite is celebrated under the 'sign' of the 'star of the *fonio.*' Indeed, this 'companion' of Sirius is the representation in the sky of the little *fonio* seed . . ." (Heusch, 1985:147). Second, if one wants to validate Sagan's hypothesis, one should, in fact, demonstrate that a European traveler hurried to the Dogon region just after the 1844 discovery by F. W. Bessel of the sinusoidal motion of Sirius. He must have taught it well for the Dogons promptly to integrate it in their myths to the point that it could perfectly function in a set of major founding symbols in time for the 1847 ritual of *sigui.* Third, the preceding supposition seems difficult since the existence of Sirius B was, in Western science, really discovered in 1862 by A. G. Clark. Dogons had already used the symbolism of the *fonio* in their 1847 and 1787 rituals of *sigui*. Specialists in "oral civilizations" can easily check this. At the same time, they should evaluate the historical credibility and context of Dyongu Seru, who according to Dogon tradition is both the one "responsible for the loss of immortality" and the inventor of the *sigui* cycle (Heusch, 1985; Griaule and Dieterlen, 1965). On the other hand, I see another problem: the Dogons' concept of *sagala*, a metal which does not exist on earth and which constitutes the nature of Sirius's companion, is strongly linked to the *sigui* mythical cycle. It thus seems to go relatively far back in the history of the ritual, whereas in Western science the hypothesis of the "relativistically degenerate nature" of Sirius B was made for the first time in the 1930s. Most scientists did not then accept the concept, which, by the way, was proposed by an Indian scholar, S. Chandrasekhar.

To conclude this long illustration of an epistemological ethnocentrism, I suppose by now it has become clear how controversial Carl Sagan's hypothesis is. Let us sum up. First, I do not believe that the Dogons got their astronomical knowledge from extraterrestrials. The "bad faith" (in the Sartrean sense) with which Sagan destroys the theses and fantasies of E. von Däniken who claims this in *Chariots of the Gods* (1970, New York) and *Gods from Outer Space* (1978, New York) makes me suspect that Sagan and von Däniken are probably closer than they suspect. Second, Sagan's way of treating the Dogons well illustrates the power of a will to truth. A *metaphor* might generalize this case. Let us imagine a theorist who is enclosed in Euclidean geometry. He thinks about, believes in, and writes on the impossibility of non-Euclidean systems. These, in effect, would incarnate the possibility of incredible contradictions such as the intellectual reality of an *intrinsic truth* (e.g., a validly demonstrated theorem in Euclidean geometry), which would be simultaneously an *extrinsic error,* that is, a validly negated proposition in the logic of a non-Euclidean geometry. As we know, there are such things as non-Euclidean geometries. Thus my metaphor could at least become a symbol: it might not make sense at all to reduce non-Euclidean systems to Euclid's, since the systems spring from radically different postulates and sets of axioms.

In brief, although presented in the second part of the twentieth century, Carl Sagan's hypothesis belongs to nineteenth-century reasoning about "primitives." In the name of both scientific power and knowledge, it reveals in a marvelous way what I shall define in the following chapter as an epistemological ethnocentrism; namely, the belief that scientifically there is nothing to be learned from "them" unless it is already "ours" or comes from "us."

Explorers do not reveal otherness. They comment upon "anthropology," that is, the distance separating savagery from civilization on the diachronic line of progress (see Rotberg, 1970). R. Thornton claims that "the discovery of Africa was also a discovery *for* paper. Had the great Victorian travellers not written anything it would not be said today that they had 'discovered' anything." Strictly speaking, however, it seems difficult to prove in a convincing way that "Livingstone, Stanley, Burton, Grant, Speke and others entered into the enterprise for the sake of the text" (Thornton, 1983:509). Other students can invoke other motives such as the classical ones of curiosity, courage, generosity, contempt (Killingray, 1973:48).

At any rate, the explorer's text is not epistemologically inventive. It follows a path prescribed by a tradition. Expedition reports only establish a very concrete, vivid representation of what paintings and theories of social progress had been postulating since the Baroque period. In what the explorer's text does reveal, it brings nothing new besides visible and recent reasons to validate a discipline already remarkably defined by the Enlightenment (Lévi-Strauss, 1973:45–56). The novelty resides in the fact that the discourse on "savages" is, for the first time, a discourse in which an explicit political power presumes the authority of a scientific knowledge and vice-versa. Colonialism becomes its project and can be thought of as a duplication and a fulfillment of the power of Western discourses on human varieties.

The development of anthropology, which up to the very end of the eighteenth century was sought within travelers' narratives, now takes a radical turn. From now on it will develop into a clearly visible power-knowledge political system. As Foucault put it:

> Ethnology has its roots, in fact, in a possibility that properly belongs to the history of the European culture, even more to its fundamental relation with the whole of history . . . *There is a certain position of the Western ratio that was constituted in its history and provides a foundation for the relation it can have with all other societies* . . . Obviously, this does not mean that the colonizing situation is indispensable to ethnology: neither hypnosis, nor the patient's alienation within the fantasmatic character of the doctor, is constitutive of psychoanalysis; but just as the latter can be deployed only in the calm violence of a particular relationship and the transference it produces, *so ethnology can assume its proper dimensions only within the historical sovereignty—always restrained, but always present—of European thought and the relation that can bring it face to face with all other cultures as well as with itself.* (Foucault, 1973:377 emphasis mine)

"African Genesis"

I would like to use Frobenius's expression "African genesis" (1937) to formulate hypotheses about the epistemological locus of Africa's invention and its meaning for discourses on Africa.

The genesis of anthropological science took place within the frame of mercantilist ideology. We know that during the eighteenth century, as G. Williams puts it, "colonies were . . . of value only insofar as they brought material benefits to the mother country" (1967:17–30). On the other hand, it is during this same century that, paradoxically, original interpretations of "savages" were proposed by Enlightenment social scientists (Duchet, 1971). And I quite agree with R. L. Meek that if we look at their work, "what shine out are its virtues rather than its vices, its brilliant intuitions rather than its occasional logical lapses, its adventurousness and novelty rather than its dogmatism" (1976:242). To defend this point, Meek quotes Marvin Harris, *The Rise of Anthropological Theory* (1968), Benjamin Keen, *The Aztec Image in Western Thought* (1971), and Sidney Pollard, *The Idea of Progress* (1958). I may add Claude Lévi-Strauss, *Anthropologie structurale II* (1973) and M. Duchet, *Anthropologie et histoire au siècle des lumières* (1971).

The problem is that during this period both imperialism and anthropology took shape, allowing the reification of the "primitive." The key is the idea of History with a capital H, which first incorporates St. Augustine's notion of *providentia* and later on expresses itself in the evidence of Social Darwinism. Evolution, conquest, and difference become signs of a theological, biological, and anthropological destiny, and assign to things and beings both their natural slots and social mission. Theorists of capitalism, such as Benjamin Kidd and Karl Pearson in England, Paul Leroy-Beaulieu in France, Friedrich Naumann and Friedrich von Bernhard in Germany, as well as philosophers, comment upon two main and complementary paradigms. These are the inherent superiority of the white race, and, as already made explicit in Hegel's *Philosophy of Right*, the necessity for European economies and structures to expand to "virgin areas" of the world (Mommsen, 1983).

From this point, various schools of anthropology developed models and techniques to describe the "primitive" in accordance with changing trends within the framework of Western experience. These different trends can easily be explained from two angles. The first is an ideological one and concerns the relationship between an individual's projection of consciousness, the norms exemplified by one's society, and the social or the scientific dominant group (see, e.g., Baudrillard, 1972:174). On the other hand, mainly since the end of the eighteenth century, natural sciences have served as models for the progressive and wavering implementation of social sciences (Duchet, 1971:229–473). *In concreto,* one thinks of those "ideological interests of strata that are in various ways privileged within a polity and, indeed, privileged by its very existence" (Weber, 1978:920). On the other hand, Aristotle's invitation to study in beings the "plane of Nature" (*Animal,* I, 5) is mathematized (Veyne, 1984:63). New methodological grids link social facts to physical phenomena. Laws of structural organization and distribution, patterns in individual or collective development, account for historical transformations. The social scientist tends to imitate the naturalist and compresses social behaviors and human cultures into "scientific paradigms." These actually remain subsumed by what is defined as the goal of knowledge. Paul Veyne recently made some strong statements about the confusion which comes out of this legacy:

> Buffon thought that the fly should not hold a greater place in the concerns of
> the naturalist than it occupies in nature; on the other hand, he maintained a
> value relationship with the horse and the swan . . . But zoology has changed a
> great deal since then and, after Lamarck had pleaded the cause of the lower
> animals, every organism became of interest in the science.

> Weber was indignant that the history of the Bantus could be studied as much
> as that of the Greeks. Let us not retort that times have changed, that the Third
> World and its nascent patriotism . . . that the awakening of the African people
> who are taking an interest in their past . . . it would be a fine time to see that
> patriotic consideration should be the criterion of intellectual interest and that
> Africans have more reasons to despise Greek antiquity than Europeans had to
> despise Bantu antiquity. (Veyne, 1984:62)

At the level of organization of discourses these two factors—the impact of
ideology and the model of natural sciences—can serve as guides to the
relative epistemological unity of social sciences since the nineteenth century.
For instance, it would be easy to draw a parallel between philology and
anthropology. We wrongly tend today to consider the former, and particularly its offshoot, linguistics, as more scientific than the latter. Morgan's
historicism in *Systems of Consanguinity and Affinity of the Human Family*
(1871) matches the positivism of Max Muller's *Lectures on the Science of
Language* (1861 and 1864), in which fidelity to August Schleicher's *Stam-
mbaumtheorie* is integrated with Darwin's general postulations. In the same
way, the *Wellentheorie* which is central in J. Schmidt's work (e.g., *Die
Verwandtschaftsverhältnisse der Indo-Germanischen Sprachen,* 1872) is
similar to the diffusionist perspective of Ankermann, Frobenius, and
Graebner in anthropology. The principles of association and difference in-
voked by Boas and Lowie resemble many hypotheses in the philological field.
Examples are the *"Junggrammatiker"* interpretations of analogy in the
evolution of language exemplified by Meyer-Lubke's work, or the perspectives opened by H. Schuchardt's *Uber die Lautgesetze,* in which the major
concept—the *Sprachmischung*—implies the necessity of subordinating general laws, such as those promoted by Darwin's disciples, to the complexity
and alterity of the objects described and studied.

I do not mean that there is an unquestionable genealogical dependence or
obvious synchronic connection between these theories. It is clear, for example, that Schuchardt deals extensively with multidimensional comparison,
while Boas avoids it. In simpler words, I mean that anthropology and
philology and all social sciences can be really understood only in the context
of their epistemological region of possibility. The histories of these sciences as
well as their trends, their truths as well as their experiences, being derived
from a given space, speak from it and, primarily, about it. Given that, one
also might agree that from the anthropology of Buffon, Voltaire, Rousseau,
and Diderot to the most modern studies, such as J. Favret-Saada's study of
witchcraft in France (1977), the basic concern of anthropology is not so

much the description of "primitive" achievements and societies, as the question of its own motives, and the history of the epistemological field that makes it possible, and in which it has flourished as retrospectivist or perspectivist philosophical discourse (see Sebag, 1964; Diamond, 1974). Thus ethnocentrism is both its virtue and its weakness. It is not, as some scholars thought, an unfortunate mishap, nor a stupid accident, but one of the major signs of the possibility of anthropology.

Some thinkers, such as Lévi-Strauss, thought that studying a diversity of cultures reduced the weight of ideology and allowed anthropologists to fight such falsehoods as those about the natural superiority of some races and traditions over others. From this ethical point of view, some scholars have wondered whether it was possible to think of an anthropological science without ethnocentrism (e.g., Leclerc, 1972). It is surely possible, as functionalism and structuralism proved, to have works that seem to respect indigenous traditions. And one could hope for even more profound changes in anthropology, as R. Wagner proposes (1981). But so far it seems impossible to imagine any anthropology without a Western epistemological link. For on the one hand, it cannot be completely cut off from the field of its epistemological genesis and from its roots; and, on the other hand, as a science, it depends upon a precise frame without which there is no science at all, nor any anthropology.

I distinguish two kinds of "ethnocentrism": an epistemological filiation and an ideological connection. In fact they are often complementary and inseparable. The first is a link to an *episteme,* that is, an intellectual atmosphere which gives to anthropology its status as discourse, its significance as a discipline, and its credibility as a science in the field of human experience. The second is an intellectual and behavioral attitude which varies among individuals. Basically this attitude is both a consequence and an expression of a complex connection between the scholar's projection of consciousness, the scientific models of his time, and the cultural and social norms of his society. Thus, for example, for the eighteenth century one might think of the differences existing between Goguet, Quesnay, and Helvétius, independently of the content of their interpretations of the stages of evolution (see Duchet, 1971; Meek, 1976). Frobenius and Lévy-Bruhl differ in the same manner, and their ethnocentrism is quite different from that of, say, Michel Leiris, Margaret Mead, or Carl Sagan. I could say that the *epistemological filiation* maintains and sustains anthropology as a system of knowledge and as a developing science; *cultural ethnocentrism* explains ideological changes and struggles in the history and practice of the social science discipline.

> The fact that universal civilization has for a long time originated from the European center has maintained the illusion that European culture was, in fact and by right, a universal culture. Its superiority over other civilizations seemed to provide the experimental verification of this postulate. Moreover, the en-

counter with other cultural traditions was itself the fruit of that advance and more generally the fruit of Occidental science itself. Did not Europe invent history, geography, ethnography, and sociology in their explicit scientific forms? (Ricoeur, 1965:277)

In the colonizing experience, the mingling of these two aspects of ethnocentrism tended, almost naturally, to be complete in both the discourse of power and that of knowledge, to the point of transforming the mission of the discipline into an enterprise of acculturation. And the anthropologist decided to take charge of controlling evolutionary processes: "Anthropology, which used to be the study of beings and things retarded, gradual, and backward, is now faced with the difficult task of recording how the 'savage' becomes an active participant in modern civilization" (Malinowski, 1938:vii).

Still, it is clear that since the beginning of the nineteenth century, explorers' reports had been useful for opening the African continent to European interests. Myths about "beastly savages," "barbaric splendours," or the "white man's grave" go along quite well with the "tropical treasure house theory," the promises of the Golden Land or New Orphir, and with the humanitarian principles for suppressing the slave trade, and for Christianizing and civilizing the Africans (Hammond and Jablow, 1977; Leclerc, 1972).

Theories of colonial expansion and discourses on African primitiveness emphasize a historicity and the promotion of a particular model of history. In other words, Mungo Park's *Journal of a Mission* (1815) or Richard and John Lander's report (1838) essentially address the same issues that R. F. Burton, V. L. Cameron, H. M. Stanley, and F. D. Lugard spelled out in different words, and on which twentieth-century anthropology focuses. This is the discrepancy between "civilization" and "Christianity" on the one hand, "primitiveness" and "paganism" on the other, and the means of "evolution" or "conversion" from the first stage to the second. From this point of view, it can be said that, for instance, J. Chaillet-Bert's programmatic theory of the steps of colonization (agriculture, commerce, industry) has the same significance as Lugard's views on the European mandate in Africa. What they propose is an ideological explanation for forcing Africans into a new historical dimension. Finally, both types of discourses are fundamentally reductionist. They speak about neither Africa nor Africans, but rather justify the process of inventing and conquering a continent and naming its "primitiveness" or "disorder," as well as the subsequent means of its exploitation and methods for its "regeneration."

In fact, the question might be a bit more complicated, and also dramatic, for the imperial power of Same, if we take into account, for example, Ricoeur's meditation on the irruption of the Other in the European consciousness:

When we discover that there are several cultures instead of just one and consequently at the time when we acknowledge the end of a sort of cultural monopoly, be it illusory or real, we are threatened with destruction by our own discovery. Suddenly it becomes possible that there are just *others,* that we ourselves are an "other" among others. All meaning and every goal having disappeared, it becomes possible to wander through civilizations as if through vestiges and ruins. The whole of mankind becomes a kind of imaginary museum: where shall we go this week-end—visit the Angkor ruins or take a stroll in the Tivoli of Copenhagen? (Ricoeur, 1965:278)

In addition to Paul Ricoeur's anguished propositions, one should note the still strong anthropological spirit exemplified by N. Barley's small book, *Adventures in a Mud Hut* (1984). In 1978, Barley decided to turn his attention to the Dowayos, "a strangely neglected group of mountain pagans in North Cameroon . . . They were interesting [for him]: they had, for example, skull cults, circumcision, a whistle language, mummies and a reputation for being recalcitrant and savage" (1984:13). The result is a brief memoir which ten years ago would have qualified as arrogant or, at best, disrespectful of both fieldwork and the peoples described. Between commentaries on "their heavily Africanized version of Marianne, the French revolutionary heroine" (1984:17) and the fact that it is "ridiculous that it should be in Africa that people of different races should be able to meet on easy, uncomplicated terms" (1984:21), one gets intrusive lessons. Among them, the following two sum up the project's scientific interest. About the "whole business" of anthropology, the author states:

> Frankly, it seemed then, and seems now, that the justification for fieldwork, as for all academic endeavour, lies not in one's contribution to the collectivity but rather in some selfish development. Like monastic life, academic research is really all about the perfection of one's own soul. This may well serve some wider purpose but is not to be judged on those grounds alone. (Barley, 1984:10)

As to the Dowayos, his adventures in a mud hut gave Barley reasons for believing that "in attempting to understand the Dowayo view of the world I had tested the relevance of certain very general models of interpretation and cultural symbolism. On the whole they had stood up pretty well and I felt much happier about their place in the scheme of things" (1984:188).

This, wrote a reviewer in *The Daily Telegraph,* is "probably the funniest book that has been produced this year." The evaluation has since served for publicizing the essay. In a more neutral manner, I would say that this book is epistemologically significant. It convincingly illustrates my two previously described dimensions of ethnocentrism in the social sciences: the pertinence of an individual's projection of consciousness and the perception of a discipline from the normative perspective of its practice and history; it comments upon itself from within a paradigmatic cultural model. Barley assumes a magnificent position which allegorically indicates the space of his introspectiveness and his African anthropology: "Face-to-face with Africa, the dif-

ferences between a French botanist and an English anthropologist seem
minimal and we talked far into the night" (1984:106).

Thus, we are not only dealing with a potential imaginary museum but with
concrete constraints produced by two major orders: a topographical dimension which explains how and why discourses on the Same and the Other are
expounded, and a cultural order which, in the disorder of what today seems
to be a common humanity, indicates clear divisions, subtle frontiers, and
sometimes the so-called openings to oneness.

I suppose that it is now clear that the trouble with Barley's text is not its
ideological orientation. In fact there seems to be none, at least no explicit
one, apart from its superb interrogation of anthropology as a business of "old
stories." What it reveals, at the end, is an absolute and almost amoral
hypercriticism and a metaphorization of cultural reading. So, for instance,
this "English alien," back in Europe, rediscovers *la ville éternelle* and notes:
"I paced the streets of Rome like a Dowayo sorcerer whose unearthly slow-
ness sets off his ritual role from everyday activities" (1984:183). Saved from
Italian robbers and sent to England by the British Embassy in Rome, one of
the most important things he remembers is being alien: "an hour after my
arrival, I was phoned by one friend who merely remarked tersely: 'Look, I
don't know where you've been but you left a pullover at my place nearly two
years ago. When are you coming to collect it?' In vain one feels that such
questions are beneath the concern of a returning prophet" (1984:186). In
effect, a topographical configuration accounts for Barley's discourse and a
cultural atmosphere might explain his addiction to cream cakes and to
anthropology. As to his impressionist message, it is a strikingly modernized
lesson on Conrad's questions in *Heart of Darkness:* Why is African culture a
"barbarous" experience? What is European civilization and in which sense is
it different?

For a history of African studies and discourses it is therefore important to
notice that apparent changes within the dominant symbols have never fundamentally modified the meaning of African conversion, but only the policies
for its ideological and ethnocentric expression and practice. Present-day
intellectual categories can allow, as demonstrated by Copans in his
periodization, a distinction between travel literature, ethnology, and applied
anthropology (Copans, 1971a). Yet it is erroneous to depend on this type of
theoretical distinction, which is concerned with differences of ideological
policies, in order to distinguish genres of "African knowledge." Travelers in
the eighteenth century, as well as those of the nineteenth and their successors
in the twentieth (colonial proconsuls, anthropologists, and colonizers),
spoke using the same type of signs and symbols and acted upon them.
During the colonial era, these consistently involved reduction of differences
into a Western historicity. This does not imply that Western inventors of an
"African genesis" did not distinguish levels and types of interpretations of
Africa. The author of *Ursprung der Afrikanischen Kulturen,* for example,
could, in an article on the origin of African civilizations, perceive that the

demands of his discipline were not met by travelers' information. "Far from bringing us answers to our questions, the travelers have increased our enigmas by many an addition" (Frobenius, 1899:637). Today, the best students, faced with contradictory reports, will ask pertinent questions: What are these reports witnessing to? Do they contribute to a better knowledge of the African past? Are they scientifically credible and acceptable? (see Vansina, 1961). If correctly answered, these propositions lead, in principle, to a new understanding of human history. As Veyne put it, "if the Bantu *Homo historicus* proved to be a more primitive organism than the Athenian, it would only add to the interest, for it would thus reveal a less known part of the plan of Nature. As for knowing—Weber . . . asks the question—how many pages are to be devoted to Bantu history and how many to Greek, the answer is simple . . . It all depends on the volume of documentation" (1984:62).

The question I am dealing with is one which would account for the possibility of anthropological knowledge, and its meaning for the foundation of both Africanist discourses and African *gnosis*. I am proposing to formulate it through a critical synthesis of Foucault's thesis on the last archaeological rupture in Western epistemology, a brief interpretation of Lévi-Strauss's notion of *savage mind*, and finally a plea for the importance of the subject in social sciences; a subject that structuralism too easily pretends to have killed. These philosophical questions of method should, I hope, affirm the usefulness of both an epistemological analysis and a critical understanding of Africanism.

II

QUESTIONS OF METHOD

Foucault's Proposition on the Disappearing Subject

> I recalled the conclusions of a noted biologist
> concerning a similar experiment: it was
> possible, he said, by so abusing an animal, to
> produce in him emotional disorders strangely
> reminiscent of neurosis in men, and sometimes
> even to send him out of his mind by repeating
> these maneuvers fairly often.
>
> P. BOULLE, *Planet of the Apes.*

In the European Classical Age, the center of knowledge was, according to Foucault's archaeology (1973), the principle of order. The means of organizing this knowledge is the discourse, the table, and the exchange. One can observe in this epistemological landscape three major systems: *(a)* General grammar, "the study of verbal order in its relation to the simultaneity that it is its task to represent." It has, as its object, the discourse in which the name dominates: "the task of Classical 'discourse' is *to ascribe a name to things and in that name to name their being.*" *(b)* Natural history, or a theory of nature understood as the characterization, ordering, and naming of the visible. Its project is "to establish a general and complete table of species, genera and classes." *(c)* A theory of wealth, rather than a political economy, analyzing "value in terms of the exchange of objects of need," or "in terms of the formation and origin of objects whose exchange will later define their value in terms of nature's prolixity" (Foucault, 1973:79–211).

In other words, during the Classical Age there was one and just one *episteme* that "defines the conditions of possibility of all knowledge, whether expressed in a theory or silently invested in practice" (Foucault, 1973:168). In the last years of the eighteenth century, a rupture appears. The *episteme* that allowed general grammar, natural history, and the theory of wealth gradually disappears. There is a radical mutation from the theme of order to that of history. In the space that systems of classical knowledge never occupied, new ways of knowing define themselves, thanks to new transcendentals: labor, life, and language. Economics replaces the theory of wealth and, since Adam Smith, labor "reveals an irreducible, absolute unit of measurement," and wealth "is broken down according to the units of labor that have in reality produced it" (Foucault, 1973:217–36). Biology supplants natural history. With Lamarck, Jussieu, and Vicq d'Azyr, the principle of organic structure becomes the basis for taxonomies and thus separates the organic from the inorganic: the first defines the living, and the second, the nonliving. In the field of analysis of language, philology takes the place of general grammar: "language no longer consists only of representations and of sounds that in turn represent the representations and are ordered among them as the links of thought require; it consists also of formal elements, grouped into a system, which impose upon the sounds, syllables, and roots an organisation that is not that of representations" (Foucault, 1973:235).

From this epistemological caesura, a new landscape develops.

> The space of order, which served as a *common place* for representation and for things, for empirical visibility and for the essential rules, which united the regularities of nature and the resemblances of imagination in the grid of identities and differences, which displayed the empirical sequence of representations in a simultaneous table, and made it possible to scan step by step, in accordance with a logical sequence, the totality of nature's elements thus rendered contemporaneous with one another—this space of order is from now on shattered: there will be things, with their own organic structures, their hidden views, the space that articulates them, the time that produces them; and then representation, a purely temporal succession in which those things address themselves (always partially) to a subjectivity, a consciousness, a singular effort of cognition, to the 'psychological' individual who from the depth of his own history, or on the basis of the relation handed on to him, is trying to know. (Foucault, 1973:240)

Thus, a new *episteme* imposes itself, different and opposed to its own history and prehistory. More importantly, according to Foucault, in the very mutation which brings it about—the metamorphosis of the theory of wealth into economics, natural history into biology, and general grammar into philology—for the first time, "man appears in his ambiguous position as both an object of knowledge and as a subject that knows" (1973:330). Foucault states that man is constituted at the beginning of the nineteenth century, and, thus:

> For man, then, origin is by no means the beginning—a sort of dawn of history from which his ulterior acquisitions would have accumulated. Origin, for man, is much more the way in which man in general, any man articulates himself upon the already-begun of labour, life and language; it must be sought for in that fold where man in all simplicity applies his labour to a world that has been worked for thousands of years, lives in the freshness of his unique, recent precarious existence a life that has its roots in the first organic formations, and composes into sentences which have never before been spoken . . . words that are older than all memory. (Foucault, 1973:330)

Simply speaking, since the epistemological mutation at the end of the eighteenth century, three models impose themselves as essential paradigms: function and norm, conflict and rule, signification and system. They constitute and concurrently cover the field of all that can be known and said about humans. They strictly define what knowledge can offer about human beings. Foucault even thinks that the brief history of social and human sciences might be studied "on the basis of these three models." It will suffice for students "to follow the dynasty of their privileges" by focusing on the temporal succession of models (biological, economic, and philological and linguistic), or by analyzing the regular shifts of categories and the meaning of their displacement. An example might be the receding of function, conflict, and signification, and the emergence of norm, rule, and system with Goldstein, Mauss, and Dumézil. Foucault also shows two major consequences of this reversal.

1. (a)   as long as the functional point of view continued to carry more weight than the normative point of view . . . it was of course necessary, *de facto,* to share the normal functions with the non-normal; thus a pathological psychology was accepted side by side with normal psychology . . . in the same way, a pathology of societies (Durkheim), of irrational and quasi-morbid forms of belief (Lévy-Bruhl, Blondel) was also accepted;

   (b)   similarly, as long as the point of view of conflict carried more weight than that of the rule, it was supposed that certain conflicts could not be overcome, that individuals and societies ran the risk of destroying themselves by them;

   (c)   finally, as long as the point of view of signification carried more weight than that of system, a division was made between significant and nonsignificant; it was accepted that there was meaning in certain domains of human behaviour or certain regions of the social area, but not others.

2. When, on the other hand, the analysis was conducted from the point of view of the norm, the rule, and the system, each area provided its own coherence and its own validity; it was no longer possible to speak of 'morbid consciousness' (even referring to the sick), of 'primitive mentalities' (even with reference to societies left behind by history), or of 'insignificant discourse' (even when referring to absurd stories, or to apparently incoherent legends). Everything may be thought within the order of the system, the rule, and the norm. By pluralizing itself—since systems are isolated, since rules form closed wholes, since norms are posited in their autonomy—the field of the human sciences found itself unified; it was no longer fissured along its former dichotomy of values. (Foucault, 1973:360–61; the arrangement of the quotation is mine)

With these suggestions, one might, for methodological purposes, classify the body of discourses on non-Western societies into two main groups. During the nineteenth century and the first quarter of the twentieth, discourses were generally characterized by a functional perspective and a self-righteous intolerance founded on the philosophical implications of the paradigms of conflict and significance. Thus the analysis, through a temporalization of the chain of being and of civilizations (Duchet, 1971; Hodgen, 1971; Meek, 1976), could simultaneously account for the normality, creative dynamism, and achievements of the "civilized world" against the abnormality, deviance, and primitiveness of "non-literate societies." This expression of a will to truth has been questioned only recently—thanks to the implications of Freud's work and the contributions of Dumézil, Mauss, Dumont, and Lévi-Strauss—to the point where today one agrees without difficulty with R. Wagner's statement that: "We might actually say that an anthropologist 'invents' the culture he believes himself to be studying, that the relation is more 'real' for being his particular acts and experiences than the things it relates" (1981:4).

Nevertheless, let us face Foucault's hypothesis of *an* archaeology of knowledge. *The order of things*, he says, is not *the* archaeology, but *an* archaeology of human sciences (1980:82). First, one might ask: what in actuality is this archaeology which, according to its author, is different from the traditional history of ideas? (Foucault, 1972:135–40). The archaeologist may treat every discourse as a "monument," and may emphasize the differential analysis of their modalities and the silent norms presiding over discursive practices. Yet their originality and their specificity are relative insofar as they are geographically determined and culturally integrated. Yes, Foucault insists on the vagueness of what "his" West really is (1980). But the succession of *epistemes*, as well as the procedures and disciplines that they allow, account for a historical activity and, indirectly, legitimate a social evolution in which knowledge essentially functions as a form of power. It is true that Foucault methodologically seeks to oppose this outcome by using four major principles. These are: reversal, in order to "recognize the negative activity of the cutting-out of discourse"; discontinuity, in order to understand discourse as "a discontinuous activity"; specificity, in order to "conceive discourse as a violence that we do to things, or, at all events, as a practice we impose upon them"; and, exteriority, in order to look for "the external conditions of existence" of the discourse (Foucault, 1982:229). These principles, along with the notions that they bring, contribute to a new understanding of the Western experience, and at the same time clearly indicate its capacity to join knowledge and power.

History might have, as Foucault states, "abandoned its attempts to understand events in terms of cause and effect in the formless unity of some great evolutionary process, whether vaguely homogeneous or rigidly hierarchized." Foucault's enterprise remarkably explains the conquering horizons of this history. Since the end of the eighteenth century, anthropological discourses represent it. They are constrained discourses and develop within the general system of knowledge which is in an interdependent relationship with systems of power and social control. Durkheim's prescriptions on the pathology of civilizations, Lévy-Bruhl's theses on prelogical systems of thought, as well as Frazer's hypothesis on primitive societies, bear witness, from a functional viewpoint, to the same epistemological space in which stories about Others, as well as commentaries on their differences, are but elements in the history of the Same and its knowledge.

The Savage Mind's Kingdom

> "Men!" Phyllis again exclaimed. "Yes, men," Jinn asserted. "That's what it says."
>
> P. BOULLE, *Planet of the Apes.*

The search for a discrete but essential order is what unites Foucault and Lévi-Strauss. In a broad sense, Lévi-Strauss's objectives in the understanding of history and anthropology are based on four principles: *(a)* true reality is never obvious and "its nature is already apparent in the care it takes to evade our attention"; *(b)* social science is not based upon events; *(c)* reality and experience might be complementary but "there is no continuity in the passage between them"; and *(d)* the social scientist's mission is "to understand being in relation to itself and not in relation to oneself" (Lévi-Strauss, 1963 and 1966).

According to Lévi-Strauss, the similarities existing between history and anthropology are more important than their differences. First, both disciplines are concerned with remoteness and otherness: while history deals with remoteness in time, anthropology deals with remoteness in space. Second, their goal is the same, namely, a better understanding of temporally or spatially different societies and, thus, a reconstruction, "a rewriting" of what "has happened" or of what "is happening" in those societies. Finally, in both cases, scientists face "systems of representations which differ for each member of the group and which, on the whole, differ from the respresentations of the investigator."

> The best ethnographic study will never make the reader a native. . . . All that the historian or ethnographer can do, and all that we expect of either of them is to enlarge a specific experience to the dimensions of a more general one, which thereby becomes accessible as experience to men of another country or another epoch. And in order to succeed, both historian and ethnographer must have the same qualities: skill, precision, a sympathetic approach and objectivity. (Lévi-Strauss, 1963:16–17)

Lévi-Strauss knows the classical distinction of methodologies. The historian's techniques are based on precise data and documents, whereas the anthropologist constructs an understanding of an "oral civilization" on the basis of observation. Nevertheless, Lévi-Strauss does not consider this distinction pertinent:

> The fundamental difference between the two disciplines is not one of subject, of goal, or of method. They share the same subject, which is social life; the same goal, which is a better understanding of man; and, in fact, the same method, in which only the proportion of research techniques varies. They differ, principally, in their choice of complementary perspectives: History organizes its data in relation to conscious expressions of social life, while anthropology proceeds by examining its unconscious foundations. (Lévi-Strauss 1963:18)

One immediately recalls the following statements of Foucault. About history, he observes: "all knowledge is rooted in a life, a society, and a language that have a history; and it is in that very history that knowledge finds the element enabling it to communicate with other forms of life, other types of society, other significations" (1973:372). About anthropology, he asserts: "ethnology situates itself in the dimension of historicity (of that perpetual oscillation which is the reason why the human sciences are always being contested, from without, by their own history)" (1973:376). The difference between the two positions, however, is clear. Foucault is emphasizing the possibility of a new anthropology and its dependence on Western historicity. As for Lévi-Strauss, he is distinguishing the methodological question from the epistemological one. The former is concerned with the future of anthropology; the latter, with ways of describing the solidarity that might exist between history and anthropology if one takes seriously Marx's statement: "men make their own history, but they do not know that they are making it" (Lévi-Strauss, 1963:23). Consequently, Lévi-Strauss thinks that it would be inaccurate to oppose the historian's method to that of the anthropologist.

> [Anthropologists and historians] have undertaken the same journey on the same road in the same direction; only their orientation is different. The anthropologist goes forward, seeking to attain, through the conscious, of which he is always aware, more and more of the unconscious; whereas the historian advances, so to speak, backward, keeping his eyes fixed on concrete and specific activities from which he withdraws only to consider them from a more complete and richer perspective. (Lévi-Strauss 1963:24)

This conception of history and anthropology as a two-faced Janus has important implications. It means a reorganization of the social disciplines: history, sociology, social philosophy, ethnography, and anthropology. More important, it signifies both a disengagement of anthropology from self-explanatory paradigms of primitiveness and a different look at "primitive societies" and at "the savage mind." *Ex hypothesi,* its momentum resides in the rejection of the antinomy between the logical and prelogical. For according to Lévi-Strauss, the savage mind is logical (1966:268).

What exactly is the "savage mind"? Lévi-Strauss affirms that "the primitive mind is not the mind of a primitive or archaic humanity but an undomesticated thinking" (1962:289). Disagreeing with Lévi-Strauss, Maurice Godelier states that "mythic thinking" is not only the thinking of savages, but also, by its status, a primitive thinking. He writes: "I think that I am disagreeing with Claude Lévi-Strauss because I do believe that mythic thinking is both undomesticated thinking and the thinking of primitives" (1973:385). Godelier's argument claims that mythical thinking is, essentially, constituted by processes of analogies, dominated by relations of similitude, as was, according to Foucault, the epistemological field of the West in the sixteenth century (1973:17–44).

> These are the analogies drawn from the field of *perception,* from serviceable knowledge, which constitute the basis with which the thinking of primitives, naturally submitted to the formal principles of undomesticated thinking, builds the organization of ideas in which is reflected infinitely the reciprocal image of humans and the world and in which spring and function the illusions the primitive being holds of himself and the world. (Godelier, 1973:386)

Godelier's position is challenging, insofar as it indicates a radical and controversial hypothesis: the possibility of cross-cultural comparison of systems of thought dominated by themes of similitude, and thus a comparative study of types of knowledge defined within an infinite proliferation of resemblances (e.g., Mudimbe, 1981b:195–97). On the other hand, one might fear that it only draws the cloak of historical materialism over the most traditional and controversial theses of social evolutionism. J. Goody has recently proposed the use of changes in communication as criteria for understanding this sort of otherness. Because those changes are critical in nature and are "multiple rather than single in character," they invalidate the dichotomy between "primitive" and "advanced" (Goody, 1977:10). Moreover, Goody delineates as a major issue the necessity of accounting for observed social transformations and types of domestication (1977:16).

In fact, one is at first struck by the apparent static character of Lévi-Strauss's analysis of the savage mind. Let us sum up the three major principles.

First, each human language is particular and expresses in an original way types of contacts that exist between man (producer of culture) and his environment (nature). Thus each language delineates in its own manner concepts, systems of classification, and knowledge. Traditionally the opposition between "primitive" and "advanced" has been explicated through the opposition of two systems of "order": magic and science. Lévi-Strauss substitutes another opposition, science of the concrete versus science of the abstract.

Second, Lévi-Strauss thinks that magic and science should not be considered two different steps in a chronological evolution, the first primitive and only a harbinger of the second. They are two different and parallel systems of knowledge. "Magic postulates a complete and all-embracing determinism" and is possibly "an expression of the unconscious apprehension of the *truth of determinism,* the mode in which scientific phenomena exist." Science, on the other hand, "is based on a distinction between levels: only some of these admit forms of determinism; on others, the same forms of determinism are held not to apply" (Lévi-Strauss, 1966:11). The parallelism would thus account for the fact that science can coexist with magic. The neolithic period shows this, being characterized by magic as well as such important discoveries and achievements as the invention of agriculture and the domestication of animals.

Third, a more pertinent opposition would therefore be the science of the concrete versus the science of the abstract; or, analogically speaking, an opposition between *"bricolage"* and "engineering," that might introduce and mean the opposition between "mythical thought" and "science." These are not "two stages or phases in the evolution of knowledge. Both approaches are equally valid" (Lévi-Strauss 1966:22). Lévi-Strauss insists on the relativity of the classical distinction between these two systems of ordering and acquiring knowledge.

> It is therefore better, instead of contrasting magic and science, to compare them as two parallel modes of acquiring knowledge. Their theoretical and practical results differ in value, for it is true that science is more successful than magic from this point of view, although magic foreshadows science in that it is sometimes also successful. Both science and magic however require the same sort of mental operations and they differ not so much in kind as in the different types of phenomena to which they are applied. (Lévi-Strauss, 1966:13)

This statement about "the science of the concrete" articulates Lévi-Strauss's reasons for the promotion and celebration of "primitive" myths as both "systems of abstract relations and as objects of aesthetic contemplation" (1964). Not only might the study of "primitive" myths open up avenues to understanding the hidden logic behind mythic thought, in its dual aspect as a logic of qualities and a logic of forms, but it might also create an opportunity for discovering ethical systems, which Lévi-Strauss thinks can "give us a lesson in humility" (1979:507).

Goody's critique of Lévi-Strauss's dichotomy emphasizes the weakness of the premises, and of the very distinction of "magic" and "myth," concepts that are "slippery to handle," and "relics of some earlier folk contrast with religion on the one hand (as in sixteenth-century England) and history on the other (as in fifth-century Athens)." More important he believes that Lévi-Strauss's opposition of "the science of the concrete" and "the science of the abstract" amounts to "a contrast between the domination of abstract science

Figure 1. Lévi-Strauss's Dichotomy

The Science of the Concrete	The Science of the Abstract

"prior" rather than primitive

Bricolage	*Engineering*
The "bricoleur" is adept at performing a large number of diverse tasks.	The engineer subordinates each task to the availability of raw materials and tools conceived and procured for the purpose of the project.
His universe of instruments is closed and the rules of his game are always to make do with whatever is at hand; the set of the bricoleur's means that it cannot be defined in terms of a project . . . It is to be defined only by its potential use.	
The bricoleur addresses himself . . . to a subset of the culture.	The engineer questions the universe.
He works by means of signs by inclination or necessity. The bricoleur always remains within the constraints imposed by a particular state of civilization.	He works by means of concepts, always trying to make his way out and go beyond the constraints imposed by a particular state of civilization.
Mythical thought	*Science*
It appears to be an intellectual form of bricolage; it builds up structured sets by using the remains and debris of events.	It is based on the distinction between the contingent and the necessary, this being also what distinguishes event and structure.
It builds structured sets by means of a structured set, namely, language. But it is not at the structural level that it makes use of (language); it builds ideological castles out of the debris of what was once a social discourse.	Science "in operation" creates its means and results in the form of events, thanks to the structures which it is constantly elaborating and which are its hypotheses and theories.

Source: *The Savage Mind* 16-22.

together with history, against the more concrete forms of knowledge" (Goody, 1977:148). Goody, contrary to Lévi-Strauss's emphasis on the synchronic dimension, insists on historical development and, specifically, on the "shift from the science of the concrete to that of the abstract." He thus relativizes one of Lévi-Strauss's caveats: the two systems are parallel and must not be thought of as chronological stages. Goody works diachronically. According to him, this shift "cannot be understood except in terms of basic changes in the nature of human communication." In other words, one must suppose a historical process accounting for "the growth of knowledge," and "this movement is related to developments in the technology of the intellect, to changes in the means of communication and, specifically, to the introduction of writing." Pushing forward a new distinction—the oral versus the written—Goody hopes to avoid both Lévi-Strauss's Grand Dichotomy and his "diffuse relativism that refuses to recognise long-term differences and regards each 'culture' as a thing on its own, a law unto itself" (1977:151).

Paradoxically, it is Lévi-Strauss's apparent diffuse relativism which appeals to me and, I think, to numerous students of non-Western *Weltanschauungen* and systems of thought (see, e.g., Heusch, 1982; Hallen and Sodipo, 1986). It makes sense not only by what it allows—a self-analytical anthropology—but also in what it relativizes. As *Tristes Tropiques* demonstrates, the usefulness of a discourse on others goes beyond the gospel of otherness: there is not a normative human culture. It becomes a means for comprehending oneself. As Lévi-Strauss put it, in an excellent metaphor, the pleasure of listening to Debussy after Chopin is intensified; for the first constitutes an organized preparation for the second, which is no longer perceived as arbitrary. "Perhaps, then, this [is] what travelling [and anthropology are], an exploration of the deserts of my mind rather than of those surrounding me" (1977:430). On the other hand, for the first time the anthropologist knows that he is the Other who may accept being in charge of reproducing a mythical state "which no longer exists, which has perhaps never existed and will probably never exist in the future" (1977:447). He can think about the impossible: in the exteriority of his own culture, he has come into contact with an *episteme* radically opposed to Western norms, which since Descartes, and despite Rousseau's invitation, have enshrined the *cogito* (1973:48–49). Presumably, Lévi-Strauss's perspective indicates a radical project of providing a body of knowledge that simultaneously could undermine a totalitarian order of knowledge and push knowledge into territories traditionally rejected as supposedly nonsensical.

Geertz states that "what Lévi-Strauss has made for himself is an infernal cultural machine" (1973:346). And regarding Foucault's enterprise, White notes that it "must seem to be little more than a continuation of a tradition of pessimistic, even decadent thought. . . . And it is true that [Foucault] not only finds little to lament in the passing of Western civilization, but also he offers less hope for its replacement by anything better" (1979:113). The diagnosis is somewhat familiar. It can be related to Lévi-Strauss's and Foucault's doubts about the history of the Same.

Lévi-Strauss is opposed to the tyranny of history. "Even history which claims to be universal is still only a juxtaposition of a few real histories within which (and between which) very much more is left out than put in" (1966:257). One could even generalize from this view and think that history is fundamentally a myth and thus enlarge Lévi-Strauss's concern: "history is never history, but history for." In effect, as Lévi-Strauss says, "what makes history possible is that a sub-set of events is found, for a given period, to have approximately the same significance for a contingent of individuals who have not necessarily experienced the events and may even consider them at an interval of several centuries" (1966:257).

Lévi-Strauss has chosen to pursue the analysis of "mythological systems" in order to write his own myth about them by using intellectual "categories" as tools for revealing an abstract and universal order of rationality (Lévi-Strauss, 1968: Overture). In this process he simultaneously promotes the kingdoms of "primitive organizations" and advances the claim that the order of cultural changes is determined everywhere by the constraints of the human mind. In doing so he methodologically replaces the Freudian unconscious by positing, as his aim, a "super-rationalism," a universal unconscious that subsumes all particularities. What is, de facto, rejected or diminished in this perspective is the sovereignty of both "dialectical reason" and "historical consciousness." Referring to Sartre's *Critique de la raison dialectique*, Lévi-Strauss can affirm that in Sartre's system, history plays exactly the part of a myth (1966:256).

Foucault seems to be an unhappy "historian of the Same." "I cannot," he writes, "be satisfied until I have cut myself off from 'the history of ideas,' until I have shown in what way archaeological analysis differs from the descriptions of 'the history of ideas' " (1982:136). In sum, as an unbelieving historian, he "rewrites" the ambiguous passion of knowledge. All his books provide good examples of this exercise, which brings to light the long, difficult, and permanent struggle of the Same and the Other. By promoting a critical archaeology of knowledge, not only does he separate himself from a history but also from its classical presuppositions, which lead to and serve the arrogance of the Same. In his *Discourse on Language*, Foucault delineates this objective: "to question [the Western] will to truth; to restore to discourse its character as an event; to abolish the sovereignty of the signifier" (1982:229).

Foucault's horizon is, one might say, a relativization of the truth of the Same in the dispersion of history; in other words "a decentralizing that leaves no privilege to any center." It is striking that one can hear, from this very practice which "deploys a dispersion that can never be reduced to a single system of difference," Lévi-Strauss's voice proclaiming after Rousseau: "Nothing is settled; everything can still be altered. What was done, but turned out wrong, can be done again. The Golden Age which blind superstition had placed behind [or ahead of] us, is *in us*" (1977:448).

I think that the positions of Lévi-Strauss and Foucault signify new critical symbols as well as invitations to redefine and rework or transform the history of the Same. I also would like to integrate Ricoeur, who, studying the crisis of Western historicity, invites us to join our efforts "under the sign of (Plato's) 'great class' which itself associates the Same and the Other. The Similar is the great category. Or better, the Analogue which is a resemblance between relations rather than between simple terms" (Ricoeur, 1984:25).

The following pages will show the real ambition of the Analogue. But in order to make it clearer, let me say that I shall be studying it with the passion of the Other, of that being which has been so far a mere object of the discourses of social and human sciences.

The masterful demonstrations by Lévi-Strauss and Foucault do not convince me that the subject in the discourse on the Same or on the Other should be a mere illusion or a simple shadow of an *episteme*. What they teach me is different; namely, that we lack a theory that could solve the dialectic tension between creative discourses and the epistemological field which makes them possible, on the one hand, and Lévi-Strauss's unconscious that sustains discourses and accounts for their organization, on the other. In fact, there is an obvious way out of this problem by means of the subject, who directly or indirectly, consciously or unconsciously, participates in the modification or the constitution of an epistemological order. M. Foucault, for example, clearly knew what his subjective will meant for the promotion of otherness and strongly urged us to reconsider what madness, as well as incarceration and sexual "abnormality," signify in a given society (see, e.g., Foucault, 1965, 1977, 1978). As for Lévi-Strauss, it strikes me that he proves well in the *Mythologiques* that empirical categories can be used as keys to a silent code, leading to universals. When analyzed, such a project in social sciences can be pertinent only with regard to the intentionality of its inventor. In our case, it is in Lévi-Strauss's praxis expressing itself within a cultural and human environment which is an obvious *practico-inert* as illustrated by his confession in *Tristes Tropiques*. The cry that closes the book—that the Golden Age is not behind nor before us but in us—expresses the power of a consciousness and its liberty. In sum, the structuralist method that Lévi-Strauss develops and applies convincingly is an intellectual tool; its condition of possibility resides in an epistemological field in which the strength of the *cogito* has led to the right of an absolute human freedom, and consequently to systematic meditations on the comparative virtues of the Same and Other.

' One might meditate upon the grave moral conclusion that ends the *Origin of Table Manners* (1979), which demonstrates that the ambiguous idea of Sartre's "hell is other people" has not been entertained by Indians, who modestly state that "hell is us" (Lévi-Strauss, 1979:422). This philosophical choice completes the lesson of Rousseau's *Confessions* on I as an Other, without negating or suppressing Lévi-Strauss's freedom to meditate on these paradoxical statements and compare them. In this particular situation, Lévi-Strauss—to use an expression he likes—is in the situation of an astronomer looking at stars. To claim "I is an Other" would be, in this case, to propose a symbolic identification. The "I" who pronounces this sentence is, in Sartrean vocabulary, in anguish, a subject thinking about how to define himself. Is he the absolute subject of the praxis that the sentence expresses symbolically or a pure reflection of the Other as meant by the copula?

An African Amplification

> After a certain period it would be the sound of
> the whistle alone that would produce the

> effect. The men would have acquired what are
> known in scientific jargon as conditioned
> reflexes.
>
> P. BOULLE, *Planet of the Apes.*

Lévi-Strauss and Foucault have brought to African consciousness new reasons for developing original strategies within the social sciences. It is not my
aim here to discuss the extent of their African presence, nor the possible
deviation that their real or supposed disciples indicate in African social
studies (see, e.g., Kinanga, 1981; N'zembele, 1983). I will rather describe an
atmosphere, that of an African *prise de parole* about philosophy and knowledge, in which one easily recognizes an amplification of Lévi-Strauss's and
Foucault's major theses. Politically, one might also find on the surface strong
coincidental resemblances to Sartre's dreams regarding liberation.

The notion of amplification implies direct or indirect causal relations. As I.
D. London put it, "amplifying effects . . . can make minor events the
progenitors of larger happenings." More precisely, one can distinguish two
main genres of effects: "an amplifying causal sequence may be seen as
producing either of two effects. (1) It may converge upon expectation, in
which case amplification is said to be convergent; (2) it may diverge from
expectation in which case amplification is said to be divergent" (1977).

The convergence is obvious, particularly in Francophone Africa, where the
prise de parole took place in the 1960s and 1970s as a discourse about
anthropology and simultaneously, a critical reflection on African culture and
its geography. The preindependence generation of African intellectuals was
mostly concerned with political power and strategies for ideological succession. Since 1960, and more visibly since the 1970s, a new generation prefers
to put forward the notion of *epistemological vigilance.* This generation
seems much more concerned with strategies for mastering intellectual paradigms about "the path to truth," with analyzing the political dimensions of
knowledge, and with procedures for establishing new rules in African studies. As E. Mveng expressed it recently, the principle of the new attitude is
different: "if political sovereignty is necessary, the scientific sovereignty is
perhaps more important in present-day Africa" (Mveng, 1983:141).

Power is still an objective. In order to comprehend the most original of
contemporary discourses, one can still refer to Aimé Césaire's wish for an
"African Copernican revolution" (1956:12). Whether or not the use of hatred
against (neo-)colonialist guardianship or policies still makes sense, it does
not seem any longer to be an important factor in the struggle for maturity.
There is an African literature that flatters condescending Western ears, in
which Africans *prove,* by means of négritude and black personality rhetoric,
that they are "intelligent human beings" who once had respectable civilizations that colonialism destroyed. This is considered by some representatives
of the present generation of African intellectuals to be a childish reaction of
overcompensation (Towa, 1971a; Rombaut, 1976). For, as Adotévi expressed
it:

> The Black person who accepts his race is a good Black, but if he forgets our fall, if he forgets himself, if he faints in mystical ecstasy, if he sees black when he should see right, he or she loses himself or herself, loses the being Black in losing perspective. (Adotévi, 1972:102)

African responsibility seems thus defined in terms of intellectual attitudes rather than in reference to an imperative political succession. Is this sort of strategy a sign of an amplification of the Western crisis of the social and human sciences? E. Mveng is explicit about the connections and their meaning: "The West agrees with us today that the way to Truth passes by numerous paths, other than Aristotelian Thomistic logic or Hegelian dialectic. But social and human sciences themselves must be decolonized" (1983:141). In a text presenting the mission of "philosophy" in Africa, P. Hountondji insists on a preliminary awareness and the necessity of destroying myths of "Africanity" and mystifications inherited from the "inventors" of Africa and her culture.

> Therefore it was necessary to begin by *demythifying* the concept of Africanity, reducing it to a status of a *phenomenon*—the simple phenomenon which *per se* is perfectly neutral, of belonging to Africa—by dissipating the mystical halo of values arbitrarily grafted on this phenomenon by the ideologues of identity. It was necessary, in order to think of the complexity of our history, to bring the theatre of this history back to its basic simplicity. In order to think of the richness of African traditions, it was necessary *to weaken* resolutely the concept of Africa, *to rid it* of all its ethical, religious, philosophical, political connotations, etc., with which a long anthropological tradition had overloaded it and the most visible effect was to close the horizon, to prematurely close history. (Hountondji, 1981:52)

The propositions are transparent. Mveng seems to be carrying Foucault's project further than the French philosopher himself would have. Hountondji emphasizes the necessity of considering Africanity as a *fait*, in the sense of an event. Its demythification should sustain a critical reinterpretation of an African history invented from its exteriority. Hountondji's invitation to *appauvrir* (impoverish or weaken) the very notion of Africa implies a radical break in African anthropology, history, and ideology. The convergence with Lévi-Strauss's and Foucault's predicaments is clear.

Although most Western anthropologists have continued up to now to argue about the best models to account for primitive societies, Lévi-Strauss, Foucault, and, since the 1960s, Africans have been destroying the classical frame of anthropology. By emphasizing the importance of the unconscious and questioning the validity of a universal subject as the center of signification, they simultaneously demand a new understanding of the strange object of the human sciences and a redefinition of at least three fields, anthropology, history, and psychoanalysis, as leading disciplines of self-criticism. Foucault dreamed of the prestige of an anthropology that will "seek its object in the area of the unconscious processes that characterize the system of a given culture" and "would bring the relation of historicity, which is constitutive of all ethnology in general, into play within the dimension in which psycho-analysis has always been deployed." The aim of this reconversion would be the definition of "a system of cultural unconsciousness." Anthropology might, then, cease to be what it has been until now, a questionable discourse on "societies without history" (1973:373–81). How can one not recall Lévi-Strauss's definition of the anthropologist's goal?

> His goal is to grasp, beyond the conscious and always shifting images which men hold, the complete range of unconscious possibilities. These are not unlimited, and the relationships of compatibility or incompatibility which each maintains with all the others provide a logical framework for historical developments, which, while perhaps unpredictable, are never arbitrary. (Lévi-Strauss, 1963:23)

The outcome of this critique of anthropology has been devastating (Towa, 1971a; Leclerc, 1972; Adotévi, 1972). It is nevertheless essentially the outcome of an external crisis (see, e.g., Schwarz, 1979, 1980). For example, Mveng explicitly refers to this reconversion and to the deconstruction of systems alleged to be the best way to truth. On Hountondji's agenda of philosophical tasks, if a radical criticism of anthropology's products is a preliminary obligation, the ultimate objective of the philosopher's task seems defined by an amplification of one specific lesson of Althusser, bearing on a theory of scientific practice whose development depends upon the actual development of scientific knowledge (Hountondji, 1977:214). Yet even a casual reader will perceive an ethnocentric tone. Mveng writes "the West agrees with us" rather than "we learn from the West." Hountondji empha-sizes the uniqueness of the European scientific tradition and, at the same time, describes the new subject of thinking, the African philosopher, as "a human being among human beings, an intellectual among his colleagues and a member of a given social class" (Hountondji, 1977:70). A glance back at the literature of 1940–1960 shows the originality of the present-day spirit. Then, as G. Balandier wrote in his *Afrique ambiguë*, the African was chal-lenging "the weaknesses" of the West, trying "to gain recognition as a subject of history," and, paradoxically, demanding "the attention of a world which has become more curious about his destiny." This period was for him a moment of an aggressive "self-expression," "after having long been an object of exchange or an instrument in the hands of foreigners." He was defining his rights to succession and dedicating himself to a possible new beginning. It was the era of Négritude and African Personality, in brief, the period of the *African event* as described by Claude Wauthier in his overview of the Africa of African intellectuals (1964). A liberal French scholar could begin his book on *L'Avènement de l'Afrique noire* . . . in a way that today would be cause for embarrassment. Blacks are awakening from a centuries-long slumber:

> Black Africa as a political event expresses itself as the slow evolution that led Blacks to participate actively on the international scene. For thousands of years, in effect, they did not seem to have taken any initiatives: neither in

antiquity, when they were nevertheless in contact with the civilizations of the Middle East and the Far East; nor during the Middle Ages when they provided slaves, gold, and incense to Arab merchants living on the coasts of Mozambique and Somalia, and where the message of Islam had reached them from North Africa across the Sahara; nor in the modern era, when Europeans had encircled the African coasts with forts and factories. (Brunschwig, 1963:7)

In the 1950s, some of the best students of African affairs were still concerned with questions of African humanity, intellectual capabilities, and moral evolution (Griaule, 1950, 1952; Guernier, 1952; Ombredane, 1969; Van Caeneghem, 1956). J. Vansina was examining how orality could actualize neat factual texts and precise knowledge which, once well understood, could be reproduced and enshrined in the frame of scientific discourses (Vansina, 1961). In America, particularly during the 1960s, at least in political science, "the major objective sought by the comparativists at the time was the development of a framework and categories that were universally valid so as to permit comparison of all types of historical and contemporary political systems (particularly Western and non-Western) irrespective of scale, structure or the cultural matrix within which they are found" (Coleman and Halisi, 1983:40).

Some Africans—after the negritude generation—have been forcibly domesticated, intellectually speaking. In principle, they should easily function in an orthodox manner within the consecrated field of normative discourse, sophisticated intelligence, and scientific textuality. But rather than reinforcing in the normative manner their own competence, most of them, in a kind of instinctual reflex, began to question its significance, interrogate the credibility of their own *prises de parole,* and challenge the evaluative scale of both scientific processes of examination and ideological presuppositions of tasks in social sciences.

Among others, the following can be considered representative of this spirit: W. E. Abraham (Ghana), O. Bimwenyi (Zaire), H. Djaït (Tunisia), F. Eboussi-Boulaga (Cameroon), A. P. E. Elungu (Zaire), P. J. Hountondji (Benin), E. Mveng (Cameroon), A. M. Ngindu (Zaire), T. Obenga (Congo). T. Okere (Nigeria), J. O. Sodipo (Nigeria), I. Sow (Guinea), M. Towa (Cameroon), and K. Wiredu (Ghana). They are all members of the same generation: the oldest, Mveng, was born in 1930; the youngest, Hountondji, in 1942. They all published their major works between 1960 and 1970. Two external characteristics give to this group a relative homogeneity: the spiritual context of their youth and their formal training. Most of them were born into Christian families, which constitute the second or the third generation of African Christians. Thus they were or still are profoundly marked by Christian principles and values. A number of them (Bimwenyi, Eboussi-Boulaga, Mveng, Okere, and Ngindu) are Roman Catholic priests, and others (Elungu and Towa, for example) at one time in their lives thought about becoming priests. The second external unifying characteristic is the type of training that these persons received. To illustrate, let us note that they were educated at some of the most respected schools and universities in Europe, principally in

Belgium and France, and hold prestigious academic degrees. For example Djaît and Hountondji attended the well-known Ecole Normale Supérieure in Paris and are both *agrégés*, in history and philosophy respectively. Abraham did his postgraduate program at the University of Oxford, where he received his D. Phil. Obenga holds an impressive list of degrees ranging from history to Egyptology and philology. Theologian and philosopher, trained within the *curriculum studiorum* of the Society of Jesus, Eboussi-Boulaga is a *docteur en philosophie* from the University of Lyon. Bimwenyi and Okere have doctorates in theology and philosophy from Louvain University; Ngindu holds a doctorate from the Catholic School of Theology in Kinshasa and a degree in social sciences from the University of Paris. Sow, an M.D., holds two *doctorats d'Etat* from the University of Paris, one in medicine, the second in human and social sciences. Elungu, Mveng and Towa, in addition to their *doctorats de troisième cycle* and various degrees in philosophy and letters, are *docteurs d'Etat* from the University of Paris.

On the basis of their academic achievements, these men hold important positions. They are university professors, and some have had important political responsibilities. For a number of years, Abraham was the *in partibus* philosopher of President Nkrumah in Ghana; Obenga has been the minister of foreign affairs in the Congo; and Hountondji and Mveng were, for years, top civil servants in their respective countries, Benin and Cameroon. Their actual power is, however, in the intellectual and spiritual field that they control de facto. They are not only teachers but also in charge of regional, inter-African, or even international agencies working for the development of the continent. Bimwenyi, for example, was until recently a powerful general-secretary of the influential Zairean episcopate. Sow is active throughout black Africa in the establishment of new programs in psycho-anthropology. Obenga brings to African history associations a critical view on Cheikh Anta Diop's theses and, at the same time, as director of a major research center in Libreville, fights for "an African perspective" and initiative in history. Sodipo, a university vice-chancellor, is the editor of *Second Order*, and Wiredu, his assistant editor. Hountondji manages the General-Secretariat of the Inter-African Council of Philosophy. Mveng, who for a long time was General-Secretary of the African Society of Culture in Paris, is now serving as the coordinator of the Ecumenical Association of Third-World Theologians; and Ngindu is the editor of the *Bulletin of African Theology* and the secretary of the Center of African Religions in Kinshasa and secretary of its journal, *Cahiers des religions africaines*.

All of these men are "in power," and no one doubts their mission in the process of modernization. Through different lenses, they all more or less define and explain conditions and possibilities of setting in motion principles of modernization and defining the meaning of being African today. This is highly ideological and one could assert that their contributions are no more than "programatic statements" or "polemics." This is a matter of subjective judgment. These intellectuals are producing a body of good works, which are both difficult, because of the amplifications that explain them, and extremely sophisticated with respect to the relationships between power and knowledge. There is no doubt that a careful study of their works would locate weaknesses. However, it would also emphasize the complexity and ambiguity of propositions for creative capacities and multiple and nonrestrictive ways to truth. Indeed, the general ambition of these propositions for spiritual and intellectual autonomy silently assumes a severe political and ideological confrontation. Abraham put it aptly:

> But what shall Africa, which is not of the West or of the East do? It would perhaps at least be an act of supine madness to ape the West or the East, indeed any point of the compass, like a new sun-worship, in ways which cannot leave the cultures of Africa the same without our having an interest in what is dominant in the external culture, or without bothering to understand its mechanics and rationale. (Abraham, 1966:35)

With the problem of truth, we are confronted with one of the most paradoxical forms of amplification and with the promotion of African alternatives. Indeed, it is on this particular question that African academics and scholars violently interrogate the European tradition. In order to clarify the meaning of this violence, let us note that since Descartes philosophy in the West has been, in a special way, concerned with the relationship between knowledge and truth: "to be a philosopher was to be concerned with the question, what is the truth? What is knowledge?" (Foucault, 1980:82). With Nietzsche, the question was modified and became: "what is the best way, the surest path to truth?" Accordingly, in his work on *The Crisis of the European Sciences,* Husserl was dealing, in actuality, with Nietzsche's promulgation. Foucault considers himself to represent a third moment, from which, looking backwards, he can ask: "What is the history of this will to truth? What are its effects? How is all this in relation to power?" (1980).

The African postulation would seem situated, metaphorically, between Nietzsche's predicament and Foucault's enterprise. More precisely, it critically jumps the *"bavardages"* of colonial discourses and its "anthropological" applications, and centers on the system of signification that allowed the "colonial propositions" and their inferences. This critical jump is negatively described by Eboussi-Boulaga as a "way of survival." Philosophizing becomes an urgent task: *"si l'on veut survivre, il faut 'vraiment' philosopher"* (in order to survive one must philosophize). Concretely, the path to truth still seems, so far, an external model accomplished in the West, imposing rules for the renunciation of the African will to be self and, simultaneously, defining the principles for the abolition of regional histories:

> It remains for the Muntu to realize for himself what is already in himself. To realize for oneself, for one's profit, by going to a good school, getting help or learning to produce, imitate, according to his capacity. His truth being realized outside of himself, he has no resource except to apply, imitate, turn to intermediaries. (Eboussi-Boulaga, 1977:95)

This principle that founded "colonial sciences" is, according to Eboussi-Boulaga, still operating in Africa. Even in the commitment of present-day

African philosophers and social scientists, one might find, subtle and silent, the acceptance of the thesis of the Western philosophical model as a *"rationalité en acte."* Because of this situation, Eboussi-Boulaga hypothesizes a critical *"récit pour soi,"* which on a regional basis and from a new "reading" of one's own particular social experience, can organize the chaos and put forward the rationality of historical sequences, the links between facts from the standpoint of their finality, or from the genesis of this finality itself. Thus, according to Eboussi-Boulaga, the *récit* is a reconstruction of history. By necessity a negation of the present, and also a negation of self, it is, at the same time, the only critical way to self. Its internal dynamism will, eventually, guarantee the reconciliation of the historical reason and a reasonable freedom for the Muntu.

> The historical reason and reasonable liberty are rested from experienced madness and arbitrariness. They are the inversion and reversal of madness and arbitrariness. The discourse which is being constituted by the being for-itself should describe in a concrete way the future of the for-itself in history, in a regional history, whose reach is universal because of the being of the subject, the subject of history. (Eboussi-Boulaga, 1977:223)

The notion of critical reading, as well as that of a *récit pour soi* that might produce a regional historical account of the global history of humankind, bring us back to Lévi-Strauss's and Foucault's annihilation of the mythologies of the Same.

From this perspective, B. Moore's classical rules on scientific strategies and their metaphors—e.g., "in science, as in art, we are compelled to make estimates about promising and unpromising lines of attack" (1958)—seem dreams of a questionable conjunction of science, knowledge, and power. Lévi-Strauss insists: Who is speaking about science? Do we know how to live with others? "The formula 'hell is other people,' which has achieved such widespread fame, is not so much a philosophical proposition as an ethnographical statement about [Western] civilization. For, since childhood, we have been accustomed to fear impurity as coming from without. When they assert, on the contrary that 'hell is ourselves,' savage peoples give us a lesson in humility which, it is to be hoped, we may still be capable of understanding" (Lévi-Strauss, 1979:507). This ethical lesson stems from an anthropological context. Eboussi-Boulaga's discourse deploys itself in the order of an amplification conceived from an African perspective. Foucault, in the conclusion of his survey of the history of insanity in the Age of Reason, notes that "Nietzsche's last cry, proclaiming himself both Christ and Dionysos, is not on the border of reason and unreason, . . . but the point where [art] becomes impossible and where it must fall silent" (1965:287). I think a number of African thinkers would identify with Nietzsche's claim, in a figurative way.

The amplification is obvious. Is it pure accident that a great number of leading African intellectuals have, between 1955 and 1970, worked strenuously publishing works on some really "compromising" European thinkers? To note just a few: Elungu specialized in Malebranche's philosophy; Hountondji chose Husserl and Comte; Senghor commented upon Teilhard de Chardin's theses; Towa was then working on Hegel, Ngindu beginning his book on Laberthonnière, and Ugirashebuja completing his research on Heidegger. In these enterprises one notes a remarkable mediation between the rigor of a philosophical exercise and the fantasies of a political insurrection: the text commented upon is a mirror which reveals the self to the reader or commentator. From an idealist epistemology come questions and propositions which, on the one hand, seem close to Sartre's political aesthetics for the liberation of the Third World and, on the other, transpose into African geography Foucault's and Lévi-Strauss's critiques of such notions as history, culture, human space, and conventions.

This clear amplification is sufficient reason for me to state that despite their violence against the rule of the Same and the history of its conquests over all regionalisms, specificities, and differences, Lévi-Strauss and Foucault, as well as a number of African thinkers, belong to the signs of the same power. What they represent could be considered an expression of the "intelligence" of the Same. As Foucault himself stated, referring to his own intellectual filiation: "Can one still philosophize where Hegel is no longer possible? Can any philosophy continue to exist that is no longer Hegelian?" And more precisely: "truly to escape Hegel involves an exact appreciation of the price we have to pay to detach ourselves from him. It assumes that we are aware of the extent to which Hegel, insidiously perhaps, is close to us; it implies a knowledge in that which permits us to think against Hegel, of that which remains Hegelian" (1982:235). One could also relate Lévi-Strauss's view to this same origin, or, more convincingly, to Kant's dream about metaphysics and anthropology (see Lévi-Strauss, 1968).

The apparent profanation represented by these projects might simply be an optical illusion. Lévi-Strauss and Foucault are engulfed in the history of the Same and its contradictions. I would not say that African intellectuals are engulfed in the same way. The passion that in Lévi-Strauss's and Foucault's works presents theories about norm, rule, and system only uncovers and seeks strictly to define this complex history of an identity. In the name of the same methodological principles, Africans tend—despite differences of language and education—to doubt the ethical value of these estimations (see e.g., Hountondji, 1977; Wiredu, 1980).

Seen from the frontiers of the Western power-knowledge system, all these choices seem stimulating. Still, one can meditate on their projects as possible symbols of a failed will to transcendence, now expressing its desire towards an ambiguous new beginning. However, it is important to note that African ideology, as a body of reflexions and questions, springs from the same lines of dissolution that, in the kingdom of the Same, allowed Lévi-Strauss's and Foucault's crises. Metaphorically speaking, in Nietzsche's confusion there is not only the silence of an art and a power-knowledge, but also, insistently, there are all the promises of Kant's old question on the possibility of an anthropology: how pertinent is it to speak about humans?

III

THE POWER OF SPEECH

The Missionary's Discourse and Africa's Conversion

> In fact, I am now so accustomed to the
> paradoxes of this planet that I wrote the
> preceding sentence without thinking of the
> absurdity it represents.
>
> P. BOULLE, *Planet of the Apes.*

It takes little imagination to realize that missionary discourses on Africans were powerful. They were both signs and symbols of a cultural model. For quite a long time, along with travelers' accounts and anthropologists' interpretations, they constituted a kind of knowledge. In the first quarter of this century, it was clear that the traveler had become a colonizer and the anthropologist, his scientific advisor, while the missionary, more vigorously than ever, continued, in theory as well as in practice, to expound the model of African spiritual and cultural metamorphosis.

The missionary's particular position in the process of Africa's conversion has led to very peculiar results (Bureau, 1962:248–62). These results, intersecting with ideological perspectives, have, on the one hand, fostered African theories of otherness and, on the other, brought about serious doubt concerning the pertinence of Western discourses on African societies. Thus, we have two magnificent actors: the missionary and his African successor, both of them presenting their views on policies of conversion, basing them on what African culture is supposed to be, and utilizing anthropology as a means of dominating or liberating African people (Hastings, 1979:119–20).

The theme to investigate is the articulation between missionary language and its African echo or negation, and the ultimate consequences of this relationship for anthropology. The investigation is appropriate in view of questionable hypotheses about missionaries' positive or negative contributions to African ideology, and, in general, of the controversial interpretations of this relationship in the crisis of African Studies.

For the sake of clarity, I shall address first the subject of missionary discourse; second, the African response; third, how they mingle historically and ideologically in an anthropological locus and have *ad valorem* responsibility in the building of an African ideology of otherness.

The more carefully one studies the history of missions in Africa, the more difficult it becomes not to identify it with cultural propaganda, patriotic motivations, and commercial interests, since the missions' program is indeed more complex than the simple transmission of the Christian faith. From the sixteenth century to the eighteenth, missionaries were, through all the "new worlds," part of the political process of creating and extending the right of European sovereignty over "newly discovered" lands (Keller, Lissitzyn, and Mann, 1938). In doing so, they obeyed the "sacred instructions" of Pope Alexander VI in his bull *Inter Caetera* (1493): to overthrow paganism and establish the Christian faith in all barbarous nations. The bulls of Nicholas V—*Dum Diversas* (1452) and *Romanus Pontifex* (1455)—had indeed already given the kings of Portugal the right to dispossess and eternally enslave Mahometans, pagans, and black peoples in general (Deschamps, 1971). *Dum Diversas* clearly stipulates this right to invade, conquer, expell, and fight (*invadendi, conquirendi, expugnandi, debellandi*) Muslims, pagans, and other enemies of Christ (*saracenos ac paganos, aliosque Christi inimicos*) wherever they may be. Christian kings, following the Pope's decisions, could occupy pagan kingdoms, principalities, lordships, possessions (*regna, principatus, Dominia, possessiones*) and dispossess them of their personal property, land, and whatever they might have (*et mobilia et immobilia bona quaecumque per eos detenta ac possessa*). The king and his successors have the power and right to put these peoples into perpetual slavery (*subjugandi illorumque personas in perpetuam servitutem*). (See Bimwenyi, 1981a:621–22).

The missionaries, preceding or following a European flag, not only helped their home country to acquire new lands but also accomplished a "divine" mission ordered by the Holy Father, *Dominator Dominus*. It was in God's name that the Pope considered the planet his franchise and established the basic principles of *terra nullius* (nobody's land), which denies non-Christian natives the right to an autonomous political existence and the right to own or to transfer ownership (Witte, 1958).

If the Reformation challenged the Holy Father's power "to give, grant and assign forever" lands to European monarchs, the new axiom, *cuius regio, illius religio,* enforced the complementarity between colonial activity and religious conversion. For instance, the Christian kingdom of Congo, was officially recognized by the Holy See and the major European seapowers in the sixteenth and seventeenth centuries. However, it lost its special status in the mercantilist and Protestant eighteenth century. The prevalent economic ideal of a "balance of trade" was inseparable from the need to increase the nation's wealth and its strength, hence the great utility of colonial trade and possessions.

The Church's involvement in establishing Western sovereignty was important both before and after the Reformation. The mass celebrated on the Guinea Coast in 1481, under a big tree displaying the royal arms of Portugal, symbolized the possession of a new territory. Among a multitude of other similar acts, Vasco Da Gama erected a pillar, engraved with the Portuguese royal arms, on the east coast in the kingdom of Melinda, and Diego Caon constructed another in 1494 at the mouth of the Congo River. These symbols were part of a formal and elaborate ceremony of appropriation of a *terra nullius*. Generally, such a ceremony presented three major characteristics (Keller et al., 1938): *(a)* the construction of a physical sign bearing the royal arms, such as a pillar (Portuguese), a landmark or even a simple pile of stones (Spanish), or a cross (English and French); *(b)* a solemn declaration, perhaps presenting the letters patent received from the king, announcing the new sovereignty and indicating that the possession is taken in the name of, or for, the king; and *(c)* a symbolization of the new jurisdiction. Explorers from Roman Catholic nations, generally, performed a mass; whereas Anglo-Saxons symbolized their control over the land with a sacred formula or legal decree. For example, on August 5, 1583, as part of the ceremony of taking possession of Newfoundland, Sir Humphrey Gilbert promulgated a code of three laws; namely, the establishment of the Church of England in the colony; the punishment as high treason of any act prejudicial to the Queen's right of possessing the new land; and, for "those uttering words to the Queen's dishonour, the penalty to be having their ears removed and their ship and goods confiscated" (see, e.g., Keller et al., 1938).

The missionary played an essential role in the general process of expropriation and, subsequently, exploitation of all the "new found lands" upon the earth. As G. Williams puts it, if in many areas his presence "helped to soften the harshness of European impact on the indigenous peoples whose lands were invaded and exploited," his "fervour was allied, rather than opposed to commercial motive" (Williams, 1967:29).

The scramble for Africa in the nineteenth century took place in an atmosphere of Christian revival: the age of Enlightenment and its criticism of religion had ended. Coleridge's phrase, "the Bible finds you," was an apt one for all Christians. In Catholic Europe, the First Vatican Council firmly reorganized Catholicism. A group of distinguished prelates even reevaluated the meaning of the so-called curse of Ham, hoping that "the interior of Africa may participate in the solemn coming joy of the Church's triumph" *(Interior Africa solemnis gaudii proximi Ecclesiae triumphi particeps fiat)* (Bimwenyi, 1981:625–26). There was, besides, a general spirit of adventure in the air (Rotberg, 1970; Betts, 1975). The European political and economic rivalries were an incentive to action overseas. The success of men like Cecil Rhodes reinforced the myth of an African treasure house and appealed to young and ambitious potential colonists. Above all, scientific curiosity and philanthropic objectives combined and confused the struggle against the slave trade, geographic explorations, and mythologies about "poor savage Africans" (Hammond and Jablow, 1977).

Three major figures, from the fifteenth century to the end of the nineteenth, determined modalities and the pace of mastering, colonizing, and transforming the "Dark Continent": the explorer, the soldier, and the missionary (Christopher, 1984). The explorer, at the end of the fifteenth century, was looking for a sea-route to India. Later on, he concerned himself with mapping out the continent and, in the nineteenth century, compiling information and organizing complex bodies of knowledge, including medicine, geography, and anthropology. The soldier constituted the most visible figure of the expansion of European jurisdiction. He built castles and forts on the coasts, was in charge of trading posts, participated in the slave-trade, and, in the nineteenth century, implemented colonial power. Finally, there was the missionary, whose objective has been, throughout the centuries, the most consistent: to expand "the absoluteness of Christianity" and its virtues.

Of all "these bearers of the African burden," the missionary was also, paradoxically, the best symbol of the colonial enterprise (see Kalu, 1977). He devoted himself sincerely to the ideals of colonialism: the expansion of Civilization, the dissemination of Christianity, and the advance of Progress. Pringle's 1820 vision sums it up nicely:

> Let us enter upon a new and nobler career of conquest. Let us subdue Savage Africa by justice, by kindness, by the talisman of Christian truth. Let us thus go forth, in the name and under the blessing of God, gradually to extend the moral influence . . . the territorial boundary also of our colony, until it shall become an Empire. (Hammond and Jablow, 1977:44)

Obviously, the missionary's objectives had to be co-extensive with his country's political and cultural perspectives on colonization, as well as with the Christian view of his mission. With equal enthusiasm, he served as an agent of a political empire, a representative of a civilization, and an envoy of God. There is no essential contradiction between these roles. All of them implied the same purpose: the conversion of African minds and space. A. J. Christopher rightly observes that "missionaries, possibly more than members of other branches of the colonial establishment, aimed at the radical transformation of indigenous society . . . They therefore sought, whether consciously or unconsciously, the destruction of pre-colonial societies and their replacement by new Christian societies in the image of Europe" (1984:83).

One might consider that missionary speech is always predetermined, pre-regulated, let us say *colonized*. It depends upon a normative discourse already given, definitely fixed, clearly meant in "a vital connection between Christianity and Western culture as a whole" (Dickson, 1984:33). Missionary orthodox speech, even when imaginative or fanciful, evolved within the framework of what, from now on, I shall call the authority of the truth. This is God's desire for the conversion of the world in terms of cultural and socio-political regeneration, economic progress and spiritual salvation. This means, at least, that the missionary does not enter into dialogue with pagans and "savages" but must impose the law of God that he incarnates. All of the non-Christian cultures have to undergo a process of reduction to, or—in missionary language—of regeneration in, the norms that the missionary represents. This undertaking is perfectly logical: a person whose ideas and mission come from and are sustained by God is rightly entitled to the use of all possible means, even violence, to achieve his objectives. Consequently, "African conversion," rather than being a positive outcome of a dialogue—unthinkable per se—came to be the sole position the African could take in order to survive as a human being.

In dealing with this kind of general theory, we need models to refer to. I propose to use three men: the seventeenth-century Italian Giovanni Francesco Romano; the nineteenth-century African Samuel Ajayi Crowther; and the twentieth-century Belgian Placide Frans Tempels. These individuals were neither the best of all missionaries, nor necessarily the most remarkable. Yet one easily recognizes that each one, in his time, was an excellent example of sound commitment to religious interests and imperial policy.

Giovanni F. Romano, a missionary in the Congo from 1645 to 1654, published in 1648 a report of fewer than one hundred pages on his voyage to, and his sojourn in, that central African kingdom (Romano, 1648). He really presents no reasons for supposing that the Congolese cannot understand the Gospel's message. His conception of mission coincides with traditional practice. It struck me that, as a missionary, he could have accomplished the same type of work with St. Boniface in Germany. He boasts of the number of people converted, masses celebrated, sacraments given, churches erected, but he cannot stand the presence of Dutch Protestants, those "enemies of the Catholic faith," *nemici della Santa Fede Cattolica,* who undermine the impression of European grandeur and unity. Romano defines his own mission as working "God's field" *la Vigna del Signore,* and "preaching God's news" *predicare la parola di Dio,* to the "poor and pagan" Congolese, *questi gentili, quei poveri,* etc. For a soldier of God, this does not exclude concern for the privileges of rank and for the continuation of this friendly Christian kingdom of Congo. Romano and his colleagues intervene in the conflict between the Congolese monarch and one of his rebel vassals, since a Christian monarch is a treasure that must be preserved at any cost. About the Catholic Congolese monarch Garcia II he wrote: "The devotion that His Majesty has showed for our religion, convent and school is a praiseworthy thing for eternity" (Romano, 1648:37).

Romano's language is a language of orthodoxy, the expression of *the Holy Faith.* Few derogatory words occur in his report. In his ethnographic description of the kingdom, the African customs are neither curious nor bizarre (Mudimbe-Boyi, 1977). Except for the king and his courtiers, all the inhabitants are *poor and pagan people.* This is not a paradox. Romano describes an African version of a Christian European kingdom with its dukes, earls and barons. With such a model, it is perfectly normal to observe a rigid hierarchy determined by social status and position or, in terms of the interpretation current in Romano's time, by God's will. The only major difference between the model and its African expression appears in a metaphor of colors—white versus black: "The natives of Congo are all of them black, some more, some less. At birth, they are not black but white and then gradually they become black" (Mudimbe-Boyi, 1977:375–83). At the heart of Romano's conviction lies the desire for the universality of God's law. At the same time he hopes to overcome Satan's presence in the African *vigna della Christianita* (field of Christianity) and promote the *essenza della verita* (essence of truth).

The second model is Samuel Ajayi Crowther. Born about 1806, this former slave and native of Yorubaland in Nigeria was educated at Fourah Bay College (Sierra Leone) and in England. Ordained a minister in 1843 within the Church Missionary Society, he became in 1864 the first Anglican bishop of "the territories of Western Equatorial Africa beyond the Queen's Dominions." An untiring missionary, he participated in several explorations, among them the voyage that he related in his *Journal of an Expedition Up the Tshadda Rivers,* published in 1855.

Crowther believed that Africa could regenerate herself without the help of others (Meester, 1980b:72; Sanneh, 1983:60–83). However, in presenting his own experience, he tends to refer to contemporary classification of "savages" and from this perspective builds his own project of converting his African brethren to civilization and Christianity. About his 1854 Niger expedition, for instance, Crowther recalls:

> I asked whether the inhabitants of Gomkoi were Pagans or Mohammedans; and was informed that they were all Pagans; that the males wore some sort of cloth around their loins, but the females only a few green leaves. On asking whether they were cannibals, I was answered in the negative. (In Hammond and Jablow, 1977:36)

What is interesting in this brief quotation is its classificatory implications, in particular the characteristics selected: paganism, nakedness, and cannibalism. Western-assimilated, Crowther intends to relate an ethnographic case objectively, but he is very clearly describing the syndrome of savagery. As D. Hammond and A. Jablow rightly put it:

> The basic attitudes which arbitrarily relate these essentially unrelated qualities—paganism, nakedness, cannibalism—are those which assign all cultural differences to the single category of savagery; and one trait as it distinguishes a savage from a European becomes an index to the existence of the other traits which are part of the syndrome. (Hammond and Jablow, 1977:36–37)

In fact, far from making Crowther responsible for this syndrome, I am inclined to look at him as expressing the signs of an *episteme.* He simply shares a pervasive evolutionary assumption, a tendency to see in Africans only these indexed features and thus subsequently to indicate the necessity of a regeneration through both a cultural and spiritual conversion (see figure 2).

Figure 2. Ideological Model of Conversion: Colonial Rule

	Premises	Mediators	Aims
Status	Primitiveness	Conversion	Civilization
Symbols or signs	Pagan (evil)	Christianity	Christian (good)
	Naked (child)	Education	Civilized (adults)
	Cannibal (beast)	Evolution	"Evolué" (human being)
Method	Anthropological presuppositions	Missiology, applied anthropology, pedagogy	Colonial sciences

My third model is the Belgian Placide F. Tempels, a missionary in Central Africa from 1933 to 1962 and author of *Bantu Philosophy*. Placide Tempels was a very serious and careful student of Bantu culture, despite allegations to the contrary made mainly by professional anthropologists and philosophers, who are inclined to emphasize formal training as the sine qua non condition of sound work. Tempels had lived more than ten years among the Luba Katanga people, sharing their language and culture when he decided to publish his experiences (1979:3–25). Rather than as a philosophical treatise, his *Bantu Philosophy* could be understood simultaneously as an indication of religious insight, the expression of a cultural doubt about the supposed backwardness of Africans, and a political manifesto for a new policy for promoting "civilization" and Christianity. But this complexity is not what is commonly discussed when specialists speak of Tempels's philosophy.

It must be remembered that *Bantu Philosophy* is based on very simple ideas. They go like this. First, in all cultures, life and death determine human behavior; or, presented differently, all human behavior depends upon a system of general principles. Second, if the Bantu are human beings, there is reason to seek the fundamentals of their beliefs and behavior, or their basic philosophical system. From this position, Tempels attempts "a true estimate of indigenous peoples," rejecting "the misunderstanding and fanaticism of the ethnology of the past and of the former attitude of aversion entertained with regard to them" (Possoz's preface in Tempels, 1959:13–15). This meant questioning the classical doctrines about evangelization, civilization and colonization (Tempels, 1959:167–89).

These three models—Giovanni Francesco Romano, Samuel Ajayi Crowther, and Placide Frans Tempels—signify the authority of the truth, its signs and discourse. We can perceive in them an expression of a common ideology. They are, all of them, people for whom commitment to God is central. Concretely, they believe that they are the ones in charge of saving

Africa. This, for them, means the promotion of the ideals of Christian civilization. Finally, they are secure in their knowledge of the correct means for Africa's conversion. In brief, they prove right M. de Certeau's observation that "the *credibility* of a discourse is what first makes believers act in accord with it. It produces practitioners" (Certeau, 1984:148).

In his evaluation of Christianity from an African point of view, Eboussi-Boulaga, the philosopher from Cameroon, holds that in general missionary discourse has always been presented as a discourse of philosophical reduction and ideological intolerance:

> Christianity is the inheritor of Greek reason and it is the continuation and the achievement of the Judaic revelation. By these two traits it is the critic of the falsehood of other religions and denounces their mythological character. Its proper element is language and history, but not the obscure regions of the cosmos nor of the imaginary. That is why it agrees with modernity and resists better than other systems the corrosion of modernity, the disillusion of the world in which it exists. (Eboussi-Boulaga, 1981:35)

Sharing this belief in the superiority of Christianity, expressed in its essential qualifications, that is, its identification with reason, history, and power, the missionary's discourse has, according to Eboussi-Boulaga, always presented five major features. First of all, it is a language of derision, insofar as it fundamentally ridicules the pagan's Gods. And one must not forget that since its birth Christianity has appropriated for itself both the only way to true communication with the divine and the only correct image of God and God's magnificence. Second, it is a language of refutation or systematic reduction: all pagan religions constitute the black side of a white transcendental Christianity, and this metaphoric opposition of colors means the opposition of evil and good, Satan and God. The third feature illuminates the missionary's pragmatic objectives: his action is supported by a language of demonstration, which reflects God's truth. In order to sustain his derision for and refutation of non-Christian beliefs and practices, the missionary emphasizes the Christian faith in terms of its historical coherence and transforming virtues. Religious and biblical categories enter into the logic of his civilization, thus making sacred a cultural model and giving it a divine seal. Consequently, there is a fourth characteristic: the rule of Christian orthodoxy which relates Faith to knowledge of the only Truth. This is the cornerstone of the belief in the supremacy of the European experience, the support of a fantastic set of principles. It accounts for the following major principles: first, that the Christian characteristic resides in the quality of Faith and not in moral grandeur; second, that it is Faith which promotes and gives sense to ethics and not the contrary. The last trait of missionary discourse relates to these two axioms and their theological significance: it is a language that conforms to these vigorous axioms. Missionary speech and praxis prove that no human enterprise can succeed as long as the true God is not acknowledged. The Christian God's spirit appears, therefore, as history's only force.

I would prefer to simplify this analytical perspective of Eboussi-Boulaga's into a simpler scheme. The missionary language of derision is basically a cultural position, the expression of an ethnocentric outlook. The aspects of refutation and demonstration rationalize the initial ethnocentric moment and are aimed explicitly towards an intellectual reduction that would complement the rules of orthodoxy and conformity. Thus we have three moments, rather than types, of violence in missionary language. Theoretically, they are expressed in the concepts of derision, refutation-demonstration, and orthodoxy-conformity.

Taking into account the missionary theology of salvation, and more precisely the general policies of *conversio gentium*, it becomes clear that the same violence is linked to the spiritual and cultural process of conversion in a hypostatic union (see figure 3). All missionaries, whatever their denominations, operate according to the same canon of conversion.

Their language depends on three major types of data always considered a given and taken for granted: premises, mediators, and objectives. All of them tend to integrate cultural and religious aims, the mission being altogether oriented towards the cultural promotion and spiritual salvation of "savages." Thus, for instance, G. F. Romano's preaching of the Holy Faith to "these needy" also implied involvement in political affairs to perpetuate a Western Christian dependent polity in Africa. Bishop Crowther was preoccupied with both Christianization and Westernization of "naked, cannibal, and pagan primitives." Tempels stated his philosophy of civilizing Bantu people in this way: "If the Bantu cannot be raised by a Christian civilization, they will not be by any other" (1959:186).

The pertinent categories arise from a structural combination. On the one hand, ethnographic commentaries on African peoples are arranged according to the prospect of their possible conversion; on the other hand, specific socio-cultural symbols designate the passage from primitiveness to civilization.

An evolutionary thesis expresses the conversion from savagery and Satan's darkness to the light of civilization and God's kingdom. The transformation is sometimes described as the introduction or restoration of health in a sick universe, the establishment of order in a world of disorder, madness, corruption, and diabolical illusions (see Pirotte, 1973; Fernandez, 1979). In its standard form, the process of conversion which is the path to a "civilized life" is presented as a gradual one: at the lowest level one finds primitives or pagans; these, infected by the "will to become Westernized" become catechumens; the zenith of their development is achieved when they become Christians or "evolués," that is, Westernized individuals. Accordingly, the missionary's language presents three major approaches: derision of so-called primitive religions and their gods, refutation and demonstration to convince

Figure 3. The Missionary Theology of Salvation

	Premises	Mediators	Aims
Status	Primitiveness	Conversion	Western Civilization and Christianity
Symbols	Illness	to introduce to restore	Health
	Disorder (madness, satanic illusions, and corruption)	to establish	Order (Christian models of faith and behavior)
	Darkness	to promote	The Light of God and Civilization
Method	Derision	Demonstration	Conformity

the evolving Africans, and imposition of rules of orthodoxy and conformity for converts.

> Quite inevitably the Christian Faith has for many years . . . been inextricably bound up with this Western aggression. But it has also to be admitted quite frankly that during these centuries the missionaries of the Christian Church have commonly assumed that Western civilization and Christianity were two aspects of the same gift which they were commissioned to offer to the rest of mankind. This assumption was sometimes quite conscious and was explicitly stated. More often it was quite unconscious and would have been indignantly denied. But in neither case are we called upon to judge our fathers. Their sincerity can hardly be disputed. (Taylor, 1963:5–6)

Fundamentally, an evolutionary assumption was expressed on the basis of a dualistic anthropology (see Ngimbi-Nseka, 1979:10 and 18–19). As Benedict XV put it in his encyclic, *Maximum Illud* (1919), missionaries must be determined to oppose Satan and to bring salvation to the "poor people of Africa victimized by evil forces." Yet one notes that Romano focused on mediators and aims rather than on premises. And Tempels absolutely doubted the classical process of conversion: he was not sure in the least that assimilation constituted the best way, and he hated the "evolués," whom he considered to be bad copies of Europeans. Moreover, he did not believe that to Christianize meant to impose a Western philosophical anthropology (Tempels, 1962). However, Tempels's position did not imply a complete negation of the essential dualism but only indicated another type of guidance for the promotion of orthodoxy and conformity. The emphasis he gave to Bantu ontology, for example, means that he had faith in the possibility of bringing about a "new Christian civilization" without destroying Bantu values or their underlying major principles, the concept and reality of "vital force" (see, e.g., Mataczynski, 1984 and Donders, 1985). This outlook is simply a new manner of demonstrating and promoting the essence of ortho-doxy, the aim remaining clearly the same: "Christianity is the only possible consummation of the Bantu ideal" (Tempels, 1959:186).

Tempels is not alone in looking for new policies for integrating Chris-tianity into African cultures, and Ethiopian Christianity, African Islam and syncretic churches all over the continent witness to the vitality of a process of indigenization (Monteil, 1980; Sundkler, 1964; Barrett, 1968; Brenner, 1984). In the 1960s, Taylor detected three main ingredients in the African challenge to Christianity: *(a)* Christian religion is "inherently Western" and "fails to correspond to the *felt* needs of Asia and Africa"; *(b)* This challenge poses a radical question: "can the Christian faith not only prove its ability to meet the deep human needs of our time but also make peoples of different backgrounds feel at home in the new world?"; *(c)* "The Christian Church has not yet faced the theological problem of 'co-existence' with other religions" (Taylor 1963:6–8).

At any rate, the apparent success of Christianity is startling. After one century of evangelization, the Christian community represents today some forty-five percent of the population of the continent. Let us note that, accord-ing to the World Bank (1984), the total population of sub-Saharan Africa, which "rose from 270 million in 1970 to 359 million in 1980, seems set to double by the turn of the century and significantly more than triple by the year 2020" (World Bank, 1984:26). Within this frame, the Catholic church has today some seventy-six million members, Protestant denominations ac-knowledge fifty million followers; the Ethiopian Coptic church, thirty mil-lion members, and some thousand autonomous local churches bring the total Christian membership to roughly 200 million. When one keeps in mind that, through conversion, and especially disproportionate population growth (see World Bank, 1984:82–83), the Christian community gains between five and six million new members each year, it becomes obvious that by the year 2000 Africa could have the largest concentration of Christians in the world (Barrett, 1970; Meester de Ravenstein, 1980a:215; Donders, 1985:1, 30). The trend is identical with the increase in the number of ministers. A 1985 Vatican statistical report shows that in Catholicism "the number of Diocesan clergy is increasing in Africa, South America and Oceania." In Central America, the figures remain "almost the same." In North America, the report notes a "modest drop," and "the most notable reduction [is] found in Europe." But the most significant shift is in the percentage of the world's major seminarians produced by different parts of the world. In Africa it jumped from 6.7 percent in 1973 to 10.7 percent in 1983, while in North America it dropped to 10.9 percent from 19.2 percent in the same period. In Europe, the percentage went down to 34.4 percent from 41.1 percent.

If European Catholicism seems to be aging dangerously, the dynamism of its African counterpart belongs either to a holy nightmare or, if one prefers, to an incredible miracle: monasteries are being built; new religious move-

ments, both activist and charismatic, are appearing and organizing themselves successfully; there are not enough schools for potential catechists, nor
are there sufficient convents for nuns. There is not enough room in semi-
naries for candidates to the priesthood, yet despite the increase in vocation,
particularly in the countries with the highest fertility rates—Kenya, Nigeria,
Tanzania, Zaïre—the number of priests is considered to be low. According to
the Vatican statistical document mentioned *above,* in 1983 Europe had 58.2
percent of the world's priests for 33.3 percent of the world's Catholics; North
America had 17.1 percent of the world's priests for 7.7 percent of its
Catholics; South America had 8.4 percent of the world's priests for 28.1
percent of the world's Catholics; and Africa had 4.3 percent of priests for
eight percent of the world's Catholics (see also Laurentin, 1977; Meester de
Ravenstein, 1980a:214). As to other Christian denominations, one notes
that, for example, the most populous Quaker community in the world lives
in the northern part of Kenya, and that it is in Uganda that one finds the most
statistically important Anglican church in the world.

The question becomes: how really Christian is this converted Africa?
A. Hastings proposes a vague, prudent answer:

> As regards Catholics and Anglicans, [the Christian] advance could probably
> be charted in a rough but not unreliable way by the decline in ecclesiastical
> marriage rates. Its vast, amorphous mass of devotion, cult, belief, superstition,
> new bonds of fellowship so often structured in ways that hardly accord with
> the rules of Rome, Geneva or Canterbury, may prove the most enduring
> ecclesiastical legacy of this quarter century. (Hastings, 1979:274)

This evaluation does not answer the question, nor does it explain why
Christianity seems so attractive. In his book on a *Non-Bourgeois Theology,*
(1985), Donders emphasizes the appeal of the miracle of God in Jesus and
the desire to be a member of a new *communitas* or communion (see also
Oduyoye 1986:97–108). He also refers to a cultural reason: the necessity of
an anthropological conversion.

> David Barret believes that one of the main reasons Africans are so attracted to
> Christianity (and to Islam) is the community it offers. It is his opinion that the
> conversion movement at the grassroots level is due to the fact that Africans are
> turning away from their local tribal religions because they see no "salvation" in
> those organizations anymore. They want to belong to a larger human and
> religious community. (Donders, 1985:32)

In fact, this seems like Baeta's classical explanation: "the mission station was
not merely a base for teaching the Christian discipline . . . and for propagat-
ing the Faith: it was also the pocket of [a] new invading civilization"
(1968:15).

In a critical analysis of African Christianity, de Meester de Ravenstein
names three antinomies: the complexity of the African critique of Western

Christianity, which implies the possibility of a zero degree of Christianity; the difficulty of bringing together African "traditional" values and the absolute gratuity of God's gift; and the fundamental opposition between Christ's religion and the African's religious heritage (1980a:43–50). These evaluations from knowledgeable observers clearly show the confusing reality of African Christianity. Let us follow its recent history.

From the 1950s onward, new orientations appeared for the indigenization of the Church (Nyamiti, 1978; Hastings, 1979). Gradually, official policies shifted from the initial step of adaptation, one that insisted on the Africanization of some external aspects (music, hymns, etc.), to an examination of the content of Christianity in an African setting. New premises established a completely different perspective: the "pagan culture" is considered and analyzed as an abandoned field in which God's signs already exist (figure 4). Thus, if there can be only one aim—Christianity—methods are arbitrary and should be modified and adapted to circumstances and cultures (Taylor, 1963:124). African intellectuals appealed "to the Church to 'come to grips' with traditional practices, and with the world view that these beliefs and practices imply" (Hastings, 1979:119; see also Kalu, 1977).

The best illustrations of this current are Gravrand's *Visage africain de l'eglise* (1962), Mulago's *Un visage africain du christianisme* (1965), Bahoken's *Clairières métaphysiques africaines* (1967), and Mbiti's *New Testament Eschatology in an African Background* (1971). In these contributions, the authors explicitly favor the search for Christianity's essential message, one which would penetrate African ways of thinking and living. A new vocabulary arises and, in principle, covers new forms of evangelization: Africanization, indigenization, naturalization, adaptation of Christianity. Some theorists even speak of "indigenizing the Gospel" and "the Message" (Bimwenyi, 1981a:231). In Roman Catholic circles, the norms of the new policy are relatively well spelled out in two official documents of Pius XII; *Evangelii Praecones* (1951) and *Fidei Donum* (1957).

What this ambivalent vocabulary introduces and means is a progressive displacement of responsibility insofar as the future of Christianity is concerned (see, e.g., Chipenda, 1977 and Setiloane, 1977). Historically, one can refer to *Des Prêtres noirs s'interrogent* (1956), a collection of black priests' articles and a solidly nationalist reflection on Christianity, as the first explicit manifestation of a new radical current. Ironically, it was during this period that positive and sympathetic contributions on African religions were produced in anthropology. They include Deschamps's *Les Religions d'Afrique noire* (1954), Parrinder's *African Traditional Religion* (1954), and *Witchcraft* (1958), Lienhardt's *Divinity and Experience* (1961), Van Caeneghem's *La Notion de Dieu chez les Balubas du Kasaï* (1956), Schebesta's *Le Sens religieux des primitifs* (1963), Damann's *Les religions de l'Afrique* (1964, a translation of his 1963 *Die Religionen Afrikas*), and *African Systems of Thought* edited by Fortes and Dieterlen (1965). African clergymen read these books looking for ways of transforming traditional religion or, at least, of

Figure 4. The Theology of Indigenization

	Premises	Mediators	Aims
Status	Pagan Culture	Conversion	Christianity
Symbols	Abandoned field	to plant, sow the African field	Adapted Christianity
		to spread the good seed	
	Stepping stones of Christianity in pagan traditions	to establish and to construct the Church	Indigenized Christianity
Method	Critical evaluation of premises	Demonstration	Conformity

using some of its elements in the process of adapting Christianity (Mulago, 1959). In the wake of independence, some of them became clearly radical: they suspected the good faith of anthropological descriptions and began to question the very meaning of the theologies of adaptation (Bimwenyi, 1980a: 172–89).

> At first, the concept of 'adaptation' was hailed on all sides, by African Christians as well as by missionaries. Even though it was not seen as commit-ting the Church to religious dialogue with African tradition, and perhaps because of this, adaptation, as the means by which the African Church could develop its own life-style, was highly welcome. It was only slowly realized that the concept of adaptation contained within itself the seeds of perpetual western superiority and domination. The reaction has been quite violent. (Shorter, 1977: 150)

The fact is that even at the time of the manifesto of black priests (1956), the search for an African Christianity was already enveloped by the themes of cultural authenticity and independence. It clearly implied a relative rejection of both anthropologists' and missionaries' interpretations of African tradi-tions and religions as well as the colonial presence.

The search had two major aspects: a nationalist reading and the introduc-tion of an intellectual rupture in colonial history. For example, Kagame questions the competence of Tempels and makes a journey back to his own roots with his *La Philosophie bantu-rwandaise de l'être* (1956), in which he describes Rwandan Bantu ontology, a criteriology, psychology, cosmology, and ethics. I am afraid Shorter confuses problems of method and ideological motivation when he states that "it is only because Kagame is inspired by European philosophy that the African thinks of trying to express the tradi-tional thought of his people as a conceptual system" (1977:24). The inspira-tion is one thing, the objective another. What Kagame did was to use the

Aristotelian model in order to demonstrate that, contrary to anthropologists' and missionaries' accepted opinions, his people had always had a well-organized and systematic "philosophy." He explicitly intended to undermine the myths which sustained both colonial policies and the Church's programs for an adapted Christianity (1976). Philosophically, one could debate Kagame's assumption about the possibility of collective and non-explicit philosophies. Ideologically, however, his work was quite important, if considered to be an answer to hypotheses on "pagan" cultures and the premises of adaptation policies (see figure 4).

In the same vein, A. Makarakiza published his *La Dialectique des Barundi* (1959), E. B. Idowu, *Olodumare. God in Yoruba Belief* (1962) and *Towards an Indigenous Church* (1965), E. Mveng, *L'Art d'Afrique noire. Liturgie et langage religieux* (1965), and F. M. Lufuluabo, a series of booklets presenting and analyzing traditional religiosity vis-à-vis Christianity (1962, 1964a and b, 1966). Significantly, the concept of African monotheism appeared and was used more and more frequently. Indeed, it refers to W. Schmidt's concept of primitive revelation (1931) and gives respectability to what was formerly called pagan and polytheist belief. One of the major assumptions of Schmidt's method is the existence of a universal theory or "philosophy" that each human community expresses in its own way and according to its own needs. This philosophy would be always and everywhere particular in its religious, cultural, and historical manifestations, but universal in its essence. Its presence marks the difference between human societies and animal communities (Schmidt, 1933–1949). A primitive revelation can thus be deduced from all human cultures and, with it, a basic monotheism. The concept of primitive revelation has not, so far, clarified the theoretical questions that it implies, despite the brilliant discussions and stimulating overviews recently presented by Mulago (1973) and Bimwenyi (1968, 1981a). K. Dickson even thinks that

> there are no easy solutions to the problem of the relation between God and the gods, and that it is much less enlightening than is thought to use such terms as monotheism and polytheism; in a sense they confuse the discussion. (Dickson, 1984:58)

On the other hand, the force of ideas for political and cultural autonomy had a direct impact on religious thinking. During the 1959 International Meeting of Black Writers and Artists in Rome, a Committee on Theology elaborated a text calling for another Christianity in Africa. Within Catholicism, two Jesuit priests from Cameroon—Mveng and M. Hebga—were active in this area and their influence marked discussions on possible ways to reconcile Christianity and Africanity (Bimwenyi, 1981a:227–30). A theology of incarnation was promoted with a particular emphasis on new premises: négritude and black personality as expressions of an African civilization, African history with its own symbols as a preparation for Christianity, and finally the experience of slavery, exploitation, and colonization as signs of the suffering of God's chosen ones (figure 5). The most striking feature of these intellectual positions resides in the theoretical distinction between the program of political liberation which should permit a transformation of the traditional civilization and that of rethinking Christianity as an integral part of the local culture (Idowu, 1965; Hebga, 1963; Tchidimbo, 1963). There is a reason for this orientation, writes M. A. Oduyoye, a woman theologian of Ghana:

> The identity crisis in Africa, especially among the urbanized, the Western-educated, and the Christians, may be attributed to the loss of a dynamic perspective on life, which comes from knowing and living one's religio-cultural history. We cannot expect those who cannot tell their story, who do not know where they come from, to hear God's call to his future. (Oduyoye, 1986:54)

I have recently proposed that in the 1960s a goal was clear and that it is now possible to discern the major trends which contributed to the progressive construction of a theology of incarnation (Mudimbe, 1983a:94–95). These trends are:

(*a*) A strong interest in the Africanization of Christianity insofar as it would permit a divorce between Christianity and Western history and culture and would introduce African features into the Church.

(*b*) A search for an African element in the field of theology and religious activities, which might keep pace with the ideological objectives for political and cultural autonomy. This trend mainly characterizes Roman Catholic African theologians.

(*c*) A vigorous interest in traditional religions, leading to the supposition that in general anthropologists' and missionaries' works are neither dependable nor acceptable. This encourages new programs and projects which will be the responsibility of African scholars (see also Chipenda, 1977; Setiloane, 1977; Oduyoye, 1986).

It would be inaccurate to pretend that most missionaries supported the new African perspective. The Church's official policies in the late 1950s and early 1960s were as confusing as those of the colonial powers (Hastings, 1979:159–74). Despite the fact that the Church had trained most of the nationalist leaders and intellectuals, and also despite widely held doubts concerning the Church's commitment to the principles of Western supremacy in Africa, many a missionary did not welcome the outcome of ideologies of otherness and did not at all like doctrines of African independence. Besides political fears, there was the feeling that these new theories were opening a new era and meant the end of missionary initiatives in Africa. As Hastings, commenting on the significance of the assembly of the International Missionary Council held in Ghana in 1958, put it:

> The churches of the third world were becoming independent and the old missionary relationship which so clearly involved a status of dependence must

Figure 5. The Theology of Incarnation

	Premises	Mediators	Aims
Status	African traditional civilization	Conversion	A modern African civilization
	(Black personality-Negritude)		(Black personality-Negritude)
Symbols	African history	Otherness	African culture
	African, Muslim, and European heritages		(African Weltanschauungen, African Christianity)
	A particular experience: slavery, exploitation, colonization		
Method	Social science	African ideology	Autonomy

inevitably end. What role would there now be for missionaries? (Hastings, 1979:120)

The question was pertinent. By the mid-1960s the initiative became African and, generally speaking, integrated the essential theses of a new model of conversion (Meester de Raventstein, 1980a). The emphasis is, then, put on new premises: négritude, blackness, African heritage and experience. It tends to present conversion in terms of critical integration into Christianity; that is, on the one hand, asserting cultural autonomy and, on the other, defining Christianization as a way of accomplishing in Christ a spiritual heritage authentically African (Mulago, 1981:43; Bimwenyi, 1981b:47–60). Eboussi-Boulaga aptly wrote that *at least for Africans,* the emergence of an African "We-Subject" was the major human phenomenon of the second half of this century (1978:339). Two major phenomena thus emerged (see figure 5). The first was a strong emphasis on history and a new anthropology as a means for a better understanding of both African tradition and identity. This led, in 1966, to the creation of centers of African religions. In pastoral institutes—in Bodija (Nigeria), Bukumbi (Tanzania), Cocody (Ivory Coast), Kinshasa and Lubumbashi (Zaïre), etc.—it generally gave birth to realistic programs taking into account native languages, local customs, and the social relations of production. Second, a striking ideological convergence became obvious: African theologians' interests blend with local nationalisms and the orientations of the African Society of Culture (ASC) and with *Présence Africaine* (Paris) on the significance of African religions (Basse, 1977:129–38; Muzorewa, 1985:37–56; Oduyoye, 1986:45–55). Further, a succession of scholarly meetings in the 1960s redefined the concept of conversion and the purposes of studying African religions, while at the same time broadening the scope of the criticism of anthropology and the philosophy of Christian missions in Africa (Agossou, 1977; Appiah-Kubi and Torres, 1977):

1955: On Africa and Christianity. Meeting. (Accra, Ghana).

1959: On Christianity, Africanity and Theology. Meeting. Sub-Committee on Theology, Second Congress of African Writers. (Rome, Italy).

1961: On African Religions. ASC-Coloquium (Abidjan, Ivory Coast). Proceedings published by Présence Africaine, Paris, 1962.

1963: ASC-publication. *African Personality and Catholicism*. Paris: Présence Africaine.

1963: Reincarnation and Mystic Life According to African Religions. Congress (Strasbourg, France). Proceedings: *Réincarnation et vie mystique en Afrique noire*. 1965.

1965: On Africa's Traditional Religions. Congress (Bouaké, Ivory Coast). Proceedings: *Les Religions africaines traditionnelles*. Paris: Seuil.

1966: On African Theology. African Churches Conference. (Ibadan, Nigeria). Proceedings: *Pour une théologie africaine*. Yaoundé: Clé, 1969.

1968: Renewal of the Church and New Churches. Colloquium. (Kinshasa, Zaire). Proceedings: *Renouveau de l'eglise et nouvelles eglises*. Mayidi: Revue de Clergé Africain, 1969.

1969: Understanding African Religions: *A la rencontre des religions africaines*. Secretariatus pro Non-Christianis. Rome: Libreria Editrice Ancora.

1970: On African Religion as a Source of Culture and Civilization. ASC-Colloquium. (Cotonou, Benin). Proceedings: *Religion africaine comme source de valeurs de culture et de civilisation*. Paris: Présence Africaine. 1972.

In the 1970s, the reconsideration of classical grids was widespread among African scholars (Hebga, 1976; Kalilombe, 1977; Ngindu, 1979). At scholarly conferences, no one really cared any longer about the scientific evidence of the past. African scholars now preferred to deal directly with the issues that involve African responsibility in theology and social sciences, as well as in the humanities (Glele, 1981; Ngindu, 1985). In religious studies, the most challenging theological meetings were the following: in 1976, the Assembly of Third World Theologians (Dar es Salaam, Tanzania) and the Pastoral Colloquium of Koumi (then Upper Volta); in 1977, the Conference on Black Civilization and the Catholic Church in Abidjan and the Accra meeting which led to the constitution of an Ecumenical Association of African Theologians (Appiah-Kubi and Torres, 1977); and, in 1978, the Kinshasa Congress on African Religions and Christianity (see Arrighi, 1979).

The result of this process may best be illustrated by two quotations from African Roman Catholics.

The first is from Malula Cardinal Joseph-Albert, Archbishop of Kinshasa:

African Christianity cannot exist without African Theology. And this implies that it should be made clear that relations exist between the authentic religion brought to us through Christ on the one hand and religions in general and more precisely African religions on the other hand. As Africa possesses today its own theologians, this task belongs in the very first place to those African theologians. (Malula, 1977:23)

The second is from Zoungrana Cardinal Paul, Archbishop, Rome:

> Beyond refusing all external domination, our wish is to link up in depth with the African cultural heritage, which for too long has been misunderstood and refused. Far from being a superficial or folkloric effort to revive some traditions or ancestoral practices, it is a question of constructing a new African society whose identity is not conferred from outside.

Cardinals, even African ones, are not customarily extremist. On the contrary. Malula's and Zoungrana's pronouncements clearly indicate the concerns of the 1980s: an analysis of the complementarity existing between Christianity and African religions; an African theology of incarnation, considered the responsibility of African theologians; and, finally, a permanent search for an identity from a positive anthropological background (Tshibangu, 1977:29–31). And McVeigh could note in 1980 that:

> Africa has reached its theological maturity and African Christianity is searching for new interpretations of its faith. It is a time of turbulence and ferment, but also a time of excitement. Something new is happening, something unique and important. (McVeigh, 1980:91)

Is this impulse towards a new discourse purely activist? Does it express at an intellectual level a confusion implying a possible transformation of ideological reference? It is obvious that new norms seem to be imposing themselves in the arena that the voices of missionaries, anthropologists, and colonial administrators have dominated so far (see, e.g., Thomas, Luneau, and Doneux, 1969; Emmet, 1972; Pratt, 1972; Hallen, 1976; Oduyoye, 1986). It may be said that what is at stake for Africans is simply the appropriation of an initiative which is based on what paradoxically founded the power and the knowledge of the colonial system (see, e.g., Mazrui, 1974). As T. Okere put it:

> Hence the peculiar originality of African culture. It means the common experience of the trauma of the slave trade, of the humiliation that was colonization, of assault on traditional religion, of new won political independence, of present economic exploitation, of the ambivalent status of standing hesitatingly on the threshold of the age of industry. (Okere, 1978:279)

The interrogations which carry the initiative sometimes slip into a sort of demagogical spiritual activism. However, that is perhaps not as important as the struggle for an orthodoxy defined in terms of historical and cultural difference.

At a very general and vague level, the main characteristic of the new discourse is its own self-definition as a discourse of succession (Mveng, 1978:267–76). Looked at carefully, it can be divided into two complementary genres. One bears upon techniques of interpreting and reworking the signs of what was called paganism and primitiveness yesterday and which, today, is qualified as religion and God's symbolic discretion. The second genre tends to focus on the right of being Other and thus on the epistemological demands of the enterprise (see, e.g., Ngindu, 1985). In the first case, studies evaluate the values of the past in terms of present exigencies and the future of African communities, thus inverting the order of anthropology's classical description. Anthropology's fecundity has been based on the approach to "primitive organizations" as closed systems (see, e.g., Mubengayi, 1966; Mulago, 1973; Bujo, 1975; Massamba, 1976; Hebga, 1979). In the second case, ideological or philosophical discussion concentrates upon the diversity of human experience. It consequently studies the relativity of cultural and political grammars, which, in their singularity, testify to an essential hidden meaning beneath the surface (e.g., Tshibangu, 1974; Boesak, 1977; Adoukounou, 1981; Eboussi-Boulaga, 1981; Bimwenyi, 1981b). In both cases, one sees that the new discourse on African difference conveys an ambitious and explicit will to truth. As such, it generates and explicates its own presence in both history and the present knowledge about African realities (e.g., Eboussi-Boulaga, 1978: 339–70; Ela and Luneau, 1981).

A third trend is clearly political: the black theology of South Africa. Influenced by Latin American liberation theology and by the North American civil rights movement of the 1960s, this current expresses itself in terms of the Exodus theme played out in a modern setting (Boesak, 1977 and 1984a & b; Tutu, 1984). Its formulation is based on three main principles: the importance of taking into account the sociopolitical context in which humans live, the obligation of espousing human dignity as the major concern, (thus theological practice meets political praxis) and the belief that Christian faith does not transcend ideologies (Boesak, 1977:99–122). Such a radical understanding of theology can only clash with the two preceding types of discourse, particularly the first. According to Buthalezi, for example, the theology of indigenization is not acceptable for two reasons: "it means doing a superficial exercise of matching the already culturally-coloured Christian teaching, and African thought . . ." and "the emphasis that this procedure places on African life and thought is not realistic since it involves conjuring up the past which is not crucial to the African in his present socioeconomic and political circumstances" (in Dickson, 1984:127–28). To my knowledge, so far only Eboussi-Boulaga (1981) has focused on the intellectual limits and ambiguities of this radical theological orientation. De facto, this trend sees itself as applied theology and explicitly submits to the politics of those who would become princes of a new organization of power. In doing so, it joins in the service of new political chauvinisms and idols, repeating the missionary's dream of conciliating God's glory and Caesar's power.

In its intention, as well as in its power, the new discourse on Christianity is clearly the result of cross-cultural breeding. One might choose to emphasize its ambiguity (Ralibera, 1959:154–87) or even review the paradoxical questions that allowed it to emerge. First, there is the question of knowing who can or should speak validly about Africa, and from which viewpoint. Second, there is the issue of promoting "discourses" on others now that we have learned an essential lesson from the criticism of anthropological and missionary discourse: "Savages" can speak, not only when their very being and their traditions are at stake, but also in order to evaluate procedures and techniques that pertain to the description of their being, traditions and beliefs (see Appiah-Kubi and Torres, 1977:189–95; Ngindu, 1985).

However, insofar as the new African discourse perceives its own course and fate in terms of epistemological rupture (Bimwenyi, 1981a; Eboussi-Boulaga, 1978 and 1981), we may stop at this claim and interrogate its situation. That can be done through three questions: Who is speaking? From which context? In what grids and in what sense are the questions pertinent? I propose that one of the best ways of answering these questions might be a careful rewriting of the relationships that have existed between African ethnography and the politics of conversion.

The Anthropologist's Influence: Ethnography and the Politics of Conversion

> I must now admit that I adapted myself with remarkable ease to the conditions of life in my cage . . . I even grew so accustomed to this situation that for more than a month, without feeling how outlandish or degrading it was, I made no attempt to put an end to it.
>
> P. BOULLE, *Planet of the Apes.*

Anthropology participated in colonization and promoted what MacGaffey calls "the mythological phase" with hypotheses "founded on a series of binary oppositions which contrasted the virtues of European civilization with their supposed absence from Africa." But I am not convinced that, as MacGaffey suggests by quoting G. I. Jones, "the early descriptive ethnographers were ill-served by the speculative constructions of the amateur anthropologists to whom they turned for theories" (MacGaffey 1981:236). I believe that amateurism has strongly contributed to a solid foundation of anthropology. Its presence had, in my opinion, exactly the same status as amateurism during the emergence of the discipline in the eighteenth and early nineteenth centuries (see, e.g., Hodgen, 1971). The Central African bibliography of anthropology, for instance, is filled with the works of amateurs, mainly missionaries, which are important documents of anthropological information. MacGaffey thinks that:

> Work by missionaries, priests and amateur ethnographers dealing with African religious beliefs or rites should not necessarily be regarded as anthropological . . . European writing about Africa presents itself in Africa with uniform authority as the product of sciences, itself a European property that Africans are told they should aspire to; an ethnographic account of this writing must recognize that much of what has been produced is of poor quality, and that what is good has not succeeded in replacing inaccurate representations of Africa in, say, the popular press. We would all like to identify our society with its best achievements, and we tend to forget or to excuse as aberration its mediocrities, horror, and blunders. (MacGaffey, 1981:265)

This is fine and correct. Nevertheless there are at least two points that I would like to discuss. The first concerns anthropological authority; the second, ethnographic interpretation.

It is in the name of science that MacGaffey makes the distinction between reliable and unreliable anthropology. In other words, science is science, and it should not be confused with its opposite. More precisely, although "good" anthropology shares the same epistemological framework as "bad," they are different in nature: the bad is bad insofar as it does not obey the rules of the "anthropological authority," that is—to use an expression of E. E. Evans-Pritchard—"a scientific habit of mind." As he put it:

> It is true that some missionaries were well educated men and had learned to speak native languages with fluency, but speaking a language fluently is very different from understanding it, as I have often observed in converse between Europeans and Africans and Arabs . . . For someone who has not made an intensive study of native institutions, habits and customs in the native's own milieu (that is, well away from administrative, missionary, and trading post) at best there can emerge a sort of middle dialect in which it is possible to communicate about matters of common experience and interest. (Evans-Pritchard, 1980:7)

I understand well Evans-Pritchard's point when he writes of evolutionist theorists that: "none of the anthropologists whose theories about primitive religion have been most influential had ever been near a primitive people. It is as though a chemist had never thought it necessary to enter a laboratory" (1980:6). However, I do not follow him in his critique of missionaries' knowledge. If some missionaries, as he notes, were "well-educated men," it is fair also to recognize that a great number of them were, by training, relatively well-read, not only in social sciences but also in scholastic anthropology. Moreover, if one speaks seriously of Westerners who, far away from Westernized posts, lived with Africans and shared their ordinary life, one is speaking of missionaries. Records and proofs exist. Contrary to most anthropologists' ten months or, at best, two or three years of field research, many missionaries spent almost their whole lives among Africans. And, in general, an objective look at the facts indicates that their existential understanding of local habits and customs is and was very often extraordinary. If there is a difference between missionaries' and anthropologists' interpretations, it comes from the intellectual particularity of their respective missions. In order to "save souls," the missionary undertakes the task of integrating his understanding of the local community into a process of reduction grounded in a theology of salvation defined within Western historicity. On the other hand, the anthropologist wants to contribute to the history of humankind by paying careful attention to all of its regional peculiarities and interpreting them according to a methodological grid of analysis and generalization which, also, depends upon the same Western historical experience (see, e.g., Stavenhagen, 1971; Schwarz, 1979, 1980).

In addition, regarding credibility, both the missionary and the anthropologist use the same argument, which might be questioned by "natives": "I know them" or "I lived with them." Writing about this principle of authority, J. Clifford aptly stated recently: "many ethnographers . . . are still cast in the experimental mode, asserting, prior to any specific research hypothesis or method, the 'I was there' of the ethnographer as insider and participant. Of course, it is difficult to say very much about experience. Like 'intuition' one has it or not, and its invocation often smacks of mystification" (Clifford, 1983:128). If one can speculate about the meaning of this authority, one could also admit that the missionary's authority does not make more sense than the anthropologist's. There is, however, a major difference. Both the missionary and the anthropologist pretend to be "bilingual" in an African setting. But the former, generally speaking, refers to an existential experience, whereas the latter uses an experiential authority; the first may fluently speak the indigenous language; the second, in general, would rather use Evans-Pritchard's "sort of middle dialect." The first seeks to reduce the "primitives" to his faith and its cultural presuppositions. For the second, "primitives" constitute an "object topic," which might or might not fit into a scientific framework and must be accounted for. Fundamentally, there are two main problems: one, of comprehending cultures, the other concerning the significance of the interpretation offered.

At a basic level, missionaries, as well as anthropologists, when they return from the "primitive context," refer to the same context. To use M. Hollis's example and words: anthropologists and missionaries knew nothing about the "natives" when they started and seem to have discovered everything they know in the end. This is very well; how do they *discover* that the natives sometimes perceive what they perceive? Insofar as the anthropologist is concerned, M. Hollis has a response: "two possible answers are that he observes their behavior and that he translates their utterances" (1981:228) This explanation is annoying, since most anthropologists only speak pidgin. How could they translate a local language that they do not know, and that, paradoxically, the missionary shares with the "natives"? In fact, this question is frightfully ill-presented. It has unduly transformed an opposition of "missions" into a problem of competence for the interpretation of cultural texts and subject matter. In any case, its exaggeration shows at least that, as matter of principles, the concept of a missionary as anthropologist should be thinkable. In effect, despite the classical bias in the discipline, nothing ontological prevents a missionary from acquiring the methodological awareness and necessary skills of a good fieldworker. He could, then, like the best trained specialists, practice anthropology, that is build bridges between two cultures, two "texts," his own and the local one, and thus produce a clear representation of his own creative experience. In this case, as well as in anthropologist's, as R. Wagner notes, "the result is an analogy, or a set of analogies, that 'translates' one group of basic meanings into the other, and can be said to participate in both meaning systems at the same time in the same way that their creator does" (1981:9).

Let us take another of Hollis's images based on the Coherence Theory. As a metaphor, we should consider the African cultural organization as a text. By his training and mission, the missionary is and must be an "unbelieving" interpreter. The anthropologist, in principle, should be "believing"; otherwise his scientific project no longer makes any sense. The missionary is concerned with a complete conversion of the text, the anthropologist with the understanding of its internal rationality. It is because the missionary has been, generally, a nonbeliever that the anthropologist tends to reject his interpretations as approximations. In passing this judgement, the anthropologist often forgets what the missionary or, worse still, the "native" might remind him—that he is not perfectly bilingual and, therefore, despite his scientific background, his intellectual construction may well be just a questionable "invention."

One might object that this is not the point. From an archaeological viewpoint, one would rather emphasize that missionaries' accounts and those of anthropologists witness to the same *episteme*. In their variety and contradictions, the discourses explicitly discuss European processes of domesticating Africa. If these discourses have to be identified with anything, it must be with European intellectual signs and not with African cultures.

Thus, Tempels can be related to M. Griaule and Evans-Pritchard, and *Bantu Philosophy* (Tempels, 1959) can be read in connection with *Dieu d'eau* (Griaule, 1948, 1965) and *Social Anthropology and other Essays* (Evans-Pritchards, 1962). All of them share a similar perspective, an idealistic faith in the potentiality of African "culture," expressed in an agrarian metaphor, and the conviction that colonization is both a providential accident and a historical benefit. The analysis of this fact and its possible evaluation (e.g., Adotévi, 1972; Leclerc, 1972; Augé, 1979), show that, as G. Vilasco aptly put it: "all the stages that found as much the ethnological project as its object are seized with a 'primary deformity' or a major vice, in other words "this obliteration of the gaze that produced an ideology of the civilization" (Vilasco, 1983:23).

Despite their critical positions, Tempels, Griaule, and Evans-Pritchard still depend on the legacy of Lévy-Bruhl, Frazer, Morgan, and Tylor, who, after

A. Comte's *loi des trois états,* promoted a split in the human condition. Allegorically, it has been well illustrated in variations of theses for or against the axiom of the identity of human nature. And we are all painfully aware of the mystifications according to which all cultures pass through a succession of evolutionary phases: from magic through religion to science; from savagery to barbarism to civilization; from sexual promiscuity through matrilineality and finally to patrilineality. Tempels, Griaule, and Evans-Pritchard all believed that the colonial administration might use their science and experience to implement the conversion of the native society. As Evans-Pritchard put it:

> If those who control policy believe in material prosperity, literacy, or whatever it may be, they feel that they have to give them to peoples of their colonial empire. Whether they are doing right or wrong is a question for moral philosophy, not for social anthropology. (Evans-Pritchard, 1962:119–20)

In other words, this idealistic perspective is likely to see and describe the value of local customs that the colonial power will not tolerate. At the same time, the decription may help administrators to understand the indigenous culture and to better dominate it. Yet the frustrated Evans-Pritchard, who would have liked to be a government advisor on colonial policy, states:

> I do not believe that [anthropological knowledge] can be applied to any extent in the arts of administration and education in any other than in this very general cultural sense—in the influence it has in shaping the attitude of the European towards native peoples. (Evans-Pritchard, 1962: 122)

Tempels and Griaule too experienced the same ambiguous feelings concerning the colonial mission. Human civilization was Western in the eyes of the colonizers, and Africans were, at least for Tempels in the 1930s, not quite human. What they were, whether pure children or incipient human beings in need of tutoring, was simply the result of the application of Western standards within a non-Western context.

One may consider this perspective general, since on a theoretical level it transcends the so-called difference between French and British anthropology. Therefore, I do not follow J. Copans (1971a) nor the traditional view which opposes the French and British, emphasizing the metaphysical aspects of the first as opposed to the pragmatism and empiricism of the second. This type of distinction is probably pertinent as far as a classification of intellectual policies is concerned. From an epistemological standpoint, the French and British approaches essentially meant the same things: reduction and acculturation (see, e.g., Harik and Schilling, 1984). Moreover, the basic ideological ground is the same. First, the importance of Durkheim's legacy in both schools accounts for the European scholar's responsibility in shaping Africa's knowledge, particularly in terms of the classification and interpretation of hierarchies in political and religious systems. Second, the essential reasons which led to the organization of the International African Institute in

Great Britain in 1926 and to the creation of the Institut d'Anthropologie in France stem from an identical philosophy of conquest.

The essence of anthropology in France and in England is the same. Its circumstantial tones and expressions vary but its aim seems identical (Leclerc, 1972). Paradoxically, Lévy-Bruhl, despite his opposition to "the English anthropological school," best reflected the Victorian ideology in which the evolution of culture as a parallel to the evolution of species explained the superiority of Europe as a result of biological and cultural achievement. But it was in England that social and cultural anthropologists made the most use of Durkheim's doctrine concerning primitive societies.

In fact, from a more general historical frame, one can observe three complementary genres of "speeches" contributing to the invention of a primitive Africa: the exotic text on savages, represented by travelers' reports; the philosophical interpretations about a hierarchy of civilizations; and the anthropological search for primitiveness. The complementarity of these speeches is obvious. It is perceived as a unity in the Western consciousness. The exotic text dominates in the seventeenth century. In the eighteenth century, it complements Enlightenment classifications of peoples and civilization. In the nineteenth century, an ideology of conquest appears in explorers' sagas, anthropologists' theories, and the implementation of colonial policy. However, until the beginning of the scramble for Africa, historical distinctions of genres can only be relative.

As far as I know, no one has yet made a detailed study of Greek and Latin writers' influence on the European invention of Africa. Miller's synthesis (1985:23–28) of the ambivalence about blackness in antiquity is too brief and, as such, a bit controversial. It refers to Snowden's thesis (1970), according to which Greeks and Romans were only culturally biased and distinguishing the civilized from the *barbaros,* independently of race: "The Greeks and Romans attached no special stigma to color, regarding yellow hair or blue eyes as a mere geographical accident and developed no special racial theory about the inferiority of darker peoples qua darker people" (Snowden, 1970:176). The problem is more complex than that. In the same vein as Snowden's argument, one could emphasize, as did A. Bourgeois, evidences of assimilation and cultural integration: "Greeks had traveled as far as Africa; inversely, blacks had visited or lived in Greece" (Bourgeois, 1971:120). It was the same in Rome. Yet what do these cases demonstrate? Here is just one of numerous counterexamples: during the reign of Hadrianus (A.D. 76–138), the poet Florus from the African province was denied a prize because, according to a witness, "the emperor . . . did not want to see Jupiter's crown going to Africa" (see, e.g., Schilling, 1944:26; Mudimbe, 1979). Miller's analysis is strictly a correction of Snowden's interpretation.

A systematic study of the Ancients' perceptions may distinguish three main problems. The first is a question of carefully locating and describing sources and then evaluating their credibility. For example, in his presentation of the

Greek sources of African history (1972), Mveng begins by noting that a rapid consultation of F. Jacoby's *Die Fragmente der griechischen Historiker* shows that, from the 943 pages of Part III, there are 276 pages referring to Egypt, sixty to Ethiopia, nine to Libya and eight to Carthage, for a total of some 355 pages (Mveng, 1972:13). This is an invitation to further research and not a closure. A vast field of research awaits scholars. The second issue concerns the content of the sources and both the physical and cultural "geographies" they unveil. How can we, today, read these texts and make sense of information and representations they offer? Finally, there is a question of method and it is twofold. On the one hand, how may we discriminate between myth and observed facts when they come out of genres so diverse as drama (e.g., Aeschylus, Aristophanes, Sophocles), poetry (e.g., Callimakos, Homer, Pindar), mythography (e.g., Apollodorus), technical and hermetic texts (e.g., Hesychius, Hippocrates, Xenophanes), and history and geography (e.g., Agatharchides, Diodorus, Herodotus, Pliny)? At the same time, in drawing together information, we have to respect a hidden movement which accounts for chronological differences in methods of describing *barbaroi* in general. To put it in a more concrete way, I feel that it is obvious that Diodorus and Pliny, who describe northern Africa five centuries after Herodotus, add to and transform an old knowledge by integrating it in the order of their contemporary culture.

Herodotus's ethnographical map is a detailed one, from the Egyptian borders to the Tritonian lake. Each "tribe" or community is well typified on the basis of some major paradigms: habitation, social space, food, physical features, religion, and marriage customs. The lake is Herodotus's reference point. He expands upon its mythological associations going back to the Argonauts (IV, 179) and, particularly, its Greek tradition in terms of sacrifice and customs: "the inhabitants of the Tritonian lake region mainly sacrifice to Athene, next to Triton and Poseidon" (IV, 189). Herodotus's account of the regions westward of the lake becomes vague. Thus, for example, the distances to the "Ammonians," "Garamantes," and other "tribes" is expressed in days of travel. He writes: "I know and can tell the names of all the peoples that dwell on the ridge as far as the Atlantes [on Mount Atlas], but no farther than that" (IV, 185). That said, he describes the nomads who live in "movable houses" (IV, 190), eat meat, drink milk, do not touch the flesh of cows (IV, 186). He notes that west of the Tritonian lake the country is savage, full of wild animals and strange creatures: "dog-headed humans," "headless peoples," and "human beings who have their eyes in their breasts," "besides many other creatures not fabulous"(IV, 191).

Pliny's chronicle follows different norms. First, it proceeds from west to east, specifically from *Mauretaniae* to the extreme eastern regions of Libya, the south of Egypt, and the Ethiopian cities of Napata and Meroë. Second, and more important, Pliny evaluates countries and peoples in terms of the presence or absence of Romans. One of the most striking illustrations may be his reflection about Ethiopia and the town of Napata: *nec tamen arma*

Romana ibi solitudinem fecerunt "It was not the forces of Rome that made the country a desert" (N.H. VI, xxxv, 182). Pliny's geography details Roman colonies and portrays ethnic groups in terms of political allegiance, relative autonomy, and opposition to the Roman power. Geography reveals the expansion of the *Imperium Romanun:* conquered kingdoms and new colonies in *Mauretania* (Traducta Julia, Julia Constantia, Zulil, Lixus etc.), cities of Roman culture on the coast of the Mediterranean Sea (Portus Magnus, Oppidum Novum, Tipassa, Rusucurium etc.), strategic outposts on the edges of the Sahara desert (Augusta, Timici, Tigavae etc.) and, finally, Roman centers in the provinces of *Numidia, Africa, and Cyrenaica.*

From the background of this normative space, which is the equivalent of Herodotus's Tritonian lake region, one seizes the meaning of "a geography of monstrosity," that is, of the unknown spaces and their inhabitants. In the fifth century B.C., Herodotus could state: "to my thinking, there is no part of Libya of any great excellence whereby it should be compared to Asia or Europe, save only in the region which is called by the same name as its river Cinypus" (IV, 198). Five hundred years later, Pliny described the north of Africa in terms of the transformations brought about by Roman civilization (NH, V, I, 14). Yet, his geography of monstrosity faithfully mirrors Herodotus's description. To Herodotus's immense space of human monsters living in the eastern part of Libya, Pliny opposes a specific area around the "black river which has the same nature as the Nile" (N.H. V, VIII, 44) Strange beings live there: peoples who do not have individual names, cave-dwellers who have no language and live on the flesh of snakes, the "Garamantes" who do not practice marriage, the "Blemmyae" who are headless, satyrs, strapfoots, etc. (NH, V, VIII, 45–46). Let us note briefly that Diodorus of Sicily's ethnography of Ethiopians (Book III) conforms to this model. It is also antithetic and presents two types of Ethiopians. There are "civilized" ones who inhabit the capital city of Napata, and whose history is transformed for the better by a Greek-educated king, Ergamenes. Then there is the majority, the other ethnic group, who are savage (*'agrioi*) and black in color (*melanes*).

For centuries, questionable facts from Herodotus, Diodorus of Sicily, and Pliny were widely accepted. In the sixteenth century, for instance, John Lok, who supposedly met West Africans, presented an account obviously derived from classical sources: he described "Negroes, a people of beastly living, without a God, law, religion"; "other people whose women are common"; "the region called Troglodytica, whose inhabitants dwell in caves and dens: for these are their houses, and the flesh of serpents their meat"; "and people without heads, having their eyes and mouths in their breast." This is a faithful recitation of Herodotus (see, e.g., Book IV), Diodorus of Sicily (see Book III), and Pliny (see Book V). At the other extreme, nineteenth-century anthropologists depict the essential paradigm of the European invention of Africa: Us/Them. Often they express the belief that the African is a negation of all human experience, or is at least an exemplary exception in terms of evolution.

The various philosophical perspectives of the Enlightenment did not negate this hypothesis (Duchet, 1971; Meek, 1976). In a more technical discourse, the Enlightenment defined the characteristics of savagery. Thus Voltaire's explanation of human inequality based on the metaphor of the inequality of trees in a forest and Buffon's principle of human advancement depending upon the use of intellectual capabilities are part of the very tradition that includes the European travelers' reports. Their particularity lies in their awareness of the possibility of translating foreign peoples' experiences and reducing them to theoretical models rather than just presenting them as exotic and incomprehensible. In his *Discourse on the Origin of Inequality* as well as in his treatise on *The Origin of Language,* Rousseau in this vein, suggests that inequality is produced by society. He claims that primitives are beyond the natural state and defines natural man as fictitious. Yet an elaborate ladder of cultures, established diachronically, emerges from his dialectic of necessity and liberty. One could even relate the Enlightenment's critical discourse on primitiveness, the historical origin of peoples, and their identification as objects of study to subsequent variations on these theories. These include Hegel's contemptuous pages on blacks and "savages" in general and Lévy-Bruhl's assertion that primitives seem frozen in a state of prelogism, thousands of years behind Western civilization. More recently, one finds K. Jaspers's interpretation of the history of primitives who simply vanish in the presence of Western culture, and B. Malinowski's theory of cultural change, involving the African's dream of becoming "if not European, then at least a master or part master of some of the devices, possessions and influences which in his eyes constitute European superiority" (see Jahn, 1961).

In fact, our three genres of speech constitute variations on a single discourse. More precisely, they reveal the same archaeological *ratio* which both creates and explains them. To the extent that this analysis is correct, the question of accounting for the dependence of these genres of speech on their epistemological locus of possibility is, in large measure, one of explaining intellectual procedures for reducing non-Western otherness to Western sameness; or, from a diachronic point of view, one of establishing their order of appearance.

I propose two periods and, therefore, two overlapping types of knowledge of Africa: before and after the 1920s, or, to use a marker, before and after Malinowski. Before 1920, this knowledge was organized in substantial congruence with Western "existence." It is in its expression the negative side of that region that Foucault describes as the sociological field "where the labouring, producing, and consuming individual offers himself a representation of the society in which this activity occurs, of the groups and individuals among which it is divided, of the imperatives, sanctions, rites, festivities and beliefs by which it is upheld or regulated" (1973:377).

Evolutionism, functionalism, diffusionism—whatever the method, all repress otherness in the name of sameness, reduce the different to the already known, and thus fundamentally escape the task of making sense of other worlds (see Ake, 1979; Copans, 1971b; Coquery-Vidrovitch, 1969a; Mafeje, 1976). It is more than a matter of methodological limitations. This limiting ethnocentrism testifies to a kind of epistemological determinism. A good example is in Evans-Pritchard's *Theories of Primitive Religion*. The book divides theories into two categories, psychological and sociological, the psychological being further divided into "intellectualist" and "emotionalist" theories. While the psychological trend is represented by works of Max Müller, Herbert Spencer, Edward Tylor, James Frazer, Andrew Lang, R. R. Marret, R. H. Lowie, and G. Van Der Leew, the sociological orientation may be found in works of Fustel de Coulanges, E. Durkheim, and Robertson Smith. Upon reading in the conclusion that none of the theories maintain popularity any longer, one's first reaction is amazement. Upon closer scrutiny, however, a careful reader realizes that what Evans-Pritchard is doing is highlighting methodological limits in the study of non-Western religions and cultures.

> All this amounts to saying that we have to account for religious facts in terms of the totality of the culture and society in which they are found . . . they must be seen as a relation of parts to one another within a coherent system, each part making sense only in relation to other institutional systems as a wider set of relations. (Evans-Pritchard, 1980:112)

Thus for Evans-Pritchard all the preceding interpretations were, at best, questionable because of two errors: the first being the evolutionary assumptions; the second, "that besides being theories of chronological origins they were also theories of psychological origins" (1980:108). Evans-Pritchard also uses the "if I were a horse" hypothesis. By this he means that each of the scholars tried to imagine how he would think if he were a primitive, then drew conclusions from these futile introspections. According to Evans-Pritchard, it is Lévy-Bruhl who comes closest to handling primitive religions in a proper manner (1980:81).

Evans-Pritchard believed that "if we are to have a general sociological theory of religion, we shall have to take into consideration all religions and not just primitive religions; and only by doing so can we understand some of its essential features" (1980:113). But he does not indicate how the present-day scholar could deal with the problems of interpretation that confronted earlier interpreters. In a recent book (1977), A. Shorter tried to analyze the most prominent schools in the study of "primitive religion." In the beautiful disorder of contradictory hypotheses and ideologies from the periods before and after the 1920s, Shorter distinguishes six schools: *(a)* the particularist approach, the classical methodology of social anthropology, which is questioned by African scholars; *(b)* the enumerative method exemplified by G. Parrinder, which generally "fails to situate the facts it studies in whole contexts" and seems "sterile"; *(c)* the hypothesis of African religious unity (W. E. Abraham, J. S. Mbiti) which is "unproven," and a "hypothesis, nothing else"; *(d)* the historical approach, (T. O. Ranger, I. N. Kimambo) which is questionable for its heavy reliance on oral history; *(e)* the comparative methodology (Evans-Pritchard) which presupposes historical method; and *(f)* the categorical and thematic approaches (M. Douglas, J. Goetz, C. H. Sawyer) which, based on theoretical models, are "designed to help a scholar understand any given situation, and [are] not a substitute for the serious study of each society in its own right" (Shorter, 1977:38–57). If progress is thinkable, Shorter states, it is on the basis of the creative potentiality that the combination of the last three methodologies represents. "The future of the comparative study of African religion appears to lie with the limited rather than the generalizing approaches" (1977:58).

A. J. Smet, a professor of philosophy at the Catholic School of Theology in Kinshasa, proposes a historical, rather than a methodological, classification. He organizes contributions based on content, emphasizing those which brought a sympathetic approach to the understanding of African "philosophy" (1980:27–107). Two names dominate this current: C. Van Overbergh and G. Van der Kerken. The first, president of the International Bureau of Ethnography, promoted the decisions of the 1905 International Meeting on Economic Expansion (Bergen) for a systematic description of African *Weltanschauungen* (Van Overbergh, 1913). The second "discovered" the rationality of African systems, through African languages, thanks to his sojourn in the Belgian Congo (Smet, 1980:96). Their analyses, contrary to contemporary descriptions, depict positive aspects in three main areas: culture, religion, and behavior (Smet, 1980:98–99). Van der Kerken is aware of the richness of the traditional literature, which is, for him, a form of a popular philosophy. He calls it practical philosophy and compares it to "the popular philosophy of the simple and unrefined folk of contemporary Europe" (Smet, 1980:102). Van der Kerken insists on the existence of an organized knowledge *(connaissances* and *croyances)* and a clear distinction of types of concrete knowledge *(savoir* and *technique):*

> It is irrefutable that the *Schools of Magicians* [in Africa] have often been at the same time, as elsewhere in the world, in addition to being *the first centers of magic, the first religious, scientific and philosophical centers,* that there was at least an oral teaching and that certain traditions passed from masters to disciples.

> [Africans] possess practical notions of *psychology* (that they used in the education of children), of *logic* (that they use to present a problem before an African court or to refute an argument of an adversary), of *ethics* (on which they rely to reproach the conduct of a member of the clan), of *politics* (which they use to govern the village, etc.). (In Smet, 1980:101–2 emphasis mine)

Van der Kerken gives us a great deal of information about this repartition of psychology, logic, ethics, and politics. He writes that they do not, in reality, constitute an order of knowledge comparable to the European one. They are, rather, embryonic systems that have not yet developed sophistication.

At the same period, 1907–1911, a young seminarian, Stephano Kaoze, published two brief texts on "Bantu Psychology" in *La Revue congolaise*. Kaoze had been studying philosophy since 1905 and the influence of evolutionary hypotheses is clear in his thinking. Civilization means for him the regeneration of Africa through both Westernization and Christianization. His article is symbolically subtitled: "The Congolese seen by a civilized Congolese." Yet within the masochistic reasoning, in which Kaoze celebrates the superiority of the European and demonstrates the relative savagery of his own country, one encounters astounding confessions. The young clergyman had hoped to impress his compatriots with questions from his newly learned philosophy. Their answers surprised him: "They reason better than I do . . . They answered better than I thought. Thus I said to myself the human being is naturally a philosopher." (Kaoze, 1979:410–12)

In the 1920s, an ambiguous expression surfaced in missionary and anthropological studies: "oral philosophy." It still implies both the traditional notions of historical backwardness and its potentiality for evolution. It refers to two different types of experience: the first is that of being human and thus having the rationality of a *Weltanschauung* specifically proper to humans; the second provides the cultural bases of a specific *Weltanschauung* through collective intellectual constructions (myths, literature, proverbs, etc.) or by reference to a personal form of reasoning. In fact the expression is not new. One can find it in the writings of Frobenius at the beginning of the century and later on in various anthropologists' texts (Smet, 1980:95–96). The novelty is that the expression has been admitted at an institutional level and therefore signifies a possible reconversion of the policies of domesticating the black continent. Benedict XV's encyclic of 1919 *(Maximum Illud)* is just one sign among others.

For a long time in anthropology the important problem has been the methodological process of analysis, following the model of natural sciences. It reduced people to the status of mere objects, so that an ethnocentric perspective could illuminate "African savagery" from Western norms (see Leclerc, 1972; Southall, 1983; Terray, 1969). MacGaffey, following D. Sperber, speaks of a "semiological illusion" and rightly suggests as a possibility that "the process of ethnocentric distortion in anthropology is much more complex than it is usually supposed to be: a two-way process, at least, in which African theories are shown to be capable of selling well in world markets" (1981:252). Even African anthropologists have described their own culture from this viewpoint, smuggling "European concepts into African contexts and [passing] them off as African religion or philosophy" (1981:248).

Between the two World Wars in Europe, particularly in France and Germany, some of the most diligent students of African societies promoted new ways of speaking about "primitives." They include scientists or missionaries like M. Delafosse, L. Frobenius, M. Rousseau, R. Schmitz, P. Schumascher, G. Tessmann, G. Van der Kerken, and C. Van Overbergh. They were all Lévy-Bruhl's contemporaries, and most of them had read his *La Mentalité primi-*

tive. Even though some of these scholars explicitly tend to accept his pervasive ideas or, unwittingly, to reinforce them, it was already clear that a change was occurring in anthropology. Lévy-Bruhl, like many professional anthropologists, used to work by proxy. Those, like M. Delafosse, O. Le Roy or P. Salkin, who had lived with Africans, could oppose him. Titles such as *Weltanschauung und Charakter des Negers, L'Ame nègre*, and *La Raison primitive*, and *Essai de réfutation de le théorie du prélogisme* constitute a new schema for research, or at any rate the possibility of interpretation from a new perspective.

However, the methodological rules remained essentially the same. They are evolutionary, or functionalist, and still imply that Africans must evolve from their frozen state to the dynamism of Western civilization. The policies of applied anthropology had taken the view of colonialism and focused on African structures in order to integrate them into the new historical process. The most imaginative Africanists, like P. Salkin, already imagined some of the consequences of political colonization and intellectual Westernization, foreseeing the independence movement and its possible outcome, namely, the relative autonomy of a Europeanized and assimilated Africa.

> Will African civilization victoriously resist the grip of European civilization? Or from reciprocal reactions of one upon the other will an intermediary civilization spring up which will conserve the African foundation and at the same time disguise it under a European cloak? (Salkin, 1916. Quoted by A. J. Smet, 1980:103)

A great variety of interpretations was proposed, particularly about African religions. But they still all followed traditional paths. First of all, the notion of religion is hardly even used to designate African beliefs and religious practices. Second, explanatory schemas, theoretical elaborations, and even empirical descriptions cautiously follow the classic nineteenth-century models. That is the case even of such achievements as Trilles's work on Pygmies (1931) and Evans-Pritchard's study of the Azande (1937). Schmidt's ambitious enterprise in *Die Ursprung der Gottesidee* and his concept of *Ur-monotheismus* (Schmidt, 1931) constituted a breakthrough in its heuristic objectives. As I have previously noted, one major assumption of the method is the existence of a universal theory that each human community expresses in its own way and according to its own needs. This "philosophy" would be always and everywhere particular in its cultural and historical manifestations, and universal in its essence.

It was also during this period that more and more Africans became aware of their traditions. In the British colonies, it was the great period of applied anthropology, but also of the first monographs on African laws and customs (Ajisafe, 1924; Danquah, 1928). One can follow the same trend in French-speaking countries: D. Delobson published *L'Empire du Mogho-Naba* (1932) and *Les Secrets des sorciers noirs* (1934), and M. Quenum, *Au pays*

des Fons (1938). *Le Bulletin de l'enseignement de l'AOF* (Afrique occidentale française) published articles by Africans (Delobson, Boubou Hama,
Ahmadou Mapate Diagne, Bendaoud Mademba, etc.) on local cultures. In
the Belgian Congo, the official norms promoted the teaching and use of
African languages. Journals, such as *Nkuruse,* written in Tshiluba, had a
large circulation. Moreover, written literature in African languages exhibited
a good beginning or, in some countries, a positive vitality. I shall cite just a
few examples. In Nigeria A. Abubakar Tafawa Balewa wrote in Hausa
(*Shaihu Umar,* 1934) and A. Abubakar Iman became editor of a Hausa
newspaper, *Gaskiya Ta Fi Kwabo.* In Malawi E. W. Chafulumire taught
history to his people and wrote in Nyanja about how to behave in contemporary times. In the same language, Yosia S. Ntara wrote Chief Msyamboza's
history and wrote of the past of the Chewa community. In Rwanda Kagame,
editor of a Kinyarwanda newspaper *(Kinyamateka)* since 1941, began his
important work of poetry in Kinyarwanda on the victorious drums and the
source of progress. The same trend was apparent in a number of other
African languages, among them Bemba (Zambia, Zaire), Ewe (Ghana),
KiKongo (Angola, Congo, Zaire), Lingala (Congo, Zaire), Lozi (Zambia),
Runyoro (Uganda), Swahili (Tanzania, Zaire), and Yoruba (Nigeria). The
most prosperous literature is surely in South African languages (Sotho,
Tswana, Xhosa, and Zulu) and was produced by such writers as J. K. Bokwe
(1855–1922), H. I. E. Dhlomo (1903–1971), M. O. M. Seboni (1912–1972),
and B. W. B. Vilakazi (1906–1947).

Yet the promotion of African literature and languages was basically a
dubious enterprise. It kept pace with the philosophy of applied anthropology
and questionable policies in education programs. Nevertheless, it seems
legitimate to consider this literature in African languages as an expression of
African condition; thus it is a voice of anthropology if one accepts the
etymological root meaning of the word: *Anthropou-logos,* a speaking about
humans. This literature heavily relies on African experiences and milieux and
can present another "view," different from that of the colonizers and Western
anthropologists. Consequently, it takes on a power which could ultimately
be used against foreign ideologies. Two other facts confer a particular weight
on this period: the collaboration, in both America and Europe, between
black Africans and black Americans (Shepperson, 1960); and, in France, the
glorification of African models in both art and literature. Of those involved,
Apollinaire, Cendrars, Derain, Guillaume, Matisse, Picasso, and Vlaminck
are the best known (Hauser, 1982). Both movements contributed to the
emergence of a black African consciousness.

This consciousness firmly relies upon an anthropological perspective but
does not always seem to follow the mainstream of anthropologists' conclusions. Within the postprimitivist era, for example, Paul Hazoumé wrote
Doguicimi (1938), an ethnological novel about the court of Abomey. In
1938, Jomo Kenyatta published *Facing Mount Kenya,* which is both a study
of Kikuyu ways and style of life and a discreet political manifesto. During

those years a very popular kind of anthropology developed. More and more Africans published traditional tales and legends (see Blair, 1976:27–30). Later on, the influence of Griaule's and Dieterlen's works and the impact of cultural anthropology led African intellectuals to distinguish "good" and "bad" works about Africa, according to their conception of the value of their own civilization. The most extreme example of this ideological process is Cheikh Anta Diop's work on the cultural experiences of Africa (1954, 1960a, 1978).

In the 1950s it was clear that independence movements, in their opposition to colonialism, also tended to reject the essentials of anthropological perspectives. African intellectuals began to question the methodological reductionism of the discipline. Later, Africa's scholars preferred to speak about African history, regarding Western colonialism and its ideology as a parenthesis in the black African experience (Ajayi, 1969; Ki-Zerbo, 1972).

> The changes that began *circa* 1950 were not the doing of Africa scholars. They were the consequence of the rise of African nationalism in the form of political movements. Nationalist movements by their very existence challenged both implicitly and explicitly, the two basic premises of the previous work of Africa scholars. First, nationalist movements asserted that the primary arena of social and political action, in terms of legitimacy and hence of study, was and ought to be the colonial state/putative nation and not the "tribe" . . . Secondly, nationalist movements asserted that the relationship between Europeans and Africans had not been one of "culture contact" at all, but rather one of a "colonial situation." Culture contact could be good or bad and . . . the anthropologists had devoted themselves politically to trying to make sure it was good rather than bad. (Wallerstein, 1983:157)

An analysis of some of the most representative works of this last period indicates a bizarre climate. Some classical methodologies of social philosophy and anthropology continued to sustain scholarly works, such as Dike's book on trade and politics in the Niger delta (1956), Idowu's study on God in Yoruba belief (1962), W. E. Abraham's hypothesis of a family resemblance which allowed him to use Akan culture as a methodological paradigm (1966), Ogot's history of the Southern Luo (1967), F. A. Arinze's account of Ibo religion (1970), Okot P'Bitek's presentation of Luo religion (1971), J. M. Agossou's study on relationships between God and man among peoples of South Dahomey (1972), and Deng's book on the Dinka (1972).

But within this apparently classical orientation, a new ideological dimension appears. For example, E. B. Idowu, in his subsequent book on African religion, questions the validity of Western scholars' works, since most of them cannot understand African languages and conduct their studies "by proxy through research assistants scattered all over the field or by library work" (1965, 1975). J. B. Danquah's attempt ([1944] 1968) to link Akan religious categories to those of the Middle East is similar to L. Olumide's objective in his study of Yoruba religion (1948), in which he claims to demonstrate the

Egyptian origin of Yoruba tradition. This assertion is similar to the theme of Cheikh Anta Diop's works on the religious, linguistic, and cultural unity of Africa (1954, 1960a, 1960b). In fact, no one will disagree that a nationalistic trend is present. More and more African scholars seem to rely on the hypothesis of African unity. The title of Abraham's book—*The Mind of Africa* (1966)—is a program. Here one can also situate Mulago's enterprise (1973), which, after the major works of P. Colle, G. Hulstaert, Van Caeneghem, and others, draws a new frame from Parrinder's approach and asserts the homogeneity of a Bantu religious vision of the world, "that some call *Untu,* Négritude, Africanity, three terms used one for the other." (Mulago, 1973:11).

It is easy to point out the paradox faced by these African scholars: on the one hand, for the sake of their own pride and identity they deny exoticism and its assumptions; on the other, they are sincerely ready for the practice of a positive social science, and so for a conscious alliance with science in the frame of its epistemological field (e.g., Hountondji, 1980, 1981). It is from this exact point that we can observe and understand the contradictions of pan-Africanist ideology in social science (Shorter, 1977:38–60). Idowu's postulations or Mulago's Africanity, as a "common factor" of African cultures and religious beliefs, are just hypotheses, in the same way as Abraham's family resemblance is an assertion and not a scientific demonstration. Mbiti's theory of the cultural unity of the continent as a foundation for the coherence of African religions and philosophy is supported by nothing except his own subjectivity (1970:2).

This paradox may account for some tedious discussions that, in Africa, repeat "alternations of European social thought" (MacGaffey, 1981:261). From this statement, however, it cannot be inferred that Africans must endeavor to create from their otherness a radically new social science. It would be insanity to reproach Western tradition for its Oriental heritage. For example, no one would question Heidegger's right to philosophize within the categories of ancient Greek language. It is his right to exploit any part of this heritage. What I mean is this: the Western tradition of science, as well as the trauma of slave trade and colonization, are part of Africa's present-day heritage. K. Nkrumah rightly pointed out, in his *Consciencism* (chapter 3), that Africans have to take these legacies along with Muslim contributions and their own past and experience (see also Mazrui, 1974).

Moreover, one might also conceive the intellectual signs of otherness not as a project for the foundation of a new science, but rather as a mode of reexamining the journeys of human knowledge in a world of competing propositions and choices (Kane, 1961; Brenner, 1984:126–40). Concretely, from the background of the colonial politics of conversion, this mode seems imperative and one would agree with R. Horton:

> The kind of comparative conceptual analysis that the "philosopher of" traditional thought could offer would do much to help the contemporary intellec-

tual in his struggle to think through the relationship between his two super-compartments (that is, tradition and modernity). It would be supremely relevant to such questions as: Should there be a global stand in favour of traditional thought patterns and against modern patterns? Or should there be a global commitment to the running-down of the traditional in order to make way for the modern? Or again, should traditional thought-patterns be encouraged to coexist with modern? And if so, in what manner? Or yet again, is traditional thought a many-stranded thing, whose various strands must be disentangled and their appropriate relations to modernity considered one by one? (Horton, 1976:71)

Beyond as well as *in* the exposition of comparative studies, the logic of the mode would institutionalize a reevaluation of preceding norms, voices, and consensus. As a test of the fruitfulness of the new formulas and answers, one would look both at the durability of the founding arguments and at processes purifying controversial assumptions in the field. I have read three rewarding and ambitious contributions: O. Nduka's brief essay on the implications of African traditional systems of thought, which is based on a "critique of principles of causation and the quality of the understanding of mechanical and organic processes" (Nduka, 1974:97); Gyekye's note on the philosophical relevance of Akan proverbs and the paradigm of the African proverb as situational (Gyekye, 1975); and Nkombe's impressive work on paremiologic symbols (1979). Using the logic of classes in order to describe metaphors and metonyms in Tetela proverbs, Nkombe succeeds in two ways: first, he makes an original contribution by demonstrating that it is possible to reformulate the logic of classes in terms of the logic of propositions; second, through this highly abstract exercise, he analyzes the originality of an African culture in its dual dimension—internal plenitude and aspiration towards universality. A final example taken from a quite different source is Horton's schema of common and contrasting features existing between African traditional thought and Western science. At the end of his demonstration, he writes: "Though I largely disagree with the way in which the 'Négritude' theorists have characterized the differences between traditional African and modern Western thought, when it gets to this point I see clearly what they are after" (1981:170).

To sum up my position more theoretically, I would say that there is a mutation which took place in the 1920s and which explains both the possibility and the pertinence of an African discourse on otherness. This mutation signifies a new foundation for organizing a plurality of historical memories within the frame of the same *episteme*. Thus, fundamentally, it does not seem to matter whether Herskovits's propositions on African cultures, Vansina's methodological proposal on oral history, or Davidson's contributions to African history and Balandier's to African sociology created or determined the emergence of a new spirit against a reigning tradition. It does not mean either that, before the 1930s, no one thought of questioning the grids through which the Same displayed its kingship. E. Blyden's thought, which I shall look at carefully below, is, for instance, an annunciating sign of the rupture. On the other hand, the very fact that in the 1930s and 1940s a Collingwood could concern himself with the theme of reenacting the glory of the Same by focusing on the documentary virtues of historical thought and its means does not invalidate my thesis. On the contrary, it rather shows the intellectual audacity of Herskovits or of Vansina, and its specificity as a question about both philosophical and historical imagination. The articulation of this mutation was already visible in the 1920s, and one of its most apparent signs is the fragmentation of the notion of civilization (see, e.g., Braudel 1980:177–217). In the first quarter of this century, critical thinkers like Blyden and Frobenius seemed to be simply transferring doxological modalities from their own rationalizations of African experiences, the first hypothesizing a black personality culture on the basis of the most controversial racist recommendations, the second anxious to grant African social formations the practicality of a classification of its culturally distinct features. However, it seems clear that Blyden and Frobenius, however unknowingly, participated in a larger epistemological shift. In the 1920s, this shift would, among other things, reveal its presence through the appearance of ideologies of existence, subjectivity, otherness, and interest in "oral philosophies" and histories. Picasso and Cendrars's celebration of primitive imagination and works, and Schmidt's description of the universal extension of an *Ur-monotheismus* were predicated upon this epistemological shift, which makes them comprehensible.

The specific question of African culture is probably the best conceivable illustration of this epistemological mutation. Within the framework of the early twentieth-century epistemology, all discourses on alterity could only, as Foucault suggested, be commentaries or exegeses on excluded areas: primitive experience, pathological societies, or non-normal functionality, subsumed by the Same defined and understood in terms of a biological model from which determining terms—function, conflict, signification—emerge as classifiers with the power of measuring the social, individual, or psychological distance vis-à-vis the model (see Foucault, 1973:360). Anthropology, as well as missionary studies of primitive philosophies, are then concerned with the study of the distance from the Same to the Other. A reversal of categories is more obvious in Schmidt's enterprise than in Malinowski's postulations. The former, by the extension of diffusionist gradients and thus the universalization of properties of the Same, was, despite his preconceptions, marking the very possibility of a grid which, using new criteria—*rule, norm,* and *system*—could eventually account for the universality and the particularity of each cultural organization according to its own rationality and historical strategies. And we have seen that the outcome of this problem in the 1950s depends on a new manner of speaking about theodicies and cosmogonies, which in their differences grant a regional coherence and at the same time witness to properties of human mind and its universal potentialities. On the other hand, the so-called relativist principles of Malinowski seem to be just

sophisticated postulates which, concretely, in the particularity of social formations as radically autonomous bodies with respect to their functional
organization, negated cross-cultural influences, or at any rate the validity of
any comparative schema. More important, Malinowski enclosed the alterity
of social formations in their own strictly limited otherness and thus very
clearly underlined the regional virtues of such paradigms as *function, conflict,* and *signification.* Thus it is no wonder that Malinowski's best creation
was applied anthropology, a technique for supposedly avoiding aberrant
mixtures of the Same and the Other. The monstrosity is represented by a
mixture "symptomatic and symbolic of culture change: the *skokian,* the
famous concoction brewed, retailed, and consumed in the notorious slum
yards of native South African locations . . . Anything which quickly increased the alcoholic content was added; calcium carbide, methylated spirits,
tobacco, molasses and sugar, blue stone, are only a few examples" (Malinowski, 1938:xxi). Independently from the significance of this violent symbol—how can anyone, *even an African,* survive after drinking such a
poison?—if we carefully look at the paradigms which produce Malinowski's
method and which, essentially, are the same that guided applied anthropology, we can state that there is no epistemological rupture between
Lévy-Bruhl's comments on prelogism and Malinowski's functionalism. All of
them, as well as Durkheim (one of the guiding stars of functionalism) work
at describing the reversed image of the Same through the models that impose
the notions of function, conflict, and signification. The real change, that is, a
reversal of grids, came later.

Yet we have to note a major difference between Lévy-Bruhl and Malinowski. The French philosopher is strictly concerned with the notion of
deviation *(écart)* and, through an exegesis of merits of the Same's function
and signification, he challenges the identity of human nature through time
and space. As everyone knows, Lévy-Bruhl was haunted by Tylor's theory
about animism and Comte's *Loi des trois états.* He used "primitives" as an
opportunity for distinguishing both the logical and the historical distance
that separates the homogeneous experience of the Same from the heterogeneity and prelogical character of the Other. Malinowski, in contrast, was
more imaginative, despite the fact that he believed, as Lévy-Bruhl did, that
humans can be mere objects of science. He substituted the concept of an
organic function of a social system for the determinism of the passage from
prelogic to logical knowledge. In doing so, Malinowski was promoting a
radical possibility, that of using and referring to such conceptual tools as
autonomous rule, social norm, and the epistemology and singularity of
regional cultural systems.

It becomes clearer that the voices which, from the 1920s to the 1950s
spoke against the historicity of the Same and its scientism do indeed repudiate anthropological policies and researches that are "anti-historical" insofar
as African communities are concerned. Particularly, they oppose the political
processes of acculturation (see Wallerstein, 1983). In order to escape these

ideological limits, some of the participants prudently or boldly chose to claim that everything in human experience was simultaneously both culture and history. They were just inferring lessons of an epistemological mutation from the margins of Malinowski's outlook. In effect, this rupture has led from an indecent curiosity about the mysteriousness of the Other to P. Veyne's statement (to which Herskovits, Lévi-Strauss, Vansina, Ajayi, or Cheikh Anta Diop could have subscribed): "the Romans existed in a manner just as exotic and just as ordinary as the Tibetans or the Nambikwara, for example, neither more nor less; so that it becomes impossible to continue to consider them as a sort of value-standard" (in Ricoeur, 1984:43).

The Panacea of Otherness

J.-P. Sartre as an African Philosopher

> Apes . . . descend from men? Some of us
> thought so; but it is not exactly that. Apes and
> men are two separate branches that have
> evolved from a point in common but in
> different directions . . .
>
> P. BOULLE, *Planet of the Apes.*

Up to the 1920s, the entire framework of African social studies was consistent with the rationale of an epistemological field and its sociopolitical expressions of conquest. Even those social realities, such as art, languages, or oral literature, which might have constituted an introduction to otherness, were repressed in support of theories of sameness. Socially, they were tools strengthening a new organization of power and its political methods of reduction, namely, assimilation or indirect rule. Within this context, negritude, a student movement that emerged in the 1930s in Paris, is a literary coterie despite its political implications. Besides, these young men— Aimé Césaire, Léon Damas, Léopold Senghor—mostly used poetry to explore and speak about their difference as blacks (Blair, 1976:143–51; Kesteloot, 1965).

It is Sartre who in 1948 with his essay, *Black Orpheus,* an introduction to Senghor's *Anthology of New Negro and Malagasy Poetry,* transformed negritude into a major political event and a philosophical criticism of colonialism. However, everyone would agree that the Indian criticism of colonialism, beginning in the 1920s, and the growing influence of Marxism from the 1930s onwards opened a new era and made way for the possibility of new types of discourses, which from the colonial perspective were both absurd and abhorrent. The most original include the negritude movement, the fifth Pan-African Conference and the creation of Présence Africaine. Eventually, these signs of an African will for power led to political and intellectual confrontations (Conferences of Bandung, Paris, and Rome). In the 1950s, one also witnessed a radical criticism of anthropology and its inherent preconceptions of non-Western cultures. Since then, a stimulating debate about the African significance of social sciences and humanities has taken place.

In his foreword to Senghor's anthology, J.-P. Sartre made the voices of negritude widely known. But what an ambiguity in raising the French existentialist to the rank of philosopher of negritude! The resources and promise of a young ideology devoting itself to the needs of a self-rediscovery were to be cast into a very critical but somehow stultifying mold. In *Black Orpheus,* Sartre presents means for a struggle against the dominant ideology and affirms the right of Africans to fashion a new mode of thought, of speech, and of life. What he proposes is much more than a brilliant game of opposites (with which Senghor might have been satisfied). "Today, these black men have fixed their gaze upon us and our gaze is thrown back in our eyes; black torches, in their turn, light the world and our white heads are only small lanterns balanced in the wind" (1976:7–8). Sartre goes further. With passion, he sets up paradigms that would allow the colonized black to assume control of a self (see Jeanson, 1949). "It is the efficiency alone which counts." "The oppressed class must first take conscience of itself." "This taking of conscience is exactly the opposite of a redescent into one's self; it has to do here with a recognition in and action of the objective situation of the proletariat." "A Jew, white among white men, can deny that he is a Jew, can declare himself a man among men. The Negro cannot deny that he is Negro nor claim for himself this abstract uncolored humanity." Sartre even specifies the exact significance of the Negro's revolt:

> The Negro who vindicates his négritude in a revolutionary movement places himself, then and there, upon the terrain of Reflection, whether he wishes to rediscover in himself certain objective traits growing out of African civilization, or hopes to find the black Essence in the wells of his soul. (Sartre, 1976:17)

The negritude which he thus affirms and celebrates is simultaneously the "triumph of Narcissism and suicide of Narcissus, tension of the soul outside of its culture, words and every psychic fact, luminous night of non-knowledge." Immediately after this celebration, he warns that negritude can neither be sufficient nor must it live forever. It is made to be negated, to be exceeded. Among the ruins of the colonial era, its singers must again rework songs, reformulate their myths, and submit them to the service and to the need of the revolution of the proletariat.

It could be said of *Black Orpheus* that while correcting the potential theoretical excesses of the ideology of negritude, it did so in a high-handed manner, thwarting other possible orientations of the movement. At the same time, it subjugated the militants' generosity of heart and mind to the fervour of a political philosophy. Sartre, in the 1940s and early 1950s, was promoting, in the name of commitment, the moral demand of choosing political sides. A substantial part of *Being and Nothingness* is devoted to the tension between the *for itself (pour-soi)* and *for others (pour-autrui)*. Now Sartre dedicated himself to the analysis of the concrete consequences of this dialectic as illustrated by colonial systems (Sartre, 1956). It was to the credit of Senghor that he was not stifled by the peremptory arguments and the vision of this first theoretician of negritude whom he had aroused: he had asked Sartre for a cloak to celebrate negritude; he was given a shroud.

Nevertheless, *Black Orpheus* is a major ideological moment, perhaps one of the most important. It displays both the potentialities of Marxist revolution and the negation of colonialism and racism: "The Negro," states Sartre, "creates an anti-racist racism. He does not at all wish to dominate the world; he wishes the abolition of racial privileges wherever they are found; he affirms his solidarity with the oppressed of all colors. At a blow the subjective, existential, ethnic notion of *Négritude* passes as Hegel would say, into the objective, positive, exact notion of the *proletariat*" (1976:59). What Sartre did was to impose philosophically the political dimension of a negativity in the colonial history. This was a compelling task for Africans. By emphasizing the relativity and the sins of Western expansionism, he gave meaning and credibility to all signs of opposition to colonialism and called for a new understanding of the significance of violence in the colonies. Thus, Pan-African Conferences, Gandhi's noncooperation movement, and the Neo-Destur party emerging in Tunisia would appear to have a dialectical and positive portent for the future: they could influence the lives of the colonized and, also fundamentally, provide the possibility of new societies.

The change from colonized to independent, from rule by divine right to liberation, may not seem to have any relation to anthropology in particular or African social studies in general. In fact, it does. First, *Black Orpheus* was in large measure responsible for the blossoming in Francophone Africa of the negritude literature of the 1950s (Blair, 1976; Wauthier, 1964). A *littérature engagée*, a highly political literature, put forward Sartre's basic positions concerning African spiritual and political autonomy. This new generation of writers born between 1910 and 1920 includes Cheikh Anta Diop, Bernard Dadié, René Depestre, Frantz Fanon, Keita Fodeba, Camara Laye, and Ferdinand Oyono, among others. Second, black intellectuals, particularly Francophones, read Sartre, discussed his anticolonialist positions and, generally speaking, upheld them. Fanon disagrees with Sartre yet offers a good example of his impact. In his *Peau noire, masques blancs*, Fanon accuses Sartre of treason, for Fanon does not believe that "Négritude is dedicated to its own destruction." Some years later, in *Les Damnés de la terre*, the West Indian theorist firmly applies Sartre's dialectical principle and bluntly states: "there will not be a Black culture," "the Black problem is a political one."

On the other hand, there is a connection between this black *littérature engagée* and the African ideology of otherness. In *Black Orpheus* Sartre proposes a Marxist paradigm. The founders of negritude do not disagree with him on this point. Some West Indians, for instance Aimé Césaire, Etienne Lero, Jules Monnerot, and Jacques Roumain, have been at one time or another members of the Communist Party. Mamadou Dia, Alioune Diop, Birago Diop, Jacques Rabemananjara, and Senghor are rather critical of communism, even when, as in the case of Senghor, they are socialists. For them communism is merely (as Sartre defined it) a traveling companion. They question the overemphasis on the fate of the international proletariat and wish to determine a strategy for promoting the individuality of African culture. As opposed to Marx's rigid interpretation of the relations between values and peoples' aspirations in society, they look for ways of reinventing a sociohistoric foundation for independent African societies (Senghor, 1962). Thus the basic premise of the African ideology of otherness: history is myth.

Is Sartre really the inspired guide of this revolution? Let us say that Sartre, philosopher *in partibus* of negritude—or, figuratively, Sartre as "Negro philosopher"—is a symbol. Since the 1920s, writers like R. Maran, A. Gide, or M. Sauvage had criticized the colonial enterprise. In anthropology, scholars such as Maurice Delafosse, Leo Frobenius, Marcel Griaule, and Théodore Monod had offered positive views of African social regimes. And in 1947, we found grouped around the press and journal, "Présence Africaine" and its founder, Alioune Diop, a significant number of French intellectuals. Georges Balandier, Albert Camus, Emmanuel Mounier, Paul Rivet, Gide, and Monod, for example, affirm the political and cultural implications of the mythical character of colonial history (Rabemananjara, s.d.:24). But Sartre established a cardinal synthesis. By rejecting both the colonial rationale and the set of culturally eternal values as bases for society, his brief treatise posited philosophically a relativist perspective for African social studies.

Sartre did not necessarily influence George Balandier or Joseph Ki-Zerbo nor does he guide all African thinkers. Nevertheless, his insights illuminated the trends and preoccupations of African scholarship. His path to liberation meant a new epistemological configuration under the sovereignty of dialectical reason (Jeanson, 1949). It is from his interpretation, rather than from communism, that the two characteristics of present-day African social studies presented by Copans (1971a) make sense: on the one hand, a radical criticism of imperialism and, on the other, a "Marxist revival" which, in effect, has taken hold of the whole theoretical domain of African studies.

Despite the importance of the negritude movement, very little attention has been given to the relationships between its textual organization, its sources, and its expressions (Melone, 1962). We have known, for instance, that negritude was a French invention but not how essentially French it was (Adotévi, 1972). We have been told that the negritude literature appears unified, but its structure and spirit are more in keeping with European sources than with immediately visible African themes (Gérard, 1964; Bastide, 1961). Hauser's voluminous book (1982) deals with these issues and is probably the most complete study to date on the negritude movement. The value of this work does not lie in any new discovery but in the manner in which it addresses the issues of negritude's significance and objectives. According to Sartre, negritude signifies, fundamentally, tension between the black man's past and future. Thus it must always be ready to redefine itself. As Hauser says, it clothes itself in mythical forms offering its meaning as a *mot de passe* and its philosophy as an inversion and a reversal of Western theses. The result is a paradox: "Poets for the Blacks, the men of the Negritude movement were read by Whites; Poets of the present, they are perceived in Africa as poets of the past" (Hauser, 1982:214). While a literary language, negritude's content reveals an ideological system and even, according to Sartre, "a revolutionary project." It comments upon a *Weltanschauung,* interprets a given world, unveils the universe (*dire le monde*), and gives a significance to it (*signifier le monde*) (Melone, 1962; Diakhate, 1965). But at the same time, because it is an ideological discourse, negritude claims to be a key to a new understanding of history. And thus the problem of the political and cultural responsibility of the negritude movement (Senghor, 1964) appears as a responsibility which Hauser considers ambiguous. Insofar as negritude's political position is concerned, Hauser states that negritude has not been a revolutionary movement nor even, with the exception of Césaire, a movement of revolt (Hauser, 1982:443). Moreover, in relation to its conditions of possibility, negritude stands as the result of multiple influences: the Bible, anthropologists' books, and French intellectual schools (symbolism, romanticism, surrealism, etc.), literary legacies, and literary models (Baudelaire, Lautréamont, Rimbaud, Mallarmé, Valéry, Claudel, St. John Perse, Apollinaire, etc.). Hauser presents multiple proofs of the Western sources of negritude and seriously doubts its African authenticity (Hauser, 1982:533).

It becomes immediately apparent from these internal contradictions of negritude that Sartre's proposition on the deadlock of the movement makes tremendous sense. Unless understood as metaphors, the signs of otherness that negritude might have promoted in literature, philosophy, history, or social science, seem to refer to techniques of ideological manipulation. R. Depestre forcefully points this out.

> The original sin of negritude—and the adventures that destroyed its initial project—come from the spirit that made it possible: anthropology. The crisis that destroyed negritude coincides with the winds that blow across the *fields* in which anthropology—be it cultural, social, applied, structural—with black or white masks, is used to carrying out its learned inquiries. (Depestre, 1980:83)

Ideologies for Otherness

In the wake of negritude, but also running parallel to it or even against it, is the affirmation of African political thought. It aimed initially at recognizing the black personality (*la personalité nègre*) and obtaining certain sociopolitical rights (Wauthier, 1964). Only later, in the 1950s, did it really serve projects for African independence (Coquery-Vidrovitch, 1974). It is commonplace to see in it one of the important elements of African nationalism. The other is resistance to colonialism, whether passive or violent. It is noteworthy that its most distinguished promoters are drawn from among those first and best assimilated to Western culture and thought. Further, one almost senses that these Westernized Africans resented the need to return to their own sources and to state the right to be different (see Kesteloot, 1965; Wauthier, 1964; Dieng, 1983).

To consider this awakening as a special turning point in the history of the West is not, in any case, to disqualify it. In 1957, Nkrumah published his autobiography, in which he explained to what extent he had been influenced by communist and socialist writings, Black American political theories (particularly Marcus Garvey's *Philosophy and Opinions*), and Padmore's view on Pan-Africanism. He also wrote that he learned much from Hannibal, Cromwell, Napoléon, Mazzini, Gandhi, Mussolini, and Hitler. Senghor (1962) also presented his own orientation, writing in first-person plural to include his friends, the co-founders of the negritude movement. If they believed in affirming their difference, it was, according to him, because of anthropologists and Black Americans. Also, in the period between the two wars they were privileged witnesses of the crisis of Western values. Moreover, their recent discovery of Marx gave them reasons for utopian dreams.

Senghor's explanation is plausible. Up to the 1960s, anthropology, Black American ideology, and Marxism had a significant impact on the African intelligentsia. For the sake of brevity, let us mention as important points of reference three major types of contributions which gradually changed colonial thinking and practice. First, there were anthropological and missionary commitments to African values: for instance, Schmidt's enterprise in the 1930s, and Tempels's, Griaule's, and Danquah's studies in the 1940s. In addition, contributions from African scholars such as Mulago (1955), and Kagame (1956), promoted the concept of African theodicy or of signs of a natural religion. They all established African religions as particular and original experiences of a universal wisdom or philosophy. Second, there was intervention by some Western sociologists and historians. Raymond Michelet in his *African Empires and Civilizations* (1945) and Basil Davidson and Georges Balandier in their numerous publications opposed widely accepted conceptions of "living fossils" or "frozen societies." Third, there was the "awakening" of African intellectuals who began to speak about their past and their culture and attacked, or at least interrogated, colonialism and its basic principles (Dieng, 1979; Guisse, 1979).

This ideological rupture sounds sincere and quite probably was in the minds of scholars who participated in it. Yet, it is a magnificent paradox, an almost illusory sacrifice of applied anthropology. It is based on two fragile principles: a methodological reversal and an intellectual discontinuity in African social studies. In their application, rather than opening up a new realm, these principles helped to confuse prospects for otherness and the significance of this concept. The significance belongs to the studied Other and is revealed to perception and given to understanding through the reality of a concrete experience. As to the discourse on this significance, it is always a project and a transcendent idea which cannot be reduced to a mental apprehension. To teach, as did Danquah, Davidson, Michelet, or Mulago, that there are, in Africa, organized social structures, sophisticated systems of relations of production, and highly complex universes of belief, is to express propositions which can be tested. To add commentaries or exegeses on black cultures which are essentially mystical, religious, and sensuous, is to decipher a possibly controversial myth and, at any rate, to elaborate on what is not the immanent significance of the object studied.

The anthropologist did not seem to respect the immanence of human experience and went on to organize, at scientific expense, methods and ways of ideological reduction: concrete social experiences were looked at and interpreted from the normativity of a political discourse and its initiatives. With a Michelet and a Herskovits, the forming of new ideological perspectives in the field produced a reversal: African experiences, attitudes, and mentalities became mirrors of a spiritual and cultural richness. There is no mystery, nor scandal in this, if we agree that we are dealing with discourses bearing upon human experience and accounted for by an *episteme*. I should also make it clear again that we are not concerned with evaluating the ethical value of discourses, but only with designating a genealogy of knowledge. Michelet's, Davidson's, Balandier's or Mulago's studies do not transform the heart of the object matter, but rather reverse, as Sartre did philosophically, a method of narration and the techniques of describing the object. A shift has occurred. A new anthropology has, silently but powerfully, put in place its basic norms, namely respectability and internal coherence for African systems and experience, as well as rules for their progressive integration into modernity.

One may observe this gradual change in some representative domains: anthropology, history, and political thinking. In anthropology, studies of traditional laws were carried out by A. Ajisafe, *The Laws and Customs of the Yoruba People* (1924), and J. B. Danquah, *Akan Laws and Customs* (1928). Analyses of African customs were published; for example, D. Delobson's, *Les secrets des sorciers noirs* (1934), M. Quenum's, *Au Pays des Fons: us et coutumes du Dahomey* (1938), J. Kenyatta's, *Facing Mount Kenya* (1938), J. B. Danquah, *The Akan Doctrine of God* ([1944] 1968), and the excellent researches of K. A. Busia and P. Hazoume, respectively, *The Position of the Chief in the Modern Political System of Ashanti* (1951) and *Le pacte du sang au Dahomey* ([1937] 1956). In the field of history, the most prominent contributions to African nationalism were J. C. de Graft-Johnson's *African Glory: The Story of Vanished Negro Civilizations* (1954) and Cheikh Anta Diop's, *Nations nègres et culture* (1954), in which he analyses the notion of Hamites and the connections between Egyptian and African languages and civilizations.

It was in the political essays that a clearly progressive awakening gradually affirmed the principles of African nationalism and international integration. In *Towards Nationhood in West Africa* (1928), J. W. de Graft-Johnson still envisaged the future of West Africa in terms of the British Empire. But nine years later, W. Azikiwe, in *Renascent Africa* (1937), was more critical of Western colonial programs. He emphasized the fact that the "renascent African" must know that his ancestors "made definite contributions to history" and he condemned imperialism and militarism. Major essays took into account the resolution of the Fifth Pan-African Congress of Manchester (1945) which stated: "we demand for Black Africa autonomy and independence," a central theme in Nkrumah's *Towards Colonial Freedom* (1947), Césaire's *Discours sur le colonialisme* (1950), and Fanon's *Peau noire, masques blancs* (1952). For a number of African intellectuals, these works have been, and probably still are, major sources for their cultural autonomy.

In her doctoral dissertation (1965), L. Kesteloot provided a brief history of the contacts with Black Americans that contributed to the awakening of the consciousness of Africans (see also Shepperson, 1960). L. G. Damas, just before his death in 1978, strongly confirmed this thesis with reference to the contributions of W. E. B. DuBois, Langston Hughes, Carter Woodson, Countee Cullen, and, in particular, Mercer Cook, all of whom he considered links between Black Americans and Africans (Damas, 1979:247–54). To these names, Senghor adds Claude MacKay and Richard Wright (Senghor, 1962).

It is difficult to say with certainty to what extent the ideological commitment of Black Americans made an impact on the African intelligentsia. It converged with the influence of the Marxist movement and particularly with that of the French Communist Party which, before World War II, was the force best organized to fight openly for the black man's cause. A number of Francophone black intellectuals became communists, including Césaire, J. Roumain, E. Lero, and J. S. Alexis. Others, like Nkrumah, Nyerere, and Senghor, allied themselves with socialist ideological principles. In any case, the association with Black Americans strongly influenced the critical views of black Africans with respect to the crisis of Western values. It also revealed differences in the sociohistorical conditions of both. Opposition had already appeared at the Second Pan-African Congress, in 1921, held successively in London (August 28), Brussels (August 29–September 2), and Paris (September 3 and 5). Surveying the history of the black race, DuBois had, to Blaise Diagne's great surprise, pleaded for the principle of the separation of races and of separate evolution. But Diagne imposed on the assembly the ethnological point of view that "the Black and the colored people were capable of progressive development which would allow [them] to reach the advanced state of other races" (Bontinck, 1980:604–605).

Nevertheless, the greatest influence on African thought from the 1930s to the 1950s was Marxism. Significant examples of its impact are the warm support that Sartre gave to the negritude movement in 1948 with his essay,

Black Orpheus, the publication by Aimé Césaire of *Discours sur le colonialisme* in 1950, and the meeting at the Sorbonne, in 1956, of the First International Congress of Black Writers and Artists.

That same year some black intellectuals stated publicly that they wished that Marxism could promote their cause, and not only the reverse. In frustration, Césaire (1956) left the French Communist Party. During the Sorbonne meeting, Marxism was at the center of the debate. A critical distance was therefore suggested, without entailing total rejection. As A. Ly would say, "the blind refusal of Marxism would be as absurd as a total alienation to the Marxist system would be fatal for the evolution of humankind" (1956). Though expressed differently, it is this spirit that dominated the debates during the first meeting of nonaligned nationalists in Bandung. Ultimately, the principle of nonalignment would be projected in politics.

In literature (see Jahn, 1968), this position is expressed in three major ways: first, in terms of domestication of political power (E. Mphahlele, Mongo Beti, and Sembene Ousmane); second, in a criticism of colonial life (Chinua Achebe, D. Chraïbi, F. Oyono); and third, in the celebration of the African sources of life (A. Loba, A. Sefrioui, Cheikh Hamidou Kane).

It is noteworthy that a number of political leaders who came to power in independent Africa declared themselves pro-Marxist or socialist or, in some cases, defined ways of indigenizing socialism. Socialists or not, the African heads of state, attempting to link thought to action, have published much, perhaps too much. In the late 1950s, one of the most prestigious leaders, Ahmed Sekou Touré, dared to refuse the progressive route to political autonomy proposed by France. In 1959, he published more than a thousand pages on his socialist projects for the development of Guinea and the promotion of Africa (1959a, 1959b, 1959c). Aimé Césaire celebrated this "courageous" and "dynamic" thought (1959–1960). In its inspiration, as in its perspectives, it is close to that of Nkrumah. With the translation of his autobiography, Nkrumah's influence, already immense in Anglophone Africa, came to French-speaking countries in 1960. His work met increasing favor, whose highest point was the welcome given to his *Consciencism.* In this work, as in others, Nkrumah incorporated fidelity to Marxism into the cause of decolonization and the struggle against imperialism. His friend Patrice Lumumba had neither the time to clarify his thought nor to refine his essays (1963) which appeared after his death. Sartre again put his talent to the service of African nationalism by introducing J. Van Lierde's book on Lumumba's political philosophy (Van Lierde, 1963).

Numerous other leaders expounded their points of view on the complex problems of independent Africa. The major issues concern the management of the State as well as the means for economic liberation. Such leaders include Ahidjo in Cameroon (1964, 1969), Badian in Mali (1964), Mamadou Dia in Senegal (1957, 1960), and Kanza in the Belgian Congo (1959a, 1959b). Nyerere in Tanzania has promoted *ujamaa* (communalism) (1968a) and M. Ngouabi (Congo) insisted on the necessity of applying scientific socialism (1975). But the paths taken in politics, when they have not led to bitter failure, have often caused serious problems. When permitted, political reaction surfaced. In any case, different schools of thought have arisen; hence, for example, the satire and the polemics found in D. Ewande's mockery of the Negro State (1968). These schools of thought were asserted in cathartic terms, especially in fiction in the 1970s, through attacks on the incompetence and the abuses of the new African administrators. The theme of ruthless colonial exploitation is replaced by an original sociopolitical subject: "we are, in the main, to blame for our misfortunes" (Casteran and Langellier, 1978; Pomonti, 1979). There is a proliferation of examples in the literary works of Kwei Armah, Kofi Awoonor, Cameron Duodu, Ahmadou Kourouma, Tierno Monenembo, Ngugi wa Thiongo, and Tati-Loutard.

Marx Africanized

The political image of Africa after 1965 is indeed distressing. Authoritarian regimes have multiplied, rules and norms of democracy have been flouted or rejected (see Gutkind and Wallerstein, 1976; O'Meara and Carter, 1986). Political dictatorships have been imposed. Some charismatic leaders have vanished into obscurity. Touré was isolated in his dictatorship and Nkrumah, challenged and insulted, died in exile (Powell, 1984). Senghor remained a model. Yet he chose to remove Mamadou Dia, his opponent, whose economic ideas were considered in the 1960s to be a necessary complement to Senghor's metaphysics of negritude. He did this to guarantee security for the African path to socialism (Kachama-Nkoy, 1963). Covered with honors, but criticized more and more by the new generation, Senghor struggled to make all his works accessible (1964, 1971, 1977, 1983). At the same time he continued, against all opposition, to define negritude as a value of dialogue and of openness and to clarify his humanist choices for socialist politics and for an economy based on an African reading of Marx (1976a). Nyerere, in these years, also appears as one of the more credible political thinkers.

Despite the crucial problems of its adaptation to the African context, socialism seemed the most fashionable doctrine. Its best known proponents are Fanon, Senghor and Nyerere. The West Indian Frantz Fanon, a solid Marxist, but also a good student of Hegel, Kierkegaard, Nietzsche, and Sartre, expressed his commitment to the African revolution in *Peau noire, masques blancs* (1952), *Les Damnés de la terre* (1962), and *Pour la révolution Africaine* (1969). His commitment is based on a concrete understanding of the Hegelian dialectic. The alienation caused by colonialism constitutes the thesis, the African ideologies of otherness (black personality and negritude), the antithesis, and political liberation should be the synthesis. The similarity with Sartre's analysis in *Black Orpheus* is striking. But Fanon, who was probably more concerned with details and practical contradictions because he knew them better, had come from a "colony," was himself black, and participated actively in the Algerian revolution. In contrast to Sartre, he could address a wider range of problems.

The alienation of colonialism entails both the objective fact of total dependence (economic, political, cultural, and religious) and the subjective process of the self-victimization of the dominated. The colonized internalizes the imposed racial stereotypes, particularly in attitudes towards technology, culture, and language. Black personality and negritude appear as the only means of negating this thesis, and Fanon expounds the antithesis in terms of antiracist symbols. Negritude becomes the intellectual and emotional sign of opposition to the ideology of white superiority. At the same time, it asserts an authenticity which eventually expresses itself as a radical negation: rejection of racial humiliation, rebellion against the rationality of domination, and revolt against the whole colonialist system. This symbolic violence ultimately turns into nationalism and subsequently leads to a political struggle for liberation. The synthesis is the conjunction of, on the one side, "national consciousness" and "political praxis," and, on the other, the contradictions created by existing social classes: national bourgeoisie, proletariat, underproletariat, and peasantry.

Whereas Fanon distinguishes the analysis of a struggle for liberation (first phase) from the promotion of socialism (second phase) Senghor tends to define African socialism as just a stage in a complex process beginning with negritude and oriented towards a universal civilization. He emphasizes three major moments: negritude, Marxism, and universal civilization.

(a) Negritude is "the warmth" of being, living, and participating in a natural, social, and spiritual harmony. It also means assuming some basic political positions: that colonialism has depersonalized Africans and that therefore the end of colonialism should promote the self-fulfillment of Africans. Thus, negritude is simultaneously an existential thesis (I am what I have decided to be) and a political enterprise. It also signifies a political choice: among European methods, socialism seems the most useful for both cultural reassessment and sociopolitical promotion.

(b) Marxism is, for Senghor, a method. In order to use it adequately, the Senegalese thinker dissociates Marxism as humanism from Marxism as a theory of knowledge. The first offers a convincing explanation of the notion of alienation in its theory of capital and value and exposes the scandal of human beings under capitalism becoming mere means of production and strangers *vis-à-vis* the product of their work. For this reason, Senghor readily accepts Marxism's conclusions insofar as they indicate a recognition of the natural rights of humans, who are and must remain free agents and creators of culture. "We are socialist," writes Senghor, "because we accept Marx and Engels and believe in the usefulness of their analysis of societies. Yet we add to Marx and Engels' works the contributions of their successors." For Senghor, Marxism as a theory of knowledge nevertheless constitutes a problem. It is one thing to use its schemas for analyzing and understanding the complexity of social formations, and another to accept the idea that social complexities universally fit into the concept of the class struggle and express the need to deny religion.

(c) Negritude and Marxist humanism are, according to Senghor, only stages in a dynamic dialectic process towards a universal civilization. Interpreting hypotheses of Pierre Teilhard de Chardin, Senghor bases his ideas of a universal civilization upon laws of evolution. He believes that the movement from microentities to more complex ones and finally consciousness expresses a natural law. This would imply at least three major theses: the principle of development of all human beings, the principle of harmony in development, and God's existence as a natural necessity. Senghor thinks that some basic African values are well expressed in this perspective: namely the idea of community, the principle of harmony between evolving humans and changing nature, and, finally, the vision of a unitary universe.

Senghor's influence on contemporary African thought, particularly in Francophone countries, is considerable. The Senegalese writer, like the Ghanaian Nkrumah, does not allow himself to be neutral. Of the African thinkers of this century, he will probably have been the most honored and the most complimented, yet probably also the most disparaged and the most insulted, particularly by the present generation of African intellectuals. It is significant that S. Azombo-Menda and M. Anobo, in their manual of African philosophy, believe they are obliged to explain the presence of Senghor in their text. "His thought has exerted on black intellectuals such influence that it would be regrettable were his principal theses to be ignored or passed in silence by sectarianism or because people felt incapable to discuss them" (Azombo-Menda and Anobo, 1978). Does including Senghor in a textbook of African philosophy really require excuses?

It is fitting to note that Senghor has become a myth that is endlessly discussed. It is true that criticism, especially African, has mainly seen in Senghor the promoter of some famous oppositions which, out of context, could appear to embrace perspectives proper to certain racist theoreticians: Negro emotion confronting hellenistic reason; intuitive Negro reasoning through participation facing European analytical thinking through utilization; or the Negro-African, person of rhythm and sensitivity, assimilated to the Other through sympathy, who can say "I am the other . . . therefore I am." On this basis, Senghor has been accused of seeking to promote a detestable model for a division of vocations between Africa and Europe, between African and European (e.g., Towa, 1971a; Soyinka, 1976). This seems quite wrong. Senghor's philosophy can be simply understood through a challenging proposition he offered to the Senagalese Socialist Party in July 1963: "Finally, what too many Africans lack, is the awareness of our poverty and creative imagination, I mean the spirit of resourcefulness" (1983:152).

Nyerere's socialism is probably the most pragmatic of all African socialisms (Duggan and Civile, 1976:181). Its basic assumption has been spelled out in simple terms. In the expression "African socialism" the most important word is not socialism but *African*. In other words, according to Nyerere, an African does not need to convert to socialism or to democracy, since his own traditional experience is socialist and democratic:

> The true African socialist does not look on one class of men as his brethren and another as his natural enemies. He does not form an alliance with the 'brethren' for the extermination of the 'non-brethren.' He regards all men as his brethren—as members of his ever-extending family. *Ujamaa*, then, or 'familihood,' describes our socialism. (Nyerere, 1968a:27)

Ujamaa, or communalism, rejects both capitalism (which "seeks to build a happy society on the basis of exploitation of man by man") and doctrinaire socialism (which "seeks to build its happy society on a philosophy of inevitable conflict between man and man"). For Nyerere, *ujamaa* means first of all the creation of a new society, a nation, based on the traditional model of family. Second, moving beyond the nation, the socialist project would imply a constant development of communalism for all peoples (Duggan and Civile, 1976:188–96).

The *Arusha Declaration,* issued by Nyerere's party in 1967, made Nyerere's program more explicit. It presented the party's creed, its socialist charter, the policy of self-reliance, the philosophy of membership, and an official statement about socialist leaders. The creed presents the rationale of *ujamaa.* In the first part, it describes the major values (sharing, equality, rejection of alienation and exploitation of man by man, etc.). In the second part, it offers as ideological deductions its main political objectives. These are: first, the independence of the nation, but a socialist nation governed by a socialist government; second, cooperation with African countries and commitment to the liberation of Africa and her unity; and third, improvement of the conditions of equality and life in the nation and, therefore, nationalization of the means of production and political control of the fields of production.

The search for the construction of a new African society has also led in other directions. Both N. Azikiwe's interpretation of political unity and the pragmatic federalism advocated by O. Awolowo in *Path to Nigerian Freedom* (1947) have followers. Nkrumah's political philosophy is still popular all over the continent, especially his concept of social revolution described in *I Speak of Freedom* (1961) and the materialism of *Consciencism* (1970), which exposes a sociopolitical system implying dialogue and the possibility of reconciling antagonistic forces and orienting them towards positive social change. Unfortunately, looking back at Nkrumah's regime in Ghana, one might think that all was just rhetoric. Though a good Marxist theorist, Nkrumah, once in power, became a bad politician and rapidly turned into a dictator. The best that can be said is that he simply failed to put his theory into practice. Yet his theoretical legacy remains, challenging and stimulating for the new generation of African Marxists looking for paradigms of revolutionary change and cultural dynamism. On a quite general level, one may still admire his critical evaluation of G. Padmore's *Panafricanism or Communism*, his views on the unity of the continent, and the pertinence of his analyses of neocolonialism (Nkrumah, 1962, 1965).

It is my feeling that in general the new African trend concentrates on the ideological significance of the failure of contemporary African society. In French-speaking countries, the criticism is carried out in the context of present-day sociopolitical contradictions rooted in both the precolonial and colonial experience, as for example, by Pathé Diagne in *Pouvoir politique traditionnel en Afrique occidentale* (1967) and G. L. Hazoume with his book *Idéologies tribalistes et nation en Afrique: le cas Dahoméen* (1972). Under the circumstances, many thinkers tend to reevaluate African socialism and insist on the usefulness of applying the Marxist lesson in a more systematic manner. Majhemout Diop suggested this in his *Contribution à l'étude des problèmes politiques en Afrique noire* (1958). Osende Afana brilliantly applied Marxist perspectives to the economic situation of West Africa in *L'Economie ouest-africaine. Perspectives de développement* (1967, 1976). The Marxist trend seems still to be dynamic, as shown by the writings of authors such as Diagne, Hountondji, and M. Ngouabi, as well as by the official ideological choices of the regimes of Angola, Benin, Congo, Ethiopia, and Mozambique. The newly created *Journal of African Marxists* is also an indication of the Marxist revival in Africa. It has succeeded in bringing together intellectuals from all over the continent and states its task in terms of "providing a platform for Marxist thought to provide that element most needed now to enable Africa to throw off imperialist domination and capitalist exploitation" (1983, no. 4:3; see also Dieng:1979).

In contrast, and mainly in West Africa, other scholars continue to give priority to questions that have been asked again and again about tradition. M. Dia, for instance, with his works on Islamic humanism (1977, 1979), joins A. Hampate Ba and Boubou Hama, prestigious survivors of an old team which, from the 1930s onward, has continued to invoke traditionalism and Islam as effective sources of regeneration (see also Brenner, 1984).

Present trends give the impression that the Africa of the 1980s is reliving the crises of the 1950s. To create myths which would give a meaning to its hopes for improvement, Africa seems to hesitate between two principal sources, Marxist and traditionalist, and to worry endlessly about the evidence about the superiority of the Same over the Other and the possible virtues of the inverse relationship. But a discrete and controverted current has quietly developed since 1954, the date of the publication of Cheikh Anta Diop's *Nations nègres et culture*. To many, this current appears as the only reasonable alternative to the present disorder. Using Marxism as a foil, it intends to study African tradition in depth, affirming the cultural unity of precolonial Africa, linguistic kinship, and common historic past (Diop,

1954, 1960a, 1967, 1981). Diop's learned investigations—assisted by the Congolese T. Obenga (1973) and the Cameroonian Mveng (1972)—seek to give Africa the moral benefit of being the cradle of humankind and of having influenced the history of ancient Egypt as well as Mediterranean civilizations. But could these potentially mobilizing myths provide, as Diop hoped (1960c), the possibility of a new political order in Africa?

IV

E. W. BLYDEN'S LEGACY
AND QUESTIONS

The Ambiguities of an Ideological Alternative

> Toute ma vie, politiquement, je me suis fait de
> la bile. J'en induis que le seul Père que j'ai
> connu (que je me suis donné) a été le Père
> politique.
>
> *Roland Barthes par Roland Barthes.*

In his foreword to *Selected Letters of Edward Wilmot Blyden* (1978) collected by Hollis R. Lynch, L. S. Senghor celebrates Blyden as the "foremost
precursor both of *Négritude* and of the *African Personality*" (Lynch
1978:xv–xxii). The father of negritude thinks that a century before the
emergence of modern African ideology, Blyden promoted its spirit. First,
because Blyden treated "both the virtues of *Négritude* and and proper modes
of illustrating these virtues: through scholarly studies, life styles and cultural
creaton." Second, because "through the stimulus of a 'revolution of mentalities'," Blyden tried "to lead Negro-Americans to cultivate what is 'authentically' theirs: their 'African Personality' . . . and advocated already the
method which is ours today: to find one's roots in the values of *Négritude*,
while remaining open to those of non-African civilizations." Third, because
as a "true universal man," Blyden "already believed, as we do today, that all
progress in a civilization can only come from a mixing of cultures." Lynch,
author of a biography of Blyden, agrees with Senghor and writes that "the
modern concept of *Négritude* . . . can find respectable historical roots in the
writings of Blyden" (1967:252). He also stresses the influence of Blyden on
such ideologues as the Nigerian Nnamdi Azikiwe and the Ghanaian Kwame
Nkrumah and states that "Blyden was the ideological father of the idea of
West African unity": "he inspired nationalism in the individual territories,"
and his "pan-Negro ideology was undoubtedly the most important pro-
genitor of Pan-Africanism" (1967:249–50).

A native of the Danish island of St. Thomas, E. W. Blyden (1832–1912)
settled in West Africa in 1851 and rapidly became one of the most careful

students of African affairs. A permanent resident of Liberia and Sierra Leone, he saw the beginning of the scramble for Africa, studied the arrival of European settlers on the West Coast, and observed the progressive establishment of colonial rule. He was the author of several works.

It is not my intention to present an exegetic interpretation of Blyden's work, nor to offer a new understanding of his life and achievements. I am concerned with a practical question in the precise field of the history of African ideologies: in what sense can we accept Senghor's and Lynch's statements about Blyden as the precursor of negritude and "African Personality"? Thus, I will not "interpret" Blyden's theses from the point of view of historical data now available, but instead will focus on their significance and limitations, and will when necessary, situate them in their "ideological atmosphere." I shall, therefore, describe the signs and symbols of Blyden's ideology as expressed by such texts as *Vindication of the Negro Race* (1857), *Liberia's Offering* (1862), *The Negro in Ancient History* (1869), *Liberia: Past, Present and Future* (1869), *Christianity, Islam and the Negro Race* (1888), and *Africa and the Africans* (1903). I use the themes of *Christianity, Islam and the Negro Race* as an organizing frame. This book, a miscellaneous collection of various texts—articles, speeches, reviews—is Blyden's major work (see Lynch, 1967:73–78). Quotations from his letters add subjectivity to some of Blyden's more formal theses.

In this first section, I will present Blyden's thesis on colonization and his interpretation of the "Negro's condition"; in the next, I will show how he sees the African and defines his own political philosophy. My conclusion on his legacy attempts a critical synthesis and studies Blyden's racial attitudes and "prophetism" and proposes a critical interpretation of Senghor's and Lynch's statements. The method used is simple. Blyden's work is not analyzed as sign or symbol of something else, but only in terms of its own density and spiritual limits, as it reveals its own irreducibility and specificity. At the same time, because this work was produced within a given historical period and a specific intellectual climate, I thought it valid to rewrite its "passion" in the manner of Foucault, as a simple discourse-object.

Given Blyden's personal situation—a West Indian Black who, denied education in the United States, emigrated to Liberia (Blyden, LO:8; Lynch, 1967:73)—one can understand that his ideas concerning colonization express both racial and nationalistic positions aimed at achieving a particular type of social revolution. On April 20, 1860, he wrote to William Gladstone, then British Chancellor of the Exchequer about Liberia: "this little Republic, planted here in great weakness, is no doubt destined, in the providence of God, to revolutionize for good the whole of that portion of Africa" (Blyden, LET:30). But in a letter written on June 9 of the same year to the Rev. John L. Wilson, Corresponding Secretary of the Board of Foreign Missions of the American Presbyterian Church, Blyden speaks of being "instrumental in doing anything towards establishing the respectability of my race." Significantly, he wishes that his efforts for the promotion of the "Alexander High

School" in Monrovia will contribute to "a partial solution" to questions
about the Negro's capabilities:

> 'The great problem to be solved is whether black men, under favorable
> circumstances, can manage their own affairs . . . with efficiency.' Will the
> efforts now put forth in the Alex High School, if efficient and successful,
> contribute to a partial solution of the problem? And, on the other hand, if
> those efforts fail, will the impression be deepened that the problem is insolva-
> ble [sic], and will the gloom which has so long rested upon the race increase in
> density? If so, then let me be forever discarded by the black race, and let me be
> condemned by the white, if I strive not with all my powers, if I put not forth all
> my energies to contribute to so important a solution. (Blyden, LET:31)

One might focus on this sign: an explicit need for over-compensation
transformed into a will-for-power. But this will for "the progress of the race"
is largely determined by an apologetic objective. For, as Blyden put it at the
end of his treatise on *The Negro in Ancient History,* "we believe that as
descendants of Ham had share . . . in the founding of cities and in the
organization of government, so members of the same family, developed under
different circumstances, will have an important part in the closing of the
great drama" (NAH:28). In this regard, he denies to whites any positive
cultural presence in Africa and frequently insists on the fact that only black
peoples can transform the continent. Yet he seriously advocates colonization
as one of the possible means of metamorphosis.

Blyden's understanding of the process of Africa's opening up to a white
presence is ambiguous:

> The modern desire for more accurate knowledge of Africa is not a mere
> sentiment; it is the philanthropic impulse to lift up the millions of that
> continent to their proper position among the intellectual and moral forces of
> the world; but it is also the commercial desire to open that vast country to the
> enterprises of trade. (Blyden, CINR, 95)

There remains the "civilizing mission." He even refers to the first years of
slavery as being positive: "The slave trade was regarded as a great means of
civilizing the blacks—a kind of missionary institution." Africans were at that
time "not only indoctrinated into the principles of Christianity, but they were
taught the arts and sciences." "The relation of the European to the African in
those unsophisticated times, was that of guardian and *protégé*" (LPPF:7–8).

Despite the fact that Blyden certainly had knowledge of Belgian atrocities
in the Congo, his stated opinion of King Leopold's enterprise in Africa was
that "everyone has confidence in the philanthropic aims and the practical and
commercial efforts of the King of Belgians in the arduous and expensive
enterprise he has undertaken in the Congo" (Lynch, 1967:208). In his *Africa
and Africans,* written in 1903, he celebrated Leopold and the Belgians as
"providential" agents for the regeneration of the continent and added that,
"retribution for their misdeeds will come from God" (Blyden, AA:45;

Lynch, 1967:209). But the same year, in a letter to John Holt, he was quite angry about "the horrible proceedings in the Congo." Identifying Leopold with a mythical and monstrous Pharaoh, he noted that the king and his aides "have the curse of God on them" (LET:474).

Blyden also focused on the commercial interest as a second explanation for colonization. He believed that the European project of colonizing Africa was an economic investment, for it would determine "the continuation of the prosperity of Europe":

> In their eager search, the explorers have discovered that Africa possesses the very highest capacity for the production, as raw material, of the various articles demanded by civilized countries. English and French, and Germans, are now in the struggles of an intense competition for the hidden treasures of that continent. (CINR:120)

We can assume that Blyden heard of the discovery of gold in Rhodesia by the German Karl Mauch in the 1860s. This discovery, widely publicized by white South African settlers, became the symbol of African treasure in the 1870s when it reached European papers. However, Blyden stressed an economic theory to explain the scramble for Africa:

> Europe is overflowing with the material productions of its own genius. Important foreign markets, which formerly consumed these productions, are now closing against them. Africa seems to furnish the only large outlet, and the desire is to make the markets of Soudan easily accessible to London, Manchester and Liverpool. The depressed factories of Lancashire are waiting to be inspired with new life and energy by the development of a new and inexhaustible trade with the millions of Central Africa. (CINR:95)

This is a classical explanation from the middle of the nineteenth century, but written near its end. The so-called anti-imperialist "little England era" of the last quarter of the eighteenth century seems a fantasy (see Robinson, Gallagher and Denny, 1961; Thornton, 1959; Langer, 1951). After J. B. Saw's thesis on economic balance and its endorsement by Mill and Bentham, almost all British economists advocated colonization as the best means to economic and social improvement at home. One of the most articulate theories, E. G. Wakefield's systematic colonization scheme, emphasized the extension of "land capital" or "field of production" as a solution to the "redundancy" of both capital and labor in England. For Wakefield, as for most of the leading theorists of this time (like R. Torrens and R. J. Wilmot-Horton), the acquisition of colonies was, to put it in John Stuart Mill's words, "the best affair of business in which the capital of an old and wealthy country can engage." Its most obvious advantages were supposed to be: first, the expansion of the field of production and employment and, therefore, the possibility of creating new wealth; second, a solution to the problem of unemployment by moving people overseas and integrating them into new fields; and third, an organic extension of markets by the export of manufactured goods and the import of food and raw materials.

Blyden seems aware of these colonial objectives (Lynch, 1967:191–209) even while accepting European "humanitarian intentions—with all its trappings for civilizing, instructing and elevating—" (CINR:338). The man is, fundamentally, a politician. He admires the British Empire and considers himself to be "acquainted with the character and temper of the men who, happily for humanity, come to the head of the Government." He sincerely rejoices in "the spirit and intention of the Imperial Government" which, according to one Mr. Bosworth Smith, whom he quotes, presents "a rule unselfish and unaggressive, benevolent and energetic, wise and just." Furthermore, he has a friendly regard for the British settlers in West Africa who "have numbered among their rulers, especially within the last twenty years, some of the best representatives of the English spirit" (CINR:298–99). As to the French presence in West Africa, he says that "France is doing her part to pacify West Africa, to improve her material conditions, and to give an opportunity for permanent progress to the sons of soil": "a work much needed, and suited to the genius of celtic race." Germany is giving "her desirable quota" and Germans "are taking their part with intelligence, energy and capital" (Lynch, 1967:200–1).

Blyden does not seem to disapprove of European colonization. In 1896, he still states that Britain "ought to have unquestioned precedence in respect of territory and political influence in West Africa" (Lynch, 1967:197; Blyden, LO:25). When, in 1906, Sir Frederick Lugard resigned, Blyden expressed his "very deep regret" to the colonial pro-Consul: "In the long list of British rulers in Africa who have deserved well of their country and of the natives, the universal sentiment will say to you 'well done, go up higher' " (LET:484). Yet there is an ambivalence in Blyden's praise of European colonization. For example, he wrote in 1878 to Sir Thomas Fowell Buxton:

> The Christianizing and civilizing mission of your country will never be carried out by commerce and military demonstrations, nor even by schools only—but by the exemplification of those great principles of justice and humanity which the Great Teacher whom you profess to follow inculcated, but which, it is sad to see, are yet far from being understood or practically applied by Christian nations in their dealings with weaker races. (LET:272)

In *Christianity, Islam and the Negro Race,* Blyden concentrated heavily on the English language as a means of African education. "Into the English, as into the bosom of a great central sea, all the streams of the past and present have poured, and are still pouring their varied contents" (LO:109). He considered English to be "the language of conquest—not of physical, but of moral and intellectual conquest" (CINR:368). He only regretted that on Western shores, English, like other European languages, has "come to the greater portion of the natives associated with profligacy, plunder, and cruelty, and devoid of any connections with spiritual things" (CINR:68). In reality, the logic of Blyden's thinking is clear: he favors both English language and colonization as means for grafting "European progress wholesale on African conservatism and stagnation" (CINR:300). In his own words:

> The native African, like all Oriental or tropical people, can see no reason or property in extra work, as long as he has enough to supply his wants. But he is imitative. And as the English language is diffused in his country, vivified by its domiciliation on the American continent . . . the native will be raised unconsciously; and, in spite of hereditary tendencies and surroundings, will work, not, then, in order to enjoy repose—the dolce farniente—but to be able to do more work, and to carry out higher objects. (CINR:368)

What is at stake is a thesis on the perfectibility of "savages," one widespread in European milieux and scholarly publications since the Age of Enlightenment (see Lyons, 1975) as well as the ideological theme of Anglo-Saxon responsibility, a view that sustained the saga of exploration during the nineteenth century. It is obvious that Blyden has no doubts about the necessity of the "regeneration" of Africa (LO:5, 28). He clearly shares Livingstone's conviction, variously presented in almost all the Anglo-American reports on African explorations: "It is on the Anglo-American race that the hope of the world for liberty and progress rest" (see Hammond and Jablow, 1977). Blyden accepts the achievements of colonization under British law and views the British colonial experience as the best model for the promotion of civilization: "Under that enlightened system of government which protects the rights, the liberty, the life and the property of every individual, of whatever race or religion, the people have been advanced in civilization and well being" (CINR:215).

It is well to keep in mind this general principle: Blyden considers colonization a way of elevating Africans to civilization and thinks that, if possible, this process must be done in English. As a theoretical explanation for the conquest of Africa it does not, at this level, differ from the philanthropic justification of Leopold II, King of the Belgians: "the extinction of Slavery and the introduction of a select civilization" (CINR:348) nor from the purposes of a multitude of colonial organizations. In his speech delivered at the anniversary of the American Colonization Society in 1883, Blyden praised the zealous curiosity of these associations which were "bringing all their resources to bear upon Africa's exploration and amelioration" (CINR:94). These were organizations such as the International African Association, created in 1876; the Italian National Association for the Exploration and Civilization of Africa; the Spanish Association for the Exploration of Africa; the German Society for the Explorations of Africa, founded in 1872; the African Society in Vienna, founded in 1876; the Hungarian African Association, created in 1877; the National Swiss Committee for the Exploration of Central Africa, etc. All these associations, wrote Blyden, bring to the task a "desire for more accurate knowledge of Africa," a "philanthropic impulse to lift up the millions of that continent to their proper position," and a "commercial desire to open that vast country to the enterprises of trade" (CINR:95).

The particular dimension of Blyden's theory of colonization resides in the assumption that the opening up and the development of the continent must be a black enterprise. In 1885, in a long letter to Sir Samuel Rowe, Governor of Sierra Leone, he expounded the essentials of his theory on colonization. The European interest "now directed to Africa" is positive in terms of its premises, since it is, according to his view, "the cause of civilization and progress." "It is gratifying to know that England is waking up to her just claims to whatever advantages those countries may yield for commercial or imperial purposes." On the basis of his "labours in connection with the Republic of Liberia, and to a limited extent with the Settlement of Sierra Leone," he gave advice on how to impose a new "system" on "Natives": "the most effectual is evidently that of annexation with a view to regular supervision and control of the annexed territories." Yet he insisted that the "settlements of civilized blacks from America" was the best policy; "the most effective way of spreading civilization in inter-tropical Africa" (LET:349–55). Blyden was convinced that "only the Negro will be able to explain the Negro to the rest of mankind" (CINR:263). For him, Liberia's case was exemplary as the most successful sign of this conviction. He wrote in "Hope for Africa" (1862) of the "fulfillment of a Divine plan":

> There are fifteen thousand civilized and Christianized Africans striving to accomplish the twofold work of establishing and maintaining an independent nationality, and of introducing the Gospel among untold millions of un-evangelized and barbarous men. (LO:19)

This is an idea he maintained till the end of his life. Equally strong were his invitations to Black Americans to emigrate to Africa. The motives he put forward were sometimes financial, sometimes psychological, and also attest to his concern for the "regeneration" of these potential immigrants. He makes this explicit in a letter of September 3, 1877, to W. Coppinger, Secretary of the American Colonization Society:

> I would be glad if you would point out to Africans in the United States these two facts:
>
> 1. There is great wealth in their fatherland of which if they do not soon avail themselves, others will get the first pick and perhaps occupy the finest sites.
>
> 2. Only in connection with Liberia or a properly established Negro nationality can they even attain to true manhood and equality. (LET:260)

Let me underscore that Blyden had a quite restrictive understanding of what *black* meant. He did not wish to have in Africa "people of mixed blood" (see, e.g., LET:174, 271, 315) who, according to him, "never get thorough sympathy with the work." This obvious racism is, paradoxically, based on the European thinking that he should be opposing. In a letter to Charles T. Geyer, he openly stated that "repatriation of civilized blacks from the Western hemisphere is indispensable in the work of African amelioration" (Blyden, LET).

Despite such clear suppositions, his reasoning emphasized Africa's mysteriousness: she is a sphinx and "must solve her own riddle at last" (CINR:127). In other words, Europe has to give up "the idea of regenerating Africa through colonies of her own subjects" (CINR:349), because "energetic colonization for Whites, must be in climates where the winter or cold weather brings its healthy and recuperative influences to body and mind" (CINR:349). Blyden sustained his argument by giving some historical precedents (CINR:358), quoting M. Stanley who wrote that "the equatorial regions of Africa have for ages defied Islam, Christianity, science and trade . . . Civilization, so often baffled, stands railing at the barbarism and savagery that presents such an impenetrable front to its efforts (CINR:345). He also emphasized the colonizers' woes: Europeans cannot survive in Africa (CINR:128); they die or become physically ill and mentally deranged (CINR:263). In sum, "the chief obstacle to the wholesome influence of Europeans in Africa is the climate. From the earliest antiquity this has been the insuperable barrier" (CINR:341). In the letter he sent to Sir Lugard in 1906, he proposed the same explanation.

> The principle of the 'man on the spot,' however applicable it may be to other countries in healthier climates, is not always to be relied on when dealing with intertropical Africa. There the *personnel* is most important. Europeans do not, as a rule, retain their normal mental state, or, perhaps, even their moral equilibrium, after six months under the influence of that climate. (Blyden, LET:484; my emphasis)

Therefore, only Blacks could colonize and reform Africa. By Blacks, he meant "civilized Americans and West Indians of African descent."

Blyden had some strange views concerning slavery, for example his belief that in the first years "it was a deportation from a land of barbarism to a land of civilization" (LO:156). Remarkable also were some of his views of Black Americans. He wrote for instance, that Africa has never lost the better classes of her people. As a rule, those who were exported belonged to "the servile and criminal classes" (CINR:126). Yet he continued to praise Black Americans and their capabilities and considered them as possible saviors of Africa. He believed that they "have never needed the stimulus of any organization of white men to direct their attention to the land of their fathers" (CINR:100). Pursuing this point of view to its furthest limits, he insisted on the particularity of this possible colonization and its racial implications:

> The exiled Negro, then, has a home in Africa. Africa is his, if he will. He may ignore it. He may consider that he is divested of any right to it; but this will not alter his relations to that country, or impair the integrity of his title. (CINR:124)

It is indeed impossible not to sympathize with the intelligent Negro, whose imagination, kindled by the prospects and possibilities of [America] the land of his birth, makes him desire to remain and share in its future struggles and future glories. But he still suffers from many drawbacks. (CINR:125)

As a rsult of their freedom and enlarged education, the descendants of Africa in [America] are beginning to feel themselves straightened. They are beginning to feel that only in Africa will they find the sphere of their true activity. (CINR:125)

In New York, Philadelphia, Baltimore, Harrisburg, and other cities Blyden preached to "colored congregations" during the summer of 1862, stating: "now, while Europeans are looking to our fatherland, ought not Africans in the Western hemisphere to turn their regards thither also?"; "We should not content ourselves with living among other races, simply by their permission or their endurance"; "We must build up negro states"; "An African nationality is our great need, and God tells us by his providence that he has set the land before us, and bids us go up and possess it" (LO:75–76), etc. The project is racially oriented; its foundation is racist:

In America we see how readily persons from all parts of Europe assimilate; [. . .] The Negro, the Indian, and the Chinese, who do not belong to the same family, repel each other, and are repelled by the Europeans. 'The antagonistic elements are in contact, but refuse to unite, and as yet no agent has been found sufficiently potent to reduce them to unity.' (LO:88)

Blyden's ideas on African colonization are based both on theories cast in terms of race and on his own experience in Sierra Leone and Liberia. Sometimes they express a personal sense of over-compensation which accounts for some of the strange reasons he proposes to Black Americans for going back to Africa. For example: "The Negro in the United States, however well educated and however qualified for it, will never have the opportunity of appearing in a diplomatic character at a European court—a privilege which the Liberian has in spite of the political insignificance of his country" (LET:260). Nevertheless, the essential point is that he envisioned the extension of Liberia's experience to all the continent, convinced that in support of "black authenticity," "whatever others may do for us, there are some things we must do for ourselves. No outward protection, no friendly intervention, no deed of gift can give those personal virtues—those attributes of manhood—self-reliance and independence" (CINR:217).

This argument on African colonization represents a departure from two related theories which were generally accepted during the nineteenth century (see Lyons, 1975:25–85). As Christopher Fyfe puts it in his introduction to one of Blyden's books, humankind "is divided into races, and . . . the movements of history and society can only be adequately explained in terms of their interaction" (CINR:xii). Blyden saw the African future in terms of racial cooperation and integration between Black Americans and Africans.

He also shared the assumption widely held in the second part of the eighteenth century and throughout the nineteenth, that only a certain race can
adapt and survive in a given climate. "East is East and West is West; and
never the twain shall meet" was a polygenist principle. With such assumptions, Blyden thought that the only alternative to the ongoing European
colonization was a Black American presence which would necessitate a
reshaping of the African environment and result in a transformation of its
peoples. This argument consequently becomes one that we should call a
tentative program for political and racial organization:

> This seems to be the period of race organization and race consolidation. The
> races in Europe are striving to group themselves together according to their
> natural affinities [. . .] The Germans are confederated. The Italians are united.
> Greece is being reconstructed. And so this race impulse has seized the African
> here. The feeling is in the atmosphere—the plane in which races move. And
> there is no people in whom the desire for race integrity and race preservation is
> stronger than in the Negro. (CINR:122)

The fundamental theme in Blyden's writings is that Africans, from a
historical point of view, constitute a universe apart and have their own
history and traditions. This point is worth analyzing, since the European
nineteenth-century literature on Africa emphasized this point too, but in a
different way (see Battle and Lyons, 1970). Nineteenth-century writers,
focusing on differences between Africa and Europe, tended to demonstrate
the complete lack of similarity between the two continents and attempted to
prove that in Africa the physical environment, the flora and fauna, as well as
the people, represent relics of a remote age of antiquity. Arthur de Gobineau's
Essai sur l'inégalité des races humaines (1853), Darwinism, and the debate
between polygenists and monogenists provided "scientific" and "social"
categories for racial thinking (see Haller, 1971). Linnaeus's classification of
types and varieties of human beings within the natural system (1758) was
then modified. G. Cuvier, for instance, offered a hierarchy of human types in
Animal Kingdom (1827); S. Morton, a table of races and their cranial and
intellectual capacity in *Crania Americana* (1833); and G. Combe, *A System
of Phrenology* (1844), in which he demonstrated the relationships between
types of brain, racial differences, and degrees of spiritual and cultural development (see Curtin, 1965; Lyons, 1975). In sum, "though they did
disagree among themselves about which European 'races' were inferior to
others, Western racial commentators generally agreed that Blacks were inferior to whites in moral fiber, cultural attainment, and mental ability; the
African was, to many eyes, the child in the family of man, modern man in
embryo" (Lyons, 1975:86–87).

This meant, in other words, that African peoples were considered as
instances of a frozen state in the evolution of humankind. They were defined
as "archaic" or "primitive" human beings, insofar as they were supposed to
represent very ancient social and cultural organizations which had been

present in Europe several thousand years earlier. Nineteenth-century anthropology was firmly based on this hypothesis and produced scholarly
works on the principles of humankind's evolution to civilization, in which
African peoples were considered signs of the initial primitiveness:

> The mistake which Europeans often make in considering questions of Negro
> improvement and the future of Africa, is in supposing that the Negro is the
> European in embryo—in the undeveloped stage—and that when, by and by, he
> shall enjoy the advantages of civilization and culture, he will become like the
> European; in other words, that the Negro is on the same line of progress, in the
> same groove, with the European, but infinitely in the rear. (Blyden,
> CINR:276)

According to the twentieth-century political philosopher Hannah Arendt:

> It is highly probable that the thinking in terms of race would have disappeared
> in due time together with other irresponsible opinions of the nineteenth
> century, if the 'scramble for Africa' and the new era of imperialism had not
> exposed Western humanity to new and shocking experiences. Imperialism
> would have necessitated the invention of racism as the only possible 'explana-
> tion' and excuse for its deeds, even if no race-thinking had ever existed in the
> civilized world. (Arendt, 1968:63–64)

This is an interesting hypothesis, which Blyden missed. For quite under-
standable reasons, Blyden had to emphasize the idealogical structure of race-
thinking. Thus the major themes of his *A Vindication of the African Race*
(1857) deal with the myth of Ham's curse and the "idea of phrenological
inferiority" (Blyden, LO:31 and 55). He dismissed racist opinions and the so-
called "scientific conclusions" by working around a provocative topic: "it was
once said that 'No good thing can come out of Nazareth'" (LO:55). His
position is one of common sense and close to that of pro-African ideologists
of the last two centuries, such as the British J. C. Prichard and the French
priest H. Grégoire. Commenting on the curse of Ham, Blyden remarked that
first, "it must be proved that the curse was pronounced upon Ham himself";
second, "that it was pronounced upon each of his sons individually"; and
third, "if pronounced upon Canaan, that he was the only offspring of Ham."
He concluded: "we know that no one of these was the fact" (LO:35–36).
Therefore, for him, the slavery experience was "no argument in favor of the
hypothesis of malediction" (LO:41). As to the phrenological theses, Blyden
did not accept them because among other good reasons, "external appearance is not always the index of the intellectual man" (LO:56), and "the
intellectual and moral character of the African in freedom" cannot be inferred "from what it is in slavery" (LO:52–53). Against the evolutionist
assumptions that emphasized the climatic conditioning, he affirmed that
"moral agencies when set in operation cannot be overborne by physical
causes" (LO:81).

Blyden did not oppose the evolutionary assumption scientifically. He simply mocked it and then took a different route, a relativist one, in order to refute it by ridiculing "the charges of superstition, etc. made against Africans and in consequence of which a hopeless 'incapacity of amelioration' is sometimes attributed to the whole race' ":

> There is not a single mental or moral deficiency now existing among Africans —not a single practice now indulged in by them—to which we cannot find a parallel in the past history of Europe, and even after the people had been brought under the influence of a nominal Christianity. (CINR:58)

He laid the same charges against both Europe and Africa: polygamy, slavery, human sacrifices, sanguinary customs (CINR:58–59). He thus defended his own view in a negative manner by showing that the African is part of humanity, even though he seems weaker. In 1869 he noted that:

> When, four hundred years ago, the Portuguese discovered this coast, they found the natives living in considerable peace and quietness, and with a certain degree of prosperity . . . From all we can gather, the tribes in this part lived in a condition not very different from that of the greater portion of Europe in the Middle Ages. (NAH:20)

The same year, in his address delivered on Mount Lebanon in Syria at the celebration of the nineteenth anniversary of the independence of Liberia, Blyden presented an ideological reading of the Liberian symbol within the "civilized world." Black responsibility has become the sign of advancement and hope. It incarnates peace and liberation against the wars, emasculation, and oppression of the traditional native cultures; it expresses an organized authority against the corruption of "aboriginal chiefs"; it institutionalizes civilization, trade, and religion against the mass of crimes and immorality of the slave trade. In brief, one has a paradoxical and romantic paradigm: here is Liberia symbolizing the New Negro opposed to both the "heathenism" of the "natives" and "the barbarism" of the slave-traders. By its very existence, Liberia implies the possibility of a radical transformation of Africa's history: "Anglo-American Christianity, liberty, and law, under the protection of the Liberian, will have nothing to impede their indefinite spread over that immense continent. I say, nothing to impede their indefinite spread" (LPPF:23). This almost mystical conviction is also present in later texts. So, for example, in 1884:

> In view of all things my consolation is that the Lord is King. In spite of the mistakes and perversity of man, His plans will be carried out. I believe that the Colonization idea was from God, and that the American Colonization Society under the necessarily imperfect conditioning of humanity have been carrying out His purposes. (LET:326)

And in 1888:

> We are unwilling . . . to admit the idea that Africans cannot acquire those trusts and convictions and that moral and spiritual development essential to human peace and guidance in this world, and to life everlasting in the world to come, without being cast in European mould. (CINR:66)

These quotations indicate Blyden's complexity. He does not refute the standard view of African "primitiveness," but rather emphasizes the relativity of social cultures and progress. This practice of arguing by means of sociological concepts, or, as he defines it, "the science of Race" (CINR:94), leads him to "the poetry" of politics:

> It is the feeling of race—the aspiration after the development on its own line of the type of humanity to which we belong. Italians and Germans long yearned after such development. The Slavonic tribes are feelig after it. Now, nothing tends more to discourage these feelings and check these aspirations, than the idea that the people with whom we are connected, and after whose improvement we sigh, have never had a past, or only an ignoble past—antecedents which were 'blank and hopeless,' to be ignored and forgotten. (CINR:197)

Blyden tends to avoid both the easy antislavery propaganda, with its myths about the "noble savage," and also the technical debates on the hierarchy of races. Rather than defining the African as a "special" counterpart of the European—a "noble savage" or a "beastly primitive"—Blyden used his literary background to describe the African as a victim of a European ethnocentrism. For instance, he considered contempt of Africans and Negroes to be a modern invention. He referred to Homer's and Herodotus's descriptions of blacks, insisted on the frequency of *kalos kagathos* (handsome and good) Ethiopian in classical literature, and discussed the aesthetic value of the color black in the Bible (NAH:14; see also Bourgeois, 1971; Mveng, 1972). In *Christianity, Islam and the Negro Race,* he affirmed that "In Greek and Latin languages and their literature, there is not, as far as I know, a sentence, a word, or a syllable disparaging to the Negro" (CINR:84). Commenting on a poem attributed to Virgil and quoting Homer's celebration of the Negro Eurybates at the siege of Troy, he states that "the disparagement began with European travellers, partly 'from a desire to be unfair' or 'from preconceived notions of the Negro,' 'and partly, also, on the principle that it is easier to pull down than to build up' " (CINR:263). These explanations do not constitute a convincing historical description. Yet, in very general terms, they situate the ideological justifications used first by travelers and then by explorers and missionaries to establish a new order in the "dark continent" (see Arendt, 1968:87). This meant opening Africa to trade, European education, and Christianity, and thus setting up and enforcing a psychological domination:

In all English-speaking countries the mind of the intelligent Negro child revolts against the descriptions given in elementary books—geographies, travels, histories—of the Negro; but, though he experiences an instinctive revulsion from these caricatures and misrepresentations, he is obliged to continue, as he grows in years, to study such pernicious teachings. After leaving school he finds the same things in newspapers, in reviews, in novels, in *quasi*-scientific works; and after a while—*saepe cadendo*—they begin to seem to him the proper things to say and to feel about his race. (Blyden, CINR:76)

Thinking of the condition of Black Americans in particular, Blyden generalized his analysis:

Those who have lived in civilized communities, where there are different races, know the disparaging views which are entertained of the blacks by their neighbours—and often, alas! by themselves. The standard of all physical and intellectual excellencies in the present civilization being the white complexion, whatever deviates from that favoured colour is proportionally depreciated, until the black, which is the opposite, becomes not only the most unpopular but the most unprofitable colour. (CINR:77)

Blyden dealt courageously with this difficult aspect of psychological dependence. He thought that the Negro was weak because he accepted the image imposed on him and that this complex of dependence could account for the "hesitancy," the "modesty growing out of a sense of inferiority" found in the Black American pupil (CINR:148), as well as for the self-depreciation seen in the adult. "It is painful in America to see the efforts which are made by Negroes to secure outward conformity to the appearance of the dominant race" (CINR:77).

As for the Negro in general, Blyden pointed out that derogatory perspectives provide the intellectual framework of this psychological war. An opposition of colors, black versus white, becomes the paramount symbol of the distance in quality and virtue between Europeans and Africans, and justifies the white man's duty toward "despised races" (CINR:138). But this duty seems a myth and its works will not last:

Victor Hugo exhorts the European nations to 'occupy this land offered to them by God.' He has forgotten the prudent advice of Caesar to the ancestors of those nations against invading Africa. The Europeans can hold the domain 'offered to them' by only a precarious tenure. (CINR:145–46)

Rejecting the theme of the barbarous Negro, Blyden focused on the connection between degeneration and Westernization. In his view, not all European accomplishments are splendid and useful. On the contrary, "things which have been of great advantage to Europe may work ruin to us; and there is often such a striking resemblance, or such a close connection between the hurtful and the beneficial that we are not always able to discriminate"

(CINR:79). Furthermore, he observed that the most visible consequence for the Kingdom of Congo, Westernized and Christianized under Portuguese influence during the seventeenth century, was its disappearance (CINR:159).

One could even think that Blyden—although he was a Christian minister—did not believe in conversion, insofar as it is an expression of Westernization: "Pagans of discernment know that the black man among them who 'calls himself a Christian and dresses himself in clothes' adheres to European habits and customs with a reserved power of disengagement" (CINR:59). He strongly ridiculed the confusion of sociocultural customs and Christian values and pessimistically noted that "the Gospel has failed to have free course in this land" (LET:115). However, he believed that the "inconsistencies of Christians" (LET:99) might account for this relative failure. In actuality, what he rejected was the "thin varnish of European civilization" that a young and inexperienced missionary propagates. "With the earnest vigour and sanguine temper which belong to youth he preaches a crusade against the harmless customs and prejudices of the people—superseding many customs and habits necessary and useful in the climate and for the people by practices which, however useful they might be in Europe, become, when introduced indiscriminately into Africa, artificial, ineffective and absurd" (CINR:64). However, Blyden seems to believe that the confusing of religious values and cultural customs is not an accident: "The Anglo-Saxon mind and the African mind trained under Anglo-Saxon influence, seem to be intolerant of all customs and practices which do not conform to the standard of European tastes and habits" (LET:114). This instance of cultural misunderstanding is neither extraordinary nor unusual. Of at least equal significance is the supposed African response to Europeans and their culture.

> There are those of other races who also sneer and scorn and 'despise.' Some of the proceedings of Baker and Stanley in Africa must frequently have impressed the natives with the feeling that those energetic travellers came from much 'darker continents' than any of their unsophisticated imaginations had ever before suggested to them. (CINR:138–9)

> Mungo Park recorded his impressions as follows: Although the Negroes, in general, have a great idea of the wealth and power of Europeans, I am afraid that the Mohammedan converts among them think but very little of our superior attainments in religious knowledge . . . The poor Africans, whom we affect to consider as barbarians, look upon us, I fear, as little better than a race of formidable but ignorant Heathen. (CINR:343)

For Blyden, these incongruities revealed the general tone of a distorted contact as it existed under slavery and colonial imperialism. Moreover, to the degree that the European presence and self-proclaimed political supremacy affect the African's culture and confidence (LO:57), Blyden felt it necessary to overemphasize certain ideological issues which would eventually foster the African's silent resistance and would bring about a new climate of ideas. The logic of this commitment led Blyden to formulate strong intellectual criticisms of Western ideology, principally through a critical evaluation of the European tradition, a new interpretation of history, and, finally, a positive evaluation of African oral tradition.

Blyden's criticism of the European tradition is based on a relativist philosophy of cultures (AA:60). He believed that even though, in religious terms, the concept of humankind is the same throughout the world, "the native capacities of mankind differ, and their work and destiny differ, so that the road by which one man may attain to the highest efficiency, is not that which would conduce to the success of another" (AA:5–8; CINR:83). Fanciful excursions in the field of comparative history provided some comparisons to support his relativism.

> The ancestors of these people [Africans] understood the use of the cotton-plant, and the manufacture of cotton, when Julius Caesar found the Britons clothing themselves in the skins of wild beasts. Visitors to the British Museum may see, in the Egyptian department, cloth of the very same material and texture wrapped around the mummies. This cloth was made by those who understood the lost art of embalming, but who, when they retired by successive revolutions, into the interior . . . lost that valuable art, but never forgot the manufacture of the cloth used in the process. (CINR:196)

This is only one of many fragile comparisons. His comments on Leo Africanus's reports about the kingdom of Mali (CINR:195), Egyptian physical characteristics (NAH:10), Ethiopian psychology (NAH:25–26), and destiny (CINR:152–3), or the civilization of the "Mohammedans of Negritia" (CINR:300) make explicit and uphold his ideas on the diversity of historical processes. This premise allowed him to state that:

> The special road which has led to the success and elevation of the Anglo-Saxon is not that which would lead to the success and elevation of the Negro, though we shall resort to the same means of general culture which has enabled the Anglo-Saxon to find out for himself the way in which he ought to go. (CINR:83)

This critical position, in fact, also required a new understanding of history. Since the kind of political and cultural domination that was taking place in Africa served the particular historical perspective on which it was based and was, in return, justified by its own success, Blyden chose to revise the concept of history altogether.

Referring to F. Harrison's classification, which distinguished "six leading epochs in the history of civilization" (Theocratic Society, Greek Age, Roman Period, Medieval Civilization, Modern Age, and the Age since the French Revolution), Blyden proposed to exclude the study of the last two ages from the African curriculum. His reasons were quite simple. He observed that it was during these periods, especially the last, that "the trans-Atlantic slave trade arose, and those theories—theological, social, and political—were invented for the degradation and proscription of the Negro." On the other hand, he considered the first periods, particularly the Greek, the Roman, and the Medieval to be exemplary: "There has been no period of history more full of suggestive energy, both physical and intellectual, than those epochs . . . No modern writers will ever influence the destiny of the race to the same extent that the Greeks and Romans have done" (CINR:82). Thus a philosophical principle of cultural relativism accompanied an ideological rejection of a part of European history and permitted Blyden to justify his claim for authenticity, and, therefore, the relevance of the African past and its proper tradition. Following Volney (NAH:5) and Hartmann, he had no doubts about "the strictly African extraction" of the pharaonic civilization (CINR:154n). But it was through an evaluation of Africa's oral traditions that he saw the basis for inspiration:

> Now, if we are to make an independent nation—a strong nation—we must listen to the songs of our unsophisticated brethren as they sing of their history, as they tell of their traditions, of the wonderful and mysterious events of their tribal or national life, of the achievements of what we call their superstitions. (CINR:91)

In sum, what Blyden put forward is a general criticism of Western ideology, not because it was wrong, but because it seemed to him irrelevant for African authenticity. This criticism, however, arose as a negation, and to some degree as a consequence, of the most intolerant "race-thinking" interpretations. Thus, it is a warping reworking of the most negative theories of the century. In a long letter to the British traveler Mary Kingsley in 1900, Blyden could agree with her: " 'The Negro must have a summit to himself'—a remark which is not the result, as has been alleged by some, of prejudice to the African, nor, as it has been held by others, of latitudenarian indifference to religious truths" (LET:461). Playing upon the ambiguous significance of Swedenborg's expression that the African is a celestial man, he could also, in a most relativist fashion, conclude that "such a man among terrestrials must have a separate place—not a hole into which some would thrust him, nor a *dead flat* where others would fix him, but a summit." Therefore, "for obvious reasons the conventional morality of Europe cannot be the conventional morality of Africa, so far as social or domestic matters are concerned" (LET:461).

Three major considerations were central to Blyden's political philosophy: the basic organized community under Muslim leadership, the concept of the African nation, and, finally, the idea of the unity of the continent.

The basic Islamic community appears to be his model of political organization. "There are no caste distinctions among them" nor "tribal barriers" (CINR:175) nor racial prejudices (CINR:15–17); "slavery and the slave-trade are laudable, provided the slaves are Kaffirs," but the "slave who embraces Islam is free, and no office is closed against him on account of his servile blood" (CINR:176). Did Blyden approve of this institutional slavery? It is not clear. One could perhaps argue that he was just presenting one case. We must keep in mind that throughout his publications he opposed slavery (e.g., LO:67–91; LO:153–67). At any rate, what he admired in the system was that for Muslims the social relations of production are not determined by racial factors but by their faith: " 'Paradise is under the show of swords,' is one of their stimulating proverbs" (CINR:9). "They gather under the beams of the Crescent not only for religious, but for patriotic reasons; till they are only swayed with one idea, but act as one individual. The faith becomes a part of their nationality, and is entwined with their affections" (CINR:231). The dynamism of these Muslim communities, their subtle and intelligent ways of proselytizing, and their trade assured Islam a brilliant future in Africa. "All careful and candid observers agree that the influence of Islam in Central and West Africa has been, upon the whole, of a most salutary character. As an eliminatory and subversive agency, it has displaced or unsettled nothing as good as itself" (CINR:174).

> None of the Nigritian tribes have ever abdicated their race individuality or parted with their idiosyncrasies in embracing the faith of Islam. But, whenever and wherever it has been necessary, great Negro warriors have risen from the ranks of Islam, and, inspired by the teachings of the new faith . . . have driven them, if at anytime they affected superiority based upon race, from their artificial ascendancy. (CINR:122)

According to Blyden, Islam is politically an excellent means of promoting an African consciousness and of organizing communities. Unfortunately, though the ideological assumptions can be accepted in principle, the historical facts badly contradict Blyden's belief in the positive capabilities of Islam. Throughout the nineteenth century in Central Africa, Islamic factions represented an objective evil and practiced a shameful slave-trade. And here, again, we face an unbelievable inconsistency in Blyden's thought: his naive admiration for Islam led him to accept the enslavement of non-Muslim peoples!

The concept of the African nation is perhaps the most puzzling, but also the most original one, in Blyden's writings. It implies the classical conception of "democracy" (LPPF:16) but with a special focus on the rejection of racial distinction, and at the same time, the paradoxical claim for the retention of racial individuality. In actuality, as a man of his time, Blyden used the romantic premises, which in the nineteenth century allowed some European theorists to rediscover their historical roots and then celebrate the authenticity of their own culture and civilization, in terms of their identity with their origins. The most conspicuous example of this process is the debate which took place among German scholars on the "Indo-European" or "Indo-Germanic" culture, in which a most remarkable confusion existed about the notions of "race," "language," "tradition," and "history" (see, e.g., Arendt, 1968:45–64). Nevertheless, European nationalisms arose, in part, from theoretical combinations of these complex and controversial notions and accounted for what Blyden called "the period of race organization and race consolidation" (CINR:122). Like his European counterparts, Blyden did not doubt that a racial phenomenon must be the basis of nationalism and the foundation of the Nation:

> On this question of race, no argument is necessary in discussing the methods or course of procedure for the preservation of race integrity, and for the development of race efficiency, but no argument is needed as to the necessity of such preservation and development. If a man does not feel it—if it does not rise up with spontaneous and inspiring power in his heart—then he has neither part nor lot in it. (CINR:122–23)

Thus, retaining the concept of racial individuality became the cornerstone in the construction of a nation. Paradoxically, Blyden wrote that he did not consider Haiti and Liberia, the two major black nations, as possible models for the African nation, because "there is a perpetual struggle between the very few who are aiming to forward the interests of the many, and the *profanum vulgus,* largely in majority" (CINR:273). Moreover, as he grew older, Blyden accepted the partition of Africa by European powers (see Lynch in LET:409), collaborated with them (LET:502), and in 1909, worked very hard for the "reconstructing [of] Liberia by the United States"; and indeed for a process of administrative "colonization."

> Let the Republic retain her Executive, Legislative and Judicial Departments. But let America take the Republic under her 'Protection' for the time being. Let the British officers, as they are doing now supervise the Customs and Treasury Departments. Let the French manage the Frontier Force under Liberian financial responsibility. Let America appoint a High Commissioner for Liberia—an experienced Southern man, if possible, surround him with the necessary white American officials to help. Abolish the American Legation at Monrovia or put a white man at the head. The High Commissioner should review the Executive, Legislative and Judicial decisions before they are sanctioned. (LET:496)

However, it is in his descriptions of Liberia and Sierra Leone that he offered his clearest view of an African nation, which must be independent, liberal, and self-reliant but must trade with other foreign countries, a "good democracy" in which racial self-elevation would be the guiding principle.

Blyden's Pan-Africanism is a sort of prophetism. He envisioned, first, a collaboration and a fusion of African Christianity and the conquering force of Islam:

> Where the light from the Cross ceases to stream upon the gloom, there the beams of the Crescent will give illumination; and, as the glorious orb of Christianity rises, the twilight of Islam will be lost in the greater light of the Sun of Righteousness. Then Isaac and Ishmael will be united. (CINR:233)

Second, he emphasized the cultural unity that Islam represents. It has placed African peoples "under the same inspiration" (CINR:229), giving them, by means of the same "language, letters, and books" (CINR:229), both a political unity and a cultural community (CINR:6). Finally, Africa will unite when it pays due attention to its experiences with Europe and America. He thus maintained the thesis that "the political history of the United States is the history of the Negro. The commercial and agricultural history of nearly the whole of America is the history of the Negro" (CINR:119; LET:476–77).

In sum, there would be unity and growth in Africa if black peoples all over the world would reflect upon their own condition. Blyden, the ideologue, became a visionary:

> In visions of the future, I behold those beautiful hills—the banks of those charming streams, the verdant plains and flowery fields . . . I see them all taken possession of by the returning exiles from the West, trained for the work of re-building waste places under severe discipline and hard bondage. I see, too, their brethren hastening to welcome them from the slopes of the Niger, and from its lovely valleys . . . Mohammedans and Pagans, chiefs and people, all coming to catch something of the inspiration the exiles have brought—to share . . . and to march back . . . towards the sunrise for the regeneration of a continent. (CINR:129)

A modern cultural and political organization would be achieved with the help of Americans of African descent.

The interpenetration of religious and political "nationalisms" expresses in Blyden's thought what we must call a policy of racial authenticity, oriented towards a cultural and political transformation of the continent. The instrumental role that he accorded Black Americans and West Indians by selecting them as "colonists" indicates his belief in "racial identity" and illustrates his peculiar philosophy about the salvation of Africa.

> The restoration of the Negro to the land of his fathers will be the restoration of a race to its original integrity, to itself; and working by itself, for itself and from itself, it will discover the methods of its own development, and they will not be the same as the Anglo-Saxon methods. (CINR:110)

Black people from America and West Indies have "served" and "suffered," and Blyden did not hesitate to compare them to the Hebrews (CINR:120). The possibility of their return to Africa becomes the hope for the promised land.

Blyden has been called the founder of African nationalism and Pan-Africanism. Surely he is, insofar as he described the burden of dependence and the drawbacks of exploitation. He put forward "theses" for liberation, insisting on the necessity of both the indigenization of Christianity and the support of Islam. Despite its romanticism and inconsistencies, Blyden's political vision is probably the first proposal by a black man to elaborate the benefits of an independent, modern political structure for the continent.

"Black Personality" as Common Locus

According to Blyden, the "Negro" that the West deals with in its literature as well as in its imperial enterprise is just a myth (Blyden, LO:52–54; 67–68). The West has produced this myth and maintains it by projecting it as a standard image. Missionaries, travelers, and colonial settlers are equally wrong in the way they portray the African personality:

> The Negro of the ordinary traveller or missionary—and perhaps, of two-thirds of the Christian world—is a purely fictitious being, constructed out of the traditions of slave-traders and slave-holders, who have circulated all sorts of absurd stories, and also out of prejudices inherited from ancestors, who were taught to regard the Negro as a legitimate object of traffic. (CINR:58)

More generally, Blyden saw this false image as both the product and the consequence of a long process which accompanied the European exploration of the world from the fifteenth century on. A prevailing ethnocentrism and a lack of sincere curiosity produced a totally absurd framework, in which African cultures and peoples constituted merely an inversion of European traditions and human types. This premise was used to justify "the indictment against a whole race" (NAH:27). For example, Sir Samuel Baker states: "Without foreign assistance, the Negro a thousand years hence will be no better than the Negro of today, as the Negro of today is in no superior position to that of his ancestors some thousand years ago" (CINR:269).

Blyden attacked this ideological positon, first by indicating the weakness of its view, stemming from an erroneous deduction; and then by criticizing the assumption that the Negro could be completely integrated into Western culture. Concerning the deduction, he wrote that the major mistake lies in a theoretical misinterpretation of the racial phenomenon and its cultural manifestations:

> There is no absolute or essential superiority on the one side, nor absolute or essential inferiority on the other side. It is a question of difference of endowment and difference of destiny. No amount of training or culture will make the Negro a European; on the other hand, no lack of training or deficiency of culture will make the European a Negro. The two races are not moving in the same groove with an immeasurable distance between them, but on parallel lines. They will never meet in the plane of their activities so as to coincide in capacity or performance. They are not *identical,* as some think, but *unequal;* they are *distinct* but *equal.* (CINR:227; my emphasis)

The difficulty of this position lies in the complexity of the concept of race, and the various and extended connotations given to it by theorists and ideologists. One could analyze the relationship between Blyden's thesis and the racial theories of his time (see, e.g., Fanoudh-Siefer, 1968; Hammond and Jablow, 1977; Hoffmann, 1973; Jordan, 1968; Lyons, 1975). Since these theories are, generally speaking, mixtures of poor philosophy, scientific speculations, and heavy ethnocentrism, it is more pertinent to look at the problem in a different way and to relate Blyden to the founders of anthropology. First of all, there is a striking similarity between Blyden's conception and that of some of the eighteenth-century anthropologists. His understanding of "anthropology," the study of "practical features" of "a system," and their influence on the natural man (CINR:232), seems to echo Rousseau. As H. R. Lynch rightly notes: "Blyden's 'natural African man' is strikingly similar to Rousseau's 'noble savage' living in a 'perfect state of nature'—a state which they both claimed was the necessary prerequisite for the development of the spiritual resources of the mankind" (Lynch, 1967:62). Blyden's theory of race makes excellent sense when it is related to Arthur de Gobineau's *Essai sur l'inégalité des races humaines* (1853) and other widespread racial conceptions. For instance, Voltaire, seeking a hierarchy of races in both his *Traité de métaphysique* (1734) and *Essai sur les moeurs,* affirmed that black peoples constitute a completely *distinct* brand of humankind. In Voltaire's anthropology, this distinction implied and explained the Negro's inferiority (see Duchet, 1971:281–321). In contrast, Buffon, a scientist, presented in his *Natural History* (1749) the principle of the distinctiveness of all human beings. To him, even "the most animal-like of human beings" does not resemble "the most human-like of animals." He called this principle an organizational identity. He also claimed to have evidence of racial distinctions, acknowledging within every race the possible existence of "human varieties" dependent upon environment and climate (See Duchet, 1971:229–80).

Believing in the distinctiveness of races, Blyden equated "purity" of race and "purity" of personality or blood. This accounts for his *"racist"* position about mulattoes. He wrote, for example, against "the introduction on a very large scale of the blood of the oppressors among their victims" (LET:488), denied even the possibility of a union between "the pure Negroes and mulattoes" (LET:388), and, in a most questionable manner, disparaged "Negroes who are as white as some white men" (LET:388). His thesis requiring the rejection of mulattoes from the "race" and from the African experience was also politically motivated: "If this difference between the Negro and the mulatto is understood hereafter, it will much simplify the Negro problem, and the race will be called upon to bear its own sins only, and not the sins also of a 'mixed multitude'" (in Lynch, 1967:59).

Blyden seems to agree also with the principle of human variety within the race but added to it the fact of ethnic difference and social influence:

> The cruel accidents of slavery and the slave-trade drove all Africans together, and no discrimination was made in the shambles between the Foulah and the Timneh, the Mandingo and the Mendi, the Ashantee and the Fantee, the Eboe

and the Congo—between the descendants of Nobles and the offsprings of slaves, between kings and their subjects—all were placed on the same level, all of black skin and woolly hair were 'niggers,' chattels . . . And when, by any course of events, these people attempt to exercise independent government, they start in the eyes of the world as Africans, without the fact being taken into consideration that they belong to tribes and families differing widely in degrees of intelligence and capacity, in original bent and susceptibility. (CINR:274)

The last sentence implies the concept of variety by establishing a relationship between "intelligence" or "capacity" and ethnic groups. This is a dangerous hypothesis, which during the last two centuries has been co-opted to legitimate every racism and has supported the foundation of the controversial science of racial differences. In Blyden's ideological perspective, this concept is a powerful claim for regional identity: Africans are not identical, their social organizations are not equal, nor necessarily similar, and, finally, their traditions do not merely reflect each other and are not the same.

Nevertheless, Blyden claimed a general distinctiveness of Africa and her people and defined it by listing some particular characteristics of the continent and its inhabitants in a clearly Rousseauist and ethnocentrist way.

Africa "has been called the cradle of civilization, and so it is." Thinking of the Egyptian past, Blyden wrote: "The germs of all sciences and of the two great religions now professed by the most enlightened races were fostered in Africa" (CINR:116; NAH:5–9). In his view, it was a brilliant world, a continent of "contentment and happiness" where people feared and loved God and showed remarkable hospitality (LO:82).

If the belief in a Common Creator and Father of mankind is illustrated in the bearing we maintain towards our neighbour, if our faith is seen in our works, if we prove that we love God, whom we have not seen, by loving our neighbour whom we have seen, by respecting his rights, even though he may not belong to our clan, tribe, or race, then I must say, and it will not be generally disputed, that more proofs are furnished among the natives of interior Africa of their belief in the common Fatherhood of a personal God by their hospitable and considerate treatment of foreigners and strangers than are to be seen in many a civilized and Christian community. (CINR:115)

To illustrate his statement on African religiosity, Blyden recalled Homer's and Herodotus's eulogies of the "blameless Black peoples" (NAH:10). Concerning hospitality, besides some ethnographic analyses on Mandingo customs (CINR:185) and Mungo Park's experience in the vicinity of Sego (CINR:206), he brought in explorers' testimonies, and among them, the amazing "long sojourn of Livingstone in that land . . . without money to pay his way, . . . another proof of the excellent qualities of the peoples" (CINR:115).

Two other characteristics of Africans, according to Blyden, are their love of music (CINR:276) and their "teachableness" (CINR:163). He focused on this last capability because of its potential for Africa's future. It seemed to him all the more important since he was convinced of a general state of "degeneration," at least among "Pagans." But "Moslems," generally, constitute an exception: "Wherever the Moslem is found on this coast . . . he looks upon himself as a separate and distinct being from his Pagan neighbour, and immeasurably his superior in intellectual and moral respects" (CINR:175).

> A century has made no change for better. Mr. Joseph Thompson [who] visited the Nigritian countries last year [says]: There is absolutely not a single place where the natives are left to their own free will, in which there is the slightest evidence of a desire for better things. The worst vices and diseases of Europe have found a congenial soil, and the taste for spirits has risen out of all proportion to their desire for clothes. (CINR:342)

Thus, general degeneration exists mainly due to intemperance (CINR:67), the climatic influences (CINR:54), and the European presence (CINR:46–47; LET:399–400). In order to stop this deadly process, Blyden proposed a course of action consisting of three principal methods for the African's conversion, all of them based on the capacity for learning.

First, there was to be an emphasis on "our past" and the objectivity of reality. For as Blyden remarked, "our teachers have of necessity been Europeans, and they have taught us books too much, and things too little." Consequently, "the notion, still common among Negroes . . . is that the most important part of knowledge consists in knowing what other men—foreigners—have said about things, and even about Africa and about themselves. They aspire to be familiar, not with what really is, but with what is printed" (CINR:220). In daily existence the expression of this failure to distinguish between "reality" and subjective "interpretation" leads Africans into absurd situations.

> The songs that live in our ears and are often on our lips are the songs which we heard sung by those who shouted while we groaned and lamented. They sang of their history, which was the history of our degradation. They recited their triumphs, which contained the records of our humiliation. To our great misfortune, we learned their prejudices and their passions, and thought we had their aspirations and their power. (CINR:91)

According to Blyden, it is likely that this cultural trend will simply lead to the Negro's destruction. One means of conversion would be the development of "black consciousness," since it is clear that "in spite of all, the "Negro race" has its part to play still—a distinct part—in the history of humanity, and the continent of Africa will be the principal scene of its activity" (CINR:276). Yet he claims that we must place the Western perception of "us" and of "our past" in perspective and look for "what we are," live it and write it according to "our own" experience.

> We have neglected to study matters at home because we were trained in books written by foreigners, and *for a foreign race,* not *for us*—or for us only so far as in the general characteristics of humanity we resemble that race . . . Therefore, we turned our backs upon our breathren of the interior as those from whom we could learn nothing to elevate, to enlighten, or to refine . . . We have had history written for us, and we have endeavoured to act up to it; where as, the true order is, that history should be first acted, then written. (CINR:221; my emphasis)

In other words, Africans have to create their own schemes for understanding and mastering social and historical data, "especially in this large and interesting country of theirs, about which the truth is yet to be found out—people and systems about which correct ideas are to be formed" (CINR:220–21). What Blyden refers to is, I suspect, the necessity to implement an African social interpretation, which should be undertaken as an African responsibility, since, as he expressed it in his address at the inauguration of Liberia College, "We have no pleasing antecedents—nothing in the past to inspire us . . . All our agreeable associations are connected with the future. Let us then strive to achieve a glorious future" (LO:120).

On a second level, Blyden struggled against the theme of mimicry of social behavior: "Fascinated by the present, [the Negro] harasses himself with the ever-recurring and ever-unsatisfying and unsatisfactory task of imitating imitators" (CINR:147). As a sign of psychological domination, imitation of the white man or the secret desire to become white expresses a dependence. In any case, research and discussion about this must take place in the determination of African culture and proposals for its future (CINR:277–78).

In addition, new and vigorous canons should be initiated immediately for young Blacks. The aim would be "to assist their power of forgetfulness—an achievement of extreme difficulty" (CINR:79) by increasing "the amount of purely disciplinary agencies" and reducing "to its minimum the amount of distracting influences" (CINR:80). The aim of these canons would also be "to study the causes of Negro inefficiency in civilized lands; and, so far as it has resulted from the training they have received, to endeavour to avoid what we conceive to be the sinister elements in that training" (CINR:80). Emphasizing the special nature of the Liberian experience, he insisted on the fact that "no country in the world needs more than Liberia to have mind properly directed" (LO:98). First, because the country is "isolated from the civilized world, and surrounded by a benighted people." Second, the experience itself seems exceptional for it means "establishing and maintaining a popular government with a population, for the most part, of emancipated slaves" (LO:98). Referring to the first settlers, he insists on the necessity of "a practical education" (LO:101).

This project leads directly to the third major step: a new policy for formal education, which ultimately would help the transformation of the continent. Using his own experience as a professional, he proposed very precise outlines for a program. Above all, he put forward this major thesis: "Lord Bacon says that 'reading makes a full man'; but the indiscriminate reading by the Negro of European literature has made him, in many instances, too full, or has rather destroyed his balance" (CINR:81). From this position it is easier to understand the complementarity between his "classical perspective" and his "nationalist outlook" with respect to the curriculum. In addition to the critical presentation of history from an African point of view, he insisted on the study of classics—the Greek and Latin languages and their literatures— mathematics, and the Bible. The study of classics—"the key to a thorough knowledge of all the languages of the enlightened part of mankind" (LO:108)—was necessary for two main reasons. First, "what is gained by the study of the ancient languages is that strengthening and disciplining of the mind which enables the student in after life to lay hold of, and, with comparatively little difficulty, to master any business to which he may turn his attention" (CINR:87). Second "the study of the Classics also lays the foundation for the successful pursuit of scientific knowledge. It so stimulates the mind that it arouses the student's interest in all problems of science" (CINR:87; LO:110). (Let us note that these are the two main reasons Senghor put forward some ninety years later to promote the teaching of Greek, Latin, and classical literature in Senegal.) Blyden also advocated the study of physics, and mathematics (LO:100), because "as instruments of culture, they are everywhere applicable" (CINR:87). Finally, the study of the Bible is essential. However, it must be a Bible "without note or comment," since "the teachings of Christianity are of universal application . . . and the great truths of the Sermon on the Mount are as universally accepted as Euclid's axioms" (CINR:89).

Blyden's "nationalist" outlook is manifest in his intention to introduce into the curriculum the study of Arabic and African languages, "by means of which we may have intelligent intercourse with the millions accessible to us in the interior, and learn more of our own country" (CINR:88). In particular, the promotion of Arabic seems important to him. In a letter to the Reverend Henry Venn, he went so far as to write that "Roman letters will never prevail or be read by Mohammedan Africa" (LET:95). Blyden advocated not only the teaching of Africa's languages but also an actual introduction to African society and its culture. And to Liberian citizens he said:

> We have young men who are experts in the geography and customs of foreign countries; who can tell all about the proceedings of foreign statesmen in countries thousands of miles away; can talk glibly of London, Berlin, Paris, and Washington . . . But who knows anything about Musahdu, Medina, Kankan, or Sego—only a few hundred miles from us? Who can tell anything of the policy or doings of Fanfidoreh, Ibrahims Sissi, or Fahquehqueh, or Simoro of Boporu—only a few steps from us? These are hardly known. Now as Negroes, allied in blood and race to these people, this is disgraceful. (CINR:88)

In sum, the potentialities of African personality are given in this impetus to promote a new perception of the past and present, the recovery of a psychological autonomy, and the introduction of an original system of education. With this argument in mind, one cay say that Blyden was really presenting a formula for the "reinvention" of the African personality, from a "racial" point of view. He wrote: "We want the eye and ear of the Negro to be trained by culture that he may see more clearly what he does see, and hear more distinctly what he does hear" (CINR:277). And in terms of the future, he dramatically asserted:

> When the African shall come forward with his peculiar gifts, he will fill a place never before occupied. Misunderstood and often misrepresented even by his best friends . . . he is, nevertheless, coming forward, gradually rising under the influences of agencies seen and unseen. (CINR:278)

It is not difficult to see Blyden's originality in these comments on African personality. Such independence of mind is, for better or worse, exceptional. At the very least, it explains Blyden's attitude towards Africanists. He advised Negroes to avoid three major categories of Europeans—"professional philanthropists," "racists," and the "indifferent." The Negro should meet with people who "treat him as they would a white man of the same degree of culture and behaviour, basing this demeanour altogether upon the intellectual or moral qualities of the man" (CINR:266).

In Blyden's conception of African personality, the most striking thing is his racial creed, with its ambivalent overtones: "first, [the African] will not fade away or become extinct before Europeans, as the American and Australian aborigines; and, second, . . . in any calculations looking at the material improvement or aggrandisement of his native home, he cannot be wisely ignored" (CINR:263).

To present Blyden's political theory, I make the distinction between two domains, the religious and the political. I will first present them separately and then comment on their interpenetration or "economy."

All Africans, wrote Blyden, believe in a "Common Creator and Father of mankind" (CINR:115) and this fundamental characteristic is the basic feature of their religion. This need not imply the existence of a formal and organized religion all over the continent. Nor does it mean, as some Africanists seem to think, that "an African's religion finds vent at his heels" (CINR:275), forgetting that the " 'Shaker element' prevails chiefly, if not entirely, among Negroes or 'coloured' people, who have been trained under the influence of the domination of which [the Africanist] himself is a distinguished ornament" (CINR:275). Blyden distinguished three religious systems: paganism, Mohammedanism, and Christianity. Concerning paganism, he recognized that he was discouraged "by what appears to us the obstinacy . . . the stubbornness of a hoary superstition." But "when we consider how large tribes . . . are kept in subordination, and fulfill many a national function without any knowledge of letters or written revelation, it must appear that there is something in the Paganism of Africa as in the Paganism of other lands—some subtle, indefinable, inappreciable influence which operates upon the people and regulates their life" (CINR:225–26). If he disapproved of pagan "fetichism," he also opposed false generalizations and erroneous accounts of African religious practices, noting once again Africanists' mystifications: "There is something lamentable—we were going to say grotesque—in the ignorance of some who assume to be authorities and guides on African matters, of the condition of things at even a little distance from the coast" (CINR:61).

At any rate, Blyden praised "the decided superiority in morality which characterised the interior natives untouched by civilisations" (LET:462) and admired the Muslims. These two groups, according to him, "possess in their conditions of life more room for vigorous individual and racial growth, and are less compressed into set shapes than any others" (LET:462–63). Despite the fact that Blyden did not hesitate to draw a brief comparison between African paganism—"this religion of the imagination, or of the fancy"—and Socrates's wisdom and Greek and Roman mysteries, he clearly considered Islam superior to pagan beliefs:

> No one can travel any distance in the interior of West Africa without being struck with the different aspects of society in different localities, according as the population is Pagan or Mohammedan. Not only is there a difference in the methods of government, but in the general regulations of society, and even in the amusements of the people. (CINR:6)

Islam seemed dynamic and well-organized. Blyden, in a letter to the Reverend Henry Venn, emphasized an external feature of Islam: its independence. Muslims, he wrote, "carry on all their institutions, educational and religious, independent of foreign aid (LET:98). Their religion is also powerful and influential. Blyden observed that he did not believe that "much can be done by attacking Islam on the coast" and proposed that "Christians should seek the favour of Muslims." Only progressively by "means of Christian Arabic books, the character of Mohammedanism may be very much modified" (LET:98–99). Not only did the system seem superior, but according to Blyden, "the Moslem [seems] immeasurably . . . superior in intellectual and moral respects" (CINR:175). Blyden expounded two major reasons which could account for the success, the strength, and the superiority of Islam: the completeness of the Koran and the aggressiveness of this socio-religious system:

> To the African Mussulman . . . the Koran is all-sufficient for his moral, intellectual, social and political needs. It contains his whole religion, and a great deal besides . . . It is his code of laws, and his creed, his homily, and his liturgy. He consults it for direction on every possible subject; and his Pagan neighbour, seeing such veneration paid to the book, conceives even more exaggerated notions of its character. (CINR:176)

> In Central Africa, Islam is an aggressive, conquering force; and it is, of course, infinitely superior to the Paganism which it has abolished. It has established in

the minds of its adherents the sense of responsibility beyond this life, and the fear of God; and this sentiment—which is the condition of all other progress—it is not only diffusing, but transmitting to posterity. This is the element which has given stability and upward impulse to the social and political forces of advanced countries; and it will have the same effect in the dark corners of this continent. (CINR:332)

Blyden wrote elsewhere that Arabic, the language of Islam, is in Africa a good preparation for Christianity (CINR:187) and an important means for an autonomous and regional policy of auto-regeneration (LET:134–38). He firmly believed that Islam could have an excellent future throughout the continent. And as far as African interests are concerned, Blyden had faith in the practical superiority of Islam over Christianity:

> Mohammedanism, in Africa, has left the native master of himself and of his home; but wherever Christianity has been able to establish itself, with the exception of Liberia, foreigners have taken possession of the country, and, in some places, rule the natives with oppressive rigour. (CINR:309)

This does not imply that Blyden could not or did not want to envisage the possibility of an African Christianity. He was a Christian minister, but refused to forget that he was black (see, e.g., LET:462). From his other views, one can see that he was bound to be skeptical about European Christianity and its processes of evangelization: "There is no evidence that Christianity, or, rather professing Christians [. . .] would have been less unscrupulous in their dealings with natives of Africa, than they have been with the natives of America, of Australia, of New Zealand" (CINR:309). His position must be understood against the background of racism and its consequences, which illuminates his reasons for stressing the generally negative influence of Christianity on Black people and "the innumerable woes which have attended the African race for the last three hundred years in Christian lands" (CINR:27). As he expressed it in his letter to Mary Kingsley in 1900: "Very few among races alien to the European believe in the genuineness of the Christianity of the white man. For neither in the teaching nor the practice of the lay white man do they see manifested, as a rule, anything of the spirit of Christianity" (LET:462).

  Although he rejoiced in the apparent failure of Roman Catholicism in Liberia (LET:388), he seemed to admire this church, which in his opinion presented remarkable characteristics: It is "an uncompromising front in the warfare against infidelity in all its forms" and "has always been and is now a protesting power . . . against those attacks upon constituted authority." Further, it is set "against the freeness and facility of divorce," "respects the integrity of the family," and "respects races." Finally, it holds to those words of St. Paul that declare that 'God hath made of one all nations of men to dwell upon the face of the earth' " (CINR:224–25). Blacks could find "Negro saints" in its calendar (CINR:39), could observe Negroes occupying important "civil, military and social positions" in Catholic countries (CINR:225), and benefitting from political freedom (CINR:46). Thus, Negroes were able to see the Church itself relying on indigenous elements and agencies for its development (CINR:167).

This eulogy of the Church of Rome is fundamentally a criticism of Protestant policies. However, Blyden recognized the relatively positive effects of five American denominations (Baptists, Methodists, Episcopalians, Presbyterians, and Lutherans) established on the West African coast, where "numerous churches have been organized and are under a native ministry, and thousands of children are gathered into schools under Christian teachers" (CINR:49). But on the whole, he judged the results to be very weak: these churches are "in their largest measure . . . confined almost exclusively to the European settlements along the coast and to their immediate neighbourhood" (CINR:49–50). At the end of his life, Blyden was quite pessimistic about missionary activities. In 1910, in a letter to R. L. Antrobus, assistant under-secretary at the British Colonial Office, he complained about "teaching mistakes" that created "a gulf between aborigines and colonists" (LET:499).

What was to be done for the successful promotion of Christianity in Africa? "In view of the serious obstacles which have so far confronted the work of African evangelization and civilization through European agency, it is a matter of serious concern among Christian workers as to how the work should be done" (CINR:160). His answer was clear and simple and followed from his racial views: only peoples of African descent could successfully evangelize the continent: "The method, the simple holding up of Jesus Christ; the instrument, the African himself" (CINR:161). Thus, at the very beginning of the second evangelization of Africa in the nineteenth century, Blyden called for an African Christianity. The new faith would be propagated by black missionaries and its significance would be transformed. He advocated the translation of the Gospel into African tongues, which would "be far more effective instruments of conveying to the native mind the truths of the Gospel than any European language" (CINR:68). Bearing in mind Islam's ideological impact on African peoples (CINR:231), he fervently envisioned an authentic African Christianity. His metaphor was the meeting of Philip the apostle and the eunuch from Ethiopia: "Philip was not to accompany the eunuch, to water the seed he had planted, to cherish and supervise this incipient work. If he desired to do so—and perhaps he did—the Spirit suffered him not, for he 'caught him away' " (CINR:161). The eunuch being the only messenger, he is the only one responsible for "a total revolution in his country through the words he had heard."

While Lynch writes that though Blyden showed "a distinct partiality for Islam," "he himself never became a Muslim" (1967:246), in spirit Blyden was a Muslim. He was truly concerned, especially in his old age, about the Muslim population and their education and commercial interests and even identified himself with their fate (see LET:402 and 409). The Muslims called

upon him to aid in their negotiations with the Liberian government
(LET:425–27). In a letter to the British Colonial Office, he recognized that
the Governor did not pay him "the courtesy due to his office because [he]
agree[d] with Mohammedans" (LET:479). In 1877, he stated that he had
"more faith in the ultimate usefulness in Africa of the pagan and Mohammedan natives, through Christian influences, than in that of the Americo-
Liberians, demoralized by slavery and deceived by a bastard Christianity"
(LET:235). In 1889, he confided to F. J. Grimké his long-standing conviction concerning "the superiority of the Soudan or Mohammedan Negroes to
others" (LET:406 and 138). He seems to have had a precise objective. In
1888 he wrote:

> My idea is that Islam is to be reformed and can be reformed. I am now writing
> . . . on 'the Koran in Africa,' discussing its theology and practical teachings in
> their effect upon the Negro race, and showing how effectively, if Christians
> understood the system, it might be utilized in the Christianization of Africa.
> (LET:399)

His aim was ambiguous. What did he mean by "reforming" Islam? This is a
mystery. What is clear is his critical rejection of "missionary" Christianity. In
any case, in 1903 his foremost desire was "to visit the College of Living
Oriental Languages in Paris" and also to "visit the famous Mohammedan
University at Cairo, the Mosque Al-Azhar, and spend a month there studying
their methods" (LET:473).

Spiritually and politically, Blyden was, at least from 1900 on, a Muslim.
He opposed "the influence of so-called Christianity and civilization" and
tended to emphasize the American lesson as he saw it: "in all the long and
weary years of the Negro's bondage in America to White Christians—the
slaves clung to Christ—but they did not believe in the religion of their white
masters" (LET:462).

Did Blyden choose between Jesus and Mohammed? There is no answer.
Nevertheless, his texts give a clue. What we are dealing with is, without
doubt, what one would call nowadays a "theology of difference," simultaneously supported by a racial consciousness and a pluralistic interpretation
of the Bible. Such a viewpoint, from Blyden's position, allows for an original
contribution by black Christians:

> There are stars, astronomers tell us, whose light has not yet reached the earth;
> so there are stars in the moral universe yet to be disclosed by the unfettered
> African, which he must discover before he will be able to progress without
> wandering into perilous seas and suffering serious injury. (CINR:151)

Complementary to this mission, which only black Christians could successfully carry out (CINR:194), is another one: the promotion of an African
nationalism and the unity of the continent.

Blyden presented as premises two relevant ideas. On the one hand, there is the fact that Europe is an invader (CINR:338; LO:73–75). Blyden accepted the truth of the following sentence, written by a European: "the eighteenth century stole the black man from his country; the nineteenth century steals his country from the black man" (CINR:337). On the other hand, there is African opposition to the invasion. Blyden praised the resistance of the Ashanti and the Zulus as an "indication of the suddenness of Africa's regeneration" (CINR:121).

The "Economy" of a Discourse

It was not the aim of this analysis to describe the historical or sociological climate in which Blyden's ideas evolved. These points have received sufficient scholarly attention (Lynch, 1967; Holden, 1967; July, 1964; Shepperson, 1960). My objective was to present Blyden's "philosophy" from an "archae-ologic" viewpoint by uncovering the specificity of his discourse in "the play of analyses and differences" of a nineteenth-century atmosphere, and by looking for discrete relationships between his discourse and some non-discursive fields. What remains to be said?

First of all, Blyden was a strange and exceptional man, who devoted his entire life to the cause he believed in. However, as C. H. Lyons rightly noted, "in seeking to answer the racists in their own terms Blyden developed a theory of race which, while vindicating the black man, derived an uncomfort-ably large measure of inspiration from late nineteenth-century European race-thinking" (Lyons, 1975:108). The frame of his thinking was a "tradi-tional" one and may be summed up in three oppositions: a racial opposition (white vs. black), a cultural confrontation (civilized vs. savage) and a religious distance (Christianity vs. paganism). His racial theory was simply a rela-tivization of the supposed superiority of the categories white, civilized, and Christian. His discourse, like the racist discourse that he opposed, is purely axiomatic. It is, in the modern sense, a discourse of intimidation; or, to put it in Barthes's language, it is "a language intended to bring about a coincidence between norms and facts, and to give a cynical reality the guarantee of a noble morality" (Barthes, 1979:103). In this sense, it clearly distinguishes itself from the language and the mythologies of the "noble savage." The "noble savage" was a romantic tool, "an aid to self-scrutiny at home" in Europe (Lyons, 1975:8). Even as an anti-slavery weapon, the "noble savage" was an idealized African presenting the most un-African features, and could, for example, "blush" and "turn pale" (Lyons, 1975:7). Blyden confronts these languages and mythologies on "blackness." A. T. Vaughan presents an accurate picture of the context:

> Virtually all descriptions of the 'dark continent' portray its inhabitants as unattractive, heathen, and grossly uncivil. In theory at least, the Africans' culture could be ameliorated; their physical characteristics could not. And,

although several aspects of African appearance—stature, facial features, and hair texture, for example—displeased the English eye, most striking and disturbing was the darkness of African skin. Descriptions of African people invariably stress their blackness, always disapprovingly. (Vaughan, 1982:919)

In this atmosphere, Blyden simply opposed one racist view to another racist view, precisely by emphasizing anti-mythologies on Africans, their cultures, and the necessity of unmixed Negro blood.

The ultimate objective of such an anti-racism becomes, almost naturally, the negation of the then-existing power relationships based on racial distinctions. This process might account for Blyden's conviction about the usefulness of American and West Indian Blacks in the transformation of the African continent, which is the basis of the project for "racial growth" and its myths about racial nationality, black creativity, and Pan-Africanism. In his own terms, the reunion of the "civilized" Christians of the West Indies and America with their "benighted" brothers in Africa would lead to a positive development from both a cultural and a religious point of view. Blyden's objectives (racial growth, cultural regeneration, Christianization) are a negation of what he considers African weaknesses. Fundamentally, the theory is both an argument against the European partition of the continent and a foundation for the ideology that allowed the creation of Liberia: "back to Africa." As Blyden grew older, his theory conflicted with his pessimistic analysis of black leadership. He continued to think in terms of opposition between "civilization" and "African degenerance." He accepted the efficiency of white colonization. However, to promote more realistically his dream for the transformation of the continent, he opposed the "American-Liberian demoralized by slavery" to the "Mohammedan native" (LET:235). He even contrasted "bastard Christianity" and its culture with the Islamic faith and its order. He also accepted the "reconstruction" of Liberia under American protection (LET:496). He knew that "the would-be rulers of the land feel it their duty to denounce [him] as a traitor to the country" (LET:235). He was flattered to be considered "the prophet of Liberia" (LET:496) and stated that he had "faith in the ultimate usefulness in Africa of the pagan and Mohammedan natives, through Christian influence" (LET:235). It is striking that a similar conviction would later lead the British government to rely on "traditional local authorities as agencies of local rule" (see, e.g., Hailey, 1970:94) for the implementation of "the dogma that civilization was a blessing that its possessors ought to spread" (Mair, 1975:252).

These theories go together in Blyden's work, contradicting each other and accounting for philosophical inconsistencies, racist propositions, and political opportunisms. As H. R. Lynch's *Edward Wilmot Blyden: Pan-Negro Patriot* convincingly demonstrates, at the end of the last century Blyden "had established an intellectual ascendancy in West Africa, and many West Africans were prepared to follow where he led, but they looked to him in vain for a firm and sustained lead, or for clear directives. Many of them thought his ideas sophistical or contradicted by his actions" (1967:246).

In what sense should we accept Senghor's statement that Blyden was the precursor of negritude and African personality? In his foreward to Blyden's *Letters*, Senghor himself recognizes that "we had, from time to time, come upon the name of Blyden, but we had not paid much attention to it . . . We had no knowledge of his correspondence, nor of his essays, nor of his weekly newspaper with the so significant title of *Negro* nor, finally, even of his major work, entitled *Christianity, Islam, and the Black [sic] Race*" (LET:xx). In his intellectual biography, *Pierre Teilhard de Chardin et la politique africaine* (1962), the name of Blyden is not even mentioned. Aimé Césaire, Léon G. Damas, and Jacques Rabemenanjara, other members of the negritude movement, never refer to Blyden. It is only in Anglophone West Africa that Blyden's real influence may be clearly seen, in Casely Hayford's ideas on West African unity, N. Azikiwe's "pan-Negro nationalism," and possibly in Nkrumah's Pan-Africanism (Lynch, 1967:248–50).

Blyden worked on racial issues in the nineteenth century. In order to oppose racist mythologies, he focused on "the virtues of black civilization" and promoted the concepts of "blackness" and "Negro personality," thus inventing positive new myths about race and the black personality. He had occasional disciples like C. Hayford and stimulated the nationalism of others, as in the case of the Nigerian Azikiwe. On the whole, the premises and even the essentials of his ideology were already in the air before he explicated his theses. They were present in the racist paradigms that his theses negated and thus might, for example, account for Mary Kingsley's relativist view on races (1965). They had already been used both politically and ideologically by the founders of Liberia (Lynch, 1967:10–31) and by the Haitian revolutionaries, who at the beginning of the nineteenth century created the first black republic. At the time of Blyden's death in the first quarter of this century, these same premises were incorporated in W. E. B. DuBois's Pan-Africanist ideology, and in the 1930s they were important in the genesis of the negritude movement in Paris (see Wauthier, 1964).

Let us now take a different look at the ideological significance of Blyden's ideology. How can we analyze it, and, more important, how might it be possible to understand it? Blyden's ideology of African identity is a "strain theory" in the sense that it should be understood against "the background of a chronic effort to correct socio-psychological disequilibrium" (Geertz, 1973:201). This interpretation should explain his suggestion for the replacement of potential European colonizers, considered as "invaders," by black peoples from America and the West Indies, who would become agents for the modernization of Africa. Thus, racial identity stands as an absolute precondition for any sociopolitical transformation of Africa. This choice seems to exclude the possibility of a methodology that, from "the background of a universal struggle for advantage," would define an "interest theory." This theory can present ideal relations: between the African process of production and the social relations of production (economic level); between the economic organization and its political reflections and interpretations (political level); and between the ideological structure and its concrete practices within the society (ideological level). This theory also does so by proposing a type of balance between the economic level and the ideological superstructures. It is, in principle, capable of generating a new African mode of production, and thus technical modernization, political democracy, and cultural autonomy.

Blyden's "strain theory" remains far from the Marxist perspective. Its roots are in the sociology of races and more precisely in the controversial principle of irreconcilable differences between races. This brings Blyden's thought closer to the romantic philosophies of otherness which flourished in Europe during the nineteenth century and which largely supported European nationalism—in Germany and Italy, for instance—or, a posteriori, explained and justified them. Nevertheless, Blyden's perspective is particular. His political ideology arose as a response to racism and to some of the consequences of imperialism. It represents an emotional response to the European process of denigrating Africa and an opposition to the exploitation that resulted from the expansionism of Europe from the fifteenth century. At the same time, in order to prove its own significance, his ideology strongly asserts the thesis of pluralism in the historical development of races, ethnic groups, and nationalities. Consequently, Blyden can reject the evolutionary assumption of "identical but unequal races" which provides grounds for the theme of the "White man's mission" and thus justifies imperialism and colonization. In its place, he puts a different assertion: "distinct but equal."

One cannot but be amazed when analyzing this thesis, which was the first articulate nineteenth-century theory of "blackness." When compared to Senghor's negritude, the relevance of Blyden's commitment is still apparent, even though the concept of race is now generally considered an ideological trap. Even in his reverence for Greco-Roman culture, Blyden announced Senghor. Despite discrepancies due to differences of sociopolitical contexts, psychological situations, and philosophical references, Senghor, on the whole, pursued Blyden's ambiguous thesis. His pronouncements emphasize the African cultural and historical identity in terms of race and consider this concept to be essential.

Blyden's ideology is, however, mostly determined by a profound understanding of the burden of slavery. It is as a negation of this experience that Blyden recommends a role for Black Americans in the modernization of Africa. This important dimension seems a defense against the experience of domination, and the prospect of Africa's transformation would appear to institutionalize a negativity. Sartre put forward a similar theoretical perspective in *Black Orpheus*. Supporting negritude in Hegelian terms he insisted on its relevance but also noted the pertinence of the dialectical contradiction: the racial moment is always the promise of another step, another contradiction. The struggle for liberty would be won in terms of a general transformation of societies and negation of social classes. This is in keeping with the logic of an "interest theory."

At any rate, Blyden established the "black personality movement" which stands for "the sum of values of African civilization, the body of qualities which make up the distinctiveness of the people of Africa." This empirical equivalent of negritude has been instrumental in sustaining the struggle for African independence by opposing colonization as a process of falsification and depersonalization of Africans and by criticizing imperialism as a means of exploitation. Blyden foresaw the immediate future of Africa. As C. Fyfe puts it, in the introduction to *Christianity, Islam and the Negro Race:*

> Looking back from the 1960s we can see that in a period equivalent to the span of Blyden's life (he lived to be nearly 80) Europeans have come and gone from the greater part of Africa, leaving Africans in political control. His reasoning may have been faulty, but his prophecy has been ultimately fulfilled. Similarly his claim that hundreds of thousands of American Negroes were ready to emigrate to Africa seemed, at the time, erroneous. Yet the passionate enthusiasm aroused in the United States, only a few years after his death, by Marcus Garvey's movement shows that here, too, he saw more deeply than his contemporaries. (CINR:xv)

Blyden expressed the essentials of the black personality movement and the Pan-Africanist program, with its focus on the ideological necessity of becoming reconciled with one's heritage and its particular sociohistorical experience and reality, which presaged Nkrumah's "Consciencism." In the works of Blyden and Nkrumah, the political philosophy is based on a framework composed of at least three major sources for inspiration: African tradition, an Islamic contribution, and a Western legacy. The difference between the two systems resides in the fact that Nkrumah accepted materialism's presuppositions as the only relevant ones and organized his political thought by integrating strain and interest theories. Because of his own assumptions, Blyden did not weld a solid programmatic juncture between the tension of his wish for power and the contradictions of his racial anxiety. This failure would account for his visionary tendency, which led him to make impressive prophecies but not always to undertake valid sociohistorical analyses.

Nonetheless, this difficulty, which is the locus of Blyden's philosophical problems (accounting for most of his inconsistencies on colonization, structural slavery, Islam's future, etc.) paradoxically allowed him to emphasize a relativist view of history and its interpretations and, therefore, the possibility of a general criticism of social sciences. He made this criticism by systematically focusing on the significance of European ethnocentrism and its various expressions. This meant, then as now, that an understanding of African personality or African culture cannot neglect a major dimension—the epistemological debate. Because of imperialism and its ideological reflections in moral and social sciences, this approach must question all discourses interpreting Africans and their culture. Blyden considered this a critical preliminary to establishing a unifying and productive rapport between African ideology and the concrete practice of knowledge. It was not until the 1920s that African intellectuals rediscovered Blyden's outlook: to benefit from the heritage of their own history rather than remaining mere objects of or obedient participants in Western social sciences, it was their duty to master knowledge of themselves and their own culture and to open a vigorous debate on the limits of anthropology. What Blyden wrote to J. R. Straton, commenting on a work of one of the most brilliant theorists of racism in France, might be applied to him in turn: "Le Bon's *Psychology of Peoples* ought to be carefully studied" (LET:466).

V

THE PATIENCE OF PHILOSOPHY

"Primitive Philosophies"

> La première question que je [me] suis posée,
> rencontrant des paysans [français] qui
> n'étaient ni crédules ni arriérés, fut alors celle-
> ci: la sorcellerie, est-ce que c'est
> inconnaissable, ou est-ce que ceux qui le
> prétendent ont besoin de n'en rien savoir pour
> soutenir leur propre cohérence intellectuelle?
> est-ce qu'un "savant" ou un "moderne" a
> besoin pour se conforter du mythe d'un
> paysan crédule et arriéré?
>
> JEANNE FAVRET-SAADA, Les Mots,
> la Mort, les Sorts.

The expression "primitive philosophy" was current in the 1920s and 1930s. In a preceding chapter, I examined at length anthropologists' discourse and both its power and its ambiguity. The concept of "primitive philosophy" is part of this system, which since the end of the nineteenth century had been colonizing the continent, its inhabitants and its realities. It also belongs to an intellectual edifice built on Lévy-Bruhl's work, particularly on such cornerstones as *Les Fonctions mentales dans les sociétés inférieures* (1910), *La Mentalité primitive* (1922), *L'Ame primitive* (1927), *Le Surnaturel et la Nature dans la mentalité primitive* (1931), and *L'Expérience mystique et les symboles chez les primitifs* (1938). They posit a radical difference between the West, characterized by a history of intellectual and spiritual reasoning, and "primitives," whose life, *Weltanschauung,* and thinking were viewed as having nothing in common with the West. As Lévy-Bruhl wrote in *La Mentalité primitive:*

> The attitude of the mind of the primitive is very different. The nature of the milieu in which he lives presents itself to him in quite a different way. Objects and beings are all involved in a network of mystical participation and exclusions. It is these which constitute its texture and order. It is then these which immediately impose themselves on his attention and which alone retain it. (In Evans-Pritchard, 1980:80)

135

From this view emerges a theory of two types of mentality. One is rational, functioning according to principles of logic and inquiring into causal determinations and relations; the other, prelogical, seems completely dominated by collective representation and strictly depends upon the law of mystical participation. Westerners participate in logical thought. In the prelogical and symbolic, one finds "such peoples as the Chinese included with Polynesians, Melanesians, Negroes, American Indians, and Australian Blackfellows" (Evans-Pritchard, 1980:88).

By 1965, Evans-Pritchard could state that "there is no reputable anthropologist who today accepts this theory of two distinct types of mentality" (1980:88). I would only note that what the present-day "grand dichotomy" implies might not be Lévy-Bruhl's model of opposed mentalities but would surely indicate a division of reason between the so-called closed and open societies. At any rate, in the 1920s and 1930s the division meant both the task of comprehending the primitive mentality as a poor and non-evolved entity and the possibility of restoring it at the beginning of the history of reason. It is within this framework that one understands such books and contributions dealing with "primitive philosophies" as Delhaisse's *Les Idées religieuses et philosophiques des Warega* (1909), Kaoze's *La Psychologie des Bantu, des Bani Marungu* (1907–1911), Correia's *Vocables philosophiques et religieux des peuples Ibo* (1925), or the well known texts of Brelsford on *Primitive Philosophy* (1935) and *The Philosophy of the Savage* (1938).

I am not saying that all who were then studying "primitive organizations" (see Smet, 1978b, 1975a, 1975b) were disciples of Lévy-Bruhl, defending the thesis of a difference in reason between the "primitive" and the "civilized." Rather, all of them, even those who, like Delafosse (1922, 1927), commented upon African structures and peoples with a vivid *Einfühlung* (sympathy), were concerned with the discrepancy between Europe and the black continent and wished to describe this difference and possibly classify it into a taxonomic grid of human cultures. The Belgian Franciscan Placide Frans Tempels, as I indicated in my analysis of missionary language, could be considered a paradigmatic illustration of this curiosity. He is a sign caught at the crossroads of several currents: evolutionary assumptions of the late nineteenth century, Lévy-Bruhl's theses on prelogism, the European self-declared mission to civilize Africans through colonization, and Christian evangelization.

Within the arrogant framework of a Belgian colonial conquest meant to last for centuries, Tempels, a missionary in Katanga, wrote a small book of philosophy that still disturbs a number of African thinkers. What Tempels knew of philosophy amounted, essentially, to the education he received during his religious training. He was not a professional philosopher, and his major preoccupations, beginning with his arrival in Africa in 1933, were of a religious nature. One of his exegetes, A. J. Smet, has suggested that Lévy-Bruhl's influence is evident in the first texts, which tended to be ethnographical in outlook, and which Tempels published before *Bantu Philoso-*

phy (Smet, 1977b:77–128). Tempels was fully committed to a mission, that of leading the black person (to whom he did not yet give the status of being a complete human) along the road to civilization, knowledge, and true religion. His style was that of a *bulamatari* (breaker of rocks), a spiritual master and authoritarian doctor (Tempels, 1962:36). *Bantu Philosophy* could be considered a testimony to a revelation and as a sign of a change in the life of Tempels:

> I must say that my goal, in this study of the Bantu was to feel myself "Bantu" at least once. I wanted to think, fell, live like him, have a Bantu soul. All that with the intention of adapting . . . There was doubtless in my attitude something more, or something else, than the simple scientific interest of an anthropologist who asks questions without the object of his science, the living man in front of him, necessarily being the objective of his investigations. My attitude perhaps included an element of sympathy towards this living individual and evoked in him a reaction of confidence towards me. (Tempels, 1962:37)

Looking back at the period that saw the publication of *Bantu Philosophy*, Tempels neatly differentiates himself from anthropologists. His aim is different, he says, and depends upon a radically different attitude, one of *Einfühlung* or sympathy. But his book had extraordinary repercussions. G. Bachelard greeted it as a treasure. Alioune Diop pledged his faith on this little work, appending a foreword to the French version and describing it as the most decisive work he had ever read (Diop, 1965). However, the book has not lacked enemies.

The story begins in Katanga, in the former Belgian Congo, where Bishop Jean-Félix de Hemptinne exercised his power to check the circulation of *Bantu Philosophy,* insisting that Rome condemn the book as heretical and that Tempels be expelled from the country (DeCraemer, 1977:29–30). The reason was that in the colonial milieu this book cast doubts on the greatness of the colonial venture. There were at the time rather respectable theoreticians who considered the right to colonize as a natural right. According to this doctrine, it was up to the most advanced humans to intervene in the "sleeping regions" of Africa and to exploit the wealth meant by God for all humanity. Through his presence and his policies, the colonizer was intended to awaken "lethargic peoples" and introduce them to civilization and true religion. For about ten years, Tempels followed this objective. In the fashion of colonial administrators, he derived two theses from his experience: that nature comes from God and that it is up to superior peoples to civilize their inferior brethren. Thus, the right to colonize was duplicated by a natural duty and a spiritual mission. A stirring metaphor very much in fashion in the 1930s supported his thesis: just as in a forest there are fragile, dependent forms of life, which can live and develop only under the protection of the stronger, so it is among human communities.

With his *Bantu Philosophy*, Tempels does not entirely reject this ideology of natural domination, notwithstanding the fears of his critics. He mainly proposes more efficient means to his avowed goal, the task of civilizing and evangelizing Bantu peoples. As a priest true to the ideals of his mission, he offers a new program for the social and spiritual improvement of the indigenous people; that is, ways to establish Christian values on a Bantu cultural basis and construct a civilization which will be in harmony with the modes of thinking and of being Bantu. Tempels was persuaded that his *Bantu Philosophy,* and particularly his ontology, is the best tool Whites can use to encounter Africans and understand them.

> Folklore alone and superficial descriptions of strange customs cannot enable us to discover and understand primitive man. Ethnology, linguistics, psychoanalysis, jurisprudence, sociology and the study of religions are able to yield definitive results only after the philosophy and the ontology of a primitive people have been thoroughly studied and written up. (Tempels, 1959:23)

Tempels's conception of Bantu philosophy may be summarized in five propositions (see Eboussi-Boulaga, 1968; Tshiamalenga, 1981).

(1) Since Bantu are human beings, they have organized systems of principles and references. These systems constitute a philosophy even if Bantu are not "capable of formulating a philosophical treatise, complete with an adequate vocabulary" (Tempels, 1959:36). In sum, the philosophy is an *implicit* one, and it is Tempels, who, interpreting Bantu answers to his questions, unveils its organized and systematic character of beliefs and customs.

(2) This philosophy is an ontology. In the West, since the Greeks, philosophy has been concerned with defining and indicating the real in terms of being, through a static perspective accounted for by such expressions as "the reality that is," "anything that exists," or "what is." Against this, Tempels notes that Bantu philosophy seems to offer a dynamic understanding by giving a great deal of attention to the being's vitality and by relating being to its force:

> We can conceive the transcendental notion of "being" by separating it from its attribute, "force," but the Bantu cannot. "Force" in his thought is a necessary element in "being," and the concept "force" is inseparable from the definition of "being." There is no idea among Bantu of "being" divorced from the idea of "force." (Tempels, 1959:50–51)

(3) Bantu ontology in its specificity implies that being, as understood in the Western tradition, signifies force in Bantu tradition, and therefore one can state that being = force, or as the Italian translator entitled his abridged version of *Bantu Philosophy: Forza = Essere* (Tempels, 1979:23). It is thus force in its mysterious presence that provides a possibility of classifying beings in a hierarchy comprising all the existing realms: mineral, vegetable, animal, human, ancestral, and divine. On the other hand, in all of them vital force appears to be the essential sign of ordering identities, differences, and

relationships. From the extreme depth up to the level of God, there is a permanent and dynamic dialectic of energy: vital force can be nourished, diminshed, or stopped altogether. It increases or decreases in every being and from one transition to another; its reference remains the order of its fulfill-ment in God.

> Bantu speak, act, live as if, for them, beings were forces. Force is not for them an adventitious, accidental reality, force is even more than a necessary attribute of beings: Force is the nature of being, force is being, being is force. (Tempels, 1959:51)

> The origin, the subsistence or annihilation of beings or of forces, is expressly and exclusively attributed to God. The term to "create" in its proper con-notation of "to evoke from not being" is found in its full signification in Bantu terminology (*Kupanga* in Kiluba). (1959:57)

> All force can be strengthened or enfeebled. That is to say, all being can become stronger or weaker. (1959:55)

Within these uninterrupted exchanges, beings are not bound in upon themselves but constitute what Tempels calls a "principle of activity" (1959:51) and by their interactions account for the "general laws of vital causality," namely,

     (*a*) "Man (living or deceased) can directly reinforce or diminish the being of another man";

     (*b*) "The vital human force can directly influence inferior force-beings (animal, vegetable, or mineral) in their being";

     (*c*) "A rational being (spirit, manes, or the living) can act indirectly upon another rational being by communicating his vital force to an inferior force (animal, vegetable, or mineral) through the intermediacy of which it influences the rational being" (1959:67–68).

(4) Bantu ontology can be thought of and made explicit only because of the conceptual frame of Western philosophy. Tempels put it in a rather direct way: "It is our job to proceed to such systematic development. It is we who will be able to tell them in precise terms, what their inmost concept of being is" (1959:36).

(5) Bantu ontology could be a guide to the ontologies of all "primitive peoples" in general. In effect, throughout his book Tempels indistinctly uses the terms Africans, Bantu, primitives, natives, and savages, clearly indicating that although he is presenting the "philosophy" of a small community in the Belgian Congo, his conclusions could be valid for all non-Western societies. At least twice he expresses this ambition. He modestly notes that "many colonials who are living in contact with Africans have assured me that I have set out nothing new, but merely set out systematically what they had grasped vaguely from their practical knowledge of Africans" (1959:37) and at the end of his first chapter, he explicitly expresses the possibility of drawing gener-

alizations: "The problem of Bantu ontology, the problem of whether it exists or not, is thus open to discussion. It is legitimate now to enter upon the task of setting out their philosophy, which is perhaps that common to all primitive peoples, to all clan societies" (1959:38).

What is one to think of *Bantu Philosophy?* Mbiti states that Tempels's main contribution is "more in terms of sympathy and change of attitude than perhaps in the actual content of his book" (1970:14). At any rate, Mbiti has doubts about the dynamic conception of Bantu ontology (1971:132). O. p'Bitek attacks Tempels for positing a possible generalization of Bantu ontology: "Tempels invites us to accept this thought-system, not only as Bantu, but as African. Can serious . . . scholars concerned with a correct appraisal and analysis of African beliefs and philosophy afford this kind of generalisation?" (1973:59). A Zairian philosopher specifies the criticism in a more satisfactory way:

> In effect, Tempels's method is simply one of sympathy *(Einfühlung)* and communion with Luba Shaba behavior, a method of rapid and superficial comparison, and premature generalization. If it is clear that sympathy can allow a hypothesis, that cannot mean that the latter is founded. (Tshiamalenga, 1981:179)

Tshiamalenga then focuses on three points. First, one cannot conclude that because the Luba Tempels studied pay a great deal of attention to the reality of force, that force is being. Second, an ontology cannot be constituted on the basis of its external signs. More important, the identification of the Bantu notion of force with the Western notion of being does not seem to make sense. (In effect, in Bantu tradition the concept of force should be understood and defined in its relationships with other concepts, while in the West, being is a notion transcending all determinations and opposing nothingness.) Third, the equivalence established between force and being should be considered as a *simulacrum* since it is unthinkable without the Western conceptual *instrumentarium* Tempels used (Tshiamalenga, 1981:179; see also Boelaert, 1946; Sousberghe, 1951). Tshiamalenga concludes that Tempels constructed a philosophy but did not *reconstruct* Bantu philosophy (1981:179).

Perhaps one should also evaluate Tempels's enterprise within the context of an era in which Lévy-Bruhl's dogmas were congruent with the colonizing objectives as well as with the Christian mission expressed in an evolutionary grid (see Pirotte, 1973; Lyons, 1975). Yet how should we interpret Tempels's own judgment about his book? He unpretentiously writes, at the beginning of his chapter on ontology, that "the present study, after all, claims to be no more than an *hypothesis,* a first attempt at the systematic development of what Bantu philosophy is" (1959:40). The debate about this "philosophy" that has since developed, and which is regularly repeated, appears to me unduly intellectual. Tempels's work is certainly ambiguous (see also Hebga, 1982). It is not, however, worth the extreme responses that it sometimes provokes. Surely one could reproach Tempels for confusing the vulgar meaning of philosophy with its technical definition, but by returning insistently and incessantly to this weakness, as though, philosophically, it constitutes a mortal sin, African philosophers obstruct more useful developments. Even though some of Tempels's disciples continue to use his controversial concept of being-force, they generally bring in stimulating African visions and conceptions (e.g., Kagame, 1956; Lufuluabo, 1962; Mujynya, 1972). Yet after Aimé Césaire (1972), one could also infer the political complicity continued in the book and better see its relationship to colonial ideology (see Eboussi-Boulaga, 1968). Yet without doubt, *Bantu Philosophy* paradoxically opened some holes in the monolithic wall of colonial ideology, as Alioune Diop noted in his foreword (1965). Of course, one is perfectly entitled to question the sociohistorical significance of the book, and to fear, with Eboussi-Boulaga, that Tempels's thesis of the evolution of Bantu thought simply means the reduction of Bantu temporality to a fixed past (Eboussi-Boulaga, 1968:5–40).

I suggest that the truth of *Bantu Philosophy* resides precisely in the tension of these contradictions. It is probable that the scholarly works of A. Smet, who has devoted years to establishing a more complete image of Tempels and his thought, will emphasize most clearly the fuzziness of a thought born of cross-breeding between ethnological curiosity, evangelical ambiguities, and colonial purpose. We should thus situate the book in the spiritual evolution of its author. While attempting to "civilize," Tempels found his moment of truth in an encounter with people of whom he thought himself the master. He thus became a student of those he was supposed to teach and sought to comprehend their version of the truth. During this encounter, there was a discrete moment of revelation, which radically complicated the convictions of the civilizer. The adventure ended in the setting up of a sort of syncretic Christian community, the Jamaa "family" (Smet, 1977c). Tempels describes its spirit in a curious book (1962). Celebrating the themes of life, love, and fertility, the movement gained ground in Central Africa before being excommunicated by the Catholic hierarchy for unorthodoxy (DeCraemer, 1977; Mataczynski, 1984).

Had Tempels chosen for his essay a title without the term "philosophy" in it, and had he simply organized his ethnographic data on Luba and commented upon them, his book would perhaps have been less provocative. At least it could have offered a representation within regional limits, in the manner of Marcel Griaule's *Conversations with Ogotemmêli* ([1948] 1965). Praising Tempels's insights, Griaule wrote what should have been the preface to the French version of *Bantu Philosophy*. It was published in *Présence Africaine* (1949, no. 7). In this brief text, Griaule established links between Bantu ontology and conceptions of the Dogons. In the preface to *Conversations,* he makes explicit their proximity:

> Ten years ago [G. Dieterlen's *Les Ames des Dogon* (1941), S. de Ganay's *Les Devises* (1941) and my own *Les Masques* (1938)] had already drawn attention to new facts concerning the "vital force" . . . They have shown the

primary importance of the notion of the person and his relations with society, with the universe, and with the divine. Thus Dogon ontology has opened new vistas for ethnologists . . . More recently . . . the Rev. Fr. Tempels presented an analysis of conception of this kind, and raised the question of whether "Bantu thought should not be regarded as a system of philosophy." (Griaule, 1965:1–2)

Griaule relied totally on an atypical informant—"Ogotemmêli, of Lower Ogol, a hunter who had lost his sight by an accident" and who was "endowed with exceptional intelligence and wisdom." In thirty-three days, Ogotemmêli introduced him to the profound knowledge of Dogon belief and tradition.

Griaule's essay is organized around the informant's interwoven monologues. From creation to the origin of social organizations, the recitation follows two threads: a mythical decoding of the universe in its being and a symbolic interpretation of the foundation of history, culture, and society. The latter, says Griaule, defines "a world system, the knowledge of which will revolutionize all accepted ideas about the mentality of Africans and of primitive peoples in general" (1965:2). The anthropological establishment decided that Griaule was lying. The conversations were a mystification: Dogons, as primitives, could not possibly conceive such a complex structuring of a knowledge which, through myths and rites, unites, orders, and explains astronomical systems, correspondences of worlds, calendrical tables, classifications of beings, and social transformations. Moreover, Griaule's book could not be really accepted: it claims to be a simple report of Ogotommêli's teaching and does not obey the sacred canons of social anthropology. As to the complexity of the "metaphysical" dimension of Ogotemmêli's recitation, Luc de Heusch, a former disciple of Griaule, has recently responded forcefully to those who could not believe that "primitives" were able to manipulate intellectually abstract symbols.

> Many of Griaule's detractors have questioned the interest of the Dogon's intellectual speculations, which seemed to them to be floating in a sociological void. As if lineage, family, existed independently of the system of representations which they arrived at in order to explain existence, as if empirical social reality could be analytically disassociated from the symbolic. It is trivial to object that the thought of the Dogon 'doctors' is not the same as that of ignorant men. In 1948 Griaule already foresaw this argument and answered it forcefully: "One would not undertake to charge the Christian dogma of the transubstantiation with esotericism on the pretext that the man in the street does not know the word and has only glimmerings of the thing itself." . . . Who would dare deny that Christianity . . . has, from its formation and throughout the centuries, established the ultimate reference point of our own social system, beyond the various modes of production which have marked its development. (Heusch, 1984:159)

At any rate, *Conversations with Ogotemmêli* indicates the far-reaching importance of myth in an African setting. The myth is a text that can break down into pieces and reveal human experience and social order. We have known this since Durkheim and Mauss. But it is Lévi-Strauss who has definitely given force to this theory and has thus invalidated the method and conclusions of a great number of inferior works, which in the 1950s were still describing "primitive philosophies" (see bibliographies in *Cahiers des religions africaines,* 1975, no. 9: 17–18), or "ethnophilosophies," as they were then called (see Smet, 1980:161). Holas's and Zahan's sound studies on African spirituality and cosmology are exceptions.

It was in mainstream anthropology that an original reevaluation of "primitive philosophies," took place. The publication in 1954 by D. Forde of a collection of essays on the African world concept was a major event. It brings together some of the most imaginative and perceptive students of Africa: M. Douglas, G. Wagner, M. Griaule, G. Dieterlen, K. Little, J. J. Maquet, K. A. Busia, and P. Mercier, all of whom explore "the significance of cosmological ideas as expressions of moral values in relation to the material conditions of life and the total social order" and, specifically, "show this intricate interdependence between a traditional pattern of livelihood, an accepted configuration of social relations, and dogmas concerning the nature of the world and the place of men within it" (Forde, 1976:x). It has thus become possible to consider myths and rites as guides to comprehending symbolic dimensions as well as mirrors of systems of thought. Publications in this vein include Fortes's *Oedipus and Job in West African Religion* (1959), Fortes and Dieterlen's *African Systems of Thought* (1965), Middleton's *Lugbara Religion: Ritual and Authority Among an East African People* (1960), de Heusch's *Le Symbolisme de l'inceste royal en Afrique* (1958), Holas's *L'Image du monde Bete* (1968), and Turner's *magna opera* (1975, 1981).

Within this new intellectual atmosphere, Leach's statement on the pertinence of myth as sociocultural code makes great sense:

> All stories which occur in the Bible are myths for the devout Christian, whether they correspond to historical fact or not. All human societies have myths in this sense, and normally the myths to which the greatest importance is attached are those which are the least probable. (Leach, 1980:1)

The most prudent (also the most trivial) generalization about African systems of thought might be that myth and society are autonomous but respond to one another. More exactly, the myth signifies human experience to the point that reality loses its meaning without it. It is, for example, a set of myths which gives the Lugbara of the Nile-Congo the history of the shifting connections between the community, its extension, and descendance (Middleton, 1980:47–61). Tiv mythology, on the other hand, fuses with genealogy, defining the overall lineage of human brotherhood and presenting itself as a cosmic order (Bohannan, 1980:315–329). In the Dogon culture also, primary myths express linkages between social organization and the cosmic universe (Heusch, 1985:126–60). Virtually all Dogon cultural signs and social features are related to the *egg of the world* with its seven vibrations and spiral motion (Griaule and Dieterlen, 1976:83–110).

Yet myth, despite its paradoxical forms and sometimes irrational contradictory versions, does not express only the mechanics of a discrete rationality giving an account of analogies, dependences, overlapping or antinomic virtues within the natural, social and cosmic orders. It is not only a collective memory for a community which often relies on *griots* and other specialists in narrating and interpreting its past. One cannot consider it merely a complicated "table of knowledge," maintaining valuable memories, important discoveries, and significant deeds and their interpretations, all handed down by ancestors. If one can look into an African myth or ritual and recognize in it, as in the case of Dogon myth (Heusch, 1985; Griaule, 1965; Dieterlen, 1941), a powerful and amazing organization of classifications, filiations, and their transformations and representations, it would be wrong to limit the meaning of the myth to this function. A careful student can always go beyond the formal systems and unveil other symbolic networks, of which the members of the community might be absolutely unaware (see e.g., Turner, 1969; Heusch, 1982). Myths are autonomous bodies, as L. de Heusch put it in his conclusion to *The Drunken King:*

> They are not the products of labor, and they defy all attempts at appropriation, whether private or collective. No copyright attaches to their telling, retelling, and transformation. They even elude the ideological function that the kings invariably try to force on them. They are borne along by the slack tides of history, but they dance with the rays of the sun and laugh with the rain, knowing no other master than themselves. (Heusch 1982:247)

The history of this new type of scholarship that searches for deep structures is the history of African anthropology in its most inspiring expressions and heresies. Tempels felt it necessary to leave the mainstream of the primitivist tradition. With his *Bantu Philosophy* he wished to counterbalance constructions on "primitive philosophies." Griaule and his fellow workers have followed a similar path. "Dogon ontology" in its elaborate expression became for them a thesis: Dogons "were thought to present one of the best examples of primitive savagery" (Griaule, 1965:1). Yet one of them, Ogotemmêli, reveals "to the European world a cosmogony as such as that of Hesiod . . . and a metaphysic that has the advantage of being expressed in a thousand rites and actions in the life of a multitude of living people" (Griaule, 1965:3). Again one may point to *Einfühlung*. It is interesting to note that D. Forde refers to the impact of this orientation in constructing a framework for his collection of texts on cosmological ideas: Tempels's book is "an arresting essay on the pervasive effects of belief in the permeation of nature by dynamic spiritual forces" and, on the other hand, field research "among some peoples of the Western Sudan, such as the Dogon, Bambara, and Akan" witnesses to "unsuspected complexity and elaboration of cosmological ideas" (1976:ix–x).

I am personally convinced that the most imaginative works that reveal to us what are now called African systems of thought, such as those of Dieterlen, de Heusch, and Turner, can be fundamentally understood through their journey into *Einfühlung*. In the case of African scholars, it often becomes a case, as with Kagame correcting Tempels, of sympathy towards oneself and one's culture.

Kagame and the Ethnophilosophical School

> I should like to reveal this astounding truth to you: not only am I a rational creature, not only does a mind paradoxically inhabit this human body, but I come from a distant planet.
>
> P. BOULLE, *Planet of the Apes*, p. 84.

Kagame explicitly wants to check the validity of Tempels's theory (1956:8) and to correct generalizations and intellectual weaknesses. A philosopher, but also a knowledgeable historian, anthropologist, linguist, and theologian (see Mudimbe, 1982c; Ntezimana and Haberland, 1984), Alexis Kagame received his doctorate in philosophy in 1955 from the Gregorian University in Rome. Member of the Belgian Academy of Overseas Sciences since 1950, university professor, author of some one hundred works, Kagame was from the 1950s onwards one of the most respected and also controversial international symbols of the African intelligentsia. He has profoundly marked the field of African philosophy with two monumental books. His first treatise, *La Philosophie Bantu-Rwandaise de l'être* (1956), deals with the Banyarwanda, a community well-defined by its history, language, and culture. The second, *La Philosophie Bantu comparée* (1976) expands this research to the whole Bantu area. Both works rely heavily on linguistic analyses of Bantu languages. These languages are a subgroup of a larger group, Benue-Congo, which also comprises the Bantoid non-Bantu languages (Nigeria, Cameroon) and Grassfields Bantu (Cameroon, partially in Nigeria). Languages of the Bantu family are spoken in Cameroon, partially in Central African Republic, Kenya and Uganda; completely or predominantly in Gabon, Equatorial Guinea, Congo, Cabinda, Zaïre, Angola, Rwanda, Burundi, Tanzania, Comores, Zambia, Malawi, Mozambique, Swaziland, Lesotho, Botswana, Zimbabwe, South Africa, and Namibia.

For Kagame, to speak of a Bantu philosophy implies above all a consideration of two conditions for its possibility, namely, the linguistic coherence of Bantu languages, which uniformly present language class structures, and the usefulness of a philosophical method inherited from the West (Kagame, 1971:591). According to Kagame, the merit of Tempels's work lies in his making the method available. However, *Bantu Philosophy* should be revised because Tempels was not a scholar. He did not pay attention to Bantu languages, and moreover, his synthesis, based strictly on his experience within the Luba-Shaba community, does not offer a comprehensive understanding of Bantu cultures (Kagame, 1971:592).

Nevertheless, Kagame's formal schema is much the same as Tempels's. It unfolds into the classic chapters of scholastics. What is Kagame's method of analysis and interpretation? He recommends a systematic search for philosophical elements within a specific language, carefully described, and then an extension of the search to include all the Bantu areas and a comparison of philosophical elements among them (Kagame, 1976:7).

> [My method is:] To look for the elements of a Bantu philosophy first within a specific language; to affirm nothing that is not based in an indisputable cultural proof, transcribed in the original language itself and translated literally into the language accessible to the foreign reader. Once in possession of these basic elements, to undertake the study on the scale of the Bantu area, to verify how each zone agrees with or differs with the results initially determined. (Kagame, 1971:592)

The method can be justified. It is quite adequate and perfectly convincing as a preliminary step towards philosophizing. But the difficulty lies in Kagame's claim that the discovery, through an Aristotelian grid, of hitherto unknown elements of Bantu cultures, is a discovery of a collective, deep, implicit philosophy: "A collective system of profound thought, lived rather than deliberated upon, [of which one can] clearly see the superiority over the solitary labor of a licensed thinker amid a literate civilization" (1976:171). According to Kagame, this silent philosophy can be described by means of a rigorous application of five major scholastic grids: formal logic, ontology, theodicy, cosmology, and ethics (1956; 1971).

Formal logic. This is concerned with the notions of idea as it is expressed in a term, of judgement as signified by a proposition, and of reasoning as exercised in a syllogism. Are these notions and relations produced in African "deep" philosophy? Kagame answers yes, noting that:

(a) Bantu distinguish the concrete from the abstract. Concerning the latter, a precondition for philosophizing, they separate the abstract of accidentality (expressing entities which do not exist independently in nature, such as *bu-gabo* [virility, courage, force]) from the abstract of substantiality (expressing entities existing independently in nature, such as *bu-muntu* [humanity]).

(b) The Bantu proposition is organized in agreement with two principles. The enunciation of actors' names is always made at the outset of the discourse. A classificatory relative, that is, a linguistic classifier incorporated into substantives, corresponds to names of each actor and allows a systematic distinction between subjects and complements in the discourse.

(c) The reasoning is elliptic. It may use a premise (major) but more

generally it states a general observation or even a proverb directly leading to a conclusion.

Bantu Criteriology and Ontology. If in general terms Bantu criteriology does not seem to be particular, nor original when compared to other "analogous" cultures (Kagame, 1971:598), the ontology or general metaphysics is well-educated, thanks to linguistic systems of classes.

> When one wishes to reach the essential thinking of the Bantu one considers any sample representing the terms belonging to any *class.* This term represents an idea, designates an object; for instance a shepherd, a child, a robber, etc.; all of these ideas thus represented lead to a unifying notion which is a *human being.* Similarly: a hoe, a spear, a knife, etc.; each one of these objects corresponds to the already unifying notion of *instrument,* surely, but if one goes further, the final unifying notion, beyond which there are no more, is the notion of thing. (Kagame, 1971:598–99)

There are ten classes in Kinyarwanda. But Kagame, and after him Mulago (1965:152–53) and Mujynya (1972:13–14), emphasize that all the categories can be reduced to four basic concepts (see also Jahn, 1961:100): *(a) Muntu* = being of intelligence, corresponds to the Aristotelian notion of *substance; (b) Kintu* = being without intelligence or *thing; (c) Hantu* expresses the *time* and *place* (presents variants such as Pa- in the eastern Bantu languages, Va- in the west and Go- + lo/ro in the south); *(d) Kuntu* indicates the modality and thus centralizes all the notions related to modifications of the being in itself (quantity or quality) or vis-à-vis other beings (relation, position, disposition, possession, action, passion). As such *kuntu* corresponds to seven different Aristotelian categories.

Bantu ontology in its reality and significance expresses itself through the complementarity and connections existing between these four categories, all of them created from the same root, *ntu,* which refers to being but also, simultaneously, to the idea of force. Kagame insists that the Bantu equivalent of *to be* is strictly and only a copula. It does not express the notion of existence and therefore cannot translate the Cartesian *cogito.* It is by enunciating *muntu, kintu,* etc., that I am signifying an essence or something in which the notion of existence is not necessarily present (1971:602).

> When essence *(ntu)* is perfected by the degree of existing, it becomes part of *the existing. The existing* cannot be used as a synonym of *being there,* since in Bantu languages, the verb *to be* cannot signify *to exist.* The opposite of the existing is *nothing.* In analyzing the cultural elements, one must conclude that the *nothing* exists and it is the entity which is at the basis of the *multiple.* One being is distinct from another, because there is the *nothing* between them. (Kagame, 1971:602–603)

Mulago specifies the basic notion of *ntu.* It cannot simply be translated by *being. Ntu* and *being* are not coextensive insofar as the *ntu* categories only subsume created beings and not the original source of *ntu,* that is God: *Imana* in Kinyarwanda and Kirundi, *Nyamuzinda* in Mashi (Mulago, 1965:153; Kagame, 1956:109–10). *Ntu* is the fundamental and referential basic being-force which dynamically manifests itself in all existing beings, differentiating them but also linking them in an ontological hierarchy:

> The being is fundamentally one and all the existing beings are ontologically attached together. Above, transcendant, is God, *Nyamuzinda,* the beginning and end of all being; *Imana,* source of all life, of all happiness. Between God and humans are intermediaries, all the ascendants, the ancestors, the dead members of the family and the old national heroes, all the armies of disencarnated souls. Below humans are all the other beings, who, basically, are only means placed at human's disposition to develop her or his *ntu,* being, life. (Mulago, 1965:155)

In sum, the *ntu* is somehow a sign of a universal similitude. Its presence in beings brings them to life and attests to both their individual value and to the measure of their integration in the dialectic of vital energy. *Ntu* is both a uniting and a differentiating vital norm which explains the powers of vital inequality in terms of difference between beings. It is a sign that God, father of all beings—*ishe w'abantu n'ebintu* (Mulago, 1965:153)—has put a stamp on the universe, thus making it transparent in a hierarchy of sympathy. Upwards, one would read the vitality that, from minerals through vegetables, animals, and humans, links stones to the departed and God. Downwards, it is a genealogical filiation of forms of beings, engendering or relating to one another, all of them witnessing to the original source that made them possible. One recalls Foucault's comment upon the prose of the world in the preclassical age of the West:

> Every resemblance receives a signature; but this signature is no more than an intermediate form of the same resemblance. As a result, the totality of these marks, sliding over the great circle of similitudes, forms a second circle which would be an exact duplication of the first, point by point, were it not for that tiny degree of displacement which causes the sign of sympathy to reside in an analogy, that of analogy in emulation, that of emulation in convenience, which in turn requires the mark of sympathy for its recognition. (1973:29)

We are dealing with an African "implicit philosophy," which, says Lufuluabo, commenting upon the Luba notion of being, is essentially dynamic because the subject lives in accordance to a cosmic dynamism (1964:22). E. N. C. Mujynya, a disciple of both Tempels and Kagame, proposes the significance of this ontological dynamism in four principles (1972:21–22): *(a)* each element in the universe that is each created *ntu* is a force and an active force; *(b)* everything being force, each *ntu* is thus always part of a multitude of other forces, and all of them influence each other; *(c)* every *ntu* can always, under the influence of another *ntu,* increase or decrease in its being; and *(d)* because each created being can weaken inferior beings or can be weakened by superior beings, each *ntu* is always and simultaneously an active and fragile force. From these principles, Mujynya deduces two corollaries: first, only one who is ontologically superior can diminish the vital force of an inferior being; second, whatever action is decided or taken by a being apropos another being modifies the latter by increasing or decreasing his, her, or its vital force. Consequently, one understands why Mulago refers to Bachelard's evaluation of Tempels's *Bantu Philosophy* and writes that it would be better to speak of Bantu *metadynamics* rather than *metaphysics* (Mulago, 1965:155–56).

Theodicy and Cosmology. Although God is the origin and meaning of *ntu,* he is beyond it to the point that, according to Kagame and Mulago, one cannot say that God is an essence (Kagame, 1968:215; 1971:603; Mulago, 1965:152). God is not a *ntu* but a causal and eternal being, who in Kinyarwanda is called the Initial One *(Iya-Kare)* or the Preexisting one *(Iya-mbere),* in Kirundi the efficient Origin *(Rugira),* and in Mashi the Creator *(Lulema).*

> It is therefore improper, in the eyes of 'Bantu' culture to call God the *Supreme Being,* since He does not belong to the category of beings and on the other hand the qualifier *Supreme* places him above beings in the same line of *ntu.* We must call Him the *Preexisting One,* an attribute that fits the Existing Eternal. (Kagame, 1971:603)

Referring to his native Luba language and carefully reviewing Kagame's documentation, Tshiamalenga strongly opposes this interpretation. God is essence. He is *ntu,* even a *muntu;* and, in the same vein, the human being is, within the dialectic of vital forces, a thing, a *kintu.* In effect, Tshiamalenga believes that Kagame and his followers, namely, Mulago and Mujynya, are wrong because they forget that prefixing classifiers are formal and arbitrary, and are used to classify and distinguish the status of substantives, not that of ontological entities (Tshiamalenga, 1973).

As to Bantu *cosmology,* according to Kagame, it is based on an implicit metaphysic principle: every body, every extension has a limit; differently stated, an unlimited extension is impossible (Kagame, 1971:606). It follows that the Bantu *Weltanschauung* distinguishes three circular and communicating worlds: the earth, center of the universe because it is the home of *muntu,* master of all existing *ntu;* above, beyond the sky, the circle of life in which God dwells; and under our earth the world in which the departed dwell (see also, e.g., Van Caeneghem, 1956; Mbiti, 1971; Bamuinikile, 1971).

Rational Psychology and Ethics. In terms of psychology, the reference here is the human being as distinct from the animal. Both are living beings, have senses and the capacity of motion. Both are marked by similar patterns in terms of birth and death. It is, however, in their passing away that a major difference can be observed. The animal's vital force or shadow completely disappears. In the case of a human being, although shadow usually vanishes, the principle of intelligence which characterizes him as human being remains, becomes the *muzimu* (*modimo, motimo,* etc.), and joins the subterranean universe. On the other hand, as long as they are alive, animals and human beings are viewed analogically as having two senses (hearing and sight) in common rather than the five senses attributed by classical Western philosophy. The other three senses are obviously experienced, but according to Kagame, the knowledge they bring is integrated into the sense of hearing (Kagame, 1956:186).

In terms of ethics, Bantu philosophy can be reduced to two essential principles.

(a) The first rule of *action* and *utilization* is based on the internal finality of the human being. Kagame notes that if one looks at the vital principle of a human being, one perceives that it is a two-pointed arrow: at one end is the faculty of knowing (intelligence) and at the other that of loving (will). Classical philosophy has put the emphasis on the first: we have *"to know* beings surrounding us in order to discern what is good and what is not good for us. We have *to love* who and what is good and avoid what is bad for us. At a second step we have *to know and love* the *Preexisting One* who made possible these beings so we can know and love them" (Kagame, 1971:608). Bantu philosophy, on the contrary, would emphasize the other point: loving, and thus procreating, perpetuating the lineage and the community of human beings. By doing this it affirms a paradigm: the vital force is immortal.

(b) The second rule is related to the preceding one. The Bantu community defines itself through blood filiation. The community stands and understands itself as a natural and social body and infers from the authority of its being and its history the laws and mechanisms for territorial occupation, political institutions, customs, and rites. The most striking and important aspect is that the Bantu community has developed two radically opposed but complementary types of laws. First, there are juridical laws that the society controls through its judges and lawyers. They do not bind individual consciences, and whoever can escape them is considered intelligent. Second, there are taboo-laws, principally of a religious nature: these are generally negative and clearly specify what should be avoided. They contain in themselves an immanent power of sanction, and God is the sole judge. Therefore, whatever the transgression, no human being—not even chief, priest, or king—can sanction or forgive the taboo-sin. The problem and its resolution lie between the transgressor and God, and also between his or her still-existing family on earth and the departed ancestors.

Kagame's views may seem controversial. They are, however, deductions of a truly impressive and well grounded linguistic analysis. No one can seriously question his talent in handling, for example, grammatical overviews of Bantu languages. Nevertheless, many points are questionable, such as the geographical extension and the meaning of the category *hantu,* or the contiguity he establishes between terms and concepts, as if the relationships existing between signifiers and signifieds were not arbitrary. At any rate, with

Kagame's work, Bantu philosophy escapes Tempels's unsupported generalizations: it is now founded on a linguistic order. A second feature marks the rupture between Tempels and Kagame. Tempels spoke of Bantu philosophy as an intellectual and dynamic system which, although implicit, exists as an organized and rational construction awaiting a competent reader or translator. Kagame is more prudent. He claims that every language and culture is sustained by a deep and discrete order. Yet he insists that his work unveils not a systematic philosophy but an intuitive organization justified by the presence of precise philosophical principles. Moreover, this organization is neither static nor permanent, as indicated by changes in present-day mentalities (1956:27). Despite the evidence of its cultural roots (1976:117, 225), it should not be reduced to an absolute alterity. The third distinction is that for Kagame it would be nonsense to proclaim an absolute otherness since such important notions as *idea, reasoning,* and *proposition* cannot be thought of as offering a Bantu particularity. In the same vein, formal logic as such does not present a definite linguistic character (1956:38–40), and insofar as criteriology and the properties of intelligence are concerned, the problems of the former are *co-naturels* to all human beings (1976:105) and those of the latter depend on philosophy as a universal discipline (1976:241). There is thus a clear universalist dimension in Kagame's philosophy. The fourth and last major point distinguishing Kagame from Tempels concerns Bantu philosophy as a collectively assumed system. For the Belgian Franciscan, this philosophy is a silent domain which has been functioning for centuries, perhaps in a sort of "frozen dynamism." Kagame, on the contrary, names the founding thinkers of a system that for him is in its being a formulation of a cultural experience and its historical transformations (1976:193, 305). These thinkers are the historical fathers of the Bantu cultures (1976:193, 238), the creators of our languages (1976:83) and the first Bantu humans (1976:76).

These four differences about Bantu philosophy—the method for revealing it, whether Bantu philosophy is a systematic or an intuitive philosophy, whether it is a strictly regional or a universalist-oriented system, and whether it is a collective philosophy with or without authors—indicate a clear discontinuity from Tempels to Kagame. Yet elements of continuity exist in both the fluctuation that these differences imply and in the objectives of Bantu philosophy itself. For Tempels, as well as for Kagame and his followers, the affirmation and promotion of African philosophy meant a claim to an original alterity. Their argument, in its demonstration, runs parallel to primitivist theories on African backwardness and savagery. If there is a dividing line between the two, it is a blurred one established primarily as a signifier of sympathy or antipathy. Tempels exploited visible signs of Bantu behavior in the name of Christian brotherhood. Kagame and most of his disciples implicitly or explicitly refer to a racial duty (Kagame, 1956:8) and stress the right to demand "an anthropological dignity" and "the assessment of an intellectual independence" (N'Daw, 1966:33). Once this difference is established, one can note the link from Tempels to Kagame and other "ethnophilosophers." It is a body of judgments stemming from their analyses and interpretation of African cultures and can be summed up in three propositions: (1) a good application of classical philosophical grids demonstrates beyond doubt that there is an African philosophy which, as a deep system, underlies and sustains African cultures and civilizations; (2) African philosophy is fundamentally an ontology organized as a deployment of interacting but hierarchically ordered forces; (3) Human vital unity appears to be the center of the endless dialectic of forces which collectively determine their being in relation to human existence (Eboussi-Boulaga, 1968:23–26; Hountondji, 1977; Tshiamalenga, 1981:178).

These principles sanction the domain of ethnophilosophy, whose geography is characterized by two features. The first is a break with the ideology inherent in the anthropologist's techniques of describing African *Weltanschauungen*. The second is a paradoxical claim according to which a satisfactory Western methodological grid is a requirement for reading and revealing a deep philosophy through an analysis and an interpretation of linguistic structures or anthropological patterns. So far, it has been possible to distinguish two principal orientations within this field: the first interrogates and explores the so-called silent philosophy (e.g., A. Makarakiza, 1959; F. Ablegmagnon, 1960; W. Abraham, 1966; Lufuluabo, 1962, 1964b; N'Daw, 1966; J. C. Bahoken, 1967; J. Jahn, 1961; Mujynya, 1972; Onyewueni, 1982). The second orientation studies this philosophy with respect to the value of those elements which could be used for the Africanization of Christianity (e.g., Gravrand, 1962; Taylor, 1963; Mulago, 1965; Lufuluabo, 1964a, 1966; Nothomb, 1965; Mubengayi, 1966; Mpongo, 1968). J. Mbiti's methodology in *New Testament Eschatology in an African Background* (1971) is a good example of this second orientation. In order to look "at the encounter between Christianity and African traditional concepts" in the Akamba setting (1971:1), he distinguishes three steps: first, the presentation and semantic analysis of Akamba concepts, which can be considered to be related to eschatology (e.g., *fire, treasure, pain, tears, heaven*); second, the presentation and theological interpretation of Christian eschatological concepts; and third, the establishing of a table of conceptual correspondences and differences, and from it deriving norms for "acclimatizing" Christianity.

One might also add a third ethnophilosophical trend. It comprises a variety of racially and culturally oriented enterprises, some of which arose independently of the thesis of an African ontology. Without any doubt they participate in the ideological climate of negritude and intellectual policies for otherness. On the other hand, they fit in the space occupied by ethnophilosophical projects with which they have been interacting strongly, particularly since the 1950s. These enterprises can be grouped under three entries: *(a)* the approach to traditional "humanisms" which in its standard forms leads to esoteric teachings (e.g., Ba and Cardaire, 1957; Ba and

Dieterlen, 1961; Fu-Kiau, 1969; Fourche and Morlighem, 1973: Zahan, 1979) and, sometimes, to a basic interpretation of the tradition from within (e.g., Ba, 1972, 1976); *(b)* the critical valorization of traditional elements as weapons for a radical criticism (e.g., Kalanda, 1967) and a reflection on present-day African modernity and its contradictions (e.g., Hama, 1972b; Dia, 1975; 1977–1981); *(c)* an exploitation of the tradition as a repository of signs and meanings of African authenticity. In its political application it has led, at least in one case, to a notorious mystification, the Zaïrian policy of "authenticity" and its dubious philosophical foundations (see, e.g., Kangafu, 1973; Mbuze, 1974, 1977).

In its conscious and erudite expressions, the search for an African authenticity raises the most fundamental questions of black identity. Césaire, for example, refers to the order of authenticity in his *Discourse on Colonialism* (1972), as well as in his explanations for leaving the French Communist Party (Césaire, 1956). A. Diop warmly acclaims Tempels's book as a tool for the possible emergence of authenticity. Recently, in a polemic article against African academic philosophy, Hebga has emphasized the demands of authenticity as imperative for cultural uniqueness (1982:38–39). Finally, it is on this very notion of authenticity that Eboussi-Boulaga established his *La Crise du Muntu: Authenticité africaine et philosophie* (1977), unfolding a problem of origin: what is an African and how does one speak of him or her and for what purpose? Where and how can one gain the knowledge of his or her being? How does one define this very being, and to what authority does one turn for possible answers? It is obvious that the significance of these questions has nothing to do with ethnophilosophy, nor with a cheap, easy exploitation of the notion of authenticity in the sense in which the Zaïrian government used it in the early 1970s. In effect, these questions originate elsewhere. They are ones I consider marked by the demands of a critical philosophy.

Aspects of African Philosophy

> You're right, Jinn. That's what I think . . .
> Rational men? Men endowed with a mind?
> Men inspired by intelligence? No, that's not
> possible.
>
> P. BOULLE, *Planet of the Apes.*

What are the major aspects of present-day African philosophy? Though we are now beyond Tempels's revolution, his ghost is still present. Implicitly or explicitly, the most inspiring trends in the field still define themselves with respect to Tempels. An African Jesuit priest, well-read in philosophy, has recently written that those scholars presently opposing Tempels and belittling the work of his followers by calling it pejoratively *ethnophilosophy* are simply ungrateful to someone who made possible their philosophizing (Hebga, 1982). In fact, this statement indicates a post-Tempels climate and a reorganization of the field, which today reveals a plurality of trends (Sodipo, 1975; Maurier, 1976; Tshiamalenga, 1981). It is possible to distinguish three main approaches in this new era. The first is the philosophical critique of ethnophilosophy, which springs mainly from an academic lecture on the conditions for the existence of a Bantu philosophy, given by F. Crahay in 1965 at the Kinshasa Goethe Institute. With his lecture, Crahay immediately imposed a new orthodoxy in the field. The second is the "foundational" trend, which since the 1960s, deliberately and in a hypercritical way, interrogates both the bases and representations of social and human sciences in order to elucidate epistemological conditions, ideological frontiers, and procedures for the practice of philosophy. The third approach is that of philological studies, critical anthropology, and hermeneutics, which indicate avenues to new praxes on African cultures and languages.

A Critique of Ethnophilosophy

The philosophical critique of ethnophilosophy is not the reverse of Tempels and Kagame's school. It is a policy discourse on philosophy aimed at examining methods and requirements for practicing philosophy in Africa. As a trend, it derives its conviction from its status as a discourse which is firmly linked to both the Western tradition of philosophy as a discipline and the academic structures which guarantee institutionally accepted philosophical practices. As such, the critique of ethnophilosophy can be understood as subsuming two main genres: on the one hand, a reflection on the methodological limits of Tempels and Kagame's school and, on the other hand (at the other pole of what ethnophilosophical exercises represent), African practices and works bearing on Western subjects and topics in the most classical tradition of philosophy.

As we have seen, until the 1960s anthropologists, European missionaries, and some African clergymen were the only ones proposing directions in the field of "African philosophy." Vaguely defined, this term conveys the meaning of *Weltanschauung*, and more generally, that of practical and traditional wisdom, rather than that of a systematically explicit and critical system of thought (Smet, 1980:97–108). A certain amount of confusion exists insofar as most hypotheses reflect, as in the case of Radin's *Primitive Man as a Philosopher* (1927), the authority of ethnographic description. Some syntheses, such as those of Frobenius (1893) and Delafosse (1922, 1927), and even Tempels (1959), Griaule (1965), and Kagame (1956, 1976), draw their textual necessity from an interpretation of patterns opposing or integrating nature and culture in order to illuminate or negate the existence of a regional rationality. Another element of confusion is, despite the recantation in *Les Carnets de Lucien Lévy-Bruhl* (1949), the pervasiveness of Lévy-Bruhl's thesis on prelogism. For a long time it was kept alive by anthropologists, colonialists, and missionaries through such notions as collective consciousness in fragmentary societies, peoples still experiencing the simplicity of the state of nature, childish Blacks incapable of managing their lives and affairs rationally, and above all, the civilizing mission themes and the policies of Christian *conversio gentium* (Lyons, 1975:123–63; Tempels, 1959:26–29; Taylor, 1963:26–27; Onyanwu, 1975:151).

Within this context, the very notion of African philosophy as used by Tempels and his first disciples seemed absurd from a technical viewpoint. Considered as a key for entrance into "native" systems and ways of life in the sense proposed by Tempels, it is generally accepted as useful. However, since 1945, some professionals have feared that it could lead to intellectual heresies, because it promotes possibilities of ambiguous commentaries on "primitive" rationality (Boelaert, 1946:90). Furthermore, it clearly seems to connote an intellectual process of manipulating African experience and traditions (Sousberghe, 1951:825).

These are some of the main questions that F. Crahay addressed in his famous speech of March 19, 1965 to Kinshasa's intelligentsia. The lecture was eventually published in *Diogenes* under the title, "Le 'Décollage' conceptuel: Conditions d'une philosophie bantoue" (1965). A former student of classics, philosophy, and psychophysiology at the universities of Louvain, Paris, and Liège where he received a doctorate in philosophy in 1954, Crahay taught logic and modern European philosophy in the 1960s at Lovanium University, a Catholic institution in Kinshasa. He had no interest in opposing Tempels's double project of guiding colonizers towards an "African soul" and stimulating original ethnographic studies. He respected the project in its practicality and intent.

> Considering this book for what is meant to be its principal objective, a kind of guide to the Bantu soul, one should limit oneself to reproaching its title without insisting too much upon it. Considering what it intended to be in addition, an incentive for systematic study in the direction indicated, one would be acting in bad faith if one took it to task for being incomplete, too general, and questionable concerning several points of detail. Through the double purpose of the book one cannot fail praising the active sympathy it reveals. (Crahay, 1965:61–62)

Crahay's intervention is a philsophical lesson which claims only to clarify the confusion surrounding the very notion of "Bantu philosophy" by evaluating Tempels's book and determining the conditions of possibility for a rigorous Bantu philosophy. He does not question the pertinence nor the usefulness of Tempels's description of a Bantu *Weltanschauung* centered on the idea of vital force, but rather studies three weaknesses of the enterprise: the title of the book, which is based on an intellectual confusion of *vécu* (lived) and *réflexif* (reflective), and of the vulgar meaning of philosophy and its strict sense; the confusing of these differences throughout the book, even when

Tempels is dealing with such specific notions as metaphysics, ontology, and psychology; and the vagueness of Tempels's philosophical terminology, leading the reader to doubt the validity of a great number of his statements (Crahay, 1965:63).

To delineate the boundaries of a proper discussion, Crahay proposes a definition of philosophy. Philosophy is a reflection presenting precise characteristics: it is "explicit, analytical, radically critical and autocritical, systematic at least in principle and nevertheless open, bearing on experience, its human conditions, significations as well as the values that it reveals" (1965:63). In a negative way, what is implied by this understanding of the discipline is that there is neither an implicit philosophy, nor an intuitive one, nor an immediate one. Philosophical language is not a language *of* experience but a language *about* experience. Given these premises, what Tempels provided is not, strictly speaking, a philosophy. Insofar as his language witnesses to and comments upon experience, it only signifies the possibility of a philosophical reflection and is at best a rationalization of a *Weltanschauung:*

> A *vision of the world,* insofar as it expresses itself, we can say is a language *of* life, language of experience (anchored in a certain experience), language of living and acting, poetic or not, and in any case filled with symbols; a vision of the world that is immediate language, not critical; and nothing prevents it from being rhapsodic and, up to a certain point, irrational. (Crahay, 1965:64–65)

The problem Tempels and his disciples pose is a methodological one: the confusion in which they indulge themselves by not distinguishing between a "vision of the world," its reflexive potentialities, and the philosophical practice which can work on them. Crahay does not hesitate to state that unless one seeks to mystify people there is to date no such a thing as an African philosophy:

> Let us speak frankly: if we do not want to compromise the very project of philosophy in Africa, confusing the technical use of this term with its vulgar use, and reduce philosophy to a simple vision of the world, we must say that until the present there has not been a Bantu philosophy. What exists surely, is a cohesive and original view of the world particular to Bantus, a kernel of wisdom. Given an ensemble of favorable circumstances, it could have brought about earlier a real philosophy. (Crahay, 1965:68)

Philosophy as an intellectual practice is different in kind from *Weltanschauung* and from ethnographic descriptions paraphrasing a tradition, its wisdom and its linguistic richness.

Yet philosophy concerns the experience of humans, although it cannot be assimilated to it; philosophy bears on experience, reflects it without being congruent with it. For the promotion of philosophy in Africa, Crahay suggests five conditions determining the possibility of a conceptual dé-

collage. These are: *(a)* the existence of a body of African philosophers living and working in an intellectually stimulating cultural milieu resolutely open to the world; *(b)* a good and critical use of external philosophical "reflectors," which through the patience of discipline, would promote in Africa a cross-cultural thought (as with Aristotle's system, which had been inherited and reworked by medieval Arabs before passing as a legacy into the hands of European scholastics); *(c)* a selective and flexible inventory of African values—be they attitudes, categories or symbols—which would possibly *donner à penser* (provoke thought) in the sense proposed by P. Ricoeur's hermeneutics (which would allow for ventures in Africa similar to Spinoza's rebuilding of a moral and political philosophy based on a critical reading of the Jewish tradition); *(d)* a clear dissociation of reflexive consciousness from mythical consciousness which would imply, and in any case, amplify major contrasts (subject versus object, I versus the Other, nature versus supernature, sensible versus metaphysical, etc.); *(e)* an examination of African intellectuals' main temptations—choices of philosophical systems apparently in accordance with African urgent needs (as in the case of Marxism and a pervasive cult of alterity which, despite its respectable objectives, might become an end in itself). In sum, Crahay's critique grants philosophy its privilege within a tradition. One could debate the validity of the definition and thus question the validity of the implications offered as conditions for the possibility of a future Bantu philosophy (see Tshiamalenga, 1977a). The real response to Crahay's lesson on philosophy is to be seen in the debate it has initiated. In any case, the formulated dichotomy establishing the opposition between philosophy and "unphilosophy" as a preliminary and necessary condition of philosophizing coincides with a historical mutation in the brief history of African philosophy (Ruch, 1974; Maurier, 1976; Tshiamalenga, 1977a and 1981; Yai, 1977). Three African philosophers—F. Eboussi-Boulaga (Cameroon), M. Towa (Cameroon) and P. Hountondji (Benin)—take on the task of completing the transformation by directing the debate towards two main issues: how and why the very question about the possibility of an African philosophy can be justified. What exactly can and cannot philosophy allow?

Eboussi-Boulaga, in a text (1968) that did not please *Présence Africaine's* editorial committee (see editor's note in Eboussi-Boulaga's "Le Bantou Problématique," 1968:4–40), dwells on "Bantu philosophy." He first comments upon the shortcomings of Tempels's method, which occur because the method does not face the problem of its own origin. It does not ask how anthropology can be a source of, or a basis for philosophy, and it defines itself as a technique for transcribing values and expressing what is fundamentally unutterable (Eboussi-Boulaga, 1968:9–10). Second, Eboussi-Boulaga elaborates on an analysis of Tempels's work, focusing on the ambiguity of the ontological hypothesis, which he thinks ultimately reduces the *Muntu* to the primitiveness of an amoral and absolutely determining order of forces (1968:19–20). Finally, Eboussi-Boulaga presents the sociohistorical contradictions of Tempels's treatise, repeating Césaire's radical question (Césaire, 1972:37–39): why was this book possible and how are we to interpret the structural similarity between the simulacrum of an ontological hierarchy and the socioeconomic hierarchy existing in the colonial experience? (Eboussi-Boulaga, 1968:24–25). Towa, in two complementary booklets (1971a and 1971b), through a general evaluation of the works of Tempels (1959), Kagame (1956), N'Daw (1966), and Fouda (1967) links the critique of ethnophilosophy to negritude's political ambivalence (Towa, 1971b:24–25). According to him, the only results of the ethnophilosophical trend are two controversial achievements: first, a dubious terminological distinction between European and African products within an ambiguously enlarged domain of philosophy; second, a confusion between anthropological structuring of beliefs, myths, and rites on the one hand, and metaphysics on the other. As such, ethnophilosophy should be considered an ideology whose methodology betrays both philosophy and anthropology:

> What ethnophilosophy praises in the past is not necessarily given by the analysis of the past. Retrojection is the method by which ethnophilosophy alters and disfigures traditional reality by secretly introducing at the descriptive onset present-day values and ideas which can be considered completely alien to Africa, rediscovering them in a militant profession of faith, "authenticated in terms of their so-called Africanity." (Towa, 1971b:32)

The second phase of the philosophical critique of ethnophilosophy begins with Hountondji's militant articles, which have made the debate an international one. His articles appear in a great variety of professional publications from the 1970s onwards: *Présence Africaine* (Paris, 1967, 61), *African Humanism–Scandinavian Culture: A Dialogue* (Copenhagen, 1970), *Etudes philosophiques* (Paris, 1970, 1), *Diogène* (Paris, 1970, 71; 1973, 84), *La Philosophie contemporaine* (Florence, 1971, vol. IV, R. Klibansky ed.), *Cahiers philosophiques africains* (Lubumbashi, 1972, 1; 1974, 3–4), *Conséquence* (Cotonou, 1974, 1), etc. He eventually collected some of them into a book, *Sur la philosophie africaine* (1977; English version, 1983), which since its publication has become the bible of anti-ethnophilosophers. Hountondji's great intellectual authority, at least in French-speaking countries, springs from several factors. First, he is a former student of the Ecole Normale Supérieure of the rue d'ulm in Paris, one of the most select and prestigious schools in the world. In philosophy, it has produced some of the most renowned modern thinkers: Merleau-Ponty, Sartre, Aron, Althusser, figures who have influenced or revolutionized the field. Second, his *agrégation de philosophie* gives him an indubitable prestige. Finally, one must consider that Hountondji's academic career in Benin, West Germany, France, and Zaïre, as well as his responsibilities in international philosophical institutions, have greatly promoted the dissemination of his ideas. Nevertheless, it is only fair to say that the brilliance of his texts, the soundness of his reasoning, and the pertinence of his arguments probably constitute the real factors in the success of his critique of ethnophilosophy.

Hountondji's position can be described in the following manner: on the one hand, he gives two main reasons for the rejection of ethnophilosophy; on the other, two other reasons for a critique and an amelioration of Crahay's lesson. Let us look at the first set. *(a)* In Hountondji's view, ethnophilosophy is an imaginary, intoxicating interpretation, which is never supported by any textual authority and depends totally on the interpreter's whims. It claims to translate a non-existent cultural text and ignores its own creative activity and therefore its own liberty. Consequently, one can say that the ethno-philosophical imagination a priori prevents itself from attaining any truth, since truth presupposes that liberty relies upon an unimaginary order and is conscious of both the evidence of a positive order and its own space of creativity. *(b)* If Western establishments have valorized ethnophilosophy, it is due to an ethnocentric bias. When, for instance, such notables as G. Bachelard, A. Camus, L. Lavelle, J. Wahl, J. Howlett, or G. Marcel readily acclaim *Bantu Philosophy* (see *Présence Africaine*, 1949, no. 7), it means that because of present-day international standards, they would accept anything (Hountondji, 1970), provided that it offers a sympathetic view of Africans. They do so even if it means entirely contradicting the theoretical implications of their own philosophical practice.

As to Hountondji's two-pronged critique of Crahay's lesson, it bears on the notion of conceptual *décollage* and on the destination of philosophical discourse. *(a)* For Hountondji, the notion of a conceptual take-off does not make sense as a general condition of existence of an African philosophy. He states that in all civilizations a conceptual take-off is always already accomplished even when human actors use or integrate mythical sequences into their discourse. By virtue of this characteristic, one could compare Parmenides's discourse to those of Confucius, Plato, Hegel, Nietzsche, or Kagame. *(b)* Hountondji believes that Crahay completely missed a major point: the destination of discourse. He rightly insists that, be it mythical or ideological, language evolves in a social environment, developing its own history and the possibility of its own philosophy (Hountondji, 1970 and 1983).

From this viewpoint, Hountondji argues that Mulago, Kagame, and most ethnophilosophers are certainly philosophers insofar as they can recognize that their own texts are philosophical, but they are totally wrong when they claim that they are restoring an African traditional philosophy.

We have produced a radically new definition of African philosophy, the criterion being the geographical origin of the authors rather than an alleged specificity of content. The effect of this is to broaden the narrow horizon which has hitherto been imposed on African philosophy and to treat it, as now conceived, as a methodical inquiry with the same universal aims as those of any other philosophy in the world. (Hountondji, 1983:66)

Hountondji's critique displays the superiority of a critical conception of philosophy. A disciple of Canguilhem and Althusser, Hountondji looks at African philosophical practices from a strictly normative viewpoint. But his philosophy seems to imply a thesis which is controversial to many: that, until now, Africa has not been philosophizing and that in her past there is nothing which might reasonably be called philosophical (Koffi, 1976; Yai, 1977; Tshiamalenga, 1977a, Laleye, 1982). It is important to note that for Hountondji, philosophy must be understood as metaphilosophy, that is, as "a philosophical reflection on discourse which [is itself] overtly and consciously philosophical."

Hountondji's texts prompted a lively debate throughout Africa on the definition of African philosophy. Generally stimulating (Ruch, 1974; Odera, 1972; Sumner, 1980), sometimes a bit too raucous (Yai, 1977; Koffi, 1977), criticisms of Towa's and Hountondji's positions focus on three main problems. The first is the validity and meaning of the question: is there an African philosophy? To this Yai responds with another question: "What is the source of this inquiry? Who, at times such as these, arrogates the right to put a question that can be innocent only in appearance?" (1977:6). The second problem concerns Hountondji's reduction of philosophy to a body of texts explicitly self-defined as philosophical in nature. The last concerns the necessary relationship between the emergence of individual philosophers and the existence of philosophy. There emerge two strong reproaches against Towa and Hountondji, but in a special way against the latter: elitism and Western dependency. It is almost a war against all African intellectuals "admitted by the conclave of the sacred collège of agrégés and doctors of philosophy" (Koffi and Abdou, 1980). According to Yai, the advocates of what he qualifies as speculative philosophy are "Young Turks who have several points in common with the Young Hegelians castigated by Marx in The German Ideology" who "find in all discussions prior to their own, nothing but mythologies" (1977:4). It is an "elite by definition" that has become "the elite of elite, a pedestal from which they are very careful not to climb down for a purpose so humble as empirical research among the masses" (1977:16). At any rate, according to Koffi and Abdou, this elite represents neocolonialism (1980:192).

In a special issue of Recherches philosophiques Africaines (1977, 1) devoted to African philosophy, members of the philosophy department of the Faculté de Théologie Catholique in Kinshasa—Tshiamalenga, Smet, and Elungu—achieved in an elegant way a provisional but organic compromise between Tempels's legacy and critical demands for the practice of African philosophy. Tshiamalenga, for example, agrees with Crahay and Hountondji on the methodological mistakes of ethnophilosophy, particularly on the absurdity of speaking of an implicit collective philosophy. On the other hand, he points out the idealizing nature of Crahay's, Towa's and Hountondji's understanding of philosophy, which as given, even within the Western philosophical experience, does not really correspond to any historically attested practice (1977a). From those positions, Tshiamalenga distinguishes two domains within African philosophy. One is that of *Negro-African traditional philosophy* constituted by explicit *énoncés* (statements and propositions) from the oral tradition pertaining to the nature of human society, the meaning of life, death, and the hereafter (cosmological and religious myths, didactic proverbs, maxims, apothegms, etc.) The other is that of contemporary African philosophy, that is, the totality of signed texts on similar subjects using a critical interpretation of the traditional philosophy or springing from reflection on the contemporary condition of the African (Tshiamalenga, 1977a:46). In the same issue, Smet dissolves the methodological and ideological oppositions between ethnophilosphers and their critics in terms of a diachronic complementarity of schools (1977a; see also, Elungu, 1978). One year later, Elungu made Smet's proposition more explicit by carefully specifying three historical trends: the first two are an anthropological philosophy or ethnophilosophy and an ideological philosophy or political philosophy—two currents that, in a mythical or nationalist way, contributed to the promotion of African dignity and political independence. More recently has emerged a post-independence trend: the critical one, which with Crahay, Hountondji and others demands a rigorous reflection on the conditions of philosophy as well as on the conditions of existing individuals and societies (Elungu, 1978).

Foundations

At the other extreme from ethnophilosophy and its critics, one finds works that have neither the form of anthropological exegeses nor the fashionable anti-ethnophilosophical vocabulary. They not only fit faithfully into the mainstream of the *philosophia perennis* but sometimes indeed deal with specifically Western topics. Many of the advanced degrees awarded in European universities to young African scholars attest to this trend. These scholars single out the universal historicity of a method. One can begin by referring to applied philosophy, as illustrated by Aguolu's study on "John Dewey's Democratic Conception and Its Implication for Developing Countries" (Aguolu, 1975) and more recently by Hallen and Sodipo's book on *Knowledge, Belief and Witchcraft* (1986). We shall refer as well to the best papers, published annually by the department of philosophy of the Faculté de Théologie Catholique in Kinshasa. (They are among those whose major references accidentally coincide with the Franco-Belgian orthodoxy in philosophy.) We shall also refer to Wiredu's very British *Philosophy and an African Culture* (1980), which among other things "teaches" us that "it is a fact that Africa lags behind the West in the cultivation of rational inquiry" (1980:43) and indicates that "the ideal way to reform backward customs in Africa must, surely, be to undermine their foundation in superstition by fostering in the people . . . the spirit of rational inquiry in all spheres of thought and belief" (1980:45).

There are in this special area quite orthodox and apparently purely speculative undertakings but also some intellectual surprises. Bodunrin's essay on "The Alogicality of Immortality" (1975b) and Wiredu's "Logic and Ontology" (1973) are exemplary. In terms of voluminous contributions I may suggest three models: Elungu's systematic study on the concept of extent in Malebranche's thought (1973b), Ugirashebuja's book on dialogue and poetry according to Heidegger (1977), and Ngindu's research on the philosophical problem of religious knowledge in Laberthonnière's thinking (1978). How can these choices of subject be justified? It is difficult to read authors' minds. The social and intellectual context in which these philosophers developed might account for their choices, just as it would for such notorious eighteenth-century cases as the African A. G. Amo's intellectual career in what was not yet Germany and his works *De Humana Mentis Apatheia* (1734), *Tractatus de Arte Sobrie et Accurate Philosophandi* (1738), and the lost *De Jure Maurorum in Europa* (1729). Another case, this one scandalous, was that of Jacobus Capitein, an African who wrote and publicly presented a study at Leiden University in the Netherlands on the nonexistent opposition between slavery and Christian freedom: *De Servitude, Libertati Christianae non Contraria* (1742). At any rate, our contemporary students of *philosophia perennis* may also be troubling. One is surely taken aback when, in examining these very classical analyses, one comes across presuppositions on African otherness in the guise of logical deduction. For example, it is a surprise to follow Ugirashebuja discovering in Heidegger's writing Banyarwanda's language as a sign of being and its nomination, and to discover in the Rwandese philosopher's text the voice of Heidegger inviting all of us—Westerners, Africans, Asians—to listen to being in our respective languages (see Ugirashebuja, 1977:227; Dirven, 1978:101–6). In the same vein, Ngindu, in a sophisticated introduction to the *fin de siècle* modernist crisis within the Roman Catholic European circles of philosophy, digs up reasons for commenting on cultural imperialism in Africa and its epistemological force of reduction (Ngindu, 1978:19).

In this philosophical practice, which is completely foreign to African culture, or at best, a marginal but powerful space in which only ways of domesticating the African experience are elaborated, slips of the pen sometimes occur and murmurs are heard which resemble ethno-philosophical dreams. On the other hand, as the School of Kinshasa has demonstrated, it is not at all certain that Hountondji and his fellow anti-ethnophilosophers are neocolonialist devils preventing people from affirming their otherness. Strangely enough, his responses to criticisms (Hountondji, 1980; 1981; 1982), reflect a well-balanced philosophical and nationalist imagination: "as Gramsci rightly used to say, only truth is revolutionary" (1982:67).

Both the ethnophilosophical trend and the critical school agree on their position about the existence of philosophy as an autocritical exercise and a critical discipline in Africa. Viewed in terms of its organic expression, this practice can be described from at least four different angles: the Ethiopian heritage, the solidity of an empiricist tradition in English-speaking countries, the debate about the epistemological foundation of an African discourse in social and human sciences, and Marxist universalism.

My brief presentation of Sumner's editions of Ethiopian texts (see appendix) shows the particular situation of the Ethiopian tradition, whose Christianity goes back as far as the fourth century. Since that time, monks and scholars have been at work on intellectual arguments, theological and political commentaries, and translations. Through the ages, a philosophy took shape. According to Sumner, *The Book of the Wise Philosophers* (see Sumner, 1974) and *The Treatise of Zär'a Yacob* (Sumner, 1978) are good examples. The first "presents itself as the quintessence of what various philosophers have said on a certain number of topics, most of which are ethical" (Sumner, 1974:100). Thus philosophy, *fälasfa*, is understood as being principally a wisdom, which includes both a knowledge of the universe and mankind's purpose in life. Adapted maxims from the Greek, Egyptian, and Arabic as well as maxims from Ethiopian tradition (as in the case of many numerical proverbs) guide the listener or the reader on topics such as matter, human physiology and psychology, man's social dimension, and moral concerns (Sumner, 1974). *The Treatise of Zär'a Yacob* also presents propositions on moral issues (Sumner, 1983) and guidance about knowledge. Yet it is a unique and important sign which suggests a critical outlook in the seventeenth-century Ethiopian culture, to the point that A. Baumstark has compared it to "the *Confessions* of a fellow African, St. Augustine" (in Sumner, 1978:5). The method of Zär'a Yacob is definitely new: it posits the light of reason as a "discriminating criterion between what is of God and what is of men" and can be compared to Descartes's clear idea (1978:70–71).

Another side of the foundation of African philosophical practice is the viability of the empiricist method in Anglophone countries. Their universities and philosophy departments are generally older. Van Parys, after a visit to twenty African countries having university departments of philosophy, noted in his evaluative synthesis that in Anglophone countries they were better organized and appeared more solid in their already tested traditions. (Van Parys, 1981:386). More directly, the quality of the biannual journal *Second Order* clearly preserves a sense of academic heritage.

> Its aim is to publish first class philosophical work of all kinds, but it is especially concerned to encourage philosophizing with special reference to African context. Although the initiators belong to the Anglo-Saxon tradition of philosophy, they see it as their job to construe their subject rather widely: to regard inter-disciplinary boundaries as made for man, not man for them, and to watch out for growing points in their subject as it applies itself to new problems. (Cover of issues: 2)

K. Wiredu's elegant book (1980) is a good example of this ambition. In fact, what determines the configuration of this empiricist practice is the very close relationship existing between Anglo-Saxon philosophers and their African colleagues. For example, *Second Order's* board of consultants includes

D. Emmet (Cambridge), E. Gellner (Cambridge), D.W. Hamilyn (London), R. Harré (Oxford), R. Horton (Ife), D. Hudson (Exeter), S. Lukes (Oxford), J.J. MacIntosh (Calgary), and A. MacIntyre (Brandeis). Also, in Anglophone countries teaching and research in philosophy are accepted as a given, and the departments are well distinguished from departments of African religions or sociology.

A third orientation in the practice of philosophy in Africa is the search for the epistemological foundation of an African discourse. We shall examine a few illustrative cases: the epistemological debate on African theology, the discussion on the significance of social sciences, and the deconstruction doctrine in philosophy.

An important debate on African theology took place in 1960 (Tshibangu and Vanneste, 1960), stemming from a public discussion between A. Vanneste, dean of the School of Theology at Lovanium University and one of his students, T. Tshibangu, who later became the Roman Catholic auxiliary bishop of the archdiocese of Kinshasa and rector of the university. When the university was nationalized in 1971 by the Mobutu government, Bishop Tshibangu became the president of the National University of Zaïre. The debate concerns the possibility of an African Christian scientific theology. Tshibangu stated that under present world conditions it makes sense to promote the feasibility of an African-oriented Christian theology that epistemologically would have the same status as the Judeo-Christian, Eastern, and Western theologies. Dean Vanneste, although believing in the future of Christian theology in Africa, insisted on the demands of theology understood in its strict sense and defined it as a universal discipline (see Nsoki, 1973; Mudimbe, 1981a; Ngindu, 1968 and 1979; Tshibangu, 1974).

At stake is the legitimacy of an exploratory inquiry: can one reconcile a universal faith (Christianity) and a culture (African) within a discipline (theology) that is epistemologically and culturally marked? (Tshibangu and Vanneste, 1960:333–352). In a great confusion, European and African scholars, notably J. Daniélou, A.M. Henry, H. Maurier, V. Mulago, Ch. Nyamiti, A. Janon, and G. Thils (see Bimwenyi, 1981a; Mudimbe, 1981a) took sides. The debate also questioned indirectly the form and the meaning of the African presence in the field of Christian theology. This debate could only lead to an evaluation of the strictly scientific orientation of the Lovanium School of Theology. The School's intellectual configuration was subordinated to a number of principles (scientific rigour, theological tradition, and dogmatic vigilance) in the manner of the best European Catholic institutions. This cult of scientific quality is exemplified in such contributions by Zaïrean theologians as Tshibangu's work on the complementarity between "speculative" and "positive" theology in the history of the Western Church (1965), Atal's philological analysis of John's prologue (1972), Monsengwo's semantic study of the Bible (1973), and Ntendika's books on patristic philosophy and theology (1966, 1971). In which sense are these highly sophisticated studies related to the concrete condition of African Christians, their human problems and spiritual hope?

The problem extends to all the social and human sciences and has been enlarged upon as both an epistemological and a political problem by the second meeting of Zaïrean philosophers in Kinshasa in 1977 (see also Adotevi, 1972; Bimwenyi, 1981a; Buakasa, 1978; Sow 1977, 1978). We have seen that anthropological discourse was an ideological discourse. In the same vein, contemporary African discourse is ideological too, and as a discourse of political power, it often depends upon the same type of ide-ologies (Hauser, 1982; Elungu, 1979). Gutkind thinks that "actual inten-sification of capitalist control over the means of production in Africa in-creasingly reduces sections of the population to a landless rural or urban proletariat in whose live ancestral traditions, however modified, no longer mean anything" (in MacGaffey, 1981). I would add that this has another significance. Large sections of the African people have nothing to do with the present-day economic and political structures within their own countries, nor with intellectuals' and universities' projects for linking Western experi-ence to the African context.

It is because of this situation that both the African Marxists and "decon-structionists"—the latter in harmony with the anti-ethnophilosophy cur-rent—base their arguments. For Towa, for example, the critical enterprise is a total vocation. The *esprit critique* must apply indiscriminately to European intellectual imperatives and to African constructions, the only acceptable "truth" being that there is nothing sacred that philosophy cannot interrogate (Towa, 1971b:30). Hountondji goes further, stating that philosophy is essen-tially history and not system, and thus there is no single doctrine that may claim truth in an absolute manner. The best understanding of truth resides in the process of looking for it. "In a way, then, truth is the very act of looking for truth, of enunciating propositions and trying to justify and found them" ([1977] 1983:73). Similar philosphical positions allowed T. Obenga to rein-vent the cultural relationships that existed between Egypt and Black Africa. In the process, he criticized European theses and pinpoints Cheikh Anta Diop's methodological weaknesses. And J. Ki-Zerbo's general history of Africa (1972) provoked a new thinking about the diversity of functions of African cultures.

All of the social and human sciences underwent this radical experience between 1950 and 1980. Fundamentally, the questioning is based on "the right to truth," implying a new analysis of three paradigms: philosophical ideal versus contextual determination, scientific authority versus so-ciopolitical power, and scientific objectivity versus cultural subjectivity. Yet there are signs that, since the end of World War II, have meant the possibility of new theories in the African field. European theorists, then, seem to invert some values of colonial sciences and analyze African experience from a perspective that gradually institutionalizes the themes of contextual determination and cultural subjectivity. In the 1950s, J. Vansina and Y. Person envisaged a new arrangement of the African past, interpreting legends, fables, and oral traditions as "texts" and "documents," which with the help of archaeological data could contribute to the foundation of an "ethnohistory," a discipline joining history and anthropology (Vansina, 1961). In the same period, G. Balandier wrote the first books on "African sociology." Moreover, with his *anthropologie dynamique,* he reorganized the discipline and described the traditional "object" of anthropology, the "native," as the only possible "subject" for his own modernization. In the psychological field, scholars such as A. Ombredane re-examined, on a regional basis, the assumptions concerning the psychology and intelligence of blacks (1969). Frantz Crahay confronted Tempels's heritage, J. Jahn's generalizations on African culture, and the limitations of Nkrumah's philosophy, and proposed conditions for a critical philosophical maturity in Africa (1965). In the 1970s G. Leclerc, with *Anthropologie et colonialisme* (1972), and J. L. Calvet, with *Linguistique et colonialisme* (1974), among others, rewrote the history of ideological conditioning in the social and human sciences.

This trend of Western scholarship has had an impact on African practice. Nevertheless, it is neither a direct ancestor nor the major reference for the African current we are examining. Although both are concerned with the same object, and both present, essentially, the same fundamental objective, there are at least two major differences that distinguish them. The first difference accounts for a paradox. These currents have the same origin in the Western *episteme,* but their beginnings did not coincide, and despite their similarity they constitute two autonomous orientations. They have all developed in the European context as "amplifications" of theses coming from two loci. The first of these is the "library" constructed by such scholars as Frobenius, Delafosse, Théodore Monod, Robert Delavignette, B. Malinowski, and Marcel Griaule; the second, the intellectual atmosphere of the 1930s–1940s and surely the 1950s, which with the rediscovery of Marx, Freud, and Heidegger produced a critical reevaluation of the significance of links between objectivity and subjectivity, history and reason, essence and existence. On the basis of these questions, new doctrines appeared: neo-Marxism, existentialism, and also negritude and black personality. These emphasized in different ways the pertinence and the importance of subjectivity, the unconscious, existence, relativity of truth, contextual difference, and otherness.

In this atmosphere, Africanism developed and took on a new visage. In the 1950s and 1960s, while in Anglophone countries M. Herskovits and B. Davidson promoted a new interest in African culture, the most dynamic schools of European Africanism in Francophone countries were Marxist-dominated and heavily influenced by Lévi-Strauss's notions of "otherness" and "savage mind." It is an Africanism of "big brothers." Y. Bénot, C. Coquery-Vidrovitch, L. de Heusch, C. Meillassoux, H. Moniot, J. Suret-Canale, B. Verhaegen, and others link the emergence of new scientific and meth-

odological approaches to the paradoxical task of teaching Africans how to
read their otherness and of helping them formulate modalities that express
their own being and their place in the world. Concurrently, in the Anglophone world, scholars such as J. Coleman, P. Curtin, J. Goody, T. Ranger,
P. Rigby, V. Turner, and Crawford Young began to bring to light new
representations of African history (Curtin, 1964, 1965; Ranger, 1967) and
synchronic analyses of sociocultural "depths" (Rigby, 1969; Turner, 1964,
1975, 1981; Young, 1965).

The "deconstruction" of colonial sciences those Western trends represented does not, however, coincide completely with the presuppositions of
the critical African trends of Ki-Zerbo, T. Obenga or Eboussi-Boulaga. The
epistemological conditioning is obviously the same, and in some cases, on
the surface, programs, projects and actions are oriented towards identical
purposes. Such is the case of Terence Ranger and the School of Dar-es-
Salaam, Peter Rigby and the Africanist team at Makerere, and B. Verhaegan
and the Zaïrean School of Political Science. However, a major difference does
exist. It has been amplified by the new generation of European scholars—
J. Bazin, J. F. Bayart, J. P. Chrétien, B. Jewsiewicki, J. C. Willame, for
example—who are more conscious of the objective limitations that their own
subjectivity and regional sociohistoric determinations impose on their dealings with African matters. M. Hauser, for example, introduces such a comprehensive work as his *Essai sur la poétique de la négritude* (1982) by
recognizing that the presuppositions that founded the project, the methods of
analysis used, determine his study in a subjective locus, itself ideologically
marked (1982:27).

On the other hand, since the 1960s African theorists and ideologues,
rather than confiding in and depending on "big brothers," have tended to use
critical analysis as a means for establishing themselves as "subjects" of their
own destiny, taking responsibility for the "invention" of their past as well as
of the conditions for modernizing their societies. Thus, the dialogue with
"big brothers" has been ambiguous, from the beginning infused with mutual
understanding and rejection, collaboration and suspicion (see Wauthier,
1964). Adotévi's *Négritude et négrologues* (1972) is a good illustration of
this trend. Although epistemologically his book is an amplification of the
Western crisis of the signification of social and human sciences, it gives a
radical account of the limits of Africanism and proposes its absolute negation
as a new "explanation" for African integration into "history" and "modernity": "revolution is not accomplished with myths, even shattered ones"
(Adotevi, 1972:81). Mabika Kalanda's study in 1966 founded the principle
of *remise en question* as a means of intellectual and political liberation.

The second difference is a consequence of the first. In its perspective, the
African critical trend displays its power as the only "common place" for both
a positive knowledge of dynamic tensions and discourses on the foundation
and justification of African human and social sciences. Thus, it tends to
define its mission in terms of three paradigms: cultural renaissance of African

nations, new scientific vocation, and developmental applications, almost grudgingly accepting the fact that non-Africans might offer contributions to this struggle for power and truth.

From this intellectual climate spring the organizing ideologies that sustain strategies for new relationships between knowledge and power and provide original frameworks for social and human studies in Africa. Hountondji represents the neo-Marxist ideology and insists on three complementary actions (1981:68): *(a)* the promotion of a philosophical critique and ideological clarification in order to oppose illusions, mystifications, and lies that continue to exist in Africa and about Africa; *(b)* rigorous studies, assimilation, and true understanding of the best in international philosophy, including Marxism, which according to the author, is the only theory to provide pertinent concepts and means for analyzing the exploitation of Africa; *(c)* and a paradoxical task—stepping out of philosophy in order to meet and have dialogue with social reality.

Most of the theorists, however, favor different views. Bimwenyi, Eboussi-Boulaga, and Sow, for instance, offer a more systematic criticism of Western philosophical anthropology as a precondition for the building of new interpretations. At the deepest level, they agree with Hountondji on the necessity of new choices. Their strategies, however, reveal the possibility of disturbing the epistemological arrangements that account for Africanism and also for Marxism. The basic assumption is a relativist one: cultures, all cultures, are blind in terms of the values they incarnate and promote (Eboussi-Boulaga). It also implies a critique of the concept of human nature. According to Sow, human nature is an abstract construction that does not really concern social and human sciences:

> We are not persuaded that when looked at carefully the specific object of social sciences is the study of one universal human nature given *a priori,* because we do not know if such a human nature exists concretely somewhere. It may be that human nature (or human being in general, natural human being, etc.) is a theoretical fiction of general philosophy, or then, the activist generalization of a limited concrete experience. (Sow, 1977:256–58)

Sow thinks that the reality of human nature makes sense only when intermingled with representations of a given anthropological tradition or perspective. His conclusion presents the following challenge: against dialectic reason and anthropology, how can intellectuals in Africa think about human nature and for what purpose?

On a more concrete level, one can observe the alternatives offered by other trends. Wiredu, for example, faces African social contradictions empirically (1980). Other theorists indicate practical policies for the implementation of strategic principles in sociocultural formulas. The paradigm of renaissance accounts for theories that essentially affirm the positivity of being oneself. As Chinweizu, Jemie, and Madobuike recently showed in their aggressive *Toward the Decolonization of African Literature* (1983), it also means the right to doubt "perennial" and "universal" values. In this sense, there is a correlation between the ideology of debates on cultural relativism in African literature and concrete policies promoting African languages and celebrating "authentic" traditions as meaningful institutions (p'Bitek, 1973). We are confronted with the difficult issue of "retraditionalization" as A. A. Mazrui and M. Tidy call it.

> Another obstacle to cultural liberation has been the confusion of the concept of modernization with Westernization. In fact, retraditionalization of African culture can take modernizing forms, especially if it becomes an aspect of decolonization. Retraditionalization does not mean returning Africa to what it was before the Europeans came . . . But a move towards renewed respect for indigenous ways and the conquest of cultural self-contempt may be the minimal conditions for cultural decolonization. (Mazrui and Tidy, 1984:283)

But this is just one side of a complex process. Mabika Kalanda posited a strict principle: to reappropriate his own cultural consciousness and invent new paradigms for his "renaissance," it is imperative for the African to reevaluate the general context of his tradition. He must expurgate it critically, since some of its inherent characteristics have predisposed him to slavery, and also explain the African tendency towards dependency.

> The Bantu global milieu can be characterized as disintegrating and depressing for the individual. Its philosophy posits as sacred law dependency, submission, effacement, the mental and therefore physical degeneracy of the Bantu. Such a milieu is predisposing to slavery . . . The individual or group mental impotency perceived intuitively or even observed in the objective realities leads people unconsciously to aggressivity towards strangers who are more advanced than we are. (Kalanda, 1967:163)

On the basis of a similar hypothesis, Eboussi-Boulaga later propounded the form of a *récit pour soi* as a critical means for understanding the past and its failures in order to be able to act differently in the future (Eboussi-Boulaga, 1977:223).

The paradigms of scientific vocation and developmental applications are probably the easiest to analyze. In the 1950s and 1960s, they meant the Africanization of personnel in universities and research centers. In other words, they sought the transfer of intellectual leadership and administrative authority to Africans (see, e.g., Bergh, 1973; Verhaegen, 1978; Mazrui and Tidy, 1984:299–315). This struggle for scientific responsibility rapidly led to myths and theories of the "Africanization of sciences." For several years, Cheikh Anta Diop's influence for example, allowed the hypostasis of African civilizations. Concurrently, African Studies centers multiplied, and African subjects were introduced into university curricula. For the classical theme "all that is European is civilized; all that is African is barbarous" was substituted "all that is African is civilized and beautiful." This intellectual nationalism depended heavily on political nationalism. As Hodgkin rightly noted, it "developed furthest in those territories where political nationalism [was] most firmly established, [and had] an effect upon practice as well as upon attitudes" (1957:175–76).

The major characteristic of the period from 1970 to the 1980s is the relative autonomy of the intellectualist side of African nationalism. The failure of dreams of independence might account for the redistribution of power. Politicians and managers have created acute contradictions between the processes of production and the social relations of production, the "economy" of power and political rhetoric (Iliffe, 1983:65–87). The intellectuals generally define their mission in terms of the deconstruction of existing systems of economic, political, and ideological control. Within the intellectual group there are, as already noted, two major tendencies: the first, increasingly Marxist-dominated, emphasizes strategies for economic and political liberation; the second, the liberal tendency, essentially focuses on the implications of a philosophy of otherness. One might think that the first group, fundamentally, promotes new theories for the Westernization of Africa. On the other hand, the second group, seems thus far caught in paradoxes created by the juncture of a will for political power and postulates of symbolic analysis. Nevertheless, both these orientations have produced significant promise in present-day African scholarship. Already, in many fields—anthropology, history, philosophy, and theology—the official orthodoxy inherited from the colonial period has been challenged. African scholars affirm new alternatives, regional compatibilities, and above all the possibility of a new economy between power and knowledge.

The process is most visible, as we have seen, in the domain of Christian theology, which is also by far the best organized field. It faced major questions in its development (Mveng, 1983). First of all, following the "Africanization" myths of the nationalist moment in the 1950s, it dealt with the challenge of a critique of Western Christianity. The aim at that time was to search for sources of confusion between colonialism and Christianity in order to achieve a better comprehension of Christianity and work for the implementation of an African Christianity. The stepping stone theory, the adaptation approach, and the incarnation interpretation are the most well-known solutions proposed for the promotion of an African Christianity (Bimwenyi, 1981b:263–81). A second question appeared almost immediately: what epistemological foundation could be proposed for African theology? Three types of visions and strategies have been offered.

We can hardly enter into details of an African reading of the Western experience because of the complexity of its purposes. Nonetheless, let us note two main methodological points: the choice of a rigorous classical analysis of the Western historical process of indigenizing the Gospel and a critical interpretation of this process, based on the ideological significance of strategic cultural selections and subservient rules and aimed at the explanation of the progressive constitution of the Church's doctrine and the development of its liturgy. Bishop Tshibangu's work on the history of theological methods in the West (1965, 1980), J. Ntendika's careful studies (1966, 1971) on patristic theology, and Kinyongo's exegetical synthesis of the meaning of Jhwh (1970) are good examples of the trend. In philosophy, the same tendency to seek a good understanding of the Western practice of philosophy, as a useful step prior to promoting African philosophy, can be observed in several cases. *Second Order's* orientation, Elungu's study of the concepts of space and knowledge in Malebranche's philosophy (1973b), Ugirashebuja's analysis of the relationship between poetry and thought in Heidegger's work (1977), and Ngindu's presentation of religious knowledge according to Laberthonière (1978) provide examples.

This critical reading of the Western experience is simultaneously a way of "inventing" a foreign tradition in order to master its techniques and an ambiguous strategy for implementing alterity. In theology, for instance, it is accepted that "African theologians have nothing to gain by withdrawing into themselves. [By so doing] they would condemn themselves to remaining second-rate theologians" (Tshibangu and Vanneste, 1960:333–52). In 1974, Tshibangu published *Le Propos d'une théologie africaine*, a brief manifesto which concentrates on linguistic and cultural relativism and upholds the evidence of ethnic understanding and expressions of Christianity, along with the fact that there are a variety of systems of thought. Tshibangu's work has become a classic and has had tremendous influence. It is already possible to study the outcome of his thesis. There are more and more anthropological and linguistic investigations of African traditions that pinpoint regions of compatibility and divergence between Christianity and African religions. Examples of this are Bimwenyi's *Discours théologique négro-africain* (1981a), Hebga's *Sorcellerie et prière de délivrance* (1982), the book published by Ela and Luneau, *Voici le temps des héritiers* (1981), and *Hearing and Knowing* (1986) by M. A. Oduyoye. Rather than insisting on the economy of cultural and religious constellations and their possible compatibility, this trend tends to emphasize the pertinence of diffraction and its relative value in a regional system of revelation. Mulago's *Cahiers des religions africaines* has been the most visible locus and vehicle for this project since 1965. Oduyoye sums up the nature of this quest:

> We . . . are confronted with this fact: those who were for a long time content to be consumers of theology have begun to be producers of theology and it is Christian theology. *They are widening the panorama of symbols, heightening the color of issues,* and demanding commitment and action. (Oduyoye, 1986:76. Emphasis mine)

I asked Tshibangu how, in this project for an intellectual discontinuity and an ideological reversal, he could explain the relationship between thought and action. He answered by specifying the philosophical frame in which this new discourse evolves and the anthropological context of its possibility.

Mudimbe: In any case concerning your project, one could wonder whether thought could precede action. Surely, this is very scholastic. But people have also said that the most important thing was to practice theology; that the specificity, the African character of the discourse would come naturally.

Tshibangu: You are correct in posing the problem of the relationship between thought and action. In reality, being, and consequently life, and action that actualizes it precede thought ontologically. But thought in turn is implied in the "form" of being that gives it the logical character of cognizability and acceptability. In fact the two are correlative and condition each other. In spiritual life, and particularly in a community of life such as the Church, life and doctrine condition one another and act one upon the other. To date the *question of African theology* is largely one of principle. Existentially concrete problems are perceived and felt specifically by African Christian communities. African theology will realize itself effectively by trying in a radical way to answer the problems posed by the principles of African culture, the evolution of African societies with numerous questions concerning spiritual and ethical problems that are not lacking. [. . .] Today given the level of awareness of cultural differences, the specificity of cultures is not worked out over a long period of time and in a spontaneous way. We know the conditions of the specificity. This specificity, however, is based on the fundamental unity of human nature. The question is one of determining the framework for the development of this specificity so that it may enrich the total realization of the potentialities that nature has granted to a humanity diversified in its historic and spatial existence.

Mudimbe: You are a professor of fundamental theology at the Faculté de Théologie Catholique in Kinshasa. By temperament and by choice you say that you are preoccupied with epistemological questions. For what reason? What exactly are you looking for?

Tshibangu: I mean by that that I am always preoccupied with the problem of justification. In the field of action everything must be grounded, and this demand imposes itself especially when in addition one accepts the law of the evolution of things, of institutions, of ideas, of customs. In order not to stray, to make mistakes, to act by simple habit or conditioning, it is necessary to reflect on the foundation of judgements and attitudes. And I intend to proceed methodologically in this search for foundations, in order to propose actions and attitudes that are themselves grounded and well justified, intellectually and with respect to the goals that humans must follow. (In Mudimbe, 1977:18)

A last trend in theology addresses a delicate issue: does it make sense to be Christian and African? As the Jesuit priest E. Mveng expressed it more concretely, why should an African believe in and promote a Christianity that not only has become a product of exportation for Western civilization but also has come to be used as a means of racial and class exploitation?

Unfortunately the West is less and less Christian; and Christianity, for a long time, has been a product of export for Western civilization, in other words, a perfect tool for domination, oppression, the annihilation of other civilizations. The Christianity preached today, not only in South Africa, but by the West as a power and civilization, is far, very far from the gospel. The question is therefore posed radically: what can be the place of Third World peoples in such a Christianity? And this question is first of all aimed at the official churches. (Mveng, 1983:140)

To face this question, another African Jesuit, Eboussi-Boulaga, has put forth for consideration his *Christianisme sans fétiche: Révélation et domination* (1981). It is a deconstruction of Christianity. Setting aside dogmas, traditional criteria, and official Church theories, he propounds a direct interpretation of revelation as a sign of liberation. In this perspective, the time and the dignity of the human being are seen and defined as the real place of God's dream for incarnation. As a consequence, according to Eboussi-Boulaga, the most important issue for followers of Jesus is the liberation of their own faith and its conversion into a practical means for a true transformation of the world. This conclusion is the postulate of theologies of liberation in South Africa (see, e.g., Tutu, 1984; Boesak, 1977, 1984a, 1984b). One of the soundest illustrations of this spirit of the Exodus is in J. M. Ela's *Le Cri de l'Homme Africain: Questions aux Chrétiens et aux Eglises d'Afrique* (1980). Ela calls for a "radical move away from the God of natural theology preached by missionaries" and an invocation of the God of Exodus, interested in history and the socioeconomic conditions of humans. Strictly speaking, this is a political discourse in the name of Christian prophetism.

We have justified slavery, violence and war; we have sanctified racism and split our churches on the issue of the preservation of white supremacy. We have discriminated against women and kept them servile whilst we hid our fear of them behind claims of "masculinity" and sanctimonious talk about Adam and Eve. We have grown rich and fat and powerful through the exploitation of the poor, which we deplored but never really tried to stop. All in the name of Jesus Christ and his gospel. Now this same gospel speaks to us, and we can no longer escape its demands. It calls us to love and justice and obedience. We would like to fulfill that calling, but we do not want to risk too much. The Reuben option. The Reuben option: Take a stand, but always cover yourself. (Boesak, 1984b:38)

A hermeneutical school appeared in this context as the site of a more culturally oriented research in African theology. I think that Okere's D.Phil. dissertation (1971) was the first major initiative. However, it is Tshiamalenga (1973, 1974, 1977b, 1980) and Nkombe (1979) who have become this school's most productive exponents. Okolo made explicit the philosophical choices of the method (1980), drawing new propositions from a brief and stimulating text by his former professor, Kinyongo (1979). Okere published in 1983 an extract of his D.Phil. dissertation concerning the foundations of the method. In this work one finds clear guidelines based on the solid principle that while "language seems to affect culture and thought at some level," it does not follow that one can "speak of philosophical and metaphysical thought as somehow predetermined linguistically" (Okere, 1983:9). The most convincing studies to date, apart from Okere's unpublished dissertation, have been those of Tshiamalenga (e.g., 1974, 1977b, 1980) and Nkombe in his methodological propositions (e.g., 1977, 1978b) and his study of metaphor and metonymy in the paroemiologic symbols of the Tetela language (1979). In terms of intellectual classification, it is possible to distinguish two main trends. The first is one of ontological hermeneutics, which at least in Kinshasa coincides with the reconversion of Tempels and Kagame's legacy to more rigourous modalities of philosophizing (see, e.g., Tshiamalenga, 1973, 1974, 1980). The second is more of a psychosocially oriented hermeneutics which integrates lessons from phenomenological methods (e.g., Laleye, 1981, 1982; Nkombe, 1979).

The question of the significance of these new intellectual strategies of "conversion" has occurred in other domains. In social sciences, T. K. Buakasa, for example, has analyzed the sociocultural determinations of scientific reason, under the provocative title, *Western Sciences: What For?* (1978; see also Okonji, 1975). Inspired by Foucault and especially by J. Ladrière's work on the philosophy of sciences, Buakasa reexamines the historicity and architecture of scientific reason in order to introduce techniques for the conversion of African "mentality" in terms of scientific reason. Another philosopher, P. E. Elungu, accepts the reality of African authenticity and the relative autonomy of its sociohistorical experience, but bases his proposals for African liberation on a unique condition: a conversion to philosophical and critical thinking. According to him, this spirit appears to be the only possible way to modernization, insofar as it will mean in African tradition the possibility of a rupture and subsequently the emergence of a scientific mentality. This is a new cultural environment characterized by: *(a)* man's capacity to break with what is simply given, in the pursuit of that which is essential and specific to him; *(b)* the seizing of this essential specificity in freedom of discourse, and *(c)* the realization that this freedom of discourse is not freedom itself, that this autonomy of discourse is not independence. (Elungu, 1976; see also Sodipo, 1975, 1983).

Examining these new rules of the game, one recalls Foucault's objectives for the liberation of discourse in *The Discourse on Language* (in appendix, 1982). Explicit references to Western schemata are also noticeable in Hountondji's program on the African practice of science, which relies on Althusser, and in Nkombe's research on African symbols inspired by Ricoeur and Lévi-Strauss. But these intellectual filiations imply methodological and ideological syntheses rather than the capitulation of otherness (Vilasco, 1983). Hountondji presents the ambiguous dream of present-day African philosophers provocatively:

> The problem . . . as regards our attitude towards our collective heritage, is
> how to respond to the challenge of cultural imperialism without imprisoning

ourselves in an imaginary dialogue with Europe, how to re-evaluate our cultures without enslaving ourselves to them, how to restore the dignity of our past, without giving room to a passeistic attitude. Instead of blindly condemning our traditions on behalf of reason, or rejecting the latter on behalf of the former, or making an absolute of the internal rationality of these traditions, it seems more reasonable to me to try and know our traditions as they were, beyond any mythology and distortion, not merely for the purpose of self-identification or justification, but in order to help us meet the challenges and problems of today. (1983: 142–43)

To sum up the rules of this deconstruction, I note three major objectives: *(a)* to understand and define the configuration of scientific practice in social and human sciences as an ideological locus determined by three major variables—time, space, and the (un)conscious of the scientist; *(b)* to analyze and understand African experiences as formed on the basis of a particular history and as witnessing to a regional *Weltanschauung;* and *(c)* to think about and propose reasonable modalities for the integration of African civilizations into modernity, this in accordance with critical thinking and scientific reason, for the purpose of the liberation of man.

It might be that all of these themes have been made possible by some of the consequences of the epistemological rupture, which according to Foucault (1973) appeared in the West at the end of the eighteenth century. The hypothesis makes sense if one looks at the progressive recession, from the nineteenth century through the 1930s, of theories about "function," "conflict," and "signification," and at the slow emergence of a new understanding of the potentialities of paradigms of "norm," "rule," or "system." In theory, this reversal accounts for all ideologies of difference (see, e.g., Ricoeur, 1984). However, it is not certain that it fully explains the functional arrangement of the "colonial library," its history and pervasive effectiveness during the nineteenth and the twentieth centuries, nor the ambiguous relationships between the myths of the "savage mind" and the African ideological strategies of otherness.

Horizons of Knowledge

The history of knowledge in Africa and about Africa appears deformed and disjointed, and the explanation lies in its own origin and development. As in the case of other histories, we face what Veyne has called "the illusion of integral reconstitution [which] comes from the fact that the documents, which provide us with the answers, also dictate the questions to us" (1984:13). Furthermore the body of knowledge itself, whose roots go as far back as the Greek and Roman periods, in its constitution, organization, and paradoxical richness, indicates an incompleteness and inherently biased perspectives. The discourse which witnesses to Africa's knowledge has been for a long time either a geographical or an anthropological one, at any rate a "discourse of competence" about unknown societies without their own "texts." Only recently has this situation been gradually transformed by the concept of ethnohistory, which in the 1950s postulated the junction of anthropological *topoi* with those of history and other social sciences, and later on integrated oral tradition and its expressions (poetry, fixed formulas, anthroponymy, toponymy). In so doing, this discourse began constructing simulacra about the relations existing between present African social organizations and history. On the whole, the discourse on African realities offers two main characteristics: on the one hand, it is a heterogenous discourse emanating from the margins of African contexts; and on the other hand, its axes as well as its language have been limited by the authority of this exteriority.

The atmosphere of the 1950s meant a new valorization in the Africanist discourse, namely, the promotion of another center: history and its ideological activity. This valorization is well represented in the shift that occurred progressively after the 1930s, moving from the anthropological authority and its negation of African historicity to the respectability of a possible historical knowledge of so-called traditional societies. This shift is illustrated by Herskovits (1962) and Vansina (1961). During the same period, other forms of languages were being derived from the same value presuppositions and freeing themselves from the anthropologist's intellectual space (see, e.g., Wallerstein, 1961, 1967). Religious thinking began to conceptualize a history and a sociology of what Schmidt called "primitive revelation" (1931) and, as in the case of *Des prêtres noirs s'interrogent* (1956), to seek regional platforms for an African Christian theology. With Griaule and Tempels, the reading and interpretation of local cultures had already challenged the narrowness of classical ethnography and the gospel of its *topoi* and raised questions of local rationalities and African philosophy.

J. Copans insists on the advent of sociology and Marxism as major events which characterize this intellectual evolution of Africanism (in Gutkind and Wallerstein, 1976). "Sociology was not just a new specialization, it constituted a complete break on several counts; empirically, as it was taking into consideration the real history of African peoples; in scale, as it moved on from the village to national social group (from 'mini' to 'maxi'); theoretically, as a materialistic and historical explanation took the place of Griaulian idealism which ignored the realities of colonialism" (1976:23). This new Marxist approach was induced in the late 1950s by what Copans calls the "collapse of anticolonial unity." This precipitated the appearance of a new theoretical field of Marxist analysis: the world economic market, struggles for political liberation, the development of social classes, capitalist economies and imperialisms, etc. Thus, after 1956, "Marxist thought found new life" insofar as from a Marxist viewpoint Africa was "a virgin theoretical field." "The use of concepts of the imperialist system or modes of production was facilitated by an explanation in terms of unstable arrangements and the dynamism of contradictions." After the 1960s, "the characteristics peculiar to neocolonialism led to research into the *economic* roots of exploitation and

into the *political* and *revolutionary* solutions to the overthrow of exploitation, and so to the adoption of a Marxist perspective" (1976:25).

By and large, I agree with Copan's diagnosis, which requires a dialectic of
analogical relations between the historical constructions of the Same and the
new compliances with and about the Other. In this prospect, Marxism
achieves a radically new approach. It does not Westernize a virgin terrain, but
rather confronts inattentivenesses, the supporting walls which suppose them,
and assembles under the roof of the analogue, relations, contradictions,
imaginations. In effect, the method results in an original type of visibility of
differences in terms of theoretical traces of *taking the place of* and *representing*. Alterity—be it socioeconomic or cultural—becomes through "models"
reenactable under the modalities of technical similarities of relations between
the Same and the Other. At the same time, these interpretative categories can
be classified in the name of their regional context (e.g., Terray, 1969; Rey,
1973). The great originality of French Marxists and their African counterparts in the 1960s resides in this. Beginning with G. Balandier's propositions
on macroperspectives in the field (1955a, 1955b), a new discourse unites
what had been kept separate and opens the way to a general theory of
historical and economic derivation as exemplified in the works of Osende
Afana (1967), J. Suret-Canale (1958), C. Meillassoux (1964, 1974), and
C. Coquery-Vidrovitch (1972).

The centrality of history is thus remarkable in what Marxism expounds in
African studies. In effect, the invention of an African history coincides with a
critical evaluation of the history of the Same. One also observes that the
possibility of an African history seems linked in a relation of necessity to a
European questioning and redefinition of both what history is not and what
it should be. For example, one notes that it is during the methodological
renewal of the 1950s that Lévi-Strauss, in order to celebrate the "savage
mind," relativizes the very concept of history, which as he put it, "is a
disconnected whole, formed of areas each of which is defined by a frequency
of its own" (1962:340). He has since been followed by L. de Heusch and
students who favor the structures of myths as pertinent loci of identity and
differences (see Heusch, 1971, 1982).

The paradox becomes clearer. The concept of "African history" marked a
radical transformation of anthropological narratives. A new type of discourse
valorizes the diachronic dimension as part of knowledge about African
cultures and encourages new representations of the "native," who previously
was a mere object within European historicity. Its Marxist version offers the
immediacy of objectivity through systems-signs of socioeconomic relations
that permit both good pictures of local organizations of power and production and intercultural comparisons. By means of a similar articulation,
structuralist postulations, without rejecting the "new historical entity" (see,
e.g., Heusch, 1971), open up areas of synchronic investigation, emphasizing
the dialectic tension and balance between regional creativity and universal
constraints of the human mind (see, e.g., Heusch, 1985). In sum, Tempels,

Griaule, and all the apostles of African otherness have been subsumed in the Marxist project of a universal discourse of the Analogue, as witnessed to by the neatly ambiguous ideology of *Présence Africaine* between 1950 and 1960. We find Sartre, Fanon, Garaudy, and Soviet communist scholars speaking to, and in dialogue with Bachelard, Senghor, Césaire, Maydieu, and Tempels. Later on, most visibly in the 1970s, structuralist methodology, in a new reflection on cultures, renewed questions of methods apropos of interpretative discourses on non-Western societies. It thus challenged an ethnohistory which tends to forget that "history is ensnared by myth which imposes its own sovereignty on kings" (Heusch, 1982:2). Structuralism proposed synchronic precepts for tabulating the forms of myths and cultures within a universal frame of relations of similarities and differences (Heusch, 1985).

I cannot wholeheartedly accept Copans's analysis of the succession of methodological paradigms from Griaule to the historical materialism applied to the African context in the 1950s and 1960s nor with respect to the advent of sociology in the same period as an epistemological event which would have transformed the entire economy of African studies and the meaning of its history. Copans's analysis is slightly misleading because the critical transformation of the 1950s is essentially and directly linked to a redefinition of both the object and aim of anthropology. This crisis expressed itself in African studies in two ways. One, a critique of and improvement upon Malinowski's functionalism, which with structuralism became a whole embodying effort for reading, commenting upon, and comparing myths and cultures independently of primitivist prejudices. As a consequence, Griaule's *Conversations with Ogotemmêli,* and Tempels's *Bantu Philosophy* stand between the ghosts of Taylor, Spencer, and Frazer, on one side and the lengthy conversation which has been uniting Malinowski, Lévi-Strauss, and de Heusch on the other. Strictly speaking, Griaule's or Tempels's idealism does not seem to belong to the past. Rather it still marks the oscillations of explanatory frameworks in programs for constituting or describing African forms of knowledge. The justification of Christianity seems an extreme case. It does not refer to a historical aberration but to a sociological fact: the universalization of a faith and a religious ideology appearing in the dispersion of both scientific and religious imaginations (see, e.g., Bimwenyi, 1981a).

Perhaps nothing has been more significant than the 1978 conference on Christianity and African Religions organized by the Roman Catholic School of Theology in Kinshasa. The Belgian scholar B. Verhaegan, who is both a Marxist and a Catholic, developed his concerns in terms of "a historical challenge":

Christian religions in Africa will be marked by this triple influence: the *capitalist* mode of production having arrived at worldwide *imperialism* and having been linked to a *colonial* past. The question that one must pose is the following: how colonial policy first, then imperialist forces and the organic structures of independent States influenced and manipulated religion in its content as well as in its forms and structures in terms of their own interests? (Verhaegen, 1979:184)

To face the combined effect of these complementary factors, Verhaegen, following G. Gutierrez's theology of liberation, proposed three genres of theological discourse: *a theology of modernity* which will link the search for social justice to the promotion of "reason, science and progress"; a *theology of charity* which will address the issue of social inequalities and poverty and offer radically new moral solutions; and, finally, a *theology of development* which will redefine modalities of development in terms of local interests (1979:188–89). Verhaegen concluded that

> three characteristics will mark the new African theology: it will be *contextual,* in other words, stemming from the life and culture of African people; it will be a theology of *liberation* because the oppression is not to be found only in cultural oppression but also in the political and economic structures; it should recognize the place of *women* as a vital part of the struggle for liberation and the struggle against all forms of sexism in the society and in the church. (Verhaegen, 1979:191)

Throughout the following years, events and research confirmed Verhaegen's analysis. The philosophy of the *Bulletin of African Theology* (an ecumenical journal of the Association of African Theologians) encourages stands similar to those expounded in Verhaegen's 1979 text. It is important to note a collective concern about otherness in cultural and spiritual matters and the implicit integration of the "Marxist reason" in an idealist perspective on spiritual, economic, and social issues. Thus Griaule and Tempels's idealism is still operating, although in a different and discrete way. Nevertheless, it is widespread and efficient to the point where one might wonder if, in countries having a high percentage of Christians, such as Cameroon and Zaire, it is not a determining ideological current, at least in the short run (see, e.g., Ela, 1985).

As to the second point of my slight disagreement with Copans's analysis, it bears on the importance of sociology in the reconversion of Africanism in the 1950s. Let us begin by noting that the crisis in the field was neither original nor unique. It signified a wider malaise well-illustrated in the debate that opposed Sartre and Lévi-Strauss on history as a dialectic totality, the universality of categories of reasoning, and the significance of the subject (e.g., Lévi-Strauss, 1962). The concepts of *model* and *structure* progressively invaded the whole field of social and human sciences, postulating both an epistemological discontinuity with traditional practices and a new understanding of the object of scientific inquiry as well as what its discourse reveals. L. Althusser's theory of scientific production (1965) epitomizes this awareness.

Commenting upon the tension existing between sociology and history, F. Braudel could write:

> The vocabulary is the same, or is becoming the same, because the problematic is becoming increasingly the same, under the convenient heading of the currently dominant two words *model* and *structure*. . . . In fact, whatever the cost, social science must construct a model, a general and particular explanation of social life, and substitute for a disconcerting empirical reality, a clearer image and one more susceptible to scientific application. (Braudel, 1980:73–74)

Thus, in the very center of human and social sciences, there is now affirmed a desire that in a radical manner interrogates the space of knowledge and the foundation of discourses expressing it. Lévi-Strauss's critique of sociology and history as two dimensions of the same figure, which in its mode of being as well as in its objective and aim is not so different from the anthropological project about "primitives," convincingly affirms the importance of new epistemological determinations (see, e.g., Lévi-Strauss, 1963:Intro.; 1968:Overture). Following Lévi-Strauss's line of reasoning, one may observe that history, as history of the Same, and its privileges are challenged. P. Veyne went further, subjecting the being of history to an evaluation and demonstrating that "history does not exist" (1984:15–30). On the other hand, he does not consecrate sociology. In the name of individual and collective identities in their differences and similarities, Veyne questioned the domain of sociological representations and the validity of its discourse: "Sociology is still at a pre-Thucydidean stage. Being history, it cannot go further than the probable, the likely" (1984:279). Comte's "sociology was a science of history 'as a whole,' a science *of* history; it was to establish the laws of history, like the 'law of the three estates,' which is the description of the movement of history taken as whole. But that science of history has revealed itself to be impossible" (1984:268). As a consequence, sociology no longer has an object, particularly when it claims to be autonomous from history.

In my view, it is under this paradoxical sign of a challenged history that new horizons have opened up in African studies and account for present-day real or potential tensions. M. Herskovits's initiatives in anthropology, G. Balandier's in sociology, J. Vansina's in history, J. Coleman's search for general paradigms in political science, are contemporaneous with this critical consciousness ensuring a new thesis that globally negates the pertinence of the inversed figure of the Same. Concretely, they impose on the field of African studies the rejection of grids leading to pathologies of societies and, after Tempels and Griaule, those positing and classifying pathologies of beliefs. The African project of succession also designates this same configuration as its locus of creativity. In effect, in the early 1960s, the African scholar succeeded the anthropologist, the "native" theologian replaced the missionary, and the politician took the place of the colonial commissioner. All of them find reasons for their vocations in the dialectic of the Same and the

Other. It is strange and significant that they tend to rationalize their missions in terms of an encounter between a narcissistic relation to the Self and the dual relation with the Other (see, e.g., Nkrumah, 1957; Senghor, 1962). Thus exegeses or commentaries on a newly discovered local rationality appear as *Gestalteneinheit;* that is, a self-sufficient language, accounting for its economy of being and defining itself as a historical culture, becomes a frame of social cooperation uniting peoples in tolerance, making events intelligible and significant, and controlling the pace of its own change (see, e.g., Abraham, 1966:26–29).

In this respect, the new knowledge and its symbols do not destroy completely the relevance of the colonial library, nor the idealism of apostles of otherness. It has brought about new standards for the collectivization and democratization of historical reason and has reformulated residual questions concerning ideological power and scientific orthodoxy. Its best and probably excessive illustration is the Africanization of diffusionism as actualized by Cheikh Anta Diop (e.g., 1954, 1960a, 1981).

Three main initiatives combined to recapture the whole of African experience and witness to it reality. They are the integration of Islamic sources and imaginations into the "newly expanded library," the constitution of a corpus of traditional texts, and a critical renewal of the anthropological authority.

The whole conception of African history had to be defined anew on the basis of Islamic contributions (Ki-Zerbo, 1972), which affect the classical historical *doctrina* by bringing up new witnesses and documents. Islamic narratives enter into the *episteme.* Some African enigmas are now examined with the aid of commentaries and descriptions by Ibn Hawkal (tenth century), El Bekri (eleventh century), Idrisi (twelfth century), and Ibn Batuta, Ibn Khaldoun, and Maqrizi (fourteenth century). The sociohistorical phenomenon of "Black Islam," as studied by V. Monteil (1980), is a primary concept for some important periods of history, and the *tarikhs,* or chronicles, have become valued sources. Islamic sources have always constituted important dimensions for the search and invention of African paradigms (see, e.g., Blyden, 1967). Islamic culture has powerfully contributed to the passion of alterity, particularly in West Africa, where it still exposes schemas and lessons on social harmony and its philosophy (e.g., Ba, 1972; Hama, 1969; 1972; Kane, 1961). But, by and large, the Islamic discourse was until the 1960s an ideological interference within the *ktèma es aei* embodied by the colonial library as, for example, represented *ad absurdum* by the life and passion of Tierno Bokar (Ba and Cardaire, 1957; Brenner, 1984).

The constitution of a corpus of African traditional texts is undeniably one of the most important achievements in the field. The most impressive collection remains the series of *Classiques Africains* created by E. de Dampierre in Paris on the model of the Greek and Latin classics of *La Collection Budé.* Note that since the first years of this century, folklorists have been publishing translations of traditional narratives under the name of "oral literature" (see Scheub, 1971, 1977). For years these collections served as professed monuments to pericivilized or marginal experiences. Frobenius's *African Genesis* (1937), for example, contributed to a scientific curiosity by transferring narratives from their original context and language into a European language and conceptual frame. They then become formulas for a diffusionist thesis. On the whole, until the 1950s, most of the published works were based on similar transference. Narratives were submitted to a theoretical order, and rather than accounting for their own being and their own meaning, they were mainly used as tools to illustrate grand theories concerning the evolution and transformations of literary genres. Kagame's project of promoting an indigenous reading of traditional narratives has been—despite its internal weaknesses—one of the most serious and least extroverted approaches to African genres. By making available some basic texts pertinent to the hypothesis of Bantu ontology, the Belgian scholar, J. A. Theuws (1954, 1983), makes a similar contribution. Narratives presented in the truth of their language and authenticity become texts of real peoples and not merely the results of theoretical manipulations.

This new perspective has been reorganizing the field for some years now. The authority of reading and classifying genres, texts, and literatures from some kind of divine position, which does not demand a knowledge of a specific social context, its culture, and language, is being progressively replaced by concrete questions bearing upon contextual authority and the necessity of linking narratives to their cultural and intellectual conditions of possibility. By way of illustration, one naturally turns to the magnificent collection of *Classiques africains* published first by Julliard and then by A. Colin under the direction of E. de Dampierre. Recently, K. Anyidoho surveyed the geography of the field (1985), H. Scheub evaluated the "state of the art" (1985), and S. Arnold described changing aspects of African literary studies (1985). Examining these articles, one finds a resolute new message: African literature studies is interested in knowledge and every text is worthy of being considered literature.

This commitment is in itself a problem, insofar as it claims to apply to all narratives, be they in African or European languages. Diverse texts produced for differing purposes and in different economic areas are all lumped together as material for one discipline. At the mercy of scientific paradigms and grids, they become almost identical memories, reflecting in the same way African social relations of production, ideological signals, and cultural geographies. Intellectual histories mix with ethnographies, imaginative works in English or French with "oral narratives." The uniformizing dichotomy of modern versus traditional organizes the competing values and merits of texts. What this sort of literary criticism does to the actual experience and meaning that the text expressed in its original cultural context does not seem to concern most students of African literature.

From an anthropology redefining itself come new possibilities and questions. L. de Heusch has brought structuralism to African studies, rediscovered Frazer's universal *mythemes* and faced the question of the being of the Analogue.

Frazer . . . curiously neglected to point out that the drama of the Passion, re-enacted on Christian altars, is a universal theme. Christianity's greatness lies in knowing how to present the political assassination perpetrated in Judea by the Roman coloniser, as the ultimate sacrifice and in having tried to build on this schema—at the price of a metaphysical illusion—a society of peace and brotherhood. That message can never again be forgotten. Yet a blind man's soft voice, which would not have been heard outside Dogon country if Griaule had not been so attentive, also deserves to be considered as a profession of sacrificial faith, based on the hope of a more humane, more balanced world . . . the sacrifice circulates "a word," destined for all, says the old Ogotemmêli. (Heusch, 1985:206)

Disciples of Ricoeur and Gadamer are also proposing ways for conciliating a critical consciousness with the authority of regional cultural texts, as in the case of Bellman's study on symbol and metaphors in *Poro* ritual (1984), or Tshiamalenga's philosophy of sin in the Luba tradition (1974), as well as his linguistic and anthropological analysis of the *ntu* vision of the human being (1973). Semiology, as an intellectual tool for examining social signs, and hermeneutics, as means and method of reading and interpreting these social signs, may indicate a future direction for African Studies. They address an apparently simple question: how can one unveil and describe African experi-ence? Is it just a matter of the methodological association of concepts, which when applied well will reveal an empirical reality, or is it a problem con-cerning the explanatory principles of scientific and philosophical models?

The main problem concerning the being of African discourse remains one of the transference of methods and their cultural integration in Africa. However, beyond this question lies another: how can one reconcile the demands of an identity and the credibility of a claim to knowledge with the process of refounding and reassuming an interrupted historicity within repre-sentations? Moreover, could not one hypothesize that, despite the cleverness of discourses and the competency of authors, they do not necessarily reveal *la chose du texte,* that which is out there in the African traditions, insistent and discrete, determining the traditions yet independent from them? Colonialism and its trappings, particularly applied anthropology and Christianity, tried to silence this. African discourses today, by the very epistemological distance which makes them possible, explicit, and credible as scientific or philosophi-cal utterances, might just be commenting upon rather than unveiling *la chose du texte.* This notion, which belongs to hermeneutics, and which according to Ricoeur's proposition calls for an *obedience* to the text in order to unfold its meaning, could be a key to the understanding of African *gnosis.* As an African responsibility, this *gnosis* emerged in the gradual and pro-gressive preeminence of history and has marked all discourses for intellectual succession.

In history, the ambition of this *gnosis* has, since the 1960s, been embodied in the work of such scholars as Ajayi, Ki-Zerbo, Obenga, and others. They brought into a dialogue the authority of historical methods and forms of life and societies which up to the 1950s were largely considered historically mute. Against the mythologies of anthropology, rightly or wrongly, the *critique historique* faced ideologies of otherness and combined with them in syntheses that claimed to represent the stimulation as well as the diachronic circulation of a dynamic African history. In effect, the project seems original, yet by the notion of alterity that is its motto, if it correctly challenges the colonial libraries, where is its obedience to the text? Moreover, which text does it obey? Do not its methodological presuppositions and techniques determine both its epistemological origin and its internal limits as historical discourse? These are classic questions that refer to the now controverted distinction between the methods of history and sociology-anthropology. On the other hand, they permit the blame to be placed on the most fruitful propositions only when these are used for what seems to go against the established tradition. Wagner recently gave us a useful lesson by noting that the "much celebrated 'Western history' is in fact *invention* placed 'out of awareness'." He also observes that "the future of anthropology lies in its ability to exorcize 'difference' and make it conscious and explicit, both with regard to its subject matter and to itself" (1981:158). In a similar vein, Paul Ricoeur could state that "man's history will progressively become a vast explanation in which each civilization will work out its perception of the world by confronting all others" (1965:283).

What African history and philosophy have been doing since their inception has been to make the difference explicit, not always calculatedly nor for utility but, paradoxically (if one keeps in mind Wagner's proposal), as the dynamic side of anthropology. This side witnesses to the explicit difference of an uninterrupted historical configuration in which, as Ajayi once put it, the colonial experience signifies a brief parenthesis.

Developments that gave rise in the 1950s to the contributions of American cultural anthropology, British social anthropology, and French Marxist anthropology are rooted in the history of the discipline and also related to changes that had occurred in African and Western societies since the 1920s. Among the most important, as we have seen, are the impact of anticolonialist movements and African criticism of anthropology. A new discourse appeared, which was not only critical of colonialism but of all the dominant colonial culture. But let us note two problems. Despite the fact that the liberation movements opposed anthropology as a structural factor of colonization, some pre- and post-independence African policies seem predicated upon the results of applied anthropology. Many African leaders, in order to legitimize a political process and to establish the right to differentiate themselves from the colonizers, accepted such colonial anthropological concepts as tribe, cultural particularism, etc. On the other hand, while new politically liberal trends were rapidly developing in anthropology, other African leaders referred to early and controversial hypotheses. The most illuminating case is Senghor's system (1962), in which anthropologists' speculations are, inter alia, combined with Marxism. Also, African personality ideology gave rise to the ambiguous social philosophy of Nkrumah (1970). In the same vein, negritude celebrated anthropologists who allowed Africans to extol the originality of their culture, and some of the present-day philosophical trends are still firmly based upon anthropology's premises (N'daw, 1983). Even in the Arab world, the advocacy of a dynamic cultural perspective relies heavily on a preliminary critique of an already given Western orientalism (see, e.g., Laroui, 1967).

These paradoxes reveal that we are dealing with ideology. Modern African thought seems somehow to be basically a product of the West. What is more, since most African leaders and thinkers have received a Western education, their thought is at the crossroads of Western epistemological filiation and African ethnocentrism. Moreover, many concepts and categories underpinning this ethnocentrism are inventions of the West. When prominent leaders such as Senghor or Nyerere propose to synthetize liberalism and socialism, idealism and materialism, they know that they are transplanting Western intellectual manicheism.

The conceptual framework of African thinking has been both a mirror and a consequence of the experience of European hegemony; that is, in Gramsci's terms, "the dominance of one social bloc over another, not simply by means of force or wealth, but by a social authority whose ultimate sanction and expression is a profound cultural supremacy." These signs of a major contradiction are manifest in the increasing gap between social classes, and within each class, of the conflict between those who are culturally Westernized Africans and the others. In order to understand the structural factors that account for the contradiction, it might be useful to analyze the effects of economic levels as well as the archaeology of cultural ideologies.

At any rate, insofar as the African *gnosis* is concerned, it seems that while Tempels, Griaule, Kagame, Mulago, Lufuluabo, and other scholars were drawing lessons from Schmidt's heritage and thinking of implementing in theology as well as in philosophy and history new policies of exploiting African culture, Malinowski's legacy was questioned *in toto*. Not until the 1970s, was Schmidt's legacy interrogated from a strictly philosophical point of view through the critique of Tempels and Kagame. From then on, two methods appeared: one turns towards a critical practice of social and human sciences; another, inverting *Einfühlung* into a method of looking at oneself, concerns itself with rigorous techniques of converting Schmidt's, Griaule's, Tempels's and Kagame's contributions into strictly hermeneutic or anthropological practices as defined by such thinkers as Gadamer, Ricoeur, and Lévi-Strauss.

Today, philosophy and sociology journals and university departments have become the loci not only for academic exercises, but also for questioning the meaning of political power and interrogating all power-knowledge systems. In the school year 1968–1969, the humanist Senghor closed the University of Dakar to silence this questioning. Mobutu of Zaire, in 1971, moved the Department of Philosophy and the School of Letters two thousand kilometers from his capital. Ahidjo in Cameroon and Houphouët-Boigny in

Ivory Coast considered themselves magnanimous for permitting the existence of departments of philosophy, history, and sociology they opposed. Kenyatta of Kenya felt similarly and his successor closed the University of Kenya at the first social disturbance that challenged his political power. These examples provoke a question: where does one place philosophy and the social sciences in Africa, if, as a body of knowledge and as the practice of essentially critical disciplines, they seem to be marginal in the power structure?

Gnosis is by definition a kind of secret knowledge. The changes of motives, the succession of theses about foundation, and the differences of scale in interpretations that I have tried to bring to light about African *gnosis* witness to the vigour of a knowledge which is sometimes African by virtue of its authors and promoters, but which extends to a Western epistemological territory. The task accomplished so far is certainly impressive. On the other hand, one wonders whether the discourses of African *gnosis* do not obscure a fundamental reality, their own *chose du texte,* the primordial African discourse in its variety and multiplicity. Is not this reality distorted in the expression of African modalities in non-African languages? Is it not inverted, modified by anthropological and philosophical categories used by specialists of dominant discourses? Does the question of how to relate in a more faithful way to *la chose du texte* necessarily imply another epistemological shift? Is it possible to consider this shift outside of the very epistemological field which makes my question both possible and thinkable?

The only answer which can bring us back to reality would consider the condition of existence of African *gnosis* and of its best sign, anthropology, as both a challenge and a promise. Perhaps this *gnosis* makes more sense if seen as a result of two processes: first, a permanent reevaluation of the limits of anthropology as knowledge in order to transform it into a more credible *anthropou-logos,* that is a discourse on a human being; and, second, an examination of its own historicity. What this *gnosis* attests to is thus, beyond its will for power and its conceptual apparatus, a dramatic but ordinary question about its own being: what is it and how can it remain a pertinent question mark?

Conclusion

THE GEOGRAPHY OF A DISCOURSE

> Concerning the historians, we must
> distinguish among them to the effect that
> many have composed works on both Egypt
> and Ethiopia, of whom some have given
> credence to false reports and others have
> invented many tales out of their own minds
> for the delectation of their readers, and so may
> justly be distrusted.
>
> DIODORUS of Sicily.

African *gnosis,* that is, both the scientific and ideological discourse on Africa, presents two main questions. The first concerns the problem of regional rationalities, which in its best expressions, Marxist anthropology and structuralism, posits de facto the thesis of an original logic or transhistoric thought. This primary rationality should be understood as both condition of history and transhistoric permanence since it cannot be conceived as part of history. On this point, Godelier thinks Lévi-Strauss and Marx would agree:

> For Lévi-Strauss: "All social life, even elementary, presupposes an intellectual activity in man of which the formal properties, consequently, cannot be reflection of the concrete organization of the society." For Marx: 'Since the thought process itself grows out of the conditions, is itself a *natural process,* thinking that really comprehends must always be the same, and can only vary gradually according to maturity of development, including that of the organ by which the thinking is done. Everything else is drivel." (Godelier, 1977:215)

The second question concerns the concept of history, which in a first approximate definition could be described as an intellectual effort of ordering human activities and social events chronologically. Specialized investigations have indeed generated important issues. I shall note only two that directly confront African *gnosis* discourses. One is the postulation that history reflects or should translate the dynamics of human needs through time. Thus a particular history could be seen as a rhetorical paradigm, giving expression to the reality of a conjunction of such variables as thought, space, and type of human being. From this postulation, one conclusion, which in fact is simply an hypothesis, could be that expounded by José Ortega y Gasset: "Each geographic space, insofar as it is a space for a possible history, is . . . a function of many variables." (Ortega y Gasset, 1973:271). A great number of theorists would agree with Ortega y Gasset when he claims that "the history of reason is the history of the stages through which the domestication of our disorderly imagining has gone. There is no other way than to understand how that refining of the human mind has continued to be produced" (Ortega y Gasset, 1973:272). Yet common sense indicate a paradox—the very concept of history is not transparent. Against the dogmatic certainties of traditional historians, one would then accept to rethink the concept of history and face the challenge presented by the French *Ecole des Annales*. F. Braudel clearly posed the basic demands of the problem:

> History exists at different levels, I would even go so far as to say three levels but that would be only in a manner of speaking, and simplifying things too much. There are ten, a hundred levels to be examined, ten, a hundred different time spans. On the surface, the history of events works itself out in the short term: it is a sort of microhistory. Halfway down, a history of conjunctures follows a broader, slower rhythm . . . And over and above the "récitatif" of the conjuncture, structural history, or the history of the *longue durée,* inquires into whole centuries at a time. It functions along the border between the moving and the immobile, and because of the long-standing stability of its values, it appears unchanging compared with all the histories which flow and work themselves out more swiftly, and which in the final analysis gravitate around it. (Braudel, 1980:74)

The problem of a history that can be thought of as a question mark or, to put it in a maore optimistic manner, as a project, is thus directly linked to both the subject and the object of history. History is both a discourse of knowledge and a discourse of power. To use Foucault's language, history, as well as all human science, has the "project of bringing man's consciousness back to its real condition, of restoring it to the contents and forms that brought it into being, and elude us within it" (1973:364).

Let us pause to clarify the difficulties brought about by these two main questions of African *gnosis*. First, there is the thesis of a transhistoric thought, which constitutes a challenge of all external determinations, including the historical. In effect, in the positions of Marx and Lévi-Strauss, thought has no history and could have one only as part of a history of matter. Second, the thesis of history as a dynamic of variables (Ortega y Gasset), or as a theoretical model combining a multi-level diachronic rhythm (Braudel), explicitly or implicitly posits thought as a major factor in the evolution of cultures, understood as different historical characters. To perceive the silently supposed importance of critical thought's initiatives, one has only to refer to the three criteria that according to Braudel (1980:202–5) should be retained for "one good definition" of a civilization. These are: a cultural area or locus with its characteristics and its particular coherence, the borrowing of cultural goods as sign of positive exchanges or traffic that never stops, and, finally, refusals, the contrary of diffusion, in which "each civilization makes its decisive choice through which it asserts and reveals itself" (Braudel, 1980:203).

Although the two theses are not necessarily contradictory (Braudel claims that he stands "shoulder to shoulder with Claude Lévi-Strauss" [1980:205]), their presence in African *gnosis* divides the geography of this discourse into two opposed spaces. On the one side, synchronically oriented discourses, generally anthropological, claim to unveil the organization of a cultural economy and its regional rationality; on the other, diachronically motivated discourses, such as Marxist history and political ideologies, present grids for both interpretation of and action upon dialectical discontinuities of social systems. This distinction does justice to a controversial yet universally and dogmatically accepted dichotomy distinguishing tradition and modernity in African *gnosis*. What this separation means in terms of pertinence and scientific validity can be evaluated on the basis of a simple illustration. Let us suppose that a social scientist decides to interpret present-day French culture by formulating and determining the signs of a tradition using only one source. He uses J. Favret-Saada's analysis of cases of witchcraft and possession in a rural sub-culture (Favret-Saada, 1977) and opposes them to the signs of a modernity system such as those studied by M. Duverger in political science and M. Crozier in sociology. Nobody would take such a *fabula* seriously. In effect, major issues are at stake: how are these two spaces to be dissociated and on the basis of what criteria? In which sense does the so-called traditional arrangement define itself as an autonomous field outside of modernity and vice-versa? In which mode of being are the concepts of tradition and modernity expressed and formulated within a cultural area?

It could be argued that in African *gnosis* anthropology, and thus the notion of a "native" tradition, preceded the body of diachronically oriented discourses pertaining to social relations of production, organization of power, and ideologies. Consequently, one ought not forget the procedures by which these discourses were founded nor that they articulated a culture that contemporary students can interrogate from the viewpoint of their modernity. Yet I am not convinced by such reasoning. In my view, it does not justify the static binary opposition between tradition and modernity, for tradition (*traditio*) means discontinuities through a dynamic continuation and possible conversion of *tradita* (legacies). As such, it is part of a history in the making. J. F. Romano's and G. Gavazzi's narratives, for example, do not offer a closed totality of the seventeenth-century Kongo but rather present systems of local customs, sociocultural signs that they believe Christianity could transform for the better.

It is the *episteme* of the nineteenth and early twentieth centuries that invented the concept of a static and prehistoric tradition. Travelers' reports localize African cultures as "beings-in-themselves" inherently incapable of living as "beings-for-themselves." Theorists such as Spencer and Lévy-Bruhl interpreted and classified these monstrosities as existing at the beginning of both history and consciousness. Functionalism, through analyses of primitive otherness, offered scientific credibility to the concept of historical deviation between prehistoric civilizations and the Western paradigm of history.

Let me clarify two major epistemological propositions. First, at the very heart of the nineteenth-century European ambition of interpreting and classifying human cultures according to a scale, one faces history as a theoretical and abstract vocation, which refers to various achievements. To use F. de Saussure's concepts, it is strictly speaking a sort of *langue* whose meaning and power are given and actualized in such *paroles* as biological characteristics of beings, evolution and organization of language, economic structures of social formation, structuration of religious beliefs and practices. These *paroles* are linked in a relation of necessity to the minds of peoples who have put them forth and, by extension, to their culture as a whole. History is not a neutral concept here. It is a normative *langue,* a being, which socializes the *cogito* and all its metaphoric duplications. It subsumes all cultural *paroles.* As such, it identifies with their locus or culture, reflects and expresses itself as both a normative *in-itself* and *for-itself.* It properly visualizes the Hegelian dream. In this sense, and in this sense only, Belgian and French colonizers were not mistaken when, following Lévy-Bruhl's famous dichotomy, they used to postulate a clear distinction between prelogism and Cartesianism, primitiveness and civilization. Yet they were both uncritical and naive in not seeing that such a separation was simply a poor transposition of a refusal to face and think the implicit, the unthought, the *An sich,* negated in their own cultural experience by the sovereignty of a history which was a mystifying socialization of the *cogito.* Foucault is perfectly correct when he observes that "the modern *cogito* does not reduce the whole being of things to thought without ramifying the being of thought right down to the inert network of what does not think" (1973:324). In sum, the discovery of primitiveness was an ambiguous invention of a history incapable of facing its own double.

My second epistemological proposition comes from taking the risk of studying and evaluating Foucault's proposition that the entire history of the human sciences from the nineteenth century onward can be retraced on the basis of three conceptual pairs: *function* and *norm, conflict* and *rule, signification* and *system.*

> These constituent models are borrowed from the three domains of biology, economics, and the study of language. It is upon the projected surface of biology that man appears as being possessing *functions*—receiving stimuli (physiological ones, but also social, interhuman, and cultural ones), reacting to them, adapting himself, evolving, submitting to the demands of an environment, coming to terms with the modifications it imposes, seeking to erase imbalances, acting in accordance with regularities, having, in short, conditions of existence and the possibility of finding average *norms* of adjustment which permit him to perform his functions. On the projected surface of

economics, man appears as having needs and desires, as seeking to satisfy them, and therefore as having interests, desiring profits, entering into opposition with other men; in short, he appears in an irreducible situation of *conflict;* he evades these conflicts, he escapes from them or succeeds in dominating them, in finding a solution that will—on one level at least, and for a time—appease their contradictions; he establishes a body of *rules* which are both a limitation of the *conflict* and a result of it. Lastly, on the projected surface of language, man's behaviour appears as an attempt to say something; his slightest gestures, even their involuntary mechanisms and their failures, have a *meaning;* and everything he arranges around him by way of objects, rites, customs, discourse, all the traces he leaves behind him, constitute a coherent whole and a *system* of signs. Thus, these three pairs of *function* and *norm, conflict* and *rule, signification* and *system* completely cover the entire domain of what can be known about man. (Foucault, 1973:357)

Now let us imagine a panoramic view of African *gnosis* as a spatial configuration. From left to right we can follow a chronological order and thus go successively from discourses on primitiveness to modernist commentaries on organization of production and those on power. The body of texts on the left side supposedly unveils a tradition; that on the right side should witness to ruptures, transformations, and challenges brought about by the efficiency of colonialism. In between, one notes a confused intermediary area. For some theorists, it is a pure blank symbolizing both a geological and an archaeological discontinuity between tradition and modernity. For others, this middle space is the locus of aberrant expressions of acculturation. At any rate, we observe that the content of discourses on tradition, that is otherness as both monstrosity and *corpus mirabiliorium,* has not qualitatively changed since the first reports of the sixteenth and seventeenth centuries. Contrary to the claims of anthropological textbooks, one can still integrate data and categories from most present-day studies into the grid proposed by Varenius in his 1650 *Geographia Generalis.* This proposes a classification based on observations of

> (1)the stature of the Natives, as to their shape, colour, length of life, Original, Meat, and Drink, etc., (2) Their Trafficks and Arts in which the inhabitants are employed, (3) Their virtues, Vices, Learning, Wit, etc., (4) Their Customs in Marriage, Christenings, and Burials, etc., (5) Their Speech and Language, (6) Their State-Government, (7) Their Religion and Church-Government, (8) Their Cities and most renowned Places, (9) Their memorable Histories, and (10) their famous Men, Artificers, and Inventions of the Natives of all Countries. (In Hodgen, 1971:168)

What makes nineteenth and twentieth century discourses on tradition pertinent is not their sophistication and so-called capacity for discriminating cultural features and organizing taxonomies, but the epistemological significance of their models and the system of values these models imply and manifest. Tempels (1945) and Griaule (1948) did not discover an African rationality but rather redescribe clearly with new metaphors that which was a pathological deviation according to Tylor, Durkheim, and Lévy-Bruhl. The shift in models does not make the new "invention" necessarily more credible than the first. It mostly postulates a different system of values by emphasizing otherness and qualifying it from its localized *norms,* regional *rules,* and *coherence.* Thus it accounts for what made it possible, a pluralization of Western social and human sciences.

This process and its contradictions are probably clearer in discourses on modernity, which implicitly or explicitly operate on the basis of a philosophy of history and study African organizations through such metaphors as political hybridism, cultural schizophrenia, economic dualism, etc., which all refer to the concept of acculturation. The debate on this issue has been exemplified by J. Jahn's *Muntu* (1961). In this book, Jahn bases his argument on Friedell's statement that "legend is not one of the forms, but rather the only form, in which we can imaginatively consider and relive history. All history is saga and myth, and as such the product of the state of our intellectual powers at a particular time: of our capacity for comprehension, the vigour of our imagination, our feeling for reality." Jahn writes:

> The Africa presented by the ethnologist is a legend in which we used to believe. The African tradition as it appears in the light of neo-African culture may also be a legend—but it is the legend in which African intelligence believes. And it is their perfect right to declare authentic, correct and true those components of their past which they believe to be so. (Jahn, 1961:17)

Let us temporarily set aside the plausibility of the thesis. The argument insists on reasons for ordering a legend as expounded by Friedell, according to whom "every age has a definite picture of all past events accessible to it, a picture peculiar to itself" (Jahn, 1961:17). This seems to outline a type of convenience history. It does not, however, postulate a priori inclinations as the only foundation and explication of historical analyses, nor does it reject methods for verifying and validating historical reconstructions. Rather it challenges the silent yet commonly accepted valorization principle that transmutes historical genres into human history and claims to explain, from the truth of the Western enunciative space of models, the articulation of history as an absolute order of both universal power and knowledge. An apt illustration is Weber's indignation about some recent textbooks: "The idea of a sort of politico-social equity in history which would want—at last! at last!—to give Bantu and (American) Indian peoples, so outrageously despised up to now, a place at least as important as to the Athenians, is quite simply naïve" (in Veyne, 1984:52). Paradoxically, against the so-called scientific ideal of historical activity which founds it, Weber's position underscores the pertinence of Jahn's pronouncement: history is a relation to values and sets itself on mechanisms of intellectual valorization. As Veyne aptly put it, "one does not prefer the Athenians to the Indians in the name of certain established values; it is the fact that one prefers them that makes them into values; a tragic gesture of unjustifiable selection would serve as a basis for every possible vision of history" (1984:51).

It is clear that as a polemic stance, Jahn's thesis is sound. In its most general ambition, it posits two types of doubt: the first, about the universalization of modalities for deciphering and interpreting Western diachronic transformations; the second, about the principle of transferring categories from one cultural field of human experience to another. More specifically, the first is applied to Jaspers's theory of history, according to which the virtues of two revolutions—the age of reflective thought between 900 and 800 B.C. and the more recent age of science and technology—endow Western civilization with a unique capacity for both development and extension that can only destroy all non-Western cultures. Jahn notes that Jaspers "foresees for them no adjustment, but only their extinction or the fate of becoming mere raw material to be processed by technological civilization" (1961:13). The second doubt concerns Malinowski's functional theory of cultural change, according to which African cultures change by the fact of European pressures and, unable to overcome the divisive effects of its own transformation, produce cultural monstrosities. To Jaspers's assessment that African cultures are destined to crumble and Malinowski's formulation of economic and cultural aberrations, Jahn proposes an alternative: a "neoculture" combining the best of European and African experience.

> The present and the future . . . will be determined by the conception that *African* intelligence forms of the African past. Neo-African culture appears as an unbroken extension, as the legitimate heir of tradition. Only where man feels himself to be heir and successor to the past has he the strength for a beginning. (Jahn, 1961:18)

It is now possible to make more explicit the tension Jahn's argument represents. On the one hand, we have the body of legends constituted by the colonial library and exemplified by primitivist anthropology. It is a constellation in which one accounts for differences with theories using functional paradigms and external causes. They depict deviations from the normativeness of a history or of a rationality. On the other hand, there is the new corpus accepted by the African intelligentsia, such as A. Césaire, J. B. Danquah, M. Deren, Cheikh A. Diop, A. Kagame, E. Mphahlele, J. H. Nketia, L. S. Senghor, etc. Although incomplete and probably a legend itself, the new corpus should reflect the authority of local systems of rules, signification, and order. Can we not understand this chronological succession, particularly when we pay attention to its complexity (from Durkheim to Cheikh Anta Diop, from Lévy-Bruhl to Tempels and Griaule, from Frobenius to Nkrumah and Senghor), as a simple modification in strategies of manipulating concepts and metaphors? In effect, orders and grids of interpretation do not and cannot change the reality they claim to translate. Yet it is not important insofar as it does not address the major issue explicit in Jahn's thesis—that of inventing these strategies. Foucault's questions on regroupings of discourses in nineteenth-century Europe are pertinent here:

> Is it necessity that links them together, makes them invisible, calls them to their right places one after another and makes of them successive solutions to one and the same problem? Or chance encounters between ideas of different origin, influences, discoveries, speculative climates, theoretical models that the patience or genius of individuals arranges into more or less well-constituted wholes? Or can one find a regularity between them and define the common system of their formation? (Foucault, 1982:64)

The cohesion of new strategies appeared in a well defined period between the 1920s and the 1950s. A reconversion of models gradually ensured new metaphors that question African society's supposedly functional pathologies, its aberrant structural conflicts, and the so-called poverty of its history and accomplishments.

By way of illustration, here are the three main types of theories I have analyzed. *(a)* African writing, in literature and in politics, proposes new horizons emphasizing the alterity of the subject and the importance of the archeological locus. Negritude, black personality, and Pan-Africanist movements are the best known strategies that postulate a major anthropological stance: nobody is at the center of human experience, and there is no human who could be defined as the center of creation. *(b)* The orthodoxy of functionalism is progressively splintered. One key lies in the contributions of German anthropology, particularly of Schmidt's diffusionist Viennese School which idealizes the concept of *philosophia perennis*. This gives impetus to Tempels's formulation of the hypothesis of a Bantu ontology. At the same time, it can be linked to Griaule's revelation: Dogon cosmology justifies and explains its own internal procedures of interpreting the universe, of organizing and accounting for the world and its past. An "ethnophilosophy" is born. Later on, after the 1960s, it will become an exacting philosophical question (Hountondji, 1983), a hermeneutical challenge (Tshiamalenga, 1980), or a proposal for a radical rethinking of both the concept of primitive revelation and the foundation of Christian theology (Bimwenyi, 1981a; Eboussi-Boulaga, 1981; Nothomb, 1965). *(c)* It is commonplace to say that anthropology, by its practical activity of describing "primitive organizations" and by its ambiguous programs of controlling them for the sake of colonialism, produced the need for an in-depth understanding of synchronic dynamics, which could only lead to the concept of African history. J. Vansina's theory of oral tradition as historical discourse (1961) is just a moment, exemplary but only one stage in the process of *reinventing* the African past, a necessity since the 1920s. Everybody knows that when oral tradition was raised to the ambiguous respectability of a historical document, a critical reading of European models about the African past led Cheikh Anta Diop and Ajayi to ask uncomfortable questions about how a truly African history is the history of Africa (Diop, 1954, 1960a; Ajayi, 1969).

The cohesion of these various strategies resides in the way they establish a dialogue between the past and the present. What distinguishes them from the nineteenth-century literature are their new models for producing knowledge. The primitivist strategies, as illustrated in travel sagas and the colonial library, negate the possibility of a plural rationality and history; the more recent theories impose them, and would even extend to the understanding of marginalized experiences in the Western culture itself. For example, on which basis can a will to knowledge define the division of reason and madness, normal and abnormal sexuality, correct and defective consciousness? (see, e.g., Foucault, 1961; 1975; 1976). To put it simply, primitivist strategies operate by means of binary oppositions at the core of a paradigmatic history, whereas the more recent theories suppose in their methods an absolute incapacity for defining, vis-à-vis functional paradigms, such things as cultural margins, morbid consciousness, primitive mentalities, insignificant legends, and so on.

It becomes clear that apart from the romantic violence of his thesis, Jahn is basically right. History is a legend, an invention of the present. It is both a memory and a reflection of our present. M. Bloch and F. Braudel say exactly the same thing when they present history as an *attempt* to establish a relation between a conceptual framework, a model, and the multi-level rhythms of the past. History's project of going beyond the fundamental arbitrariness of the signifier and signified model in order to describe a relation of necessity between our understanding and the past depends on three systems. These are: *(a)* the subjectivity of the author, which is so evident that P. Ricoeur proposed to understand objectivity in history as a good and critical usage of one's subjectivity; *(b)* the collection of tools, techniques, theoretical grids, and "libraries" of events and their interpretation; *(c)* and especially important, the epistemological conditions that make the project both thinkable and feasible.

Theories of cultural hybridism, schizophrenia, and other metaphoric diseases (see, e.g., Levine, 1986:159–73) seem, therefore, to be by-products of a normative conception of history. They look at and comment upon positivities from the arrogance of a Hegelian dialectic and thus fail to witness to concrete temporal and localized figures. We know now, thanks to M. Mauss, G. Dumézil, and Lévi-Strauss, that all cultural figures determine their own specificity in apparently regional ruptures and continuities, whereby the otherness of their being appears as dynamic event, and thus history. All temporal pasts expose an otherness of the same ontological quality as the otherness unveiled by anthropologists, be they primitivists or not. This implies methodological challenges. The first, as proposed by Lévi-Strauss, is reconceptualizing the complementarity of history and sociology-anthropology (Lévi-Strauss, 1963: Introduction). The second challenge, as stated by Veyne (1984:285), lies in overcoming the restriction of the unities of time and space, envisaging a shift from continuous or regional history to a comparative or general history. Granted, this is still a dream. Yet, we already have enough evidence to understand that acculturation is not an African disease but the very character of all histories. In the sequences, mutations, and transformations that we can read, all histories deploy in effect the dispersion of the violence of the Same, which from the solid grounding in the present, invents, restores, or endows meaning to the Other in a past or in geographically remote synchronic cultures.

Can I affirm that Marxist analysis does not achieve a positive interplay between regional formations and general history to the point that such concepts as historical deviation, cultural schizophrenia, or economic aberration become pertinent? First of all, let us note that Marxist methodology operates from the supposed universal pertinence of its presuppositions. Marxism is, and I am travestying A. Koyré's thought, a fundamental and absolute science in its own intellectual right. The variability of all archaeological regionalities is subsumed in the logic of historical and dialectical materialism and can be localized thanks to the rules of this grid. Marxist Africanist discourses witness to this. Let us take two examples: the first, theoretical, on the question of modes of production and its subsequent concept of articulation; the second, more concrete, on how intellectual discourse should describe social contradictions and espouse the fate of socialism.

Marx's schemes and remarks on precapitalist modes of production promoted a number of categories related to the dominant relation of production: Slave, German, Feudal, Asiatic, etc. In Marxist exegeses, modes of production rapidly became structural stages reflecting the historical succession of types of combinations of forces and relations of production. After the debate created by the volumes from the Centre d'Etudes et de Recherches Marxistes (CERM) on Asiatic modes of production (1969, 1973), Marxist analysis reworked the historical tempo in a perfectly evolutionist and functional grid as an almost mechanical succession of modes of production determined by productive forces and class struggle. Paradoxically, this conception goes along with a theoretical claim concerning the plurality of historical experiences. It both posits a critique of the concept of a paradigmatic history and promotes the principle of historical specificity (Jewsiewicki and Letourneau, 1985:4–5). The precolonial modes of production are, at any rate, supposed at the outset of the historical canon, and the general argument takes the route from lineage systems to capitalist modes of production. Arranged in a table (Coquery-Vidrovitch, 1985:13–16), one sees on one side precapitalist modes. These are defined by two main factors: first, in a space where private property does not exist, buying or selling land is an impossibility and second, production relations are dependent upon a system of lineage relationships. On the other side one sees the capitalist mode, the dominant exterior force. In between are found dependent or precapitalist modes, generally known as peripheral capitalisms. The process of social transformation is isomorphic with the society's capacity to innovate and adjust to capitalism. Jewsiewicki's classification of dominant models facing the challenge represented by this process and its signification, namely, types of mode of production (e.g., Rey, 1966; Jewsiewicki and Letourneau, 1985), particularly those of dependent (e.g., Amin, 1964, 1965, 1967, 1969) and marginal society (e.g., Meillassoux, 1975), brings us back to the problematic articulation of binary oppositions: primitiveness versus civilization, tradition versus modernity, lineage mode versus capitalist mode of production, underdevelopment versus development.

It could be argued that even materialist models tend to reduce otherness. The unfamiliar is subsumed in metaphors, standardized procedures deduce patterns and their meaning relative to Marxist paradigms. John Saul's magnificent "socialist lesson" (1977) apropos of I. Kimambo and A. Temu's *A History of Tanzania* may serve as an illustration. From the book's "too straightforward a focus 'on the African himself,' " he deduces four main dangers. These are: *(a)* a playing down of "the overall imperialist framework within which African initiatives are taken," which *(b)* "can encourage a blurring of relevant distinctions and differentiations within the African community itself" *(c)* "with the result that the full *meaning* and *significance* of African initiatives is lost and, moreover *(d)* the accomplishments of Africans . . . are, therefore, over-valued, at the expense of a frank discussion of the very challenges which remain (the realization of socialism and self-reliance, and the fulfillment of the country's productive potential)." In sum, as Saul puts it himself:

> The contention (. . .) is that the questions which underlie the Kimambo-Temu volume are too exclusively those relevant to a nationalist perspective on Tanzania history, at a moment when a socialist perspective and a set of socialist questions are increasingly imperative. (Saul, 1977:138)

Saul's language is one of universal and normative orthodoxy. It does not reject the necessity for an obedience to events and facts but explicitly insists on the paramount value of socialist imperatives. It does not question the pertinence of Tanzania's history as specificity but indicates that narratives about it can be situated within a socialist perspective only on well-determined conditions. What Saul's discourse witnesses to is the silent yet powerful sovereignty of the Same.

The discourse of orthodoxy has revised its categories since the 1920s policy of *mise en valeur* of colonial territories. However, it still holds the keys to norms and rules, thus accounting for African systems and the modalities of their adjustment to modernity as represented by either the capitalist or socialist paradigms. Thus, Saul's position is part of a more general epistemological process. It belongs to a set of models claiming to reflect and explain historical dynamics and establish the validity of a method. Here is another example which is also a generalization. The African political economy discourse, with it concepts of and models on diachronic and synchronic structural deviations, economic dualism, mechanisms of underdevelopment, technology of transfer, etc., comments upon hypothetical dogmas of transition from tradition to modernity, using terms similar to the Durkheimian opposition (1947) between, on the one hand, specific and abnormal and, on the other, general and normal.

Structuralist anthropology, a somewhat enigmatic discourse, seems to transcend contradictory representations about the interaction between tradition and modernity. Rooted in the same epistemological ground which permitted the reconversion of African *gnosis,* it rises above typological models of historical transformations and defines itself as both reflection and comment on transhistoricity. More concretely, it introduces an obvious evidence, namely that there is more to say about being human than mechanized tautologies can offer about a history of the Same. In the name of explaining the reality of human fate, the discourse about the Same incessantly repeats its own fantasies and the incoherences defining it as normative.

> The solidity of the self, the major preoccupation of the whole of Western philosophy, does not withstand persistent application to the same object, which comes to pervade it through and through and to imbue it with an experiential awareness of its own unreality. For the only remnant of reality to which it still dares to lay claim is that of being a "singularity," in the sense in which astronomers use the term: a point in space and a moment in time, relative to each other, and in which there have occurred, are occurring or will occur events whose density . . . makes possible its approximate definition, always remembering of course that this nodal point of past, present and probable events does not exist as a substratum, but only in the sense that phenomena are occurring in it . . . (Lévi-Strauss, 1981:625–26)

One could also refer to Veyne's strong critique of a history of the Same that, in reality, does not exist despite its ambitions (Veyne, 1984:15–30). Most important, at least in African *gnosis,* are the implications of this new perspective: *(a)* an interrogation about the subject of discourse; *(b)* a reevaluation of the concept of rationality from the viewpoint of intrinsic properties of categories functioning in regional texts, myths and interpretations; *(c)* a reconceptualization of scientific method and the relationships that "scientific knowledge" might have with other forms or types of knowledge; and *(d)* a redefinition of human freedom. These are not small issues, and because of their range, structuralism, to use an unfortunate expression of M. P. Edmond, has been perceived as a process of de-Westernizing scientific knowledge (Edmond, 1965:43–44).

Let me be frank: twenty years of careful study of structuralism have convinced me that although there is an impressive body of good and comprehensive analyses on structuralism in which one finds stimulating and highly technical criticisms (e.g., Beidelman, 1966; Turner, 1969) and philosophical challenges (e.g., Ricoeur, 1969), a great number of criticisms of Lévi-Strauss are consciously or unconsciously ideological, even, I would say, racially motivated. They can often be reduced to the two following statements: Is not structuralism a Jewish enterprise against the achievements of the Christian West? And, as one of my European students put it, forgetting my origin: "Lévi-Strauss does them too much honor."

Concerning the methodology of describing African cultural dynamics, the difficult exchange that exists nowadays between J. Vansina and L. de Heusch, T. Obenga and his opponents, P. Hountondji and his critics, is a sign of the organic richness of discourses focusing on the individuality of norms, rules, and systems. These discourses show the perilous path of the future. On the other hand, they point to the delicate validity of patient translations and interpretations of regional cultural economies, such as the work of Lienhardt (1961), Buakasa (1973), Jackson (1982), and Izard (1985). This orientation is revealed most explicitly in Bird and Karp's collection of specialized studies, *Explorations in African Systems of Thought* (1980), and in Beidelman's study on Kaguru modes of thought (1986). The domain of a universal language (*langage*) or megarationality has been replaced by the criterion of experiential authority "inventing" itself as translation and exegesis of institutional and well-delineated languages (*langues*) founded by concrete performances (*paroles*). What one gets is thus a decisive critique of traditional methods of correlating the Same to the Other. In B. Barnes's words, these enterprises from within indicate that "making a demarcation in actors' own terms is useful for explanatory purposes. Such a demarcation is part of the actors' perception of the situation; and action is intelligible only as a response to that perception . . . Making a demarcation by external standards, on the other hand, is useless for explanatory purposes . . ." (1974:100). It is obvious that such a method should define itself as a critical system of making statements, which could only partially unveil the social and cultural archives of a society.

What then should we do with the problem of a transhistoric thought? From the rhetorical margins of history, it opens upon a paradox: something like the pure reflection of consciousness in a pure language. It enlarges and universalizes regional archives and brings them into contact with the analyst's mind, thus inventing in a dynamic manner both understanding and history. It is useful "for history to move away from us in time or for us to move away from it in thought, for it to cease to be internalizable and to lose its intelligibility, a spurious intelligibility attaching to a temporary internality" (Lévi-Strauss, 1966:225). This does not constitute the negation of the truth of social forms as expressed and generated by the dialectic between *Leben* (living and sharing with others) and *Gemeinsamkeit* (a permeating community). On the contrary, a permanent recapitulation of this dialectic should remain as an endless task of reading, commenting upon the permanent production of cultural legends and *"une parole pour-soi."*

Foucault once said that he deprived "the sovereignty of the subject of the exclusive and instant right to discourse." That is good news. I believe that the geography of African *gnosis* also points out the passion of a subject-object who refuses to vanish. He or she has gone from the situation in which he or she was perceived as a simple functional object to the freedom of thinking of himself or herself as the starting point of an absolute discourse. It has also become obvious, even for this subject, that the space interrogated by the series of explorations in African indigenous systems of thought is not a void.

APPENDIX

ETHIOPIAN SOURCES OF KNOWLEDGE

"If Abyssinia had been a colony, for example, the most ardent believer in the preservation of native culture would not have advocated the recreation of the pre-Christian religion" wrote L. P. Mair (Malinowski and others, 1938:4). In the Marxist Ethiopia of today, a Canadian scholar, C. Sumner, has made a major contribution to the search for a new outlook on "African philosophy." He thinks that "there is an urgent need that philosophy, taught in Ethiopia at a university level, should not be entirely alien, but integrate values found at home, in the fertile native ground" (Sumner, 1974:3). He has so far made available the following major sources.

(1) *The Book of the Wise Philosophers* has been known since 1875 thanks to C. H. Cornill (*Das Buch der Weisen Philosophen nach dem Aethiopischen untersucht*, Leipzig) and A. Dillmann (*Chrestomathia Aethiopica*, 1950, Berlin). It is an anthology of sayings, most attributed to such philosophers as Socrates, Plato, Aristotle, and Galen. "The majority of the sayings were exhortations and advice, often addressed by a wise man to a disciple or to his son" (Sumner, 1974:4). The text used is a Geez translation from an Arabic original compiled between 1510 and 1522 by Abba Mikael, an Arabic-speaking Egyptian. It is profoundly marked by Greek and Christian influences, as shown in references to Socrates's life and to platonic philosophy and in quotations of early church fathers such as Gregory and Basil.

(2) *The Treatise of Zär'a Yacob and of Walda Heywat.* The corpus of these seventeenth-century texts was established for the first time in 1904 by E. Littman (Philosophia Abessini, *Corpus Scriptorum Christianorum Orientalium* 18, (1):Paris). Sumner's edition (1976, 1978) is the first complete English version (1976:3–59). The work comprises two *hatätas*, autobiographical meditations. The *Zär'a Yacob* (seed of Jacob) is divided into twenty-five chapters bearing on the author's life, the eternity of God, division among believers, the meaning of faith and prayer, the law of God and the law of man, Mosaic law and Mohammed's meditation, physical and spiritual work, marriage, and the nature of knowledge. Composed of thirty-five brief chapters, the *Treatise of Walda Heywat* (son of life) examines such topics as creation, knowledge, faith, the nature of the soul, law and judgement, social life, the use of love, virtues and human weaknesses, education, time, and culture.

In his 1904 edition, Littmann noted the intellectual power and originality of these works.

While the greater part of Ethiopian literature is translated from foreign languages, these two books written by Abyssinians are imbued with their own
native character . . . However, I would say that these flowers could not grow
solely from the Ethiopian ground, unless they had been irrigated by external
waters. (In Sumner, 1976:63)

In 1916, Carlo Conti Rossini hypothesized that the treatises were of European origin and suggested the author might have been Giusto D'Urbino, an
Italian missionary. Eventually, the two *hatätas* came to be considered nineteenth-century Italian works. Sumner has worked to prove the contrary and
to reestablish the Ethiopian origin of the texts (Sumner, 1976:250–75).
However, in his extensive analysis, Sumner compares Zär-a Yacob to Mani,
Luther, Herbert of Cherbury, René Descartes and Jean-Jacques Rousseau
(1978:65–73). He thinks that "many of the ideas developed in the *Hatäta* are
similar to, and in some instances identical with, the *Tractatus de Veritate*
and the *Discours sur la méthode*. But the convergence would not apply
beyond the logical level of a common rationalistic approach and of epistemological investigations" (1978:61).

(3) *The Life and Maxims of Skandes* is an Ethiopic version of the well-
known text of Secundus, whose roots go back to the first centuries of the
Roman Empire. It has survived in two lineages: Western (Greek and Latin)
and Eastern (Syriac, Arabic, and Ethiopic). Sumner reproduces the edition
established by Bachmann: *Das Leben und die Sentenzen des Philosophen
Secundus das Schweigsamen* (1887, Halle). This Geez version belongs to the
1434–1468 literary period and is a translation of an earlier Arabic text. The
theme of the book is a question: what is the relation between a woman's will
and her instinctive tendencies? It is also a commentary on the shocking
maxim that all women are prostitutes. According to Sumner, the Ethiopian
version is, from a literary viewpoint, original. "The translator very often
departs from the Arabic original. He both subtracts and adds" (1981:437).

Sumner is preparing two other volumes for publication: *The Fisalgwos*
and *Basic Ethiopian Philosophical Texts*. Greeting the publication of *The
Book of the Wise Philosophers*, L. Nusco, of the then Haile Selassie I
University, remarked that the book "is not a work of philosophy in the
technical sense of the word," adding that "such a classification would cause
the indignation of all professional philosophers" (Sumner, 1974). In his
evaluation of the 1976 Addis Ababa Seminar on African philosophy, Van
Parys asked whether or not these treatises are really Ethiopian, since at least
the first and the third are translations. His answer is prudent: they are
original and creatively Ethiopian, but apart from the second, they are not
really critical. "It is in the comparisons between Arab and Greek on one
hand and Ethiopian on the other that is found Ethiopian originality. However
none of these works show the critical spirit that characterizes modern
thinking" (Van Parys, 1978:65).

This is possibly a matter of opinion. The body of ancient Ethiopian texts does not conceal its sources. Nevertheless one cannot ignore that some of them, such as the books of Zär'a Yacob and Walda Heywat, witness to a regional inspiration. In any case, all these texts are somehow "subjects" commenting upon themselves and their restlessness. The fact is that, as in the case of most intellectual contributions, there is a mystery on two sides: the genealogical reciprocity existing between the Ethiopian versions and their historical references, and, on the other hand, the privileges of their own textuality. In a paper focusing on the ethical aspects of this literature, Sumner has emphasized the complementarity of these two aspects:

> If we consider together the two expressions of Ethiopian Philosophy: transla-
> tion, adaptation and personal reflection, popular-traditional wisdom and
> rationalism . . . we come to a few conclusions which can be summarized
> under four headings: centrality, comprehensiveness, richness, theological
> basis. (Sumner, 1983:99)

For Sumner, the notion of centrality is linked to that of moral importance or prevalence that "characterizes all types of Ethiopian thought." That of comprehensiveness implies that "all aspects, objective and subjective, proximate and ultimate, are taken into consideration in the assessment of the norms of morality." The concept of richness is a theoretical image expressing connotations and implications stemming from "the key word of 'heart,' the radiating polarity of 'conscience'" in the texts. Finally, there is the theological basis, which is radically anthropocentric. About the sixteenth-century *Book of the Wise Philosophers* and the seventeenth-century philosophical treatises of Zär'a Yacob and his disciple Walda Heywat, Sumner proposes hypotheses that clearly discriminate them from the tradition that produced them:

> Both are opposed to any kind of religious revelation, and hence are not
> Christian in any way; they are, in that sense, explicitly anti-Christian. And yet
> their rationalism led them to a clear, pure, abstract theism. For the natural
> light of reason, however opposed to any revealed positive light, is nonetheless a
> penetration of the divine into the creatural. (Sumner, 1983:100)

Thus, one can provisionally note that textual deviations mean what they silently or explicitly negate: the intellectual locus of their possibility. At the same time and more important, by their very presence they also indicate a remarkable instance of a culturally regional authority in terms of creativity.

BIBLIOGRAPHY

ABANDA NDEGUE, M. J. (1970). *De la négritude au négrisme*. Yaoundé: Clé.

ABLEGMAGNON, F.M. (1957). "Du 'temps' dans la culture Ewe." *Présence Africaine* nos. 14–15: 222-32.

———. (1958). "Personne, tradition et culture." In *Aspects de la culture noire*. Paris: Fayard.

———. (1960). "L'Afrique noire: La Métaphysique, l'ethique, l'évolution actuelle." *Comprendre* nos. 21–22:74–82.

———. (1962). "Totalités et systèmes dans les sociétés d'Afrique noire." *Présence Africaine* no. 41:13–22.

ABRAHAM, W. E. (1966). *The Mind of Africa*. Chicago: The University of Chicago Press.

ADELE JINADU, L. (1976). "The Moral Dimensions of the Political Thought of Frantz Fanon." *Second Order* 5 (1).

ADOTEVI, S. (1972). *Négritude et négrologues*. Paris: Plon.

ADOUKOUNOU, B. (1981). *Jalons pour une théologie africaine*. 2 vols. Paris: Lethielleux.

AFANA, O. ([1967] 1976). *L'Economie de l'ouest africain*. Paris: Maspero.

AGASSI, J. (1963). *Towards an Historiography of Science*. The Hague: North Holland Publishing Company.

AGOSSOU, J. M. (1972). *Gbet'o et Gbedo'to*. Paris: Beauchesne.

———. (1977). "Pour un Christianisme africain." *Cahiers des religions africaines* 11, 21–22, I.

AGUOLU, C. (1975). "John Dewey's Democratic Conception and its Implication for Developing Nations." *Second Order* 4 (2).

AHIDJO, A. (1964). *Contribution à la construction nationale*. Paris: Présence Africaine.

———. (1969). *Nation et développement dans l'unité*. Paris: Présence Africaine.

AJAYI, J. F. A. (1969). "Colonialism: An Episode in African History." In *Colonialism in Africa 1870–1960*, L. H. Gann and P. Duignan, eds. vol. 1 of *The History and Politics of Colonialism*. Cambridge: Cambridge University Press.

AJAYI, J. F. A. and CROWDER, M. (1972). *History of West Africa*. London: Longmans.

AJISAFE, A. K. (1924). *The Laws and Customs of the Yoruba People*.

AKE, C. (1979). *Social Science as Imperialism: The Theory of Political Development*. Lagos: University of Ibadan Press.

ALLIER, R. (1925). *La Psychologie de la Conversion chez les Peuples non-civilisés*. Paris: Payot.

ALMOND, A. G., and COLEMAN, J. S., eds. (1960). *The Politics of Developing Areas*. Princeton: Princeton University Press.

ALTHUSSER, L. (1965). *Pour Marx*. Paris: Maspero. (*For Marx*, New York: Pantheon).

AMIN, S. (1964). *Neo-Colonialism in West Africa*. Harmondsworth: Penguin.

———. (1965). *Trois expériences africaines de développement: le Mali, la Guinée et le Ghana*. Paris: Presses universitaires de France

———. (1967). *Le Développement du capitalisme en Côte d'Ivoire*. Paris: Editions de Minuit.

———. (1969). *Le Monde d'affaires sénégalaises*. Paris: Editions de Minuit.

———. (1973). *Le Développement inégal. Essai sur les formations sociales du capitalisme périphérique*. Paris: Editions de Minuit. (*Unequal Development*. New York: Monthly Review Press).

———. (1974). *L'Accumulation à l'échelle mondiale.* Paris: Anthropos. (*Accumulation on a World Scale: A Critique of the Theory of Underdevelopment,* New York: Monthly Review, 1974).

———. (1979). *Classe et nation dans l'histoire et la crise contemporaine.* Paris: Editions de Minuit.

AMIN, S., and COQUERY-VIDROVITCH, C. (1969). *Histoire économique du Congo, 1880–1968.* Paris: Anthropos.

AMSELLE, J. L. (1979). *Le Sauvage à la mode.* Paris: Le Sycomore.

ANYIDOHO, K. (1985). "The Present State of African Oral Literature Studies." In *African Literature Studies. The Present State/L'Etat Présent,* Arnold, S., ed. Washington, D.C.: Three Continents Press.

APOLLINAIRE, G. (1913). *Les Peintres cubistes.* Paris: E. Figuière.

APPIAH-KUBI, K., and TORRES, S. (1977). *African Theology en Route.* New York: Orbis.

ARENDT, H. (1968). *Imperialism: Part Two of the Origins of Totalitarianism.* New York: Harcourt Brace Jovanovich.

ARINZE, F. A. (1970). *Sacrifice in Ibo Religion.* Ibadan.

ARNOLD, S. (1985). "African Literary Studies: The Emergence of a new discipline." In *African Literature Studies. The Present State/L'Etat Présent,* S. Arnold, ed. Washington, D.C.: Three Continents Press.

ARRIGHI, R. (1979). *Libération ou Adaptation. La Théologie africaine s'interroge. Le Colloque d'Accra.* Paris: L'Harmattan.

ASAD, T., ed. (1973). *Anthropology and the Colonial Encounter.* New York: Humanities Press.

ASHBY, E. (1966). *Universities: British, Indian, African: A Study in the Ecology of Higher Education.* London: Weidenfeld & Nicolson.

ASTIER-LOUTFI, M. (1971). *Littérature et colonialisme: L'Expansion coloniale vue dans la littérature française.* Paris: Mouton.

ATAL, D. (1972). *Structures et signification des cinq premiers versets de l'hymne johannique au logos.* Louvain-Paris: Béatrice-Nauwelaerts.

ATANGANA, N. (1971). *Travail et développement.* Yaoundé: Clé.

AUGE, M. (1979). *Symbole, fonction, histoire. Les interrogations de l'anthropologie.* Paris: Hachette.

AWOLOWO, O. (1947). *Path to Nigerian Freedom.* London: Faber and Faber.

———. (1968). *The Peoples' Republic.* Ibadan: Oxford University Press.

AYANDELE, E. (1966). *The Missionary Impact on Modern Nigeria, 1842–1914.* London: Longman.

AZIKIWE, N. (1937). *Renascent Africa.* New ed. 1969. London: Cass.

———. (1961). *Zik: A Selection from the Speeches.* Cambridge: Cambridge University Press.

AZOMBO-MENDA, S. M., and ANOBO, K. (1978). *Les Philosophes africains par les textes.* Paris: Nathan.

BA, A. H. (1972). *Aspects de la civilisation africaine.* Paris: Présence Africaine.

———. (1976). *Jésus vu par un musulman.* Dakar-Abidjan: Nouvelles editions africaines.

BA, A. H., and CARDAIRE, M. (1957). *Tierno Bokar, le sage de Bandiagara.* Paris: Présence Africaine.

BA, A. H., and DIETERLEN, G. (1961). *Koumen. Texte initiatique des pasteurs Peul.* Paris: Mouton.

BADIAN, S. (1964). *Les Dirigeants africains face à leur peuple.* Paris: Maspero.

BAETA, C. G., ed. (1968). *Christianity in Tropical Africa.* Oxford: Oxford University Press.

BAHOKEN, J. C. (1967). *Clairières métaphysiques africaines. Essai sur la philosophie et la religion chez les Bantu du Sud-Cameroun.* Paris: Présence Africaine.

BAIROCH, P. (1971). *Le Tiers Monde dans l'impasse*. Paris: Gallimard.

BAL, W. (1963). *Le Royaume du Congo aux XVᵉ et XVIᵉ siècles. Documents d'histoire*. Léopoldville (Kinshasa): Institut National d'Etudes Politiques.

BALANDIER, G. (1955a). *Sociologie des Brazzavilles noirs*. Paris: A. Colin.

———. (1955b). *Sociologie actuelle de l'Afrique noire*. Paris: Presses universitaires de France.

———. (1957). *Afrique ambiguë*. Paris: Plon.

———. (1967). *Anthropologie politique*. Paris: Presses universitaires de France.

BAMUINIKILE, S. (1971). *La Mort et l'au-delà chez les Baluba du Kasai*. Lubumbashi: CEPSI.

BARAN, P. (1957) *The Political Economy of Growth*. New York: Modern Reader Paperbacks.

BARLEY, N. (1984). *Adventures in a Mud Hut*. New York: The Vanguard Press.

BARNES, B. (1974). *Scientific Knowledge and Sociological Theory*. London: Routledge & Kegan Paul.

BARRETT, D. B. (1968). *Schism and Renewal in Africa*. Nairobi: Oxford University Press.

———. (1970). "A.D. 2000—350 Million Christians in Africa." *International Review of Missions*, 59 (233):39–54.

———, ed. (1974). *African Initiatives in Religion*. Nairobi: East African Publishing House.

BARTHES, R. (1979). *The Eiffel Tower and Other Mythologies*. New York: Hill and Wang.

BASSE, E.C. (1977). "Itinéraire de Présence Africaine: Problème de l'église en Afrique." *Cahiers des religions africaines* 11, 21–22, 1.

BASTIDE, R. (1961). "Variations sur la négritude." *Présence Africaine* no. 36.

———. (1967). "Color, Racism, and Christianity." *Daedalus* 96 (2):312–27.

BATTLE, V. M., and LYONS, C. H. eds. (1970). *Essays in the History of African Education*. New York: Teachers College Press.

BAUDRILLARD, J. (1972). *Pour une critique de l'économie politique du signe*. Paris: Gallimard.

———. (1977). *Le Miroir de la production: ou L'Illusion critique du matérialisme historique*. Tournai: Casterman. (*The Mirror of Production*. St. Louis: Telos, 1975).

BAYART, J. F. (1979). *L'Etat au Cameroun*. Paris: Presse de la Fondation Nationale des Sciences Politiques.

———. (1983). "La Revanche des sociétés africaines." *Politique africaine* 1:95–127.

BEATTIE, J. (1973). "Understanding Traditional African Religion: A Comment on Horton." *Second Order* 2, (2).

BEIDELMAN, T. O. (1966). "Swazi Royal Ritual." *Africa* 34 (4):373–405.

———. (1986). *Moral Imagination in Kaguru Modes of Thought*. Bloomington: Indiana University Press.

BEIER, U., ed. (1966). *The Origin of Life and Death*. London: Heinemann.

BELLMAN, B. L. (1984). *The Language of Secrecy: Symbols and Metaphors in Poro Ritual*. New Brunswick: Rutgers University Press.

BERGH, P. VAN DEN. (1973). *Power and Privilege at an African University*. London: Routledge & Kegan Paul.

BETTS, R. F. (1975). *The False Dawn: European Imperialism in the XIXᵗʰ Century*. Minneapolis: University of Minnesota Press.

BIGO, P. (1974). *L'Eglise et la révolution du tiers monde*. Paris: Presses universitaires de France.

BIMWENYI, O. (1968). "Le Muntu à la lumière de ses croyances en l'au-delà," *Cahiers des religions africaines* 8:137–51; 9 (1971):59–112.

————. (1981a). *Discours théologique négro-Africain. Problèmes de fondements.* Paris: Présence Africaine.

————. (1981b). "L'Inculturation en Afrique et attitude des agents de l'evangélisation." *Aspects du catholicisme au Zaire.* Kinshasa: Faculté de Théologie Catholique.

BINSBERGEN, W. M. J. VAN. (1981). *Religious Change in Zambia: Exploratory Studies.* London: Routledge & Kegan Paul.

BINSBERGEN, W. M. J. VAN, and SCHOFFELEERS, M., eds. (1985). *Theoretical Explorations in African Religion.* London: Routledge & Kegan Paul.

BIRD, C. S. and KARP, I., eds. (1980). *Explorations in African Systems of Thought.* Bloomington: Indiana University Press.

BJORNSON, R., and MOWOE, I. J., eds. (1986). *Africa and the West.* New York: Greenwood Press.

BLACK, M., (1962). *Models and Metaphors.* New York, Ithaca: Cornell University Press.

BLAIR, D. (1976). *African Literature in French.* Cambridge: Cambridge University Press.

BLOCH, M., (1961). *Feudal Society.* Chicago: The University of Chicago Press.

BLYDEN, E. W. (1862). *Liberia's Offering,* New York, 1862. (LO) It contains the following texts:
  (1) "Hope for Africa," 5–28.
  (2) "A Vindication of the African Race," (Liberia, 1857):31–64.
  (3) "The Call of Providence to the Descendants of Africa in America," 67–91.
  (4) "Inaugural Address at the Inauguration of Liberia College," 95–123.
  (5) "Eulogy on Rev. John Day," 127–149.
  (6) "A Chapter in the History of the African Slave-Trade," 153–167.
  (7) "A Note to Benjamin Coates on 'The Colonization and Abolition Movements'," 169–181.

————. (1869a). *Liberia: Past, Present, and Future.* (LPPF) Washington.

————. (1869b). *The Negro in Ancient History.* (NAH) Washington.

————. (1888). *Christianity, Islam and The Negro Race.* (CINR) London. New edition, 1967, at Edinburgh University Press.

————. (1903). *Africa and Africans.* (AA) London.

————. (1978). *Selected letters of Edward Wilmot Blyden,* (LET) ed., Hollis R. Lynch. New York: KTO Press.

BODUNRIN, P. O. (1975a). "Values and Objectivity in the Social Sciences." *Thought and Practice* 2, (1).

————. (1975b). "The Alogicality of Immortality." *Second Order* 4 (2).

————. (1978). "Witchcraft, Magic and E.S.P." *Second Order* 7 (1 and 2).

BOELAERT, E. (1946). "La Philosophie bantoue selon le R. P. Placide Tempels." *Aequatoria* 9:81–90.

BOESAK, A. A. (1977). *Farewell to Innocence: A Socio-Ethical Study on Black Theology and Black Power.* New York: Orbis.

————. (1984a). *Black and Reformed: Apartheid, Liberation and the Calvinist Tradition.* New York: Orbis.

————. (1984b). *Walking on Thorns: The Call to Christian Obedience.* Grand Rapids: W. B. Eerdmans Publishing Company.

BOHANNAN, P. ([1953] 1980). "Concepts of Time among the Tiv of Nigeria." In *Myth and Cosmos,* Middleton, J., ed. Austin: University of Texas Press.

BONTE, P. (1976). "Marxisme et anthropologie: Les Malheurs d'un empiriste." *L'Homme* 16 (4):129–36.

BONTINCK, F. (1980). "Mfumu Paul Panda Farnana (1888–1930) Premier (?) nationaliste congolais." In *Africa's Dependence and the Remedies,* V. Y. Mudimbe, ed. Paris: Berger-Levrault.

BOOTH, N. S., ed. (1977). *African Religions: A Symposium*. New York: Nok.
BOURDIEU, P. (1973). "The Three Forms of Theoretical Knowledge." *Social Science Information* 14 (6):19–47.
BOURGEOIS, A. (1971). *La Grèce antique devant la négritude*. Paris: Présence Africaine.
BRAUDEL, F., (1980). *On History*. Chicago: The University of Chicago Press.
BRELSFORD, V. (1935). *Primitive Philosophy*. London: J. Bale
———. (1938). "The Philosophy of the Savage." *Nada*, 15.
BRENNER, L. (1984). *West African Sufi: The Religious Heritage and Spiritual Search of Cerno Bokar Saalif Taal*. Berkeley/Los Angeles: University of California Press.
BROWN, R., ed. (1973). *Knowledge, Education and Cultural Change*. London: Tavistock.
BRUNSCHWIG, H. (1963). *L'Avènement de l'Afrique noire du XIXe siècle à nos jours*. Paris: A. Colin.
BUAKASA, T. K. M. (1973). *L'Impensé du discours. Kindoki et nkisi en pays Kongo du Zaire*. Kinshasa: Presses Universitaires du Zaire.
———. (1978). "Les Sciences de l'occident: Pour quoi faire?" *Philosophie et libération*, Kinshasa: Faculté de Théologie Catholique.
BÜHLMANN, W. (1978). *The Coming of the Third Church*. New York: Orbis.
———. (1979). *The Missions on Trial*. New York: Orbis.
———. (1980). *All Have the Same God*. New York: Orbis.
———. (1982). *The Chosen Peoples*. New York: Orbis.
BUJO, B. (1975). *Morale africaine et foi chrétienne*. Kinshasa: Faculté de Théologie Catholique.
BUREAU, R. (1962). "Les Missions en question. La Conversion des cultures." *Christus* no. 9:34.
BUSIA, K. H. (1951). *The Position of the Chief in the Modern Political System of Ashanti*. London.
———. (1962). *The Challenge of Africa*. London: Pall Mall.
CALVET, J. L. (1972). *Linguistique et colonialisme*. Paris.
CASTERAN, C., and LANGELLIER, J. P. (1978). *L'Afrique déboussolée*. Paris: Plon.
CENDRARS, B. (1921). *Anthologie nègre*. New ed. 1972. Paris: Buchet-Chastel.
CERM. (1969). *Sur le mode de production asiatique*. Paris: Editions Sociales.
———. (1973). *Sur les sociétés précapitalistes. Textes choisis de Marx, Engels, Lénine*. Paris: Editions Sociales.
CERTEAU, M. DE. (1969). *L'Etranger ou l'Union dans la différence*. Paris: Desclée de Brouwer.
———. (1984). *The Practice of Everyday Life*. Los Angeles: University of California Press.
CESAIRE, A. (1950). *Discours sur le colonialisme*. Paris: Présence Africaine (*Discourse on Colonialism*. New York: Monthly Review Press, 1972).
———. (1956). *Lettre à Maurice Thorez*. Paris: Présence Africaine.
———. (1959–60). "La Pensée Politique de Sekou Touré." *Présence Africaine* no. 29.
CHENU, B. (1977). *Dieu est noir*. Paris: Le Centurion.
CHILCOTE, R. H. (1981). *Dependency and Marxism*. Boulder: Westview Press.
CHINWEIZU, JEMIE, MADUBUIKE. (1983). *Toward the Decolonization of African Literature*. Washington, D.C.: Howard University Press.
CHIPENDA, J. B. (1977). "Theological Options in Africa Today." In *African Theology En Route*, Appiah-Kubi and Torres, eds. New York: Orbis.
CHRISTOPHER, A. J. (1984). *Colonial Africa*. Totowa, New Jersey: Barnes and Noble.
CLARENCE-SMITH, W. G. (1977). "For Braudel: A Note on the Ecole des Annales and the Historiography of Africa." *History in Africa* 4:275–81.
———. (1985). *The Third Portuguese Empire 1825–1975: A Study in Economic Imperialism*. Manchester: Manchester University Press.

CLARK, G. (1936). *The Balance Sheets of Imperialism.* New York: Columbia University Press.

CLIFFORD, J. (1983). "On Ethnographic Authority." *Representations* 1 (2).

COHEN, R. (1977). "Oedipus Rex and Regina: the Queen Mother in Africa." *Africa* 47 (1).

COLEMAN, J. S. (1956). *Togoland.* New York: Carnegie Endowment for International Peace.

———. (1965). *Nigeria: Background to Nationalism.* Berkeley: University of California Press.

COLEMAN, J. S., and ALMOND, G. A., eds. (1960). *The Politics of the Developing Areas.* Princeton: Princeton University Press.

COLEMAN, J. S., and HALISI, C. R. D. (1983). "American Political Science and Tropical Africa: Universalism vs. Relativism." *African Studies Review* 26 (3/4):25–62.

COLEMAN, J. S., and ROSBERG, C. G. Jr., eds. (1964). *Political Parties and National Integration in Tropical Africa.* Berkeley: University of California Press.

COLLINGWOOD, R. G. (1946). *The Idea of History.* London: Oxford University Press.

COPANS, J. (1971a). "Pour une histoire et une sociologie des études africaines." *Cahiers d'études africaines* 11, 43. Repr. as "African Studies: A Periodization." In *African Social Studies: A Radical Reader,* P. Gutkind and P. Waterman, eds. (New York: Monthly Review Press, 1978).

———. (1971b). *Critiques et politiques de l'anthropologie.* Paris: Maspero.

———. (1974). *Anthropologie et impérialisme.* Paris: Maspero.

COQUERY-VIDROVITCH, C. (1969a). "Anthropologie politique et histoire de l'Afrique." *Annales* 24 (1):142–63.

———. (1969b). "Recherches sur un mode de production africaine." *La Pensée,* no. 144:61–78.

———. (1972). *Le Congo au temps des grandes compagnies concéssionaires.* Paris: Mouton.

———. (1980). "Analyse historique et concept de mode de production dans les sociétés capitalistes." *L'Homme et la société* 55–58, 104–44.

———. (1984). "Réflexions d'historienne." In *Mode of Production: The Challenge of Africa,* B. Jewsiewicki and J. Létourneau, eds. Ste-Foy, Canada: Safi.

———, and MONIOT, H. (1974). *L'Afrique noire de 1800 à nos jours.* Paris: Presses universitaires de France.

CORDELL, D. D. (1985). *Dar al-Kuti and the Last Years of the Trans-Saharan Slave Trade.* Madison: University of Wisconsin Press.

CORREIA, J. A. (1925). "Vocables philosophiques et religieux des peuples Ibo." *Bibliotheca Ethnologica Linguistica Africana* 1.

COSMAO, V. (1979). *Changer le monde.* Paris: Cerf.

COUNT, E. W., ed. (1950). *This is Race: An Anthology Selected from the International Literature on the Races of Man.* New York: Schuman.

CRAHAY, F. (1965). "Le Décollage conceptuel: conditions d'une philosophie bantoue." *Diogène,* 52, 61–84.

CURTIN, P. D. (1961). "'The White Man's Grave': Image and Reality, 1780–1850." *Journal of British Studies* 1:94–110.

———. (1964). *Africa Remembered: Narratives by West Africans from the Era of the Slave Trade.* Madison: University of Wisconsin Press.

———. (1965). *The Image of Africa: British Thought and Action 1780–1850.* Madison: University of Wisconsin Press.

DAMANN, E. (1964). *Les Religions d'Afrique noire.* Paris: Payot.

DAMAS, L. G. (1979) "The Last Public Statement of L.-G. Damas." *Hommage Posthume à L. G. Damas.* Paris: Présence Africaine.

DANQUAH, J. B. (1928). *Akan Laws and Customs.*

———. (1968) *The Akan Doctrine of God.* London: Cass.

DAVIDSON, B. (1959). *The Lost Cities of Africa*. Boston: Little, Brown.
————. (1970). *The African Genius*. Boston: Little, Brown.
DECRAEMER, W. (1977). *The Jamaa and the Church*. Oxford: Clarendon.
DELAFOSSE, M. (1922). *L'Ame nègre*. Paris: Payot.
————. (1927). *Les Nègres*. Paris: Rieder.
DELANGE, J. (1967). *Arts et peuples d'Afrique noire*. Paris: Gallimard.
DELAVIGNETTE, R. (1962). *L'Afrique noire et son destin*. Paris: Gallimard.
DELEUZE, G., and GUATTARI, F. (1972). *L'Anti-Oedipe*. Paris: Editions de Minuit.
DELHAISE, C. (1909). "Les Idées religieuses et philosophiques des Waregas." *Mouvement géographique* 29.
DELOBSON, D. (1932). *L'Empire du Mogho-Naba*. Paris: Domat Montchrétien.
————. (1934). *Les Secrets des sorciers noirs*. Paris.
DENG, F. M. (1972). *The Dinka of the Sudan*. New York: Holt, Rinehart and Winston.
DEPESTRE, R. (1980). *Bonjour et adieu à la négritude*. Paris: Laffont.
DESCHAMPS, H. (1971). *Histoire de la traite des noirs de l'antiquité à nos jours*. Paris: Fayard.
————. (1954). *Les Religions de l'Afrique noire*. Paris: Presses universitaires de France.
DESMOND CLARK, J., and BRANDT, S. A., eds. (1984). *From Hunters to Farmers*. Berkeley and Los Angeles: University of California Press.
DHOQUOIS, G. (1966). "Le Mode de production asiatique." *Cahiers internationaux de sociologie* 41, 83–92.
DIA, M. (1957). *L'Economie africaine*. Paris: Presses universitaires de France.
————. (1960). *Nations africaines et solidarité mondiale*. Paris: Presses universitaires de France.
————. (1975). *Islam, sociétés africaines et culture industrielle*. Dakar: NEA.
————. (1977–1981). *Essais sur l'Islam*. 3 vols. 1. *Islam et humanisme*. 2. *Socio-Anthropologie de l'Islam*. 3. *Islam et civilisations négro-africaines*. Dakar: Nouvelles editions africaines.
DIAGNE, M. (1976). "Paulin J. Hountondji ou La Psychanalyse de la conscience ethno-philosophique." *Psychopathologie Africaine*, 3, XII.
DIAGNE, P. (1967). *Pouvoir politique traditionnel en Afrique occidentale. Essai sur les institutions précoloniales*. Paris: Présence Africaine.
————. (1972). *Pour l'unité ouest-africaine. Micro-Etats et intégration economique*. Paris: Anthropos.
DIAKHATE, L. (1965). "Le Processus d'acculturation en Afrique noire et ses rapports avec la négritude." *Présence Africaine*, no. 56.
DIAMOND, S. (1974). *In Search of the Primitive: A Critique of Civilization*. New Brunswick.
DICKSON, K. A. (1984). *Theology in Africa*. New York: Orbis.
DIENG, A. L. (1979). *Hegel, Marx, Engels et les problèmes de l'Afrique noire*. Dakar: Sankoré.
————. (1983). *Contribution à l'etude des problèmes philosophiques en Afrique noire*. Paris: Nubia.
DIETERLEN, G. (1941). *Les Ames des Dogons*. Paris: Institut d'Ethnologie.
————. (1971). "Les Cérémonies soixantenaires du Sigui chez les Dogons." *Africa* 41 (1).
DIKE, K. O. (1956). *Trade and Politics in the Niger Delta, 1830–1885*. Oxford: Clarendon.
DIODORUS SICULUS. (1935). An English translation by C. H. Oldfather. Cambridge: Harvard University Press.
DIOP, A. (1965). "Niam M'Paya." Preface to *La Philosophie Bantoue* by P. Tempels. Paris: Présence Africaine.

DIOP, C. A. (1954). *Nations nègres et culture*. Paris: Présence Africaine.
———. (1960a). *L'Afrique noire précoloniale*. Paris: Présence Africaine.
———. (1960b). *Les Fondements culturels, techniques et industriels d'un futur etat fédéral d'Afrique noire*. Paris: Présence Africaine.
———. (1960c). *L'Unité culturelle de l'Afrique noire*. Paris: Présence Africaine.
———. (1967). *Antériorité des civilisations nègres*. Paris: Présence Africaine.
———. (1978). *Parenté génétique de l'égyptien pharaonique et les langues négro-africaines*. Dakar-Abidjan: Nouvelles éditions africaines.
———. (1981). *Civilisation ou Barbarie*. Paris: Présence Africaine.
DIOP, M. (1958). *Contribution à l'étude des problèmes politiques en Afrique noire*. Paris: Présence Africaine.
———. (1972). *Histoire des classes sociales dans l'Afrique de l'Ouest*. Paris: Maspero.
DIRVEN, E. (1978). "Philosopher en Africain." *Mélanges de philosophie africaine*. Kinshasa: Faculté de Théologie Catholique.
DOGBE, E. (1980). *Négritude, culture et civilisation. Essai sur la finalité des faits sociaux*. Mée-sur-Seine (France): Akpagnon.
DONDERS, J. G. (1985). *Non-Bourgeois Theology*. New York: Orbis.
DOUGLAS, M. (1963). *The Lele of the Kasai*. London: Oxford University Press.
———. (1970). *Natural Symbols*. London: Barrie Jenkins.
DUCHET, M. (1971). *Anthropologie et histoire au siècle des lumières*. Paris: Maspero.
DUGGAN, W. R., and CIVILE, J. R. (1976). *Tanzania and Nyerere*. New York: Orbis.
DURKHEIM, E. (1912). *Les Formes élémentaires de la vie religieuse*. Paris: Alcan. (*The Elementary Forms of the Religious Life*. New York: Free Press.)
EBOUSSI-BOULAGA, F. (1968). "Le Bantou Problématique." *Présence Africaine* no. 66:4–40.
———. (1977). *La Crise du Muntu. Authenticité africaine et philosophie*. Paris: Présence Africaine.
———. (1978). "Pour une catholicité africaine." *Civilisation noire et église catholique*. Paris: Présence Africaine.
———. (1981). *Christianisme sans fétiche. Révélation et domination*. Paris: Présence Africaine.
EDMOND, M. P. (1965). "L'Anthropologie structuraliste et l'histoire." *La Pensée* no. 123.
ELA, J.-M. (1980) *Le Cri de l'homme africain*. Paris: L'Harmattan.
———. (1985). *Ma foi d'africain*. Paris: Karthala.
ELA, J. M., and LUNEAU, R. (1981). *Voici le temps des héritiers. Eglises d'Afrique et voies nouvelles*. Paris: Karthala.
ELUNGU, P. E. (1973a). " 'Authenticité' et Culture." *Revue zairoise de psychologie et de pédagogie* 2, 1, 71–74.
———. (1973b) *Etendue et connaissance dans la philosophie de Malebranche*. Paris: Vrin.
———. (1976). "La Philosophie, condition du développement en Afrique aujourd'hui." *La Place de la philosophie dans le développement humain et culturel du Zaire et de l'Afrique*. Lubumbashi: Département de Philosophie.
———. (1977). "La Philosophie, condition du développement en Afrique aujourd'hui." *Présence Africaine* no. 103:3–18.
———. (1978). "La Libération africaine et le problème de la philosophie." *Philosophie et Libération*. Kinshasa: Faculté de Théologie Catholique.
———. (1979). *Du Culte de la vie à la vie de la raison. De la crise de la conscience africaine*. Doctoral thesis. Paris: Université de Paris.
———. (1980) "La Philosophie africaine hier et aujourd'hui." *Mélanges de philosophie africaine* no. 3:9–32. Kinshasa: Faculté de Théologie Catholique.
EMMANUEL, A. (1969). *L'Echange inégal*. Paris: Maspero.

EMMET, D. (1972). "Haunted Universes." *Second Order* 1 (1).
EVANS-PRITCHARD, E. E. (1937). *Witchcraft, Oracles and Magic among the Azande.* London: Oxford University Press.
———. (1946). "Applied Anthropology." *Africa.*
———. (1956). *Nuer Religion.* London: Oxford University Press.
———. (1962). *Social Anthropology and Other Essays.* New York: The Free Press.
———. (1980). *Theories of Primitive Religion.* Oxford: The Clarendon Press.
EWANDE, D. (1968). *Vive le président. La Fête africaine.* Paris: A. Michel.
FABIAN, J. (1969). "An African Gnosis." *History of Religion* 9.
FACELINA, R., and RWEGERA, D. (1978). *Africain Theology. Théologie Africaine.* Strasbourg: Cerdic Publications.
FANON, F. (1952). *Peau noire, masques blancs.* Paris: Seuil.
———. (1961). *Les Damnés de la terre.* Paris: Maspero.
———. (1969). *Pour la révolution africaine.* Paris: Maspero.
FANOUDH-SIEFER, L. (1968). *Le Mythe du nègre et de l'Afrique noire dans la littérature française (de 1800 à la seconde guerre mondiale).* Paris: Klincksieck.
FAVRET-SAADA, J. (1977). *Les Mots, la mort, les sorts.* Paris: Gallimard. (*Deadly Words.* Cambridge University Press, 1980).
FERNANDEZ, J. W. (1979). "Africanization, Europeanization, Christianization." *History of Religions* 18 (3).
———. (1982). *Bwiti: An Ethnography of the Religious Imagination in Africa.* Princeton: Princeton University Press.
FIELDHOUSE, D. K. (1981). *Colonialism 1870–1945: An Introduction.* London: Weidenfeld and Nicolson.
FIELDS, K. (1985). *Revival and Rebellion in Colonial Central Africa.* Princeton: Princeton University Press.
FINNIGAN, R. (1970) *Oral Literature in Africa.* Oxford: Oxford University Press.
FLEISCHMAN, E. (1970). *Le Christianisme 'mis à nu'.* Paris: Plon.
FORDE, D., ed. ([1954] 1976). *African Worlds.* London: Oxford University Press.
FORTES, M. (1959). *Oedipus and Job in West African Religion.* Cambridge: Cambridge University Press.
FORTES, M., and DIETERLEN, G., eds. (1965). *African Systems of Thought.* London: Oxford University Press.
FOUCAULT, M. (1961). *L'Histoire de la folie.* Paris: Gallimard. (*Madness and Civilization.* New York: Random House, 1965.)
———. (1966). *Les Mots et les Choses.* Paris: Gallimard. (*The Order of Things.* New York: Pantheon, 1973.)
———. (1969). *L'Archéologie du savoir.* Paris: Gallimard. (*The Archaeology of Knowledge.* New York: Pantheon, 1982.)
———. (1975). *Surveiller et Punir.* Paris: Gallimard. (*Discipline and Punish.* New York: Pantheon, 1977.)
———. (1976). *La Volonté de savoir I.* Paris: Gallimard. (*The History of Sexuality I,* New York: Pantheon, 1978.)
———. (1980). *Power/Knowledge: Selected Interviews and Other Writings 1972–1977.* New York: Pantheon.
FOUDA, B. J. (1967). *La Philosophie africaine de l'existence.* Doctoral dissertation. Lille: Faculté des Lettres.
FOURCHE, J. A. T., and MORLIGHEM, H. (1973). *Une bible noire.* Brussels: Max Arnold.
FRAZER, J. (1922). *The Golden Bough.* London: MacMillan.
FROBENIUS, H. (1893). *Die Heiden-Neger des "agyptischen Sudan."* Berlin: Nitschke und Loechner.
———. (1899). "The Origin of African Civilization." *Annual Report of the Board of*

Regents of the Smithsonian Institution. Washington: Government Printing Office.

———. (1936). *Histoire de la civilisation africaine.* Paris: Gallimard.

———. (1937). *African Genesis.* New York: Stackpole Sons.

———. (1940). *Le Destin des civilisations.* Paris: Gallimard.

FROELICH, J. C. (1964). *Animismes, les religions païennes de l'Afrique de l'ouest.* Paris: Orante.

———. (1969). *Nouveaux dieux d'Afrique noire.* Paris: Orante.

FRY, R. (1940). *Vision and Design.* New York: Penguin.

FU-KIAU, A. (1969). *Le Mukongo et le monde qui l'entourait.* Kinshasa: Office National de la Recherche Scientifique.

FULCHIRON, B., and SCHLUMBERGER, C. (1980). *Poètes et romanciers noirs.* Paris: Nathan.

GEERTZ, C. (1973). *The Interpretation of Cultures.* New York: Basic Books.

GERARD, A. (1964). "Origines historiques et destin littéraire de la négritude." *Diogène 48.*

GILBERT, F., and GRAUBARD, S. R., eds. (1972). *Historical Studies Today.* New York: Random House.

GLELE, M. (1981). *Religion, culture et politique en Afrique noire.* Paris: Présence Africaine.

GODELIER, M. (1970). *Sur les sociétés précapitalistes.* Paris: Editions Sociales.

———. (1973). *Horizons, trajets marxistes en anthropologie.* Paris: Maspero.

———. (1977). *Perspectives in Marxist Anthropology.* Cambridge: Cambridge University Press.

GOODY, J. (1968). *Literacy in Traditional Societies.* Cambridge: Cambridge University Press.

———. (1977). *The Domestication of the Savage Mind.* Cambridge: Cambridge University Press.

GOROG, V., and CHICHE, M. (1981). *Littérature orale d'Afrique noire. Bibliographie analytique.* Paris: Maisonneuve et Larose.

GRAFT-JOHNSON, J. C. de. (1954). *African Glory: The Story of Vanished Negro Civilizations.* New York: Praeger.

GRAFT-JOHNSON, J. W. DE. (1928). *Towards Nationhood in West Africa.* New ed. 1971. London: Cass.

GRAVRAND, H. (1962). *Visage africain de l'église. Une experience au Sénégal.* Paris: Orante.

GREGOIRE, H. B. (1808). *De la littérature des nègres.* Paris: Maradan.

GRIAULE, M. (1948). *Dieu d'eau. Entretiens avec Ogotemmêli.* Paris: Chêne. (*Conversations with Ogotemmêli.* Oxford University Press, 1965.)

———. (1950). "Philosophie et Religion des Noirs." *Présence Africaine* 8–9:307–12.

———. (1952). "Le Savoir des Dogon." *Journal de la société des africanistes* 22, 27–42.

GRIAULE, M. and DIETERLEN, G. (1965). *Le Renard pâle.* Paris: Institut d'Ethnologie.

———. (1976). "The Dogon of the French Sudan." In *African Worlds,* D. Forde, ed. London: Oxford University Press.

GRIMAL, H. (1965). *La Décolonisation 1919–1963.* Paris: A. Colin.

GUERNIER, E. (1952). *L'Apport de l'Afrique à la pensée humaine.* Paris: Payot.

GUISSE, Y. M. (1979). *Philosophie, culture et devenir social en Afrique noire.* Dakar: Nouvelles éditions africaines.

GUNDER-FRANK, A. (1969). *Capitalism and Underdevelopment in Latin America.* New York: Monthly Review Press.

GUTKIND, P. C. W., and WALLERSTEIN, I., eds. (1976). *The Political Economy of Contemporary Africa.* Beverly Hills: Sage.

GYEKYE, K. (1973). "Al-Ghazali on Causation." *Second Order* 2 (1).

————. (1975). "Philosophical Relevance of Akan Proverbs." *Second Order* 4 (2).

HAEFFNER, G. (1978). "Philosophie Afrika." *Stimmen der Zeit* 103.

HAILEY, M. (1970). "Colonial Government through Indirect Rule: The British Model." In *The African Reader: Colonial Africa,* W. Cartey and M. Kilson, eds. New York: Vintage Books.

HALLEN, B. (1976). "Phenomenology and the Exposition of African Traditional Thought." *Second Order* 5 (2).

HALLEN, B., and SODIPO, J. O. (1986). *Knowledge, Belief and Witchcraft: Analytical Experiments in African Philosophy.* London: Ethnographica.

HALLER, J. H. (1971). *Outcasts from Evolution: Scientific Attitudes of Racial Inferiority.* Urbana: University of Illinois Press.

HAMA, B. (1968). *Essai d'analyse de l'éducation africaine.* Paris: Présence Africaine.

————. (1969). *Kotia-Nima.* 1. *Rencontre avec l'Europe;* 2. *Rencontre avec l'Europe;* 3. *Dialogue avec l'Occident.* Paris: Présence Africaine.

————. (1972a). *Le Retard de l'Afrique. Essai philosophique.* Paris: Présence Africaine.

————. (1972b). *Cet 'autre' de l'homme.* Paris: Présence Africaine.

HAMMOND, D., and JABLOW, A. (1977). *The Myth of Africa.* New York: The Library of Social Science.

HANNA S. (1963). *Who are the Copts?.* Cairo: Costa Tsouma.

HARIK, E. M., and SCHILLING, D. G. (1984). *The Politics of Education in Colonial Algeria and Kenya.* Athens, Ohio: University Center for International Studies.

HASTINGS, A. (1979). *A History of African Christianity 1950–1975.* Cambridge: Cambridge University Press.

HAUSER, M. (1982). *Essai sur la poétique de la négritude.* Lille: Université de Lille III.

HAZOUME, G. L. (1972). *Idéologies tribalistes et nation en Afrique: le cas dahoméen.* Paris: Présence Africaine.

HAZOUME, P. (1937). *Le Pacte du sang au Dahomey.* Paris: Travaux et Mémoires de l'Institut d'Ethnologie.

————. (1938). *Doguicimi.* Paris: Larose.

HEADRICK, D. (1981). *The Tools of Empire.* Oxford: Oxford University Press.

HEBGA, M. (1958). "Plaidoyer pour les logiques de l'afrique noire." *Aspects de la culture noire* 104–116. Paris.

————. (1976). *Emancipation d'églises sous-tutelle. Essai sur l'ère post-missionnaire.* Paris: Présence Africaine.

————. (1979). *Sorcellerie, chimère dangereuse?* Abidjan: Inades.

————. (1982). "Eloge de l'ethnophilosophie." *Présence Africaine,* no. 123.

HEBGA, M., ed. (1963). *Personnalité africaine et catholicisme.* Paris: Présence Africaine.

HERDECK, E. D., ed. (1973). *African Authors: A Companion to Black African Writing 1300 1973.* Washington, D.C.: Black Orpheus Press.

HERODOTUS. (1921). *Books III and IV.* With an English translation by A. D. Godley. London: W. Heinemann.

HERSKOVITS, M. J. (1962). *The Human Factor in Changing Africa.* New York: Knopf.

HERSKOVITS, M. J. and HERSKOVITS, F. (1958). *Dahomean Narrative.* Evanston: Northwestern University Press.

HERTEFELT, M. D' (1962). *Les Anciens Royaumes de la zone interlacustre méridionale.* Tervuren: Musée Royal de l'Afrique Centrale.

HESSE, M. (1963). *Models and Analogies in Science.* London: Sheed & Ward.

HEUSCH DE, L. (1958). *Le Symbolisme de l'inceste royal en Afrique.* Brussels: Université Libre de Bruxelles.

————. (1971). *Pourquoi l'épouser et autres essais.* Paris: Gallimard. (*Why Marry Her?* Cambridge University Press, 1981).

———. (1972). *Le Roi Ivre*. Paris: Gallimard. (*The Drunken King*. Bloomington: Indiana University Press, 1982.)

———. (1973). "Le Sorcier, le père Tempels et les jumeaux mal venus." In *La Notion de Personne en Afrique Noire*. Paris: Editions du Centre National de la Recherche Scientifique.

———. (1982). *Rois nés d'un coeur de vache*. Paris: Gallimard.

———. (1985). *Sacrifice in Africa*. Bloomington: Indiana University Press.

HOBSON, J. A. ([1902] 1972). *Imperialism: A Study*. Ann Arbor: University of Michigan Press.

HODGEN, M. T. (1971). *Early Anthropology in the Sixteenth and Seventeenth Centuries*. Philadelphia: University of Pennsylvania Press.

HODGKIN, T. (1957). *Nationalism in Colonial Africa*. New York: New York University Press.

HOFFMANN, (1973). *Le Nègre romantique. Personnage littéraire et obsession collective*. Paris: Payot.

HOLAS, P. (1954). *Le Culte de Zié*. Dakar: Ifan.

———. (1965). *Le Séparatisme religieux en Afrique noire*. Paris: Presses universitaires de France.

———. (1968a). *Les Dieux de l'Afrique*. Paris: Geuthner.

———. (1968b). *L'Image du monde bete*. Paris: Presses universitaires de France.

HOLDEN, E. (1967). *Blyden of Liberia*. New York: Vantage.

HOLLIS, M. (1981). "The Limits of Irrationality." In *Rationality*, B. R. Wilson, ed. Oxford: Basil Blackwell.

HORTON, R. (1961). "Destiny and the Unconscious in West Africa." *Africa* 31 (2):110–16.

———. (1972). "Spiritual Beings and Elementary Particles." *Second Order* 1 (1).

———. (1976). "Traditional Thought and the Emerging African Philosophy Department: A Comment on the Current Debate." *Second Order* 6 (1).

———. (1981). "African Traditional Thought and Western Science." In *Rationality*, B. R. Wilson, ed. Oxford: Basil Blackwell.

HOUNTONDJI, P. (1970). "Remarques sur la philosophie africaine contemporaine." *Diogène* no. 71.

———. (1977). *Sur la philosophie africaine*. Paris: Maspero (*African Philosophy: Myth and Reality*. Bloomington: Indiana University Press, 1983).

———. (1980). "Distances." *Recherche, pédagogie et culture* 49, 27–33.

———. (1981). "Que peut la philosophie?" *Présence Africaine* no. 119:47–71.

———. (1982). "Occidentalisme, Elitisme: réponse à deux critiques." *Recherche, pédagogie et culture* 9, 56.

———. (1983). "Reason and Tradition." In *Philosophy and Cultures*, O. Oruka, ed. Nairobi: Bookwise Limited.

HOWLETT, J. (1974). "La Philosophie africaine en question." *Présence Africaine* 91:14–25.

IDONIBOYE, D. E. (1973). "The Concept of 'Spirit' in African Metaphysics." *Second Order* 2 (1).

IDOWU, E. B. (1962). *Olodumare: God in Yoruba Belief*. London: Longmans.

———. (1965). *Towards an Indigenous Church*. Oxford University Press.

———. (1975). *African Traditional Religion: A Definition*. New York: Orbis.

ILIFFE, J. (1983). *The Emergence of African Capitalism*. Minneapolis: University of Minnesota Press.

ISICHEI, P. A. C. (1975). "Two Perspectives to the Past: History and Myth." *Second Order* 4 (2).

IYEKI, J. F. (1956). *Essai de psychologie du primitif*. Leopoldville (Kinshasa): Editions de la Voix du Congolais.

IZARD, M. (1985). *Gens du pouvoir. Gens de la terre*. Cambridge: Cambridge University Press.

JACKSON, M. (1982). *Allegories of the Wilderness: Ethics and Ambiguity in Kuranko Narratives*. Bloomington: Indiana University Press.

JAHN, J. (1961). *Muntu: An Outline of the New African Culture*. New York: Grove Press.

———. (1965). *Die Neoafrikanische Literatur. Gesamtbibliographie von den Anfängen bis zur Gegenwart*. Dusseldorf-Köln: Eugen Diederichs.

———. (1968). *A History of Neo-African Literature*. London: Faber and Faber.

JEANSON, F. (1949). "Sartre et le monde noir." *Présence Africaine* no. 7.

JEWSIEWICKI, B. (1980). "L'Histoire en Afrique ou Le Commerce des idées usagées." In *Les Faux Prophètes de l'Afrique*, A. Schwarz, ed. Quebec: Presses de l'Université de Laval.

———. (1981). "Lineage Mode of Production: Social Inequalities in Equatorial Central Africa." In *Modes of Production in Africa*, D. Grummey and C. C. Stewart, eds. Beverly Hills: Sage.

———. (1985). *Marx, Afrique et occident*. s.l.: McGill University Center for Developing Area Studies.

JEWSIEWICKI, B., and LETOURNEAU, J., eds. (1985). *Mode of Production: The Challenge of Africa. Canadian Journal of African Studies* 19 (1) special issue.

JEWSIEWICKI, B., and NEWBURY, D. eds. (1985). *African Historiographies*. Beverly Hills: Sage.

JORDAN, W. D. (1968). *White over Black: American Attitudes Towards the Negro, 1550–1812*. Chapel Hill.

JULES-ROSETTE, B. (1975). *African Apostles: Ritual and Conversion in the Church of John Maranke*. Ithaca: Cornell University Press.

———. (1984). *The Message of Tourist Art*. New York: Plenum Press.

JULY, R. (1964). "Nineteenth Century Negritude: Edward W. Blyden." *Journal of African History* 5 (1).

KABA, L. (1974). *The Wahhabiyya: Islamic Reform and Politics in French West Africa*. Evanston: Northwestern University Press.

KACHAMA-NKOY, J. (1963). "De Karl Marx à Pierre Teilhard de Chardin dans la pensée de L. S. Senghor et Mamadou Dia." In *Voies Africaines du Socialisme*. Leopoldville (Kinshasa): Bibliothèque de l'Etoile.

KAGAME, A. (1943). *Inganji Karinga* (The Victorious Drums) and (1949–51). *Isoko y'ámajyambere* (Sources of Progress). Kabgayi: Editions Morales. (*La Divine Pastorale*. Brussels: Editions du Marais, 1952).

———. (1950). *Bref aperçu sur la poésie dynastique du Rwanda*. Brussels: Editions universitaires.

———. (1952–53). *Umuliribya wa Nyiliibiremwa*. Astrida: Butare.

———. (1956). *La Philosophie bantu-rwandaise de l'être*. Brussels: Académie Royale des Sciences Coloniales.

———. (1968). "La Place de Dieu et de l'homme dans la religion des Bantu." *Cahiers des religions africaines* 4:213–22 and 1969, 5:5–11.

———. (1970). *Introduction aux grands genres lyriques de l'ancien Rwanda*. Butare: Editions universitaires du Rwanda.

———. (1971). "L'Ethno-Philosophie des Bantu." In *La Philosophie Contemporaine*, R. Klibansky, ed. Florence: La Nuova Italia.

———. (1972). *Un abrégé de l'ethno-histoire du Rwanda*. Butare: Editions universitaires du Rwanda.

———. (1976). *La Philosophie bantu comparée*. Paris: Présence Africaine.

KALANDA, M. A. (1967). *La Remise en question. Base de la décolonisation mentale*. Brussels: Remarques Africaines.

KALILOMBE, P. A. (1977). "Self-Reliance of the African Church: A Catholic Perspective." In *African Theology En Route*, Appiah-Kubi, K., and S. Torres, eds. New York: Orbis.

KALU, O. U. (1977). "Church Presence in Africa: A Historical Analysis of the Evangelization Process." In *African Theology En Route*, Appiah-Kubi, K., and S. Torres, eds. New York: Orbis.

KANE, C. H. (1961). *L'Aventure ambigue*. Paris: Julliard.

KANE, M. (1982). *Roman Africain et Tradition*. Dakar: Nouvelles éditions africaines.

KANGAFU, K. (1973). *Discours sur l'authenticité*. Kinshasa: Presses Africaines.

KANZA, T. (1959a). *Le Congo à la veille de son indépendance*. Bruxelles: Les Amis de Présence Africaine.

———. (1959b). *Propos d'un Congolais naïf*. Bruxelles: Les Amis de Présence Africaine.

KAOZE, S. (1907–1911). *La Psychologie des Bantus et quelques lettres*. Anastatic reproduction by A. J. Smet (1979). Kinshasa: Faculté de Théologie Catholique.

KASHAMURA, A. (1973). *Famille, sexualité et culture*. Paris: Payot.

KAUMBA, L. (1986). *Dimensions de l'identité. Approche phénoménologique de l'univers romanesque de Mudimbe*. Louvain-La-Neuve: Unpublished Ph.D. dissertation.

KAUNDA, K. D. (1966). *A Humanist in Africa: Letters to Colin M. Morris*. London: Longmans.

KELLER, A. S.; LISSITZYN, O.; and MANN, J. F. (1938). *Creation of Rights of Sovereignty Through Symbolic Acts 1400–1800*. New York: Columbia University Press.

KENYATTA, J. (1938). *Facing Mount Kenya*. London: Secker and Warburg. New edition, 1962. New York: Vintage.

KESTELOOT, L. (1965). *Les Ecrivains noirs de langue française: Naissance d'une littérature*. Brussels: Institut de Sociologie.

———. (1968). *Négritude et situation coloniale*. Yaoundé: Clé.

KILLINGRAY, D. (1973). *A Plague of Europeans*. Harmondsworth: Penguin Education.

KIMONI, I. (1975). *Destin de la littérature négro-africaine ou Problématique d'une culture*. Kinshasa: Presses universitaires du Zaire.

KINANGA, M. (1981). "L'Archéologie foucauldienne. Une méthode d'analyse du discours." In *Langage et philosophie*. Kinshasa: Faculté de Théologie Catholique.

KINGSLEY, M. H. (1965). *Travels in West Africa*. (Abridged version of 1900 edition). London: Cass.

KINYONGO, J. (1970). *Origine et signification du nom divin Yahvé*. Bonn: Bonner Biblische Beiträge.

———. (1973). *L'Etre manifesté. Méditation philosophique sur l'affirmation de soi, la participation et l'authenticité au Zaire*. Lubumbashi: Synthèse.

———. (1979). "Essai sur la fondation épistémologique d'une philosophie herméneutique en Afrique: Le Cas de la discursivité." *Présence Africaine* no. 109:12–26.

———. (1982). "La Philosophie africaine et son histoire." *Les Etudes philosophiques* 4:407–18.

KI-ZERBO, J. (1972). *Histoire de l'Afrique d'hier à demain*. Paris: Hatier.

———. (1980). "De l'Afrique ustensile à l'Afrique parternaire." In *Africa's Dependence and the Remedies*, V. Y. Mudimbe, ed. Paris: Berger-Levrault.

KOFFI, N. (1976). "L'Impensé de Towa et de Hountondji." Paper presented at the International Seminar on African Philosophy, Addis-Ababa, Dec. 1976.

———. (1977). "Les Modes d'existence matérielle de la philosophie et la question de la philosophie africaine." *Koré, Revue ivoirienne de philosophie et de Culture* nos. 5, 6, 7, and 8.

KOFFI, N., and ABDOU, T. (1980) "Controverses sur l'existence d'une philosophie africaine." In *African Philosophy*, C. Sumner, ed. Addis-Ababa: Chamber Printing House.

KOM, A., ed. (1983). *Dictionnaire des oeuvres littéraires négro-africaines de langue française des origines à 1978*. Sherbrooke: Editions Naaman.

KOYRE, A. (1968). *Metaphysics and Measurement*. London: Chapman & Hall.

KRADER, L. (1973). "The Works of Marx and Engels in Ethnology Compared." *International Review of Social History* 18 (2).

KUNST, H. J. (1967). *L'Africain dans l'art européen*. Cologne: Dumont Presse.

LADRIERE, J. (1979). Foreword to *Métaphore et Métonymie dans les Symboles Parémiologiques*, by O. Nkombe. Kinshasa: Faculté de Théologie Catholique.

LALEYE, I. (1970). *La Conception de la personne dans la pensée traditionnelle yoruba*. Berne: Lang.

———. (1975). *La Philosophie? Pourquoi en Afrique? Une phénoménologie de la question*. Berne: Lang.

———. (1981). "Philosophie et réalités africaines." *Langage et philosophie*. Kinshasa: Faculté de Théologie Catholique.

———. (1982). "La Philosophie, l'Afrique et les philosophes africains. Triple malentendu ou possibilité d'une collaboration féconde." *Présence Africaine* no. 123: 42–62.

LANGER, W. L. (1951). *The Diplomacy of Imperialism 1890–1902*. New York.

LAROUI, A. (1967). *L'Idéologie arabe contemporaine*. Paris: Maspero.

LATOUCHE, S., (1982). "L'Impérialisme précède le développement du capitalisme." *Les Temps modernes* no. 434:515–38.

LAUDE, J. (1979). *L'Art d'Afrique noire*. Paris: Chêne.

LAURENTIN, R. (1977). "Données statistiques sur les chrétiens en Afrique." *Concilium* 126.

LEACH, E. R. (1965). "Frazer and Malinowski." *Encounter*, no. 25:24–26.

———. (1980). "Genesis as Myth." In *Myth and Cosmos*, J. Middleton, ed. Austin: University of Texas Press.

LECLERC, G. (1972) *Anthropologie et colonialisme*. Paris: Fayard.

LEGUN, C. (1958). *Bandoeng, Cairo, Accra*. London: The African Bureau.

LEIRIS, M. (1934). *L'Afrique fantôme*. Paris: Gallimard.

LEUSSE, H. DE. (1971). *Afrique et occident. Heurs et malheurs d'une rencontre, les romanciers du pays noir*. Paris: Orante.

LEUZINGER, E. (1962). *Afrique. L'Art des peuples noirs*. Paris: A. Michel.

LEVINE, V. T. (1986). "Political Cultural Schizophrenia in Francophone Africa." In *Africa and the West*, R. Bjornson and I. J. Mowoe, eds. New York: Greenwood Press.

LEVI-STRAUSS, C. (1955). *Tristes tropiques*. Paris: Plon. (New York: Washington Square Press, 1977.)

———. (1958). *Anthropologie structurale*. Paris: Plon. (*Structural Anthropology*. New York: Basic Books, 1963.)

———. (1962). *La Pensée sauvage*. Paris: Plon. (*The Savage Mind*. Chicago: University of Chicago Press, 1966.)

———. (1964). *Le Cru et le cuit, Mythologiques I*. Paris: Plon. (*The Raw and the Cooked*. New York: Harper and Row, 1968.)

———. (1966). *Du Miel au cendres, Mythologiques II*. Paris: Plon. (*From Honey to Ashes*. London: J. Cape, 1973.)

———. (1968). *L'Origine des manières de table, Mythologiques III*. Paris: Plon. (*The Origin of Table Manners*. New York: Harper and Row, 1979.)

———. (1971). *L'Homme nu*. Paris: Plon. (*The Naked Man*. New York: Harper and Row, 1981.)

———. (1973). *Anthropologie structurale II*. Paris: Plon.

LEVY-BRUHL, L. (1949). *Les Carnets de Lucien Lévy-Bruhl*. Paris: Presses universitaires de France.

———. (1963). *L'Ame primitive*. Paris: Presses universitaires de France.

LIENHARDT, G. (1961). *Divinity and Experience: The Religion of the Dinka.* Oxford: Oxford University Press.

LISSOUBA, P. (1975). *Conscience du développement et démocratie.* Dakar-Abidjan: Nouvelles éditions africaines.

LOFCHIE, M. F. (1968). "Political Theory and African Politics." *Journal of Modern African Studies 6.*

LOKADI, L. (1979). *Différence entre la généralité II du matérialisme dialectique et la généralité II du matérialisme historique. Contribution à la critique de l'epistémologie althussérienne.* Doctoral dissertation. Lubumbashi: Faculté des Lettres.

LONDON, I. D. (1977). "Convergent and Divergent Amplification and its Meaning for Social Science." *Psychological Reports* no. 41: 111–23.

LUFULUABO, F. M. (1962). *Vers une théodicée bantoue.* Paris-Tournai.

———. (1964a) *Orientation préchrétienne de la conception bantoue de l'etre.* Léopoldville (Kinshasa): Centre d'Etudes Pastorales.

———. (1964b). *La Notion luba-bantoue de l'etre.* Tournai: Casterman.

———. (1966). *Perspective théologique bantoue et théologie scholastique.* Malines.

LUGARD, F. (1905). *A Tropical Dependancy.* London: J. Nisbet.

———. (1965). *The Dual Mandate in British Tropical Africa.* London: Cass.

LUMUMBA, P. (1963). *Le Congo, terre d'avenir, est-il menacé?* Brussels: Office de Publicité.

LY, A. (1956) *Les Masses africaines et l'actuelle condition humaine.* Paris: Présence Africaine.

LYNCH, H. R. (1967). *Edward Wilmot Blyden: Pan-Negro Patriot 1832–1912.* London: Oxford University Press.

———, ed., (1978). *Selected Letters of Edward Wilmot Blyden.* New York: KTO Press.

LYONS, R. H. (1975). *To Wash an Aethiop White.* New York: Teachers College Press.

MACGAFFEY, W. (1981). "African Ideology and Belief: A Survey." *African Studies Review* 24 (2/3).

MAFEJE, A. (1976). "The Problem of Anthropology in Historical Perspective: An Inquiry into the Growth of the Social Sciences." *Canadian Journal of African Studies* 10 (2).

MAGUBANE, B. (1968). "Crisis in African Sociology." *East African Journal* 5 (12).

MAIR, L. (1975). *Primitive Government.* Gloucester (Mass.): Peter Smith.

MAKARAKIZA, A. (1959). *La Dialectique des Barundi.* Brussels: Académie Royale des Sciences Coloniales.

MALANDA, D. (1977a). *La Mentalité africaine et l'avenir de la science.* Kisangani: Editions du base.

———. (1977b). *Science et psychologie.* Kisangani: Editions du base.

MALINOWSKI, B. and others. (1938). *Methods of Study of Culture Contact in Africa.* Oxford: Oxford University Press.

MALLOWS, W. (1984). *The Mystery of the Great Zimbabwe.* New York: Norton.

MALULA, J. A. (1976). *L'Eglise de Dieu qui est à Kinshasa vous parle.* Kinshasa: Saint Paul.

———. (1977). "Inaugural Address." *Cahiers des religions africaines* 11, 21–22, 1.

MARTINS VAZ, J. (1970). *Filosofia Tradicional dos Cabindas.* 2 vols. Lisbon: Agencia Geral do Ultramar.

MARX, K. (1975). *Pre-Capitalist Economic Formations.* New York: International Publishers.

MASSAMBA MA MPOLO. (1976). *La Libération des envoûtés.* Yaoundé: Clé.

MATACZYNSKI, D. A. (1984). *A Re-examination of the Jamaa: "Thick Description."* Thesis in Religion. Haverford College.

MAURIER, H. (1974). "Métholodogie de la philosophie africaine." *Cultures et développement* 6.

———. (1976). *Philosophie de l'Afrique noire.* St. Augustin bei Bonn: Verlag des Anthropos-Instituts.

MAZRUI, A. A. (1974). *World Culture and the Black Experience* Seattle: University of Washington Press.

MAZRUI, A. A., and TIDY, M. (1984). *Nationalism and New States in Africa.* London: Heinemann.

MBITI, J. S. (1970). *African Religions and Philosophy.* New York: Anchor.

———. (1971). *New Testament Eschatology in an African Background.* Oxford: Oxford University Press.

MBUZE, L. (1974). *Révolution et humanisme.* Kinshasa: Presses africaines.

———. (1977). *Aux sources d'une révolution.* Kinshasa: Presses africaines.

MCVEIGH, M. J. (1974). *God in Africa.* Boston: Stark.

———. (1980). "La Notion de la religion dans les théologies chrétiennes." *Concilium* 156.

MEEK, R. L. (1976). *Social Science and the Ignoble Savage.* Cambridge: Cambridge University Press.

MEESTER DE RAVENSTEIN, P. DE. (1980a). *Où va l'eglise d'Afrique?* Paris: Cerf.

———. (1980b) *L'Eglise d'Afrique.* Lubumbashi: Saint Paul.

MEILLASSOUX, C. (1964). *Anthropologie économique des Gouro de la Côte d'Ivoire.* Paris: Mouton.

———. (1974). *L'Esclavage dans l'Afrique pré-coloniale.* Paris: Maspero.

———. (1975). *Maidens, Meal and Money.* Cambridge: Cambridge University Press.

MELONE, T. (1962). *De la négritude dans la littérature négro-africaine.* Paris: Présence Africaine.

MEMEL-FOTE, H. (1962). "Rapport sur la civilisation animiste." *Colloque sur les Religions,* 31–58.

———. (1965). "De la paix perpétuelle dans la philosophie pratique des Africains." *Présence Africaine* no. 55: 15–31.

MEMMI, A. (1966). *Portrait du colonisateur précédé du portrait du colonisé.* Paris: Pauvert. (*The Colonizer and the Colonized.* Boston: Beacon Press)

MICHELET, R. (1945). *African Empires and Civilisations.* London.

MIDDLETON, J. (1960). *Lugbara Religion: Ritual and Authority Among an East African People.* London: Oxford University Press.

———., ed. (1980 [1963]). *Myth and Cosmos.* Austin: University of Texas Press.

MILLER, C. L. (1985). *Black Darkness: Africanist Discourse in French.* Chicago: University of Chicago Press.

MOMMSEN, W. J. (1983). *Theories of Imperialism.* London: Weidenfeld and Nicolson.

MONSENGWO PASINYA, L. (1973). *La Notion de nomos dans le pentateuque grec.* Rome: Biblical Institute Press.

MONTEIL, V. (1980). *L'Islam noir.* Paris: Seuil.

MOORE, B. (1958). *Political Power and Social Theory.* Cambridge: Harvard University Press.

MOSELY, A. (1978). "The Metaphysics of Magic." *Second Order* 7 (1 and 2).

MOURALIS, B. (1981). "Mudimbe et le savoir ethnologique." *L'Afrique littéraire et artistique* 58, 1, 112–25.

———. (1984a). "V. Y. Mudimbe et l'odeur du pouvoir." *Politique africaine* no. 13.

———. (1984b). *Littérature et développement.* Paris: Silex-ACCT.

MPONGO, L. (1968). *Pour une anthropologie chrétienne du mariage au Congo.* Kinshasa: Centre d'Etudes Pastorales.

MPOYI-BWATU, T. (1983). "V. Y. Mudimbe ou Le Rêve du promontoir et le blocage dans l'ascenseur. Sur *L'Ecart.*" *Peuples noirs/peuples africains* 33.

MUBENGAYI, C. L. (1966). *Initiation africaine et initiation chrétienne.* Kinshasa: Centre d'Etudes Pastorales.

MUDIMBE, V. Y. (1973). *L'Autre Face du royaume. Une introduction à la critique des langages in Folie.* Lausanne: L'Age d'homme.

———. (1977). "Entretien avec Monseigneur Tshibangu Tshishiku." *Recherches, pédagogie et culture* VI, 32, 16–19.

———, ed. (1980). *Africa's Dependence and the Remedies.* Paris: Berger-Levrault.

———. (1979). "Le Chant d'un Africain sous les Antonins: Lecture du 'Pervigilium Veneris'." *Africa et Roma: Acta Omium Gentium ac Nationum Conventus Latinis Litteris Linguaeque Fovendis.* Rome: 'l'Erma' di Bretschneider.

———. (1981a). *Visage de la philosophie et de la théologie contemporaines au Zaire.* Brussels: Cedaf.

———. (1981b) "Signes thérapeutiques et prose de la vie en Afrique noire. *Social Sciences and Medicine,* 15B.

———. (1982a). "La Pensée africaine contemporaine 1954–1980. Répertoire chronologique des ouvrages de langue française." *Recherche, pédagogie et culture* 56, IX, 68–73.

———. (1982b). *L'Odeur du père. Essai sur des limites de la science et de la vie en Afrique noire.* Paris: Présence Africaine.

———. (1982c) "In Memoriam: Alexis Kagame (1912–1981)." *Recherche, pédagogie et culture,* 56.

———. (1983a). "An African Criticism of Christianity." *Geneva-Africa* 21 (2).

———. (1983b). "African Philosophy as an Ideological Practice: The Case of French-Speaking Africa." *African Studies Review* 26, 3–4.

MUDIMBE-BOYI, M. (1977). *Testi e Immagini. La Missione del "Congo" nelle Relazioni dei Missionari Cappucini Italiani 1645–1700.* Dissertation. Lubumbashi.

MUJYNYA, E. N. C. (1972). *L'Homme dans l'univers des Bantu.* Lubumbashi: Presses universitaires du Zaire.

MULAGO, V. (1955). *L'Union vitale bantu chez les Bashi, les Banyarwanda, et las Barundi face à l'unité vitale ecclésiale.* Dissertation. Rome: Propaganda.

———. (1959). "La Théologie et ses responsabilités." *Présence Africaine* no. 27–28.

———. (1965). *Un visage africain du christianisme.* Paris: Présence Africaine.

———. (1973). *La Religion traditionnelle des Bantu et leur vision du monde.* Kinshasa: Presses universitaires du Zaire.

———. (1981). "Evangélisation et Authenticité." *Aspects du catholicisme au Zaire.* Kinshasa: Faculté de Théologie Catholique.

MURDOCK, G. P. (1959). *Africa: Its Peoples and Their Culture History.* New York: McGraw Hill.

MUZOREWA, G. H. (1985). *The Origins and Development of African Theology.* New York: Orbis.

MUZUNGU, B. (1974). *Le Dieu de nos pères.* Bujumbura: Presses Lavigerie.

MVENG, E. (1965). *L'Art d'Afrique noire. Liturgie et Langage religieux.* Paris: Mame.

———. (1972). *Les Sources grecques de l'histoire négro-africaine.* Paris: Présence Africaine.

———. (1978). "De la sous-mission à la succession." *Civilisation noire et église catholique.* Paris: Présence Africaine.

———. (1983). "Récents développements de la théologie africaine." *Bulletin of African Theology* 5, 9.

N'DAW, A. (1966). "Peut-on parler d'une pensée africaine?" *Présence Africaine* no. 58:32–46.

———. (1983). *La Pensée africaine. Recherches sur les fondements de la pensée négro-africaine.* Dakar: Nouvelles éditions africaines.

NDUKA, O. (1974). "African Traditional Systems of Thought and Their Implications for Nigeria's Education." *Second Order* 3 (1).

NGIMBI-NSEKA. (1979). "Théologie et anthropologie transcendentale." *Revue africaine de théologie* 3, 5.

NGINDU, A. (1968). "La Quatrième Semaine Théologique de Kinshasa et la problématique d'une théologie africaine." *La Revue du Clergé Africain* 2, 4.

———. (1978). *Le Problème de la connaissance religieuse d'après Lucien Laberthonnière*. Kinshasa: Faculté de Théologie Catholique.

———. (1979). "La Théologie africaine. De la polémique à l'irénisme critique." *Bulletin of African Theology*, *1*, (*1*).

———, ed. (1985). *The Mission of the Church Today*. Kinshasa: Saint Paul.

NGOMA, B. (1975). "Pour une orientation authentique de la philosophie en Afrique: l'herméneutique." *Zaire-Afrique* no. 113.

———. (1978). "La Récusation de la philosophie par la société africaine." *Mélanges de philosophie africaine* 3, 85–100. Kinshasa: Faculté de Théologie Catholique.

NGOUABI, M. (1975). *Vers la construction d'une société socialiste en Afrique*. Paris: Présence Africaine.

NGUVULU, A. (1971). *L'Humanisme négro-africain face au développement*. Kinshasa: Okapi.

NJOH-MOUELLE, N. (1970a). *De la médiocrité à l'excellence*. Yaoundé: Clé.

———. (1970b). *Jalons. Recherches d'une mentalité neuve*. Yaoundé: Clé.

———. (1975). *Jalons II. L'Africanisme aujourd'hui*. Yaoundé: Clé.

NKOMBE, O. (1977). "Méthode et point de départ en philosophie africaine: authenticité et libération." *La Philosophie africaine* 69–87. Kinshasa: Faculté de Théologie Catholique.

———. (1978a). "Essai de sémiotique formelle: les rapports différentiels." *Mélanges de philosophie africaine* 3:131–48. Kinshasa: Faculté de Théologie Catholique.

———. (1978b). "Sagesse africaine et libération." *Philosophie et Libération*. Kinshasa: Faculté de Théologie Catholique.

———. (1979) *Métaphore et métonymie dans les symboles parémiologiques. L'Intersubjectivité dans les proverbes tetela*. Kinshasa: Faculté de Théologie Catholique.

NKOMBE, O., and SMET, A. J. (1978). "Panorama de la philosophie africaine contemporaine." *Mélanges de philosophie africaine* 3:263–82. Kinshasa: Faculté de Théologie Catholique.

NKRUMAH, K. (1957). *Ghana. The Autobiography of Kwame Nkrumah*. London: Thomas Nelson.

———. (1961). *I Speak of Freedom*. London: Heinemann.

———. (1962). *Towards Colonial Freedom*. London: Heinemann.

———. (1963). *Africa Must Unite*. London: Heinemann.

———. (1965). *Neo-Colonialism: The Last Stage of Imperialism*. London: Heinemann.

———. (1970). *Consciencism*. London: Panaf Books.

NORDMANN-SEILER, A. (1976). *La Littérature néo-africaine*. Paris: Presses universitaires de France.

NOTHOMB, D. (1965). *Un humanisme africain*. Brussels: Lumen Vitae.

NSOKI, K. (1973). *Problématique de la théologie africaine. Dix ans de débats 1960–1970*. Unpublished thesis. Louvain University.

NTENDIKA, J. (1966). *L'Evolution de la doctrine du purgatoire chez St. Augustin*. Paris: Etudes augustiniennes.

———. (1971). *L'Evocation de l'au-delà dans la prière des morts. Etude de patristique et de liturgie latines*. Louvain-Paris: Béatrice Nauwelaerts.

———. (1977). "Les Responsabilité du département de philosophie et religions africaines de la Faculté de Théologie." *La Philosophie africaine* no. 1:9–20. Kinshasa: Faculté de Théologie Catholique.

———. (1977–79). "La Théologie africaine. Bibliographie sélective." *Revue africaine de théologie* 2, 3, 4, and 6.

NTEZIMANA, E.; HABERLAND, E; and others (1984). "Dossier: Alexis Kagame." *Dialogue* (Kigali), no. 102:19–81.

NYAMITI, C. (1978). "New Theological Approach and New Vision of the Church in Africa." *Revue africaine de théologie* 2, (3).

NYEME, T. (1975). *Munga. Ethique en milieu africain. Gentilisme et christianisme.* Ingenbohl: Imprimerie du P. Théodose.

NYERERE, J. (1967). *Freedom and Unity.* Oxford: Oxford University Press.

———. (1968a). *Ujamaa. Essays on Socialism.* London: Oxford University Press.

———. (1968b). *Freedom and Socialism.* Oxford: Oxford University Press.

———. (1973). *Freedom and Development.* Oxford: Oxford University Press.

NZEGE, A. (1980). *Intelligence et guerre. Essai sur la philosophie politique de H. Bergson.* Doctoral dissertation. Lubumbashi: Faculté des Lettres.

N'ZEMBELE, L. (1983). "L'Avenir d'une dérision: l'ordre du discours africain." *Peuples noirs/peuples africains,* no. 31.

OBBO, C. (1980). *African Women: Their Struggle for Economic Independence.* London: Zed Press.

OBENGA, T. (1973). *L'Afrique dans l'antiquité.* Paris: Présence Africaine.

———. (1980). *Pour une nouvelle histoire.* Paris: Présence Africaine.

ODERA, H. O. (1972). "Mythologies as African Philosophy." *East African Journal* 9, 10.

———, ed. (1983). *Philosophy and Cultures.* Nairobi: Bookwise Limited.

ODUYOYE, M. A. (1986). *Hearing and Knowing. Theological Reflections on Christianity in Africa.* New York: Orbis.

OFORI, P. E. (1977). *Black African Traditional Religions and Philosophy: A Select Survey of the Sources from the Earliest Times to 1974.* Nendeln: Kto Press.

OGILBY, J. (1670). *Africa: being an accurate description of the regions of Aegypt, Barbary, Lybia, and Billedulgerid, the land of the Negroes, Guinée, Aethiopia and the Abyssines.* London: Thomas Johnson.

OGOT, B. A. (1967). *History of the Southern Luo.* Nairobi: East African Publishing House.

OKERE, T. (1971). *Can There Be an African Philosophy? A Hermeneutical Investigation with Special Reference to Ibgo Culture.* Thesis. Louvain University.

———. (1978). "The Assumptions of African Values as Christian Values." *Civilisation noire et église catholique.* Paris: Présence Africaine.

———. (1983). *African Philosophy.* Washington, D.C.: University Press of America.

OKOLO, O. (1979). *Tradition et destin. Essai sur la philosophie herméneutique de P. Ricoeur, M. Heidegger et H. G. Gadamer.* Doctoral dissertation. Lumbumbashi: Faculté des Lettres.

———. (1980). "Tradition et destin: horizons d'une herméneutique philosophique africaine." *Présence Africaine* no. 114.

OKONJI, M. O. (1975). "The Decolonization of the Social Sciences in Africa and Traditional African Psychology." *Thought and Practice* 2 (2).

O'LAUGHLIN, B. (1975). "Marxist Approaches in Anthropology." *Annual Review of Anthropology* 4:341–70.

OLIVER, R. (1956). *How Christian is Africa?* London: Highway Press.

OLUMIDE, L. J. (1948). *The Religion of the Yorubas.* Lagos.

OMBREDANE, A. (1969). *L'Exploration de la mentalité des noirs.* Paris: Presses universitaires de France.

O'MEARA, P., and G. M. CARTER, eds. (1986). *African Independence: The First Twenty-Five Years*. Bloomington: Indiana University Press.

OMOYAJOWO, A. (1984). *Diversity and Unity: The Development and Expansion of the Cherubim and Seraphim Church in Nigeria*. New York: University Press of America.

ONYANWU, K. C. (1975). "African Religion as an Experienced Reality." *Thought and Practice* 2 (2).

ONYEWUENI, I. C. (1982). "A Philosophical Reappraisal of African Belief in Reincarnation." *Présence Africaine* no. 123.

ORTEGA Y GASSET, J., (1973). *An Interpretation of Universal History*. New York: Norton.

ORTIGUES, M. C., and ORTIGUES, E. (1973). *Oedipe Africain*. Paris: U. G. E.

OWUSU, M. (1970). *Uses and Abuses of Political Power*, Chicago: University of Chicago Press.

———. (1978). "The Ethnography of Africa: The Usefulness of the Useless." *American Anthropologist* 80 (2):310–34.

PADMORE, G. (1971). *Pan-Africanism or Communism*. New York: Doubleday.

PARRINDER, G. (1954). *African Traditional Religion*. London: Hutchinson's University Library.

———. (1958). *Witchcraft*. London: Penguin.

P'BITEK, O. (1970). *African Religions in Western Scholarship*. Nairobi: East African Literature Bureau.

———. (1971). *Religion in Central Luo*. Nairobi.

———. (1973). *Africa's Cultural Revolution*. Nairobi: Macmillan.

PERSON, Y. (1968–1975). *Samori*. 3 vol. Dakar: Institut Fondamental d'Afrique Noire.

PIROTTE, J. (1973). *Périodiques missionaires belges d'expression française. Reflets de cinquante années d'evolution d'une mentalité*. Louvain: Publications Universitaires.

PLINY. (1942). *Natural History*. An English translation by H. Rackham, Cambridge: Harvard University Press.

POMONTI, J. C. (1979). *L'Afrique trahie*. Paris: Hachette.

POPPER, K. (1949). *The Poverty of Historicism*. London: Routledge & Kegan Paul.

PORTERES, R. (1950). "Vieilles agricultures de l'Afrique intertropicale." *Agronomie tropicale* 5:489–507.

———. (1962). "Berceaux agricoles primaires sur le continent africain." *Journal of African History* 3:195–210.

POUILLON, F., (1976). *L'Anthropologie économique: courants et problèmes*. Paris: Maspero.

POWELL, E. (1984). *Private Secretary (Female)/Gold Coast*. New York: St. Martin's Press.

PRATT, V. (1972). "Science and Traditional African Religion." *Second Order* 1:(1). *Prêtres noirs s'interrogent (Des)* (1957). Paris: Cerf.

RABEMANANJARA, J. (s.d.). "Alioune Diop, le cénobite de la culture noire." *Hommage à Alioune Diop fondateur de Présence Africaine*. Rome: Editions des Amis de Présence Africaine.

RADIN, P. (1927). *Primitive Man as Philosopher*. New York-London: Appleton.

RALIBERA, R. (1959). "Théologien-Prêtre africain et le développement de la culture africaine." *Présence Africaine* nos. 27–28.

RANDALL-MACIVER, D. (1906). *Medieval Rhodesia*. London: Macmillan.

RANGER, T. (1967). *Revolt in Southern Rhodesia 1896–97: A Study in African Resistance*. London: Heineman.

———. (1969). *The African Churches of Tanzania*. Nairobi: East African Publishing House.

———. (1985). "Religious Movements and Politics in Sub-Saharan Africa." Review essay for the SSRC/ACLS Joint Committee on African Studies, ASA annual meeting, New Orleans.

RANGER, T. and KIMAMBO, I., eds. (1972). *The Historical Study of African Religion.* London: Heinemann.

REED, C. A., ed. (1977). *Origins of Agriculture.* The Hague: Mouton.

RENCONTRES INTERNATIONALES DE BOUAKÉ. (1965). *Tradition et modernisme en Afrique noire.* Paris: Seuil.

———. (1965). *Les Religions africaines traditionnelles.* Paris: Seuil.

REY, P. P. (1966). "The Lineage Mode of Production." *Critique of Anthropology,* 3:27–79.

———. (1971). *Colonialisme, néo-colonialisme et transition au capitalisme. Exemple de la "comilog" au Congo-Brazzaville,* Paris: Maspero.

———. (1973). *Les Alliances de classes.* Paris: Maspero.

RICOEUR, P. (1955). *Histoire et vérité.* Paris: Seuil. (*History and Truth.* Evanston: Northwestern University Press, 1965.)

———. (1969). *Le Conflit des interprétations: Essais d'herméneutique.* Paris: Seuil (*The Conflict of Interpretations.* Evanston: Northwestern University Press).

———. (1984). *The Reality of the Historical Past.* Milwaukee: Marquette University Press.

RIESMAN, P. (1985). "The Person and the Life Cycle: African Social Life and Thought." Review essay for the SSRC/ACLS Joint Committee on African Studies, ASA annual meeting, New Orleans.

RIGBY, P. (1969). *Cattle and Kinship among the Gogo.* Ithaca: Cornell University Press.

———. (1985). *Persistant Pastoralists: Nomadic Societies in Transition.* London: Zed.

ROBINSON, R.; GALLAGHER, J.; and DENNY, A. (1961). *Africa and the Victorians: The Climax of Imperialism in the Dark Continent.* New York: St. Martin's Press.

RODEGEM, F. M. (1961). *Sagesse kirundi.* Tervuren: Musée Royal de l'Afrique Centrale.

———. (1973). *Anthologie rundi.* Paris: A. Colin.

RODNEY, W. (1981). *How Europe Underdeveloped Africa.* Washington, D.C.: Howard University Press.

ROMANO, G. F. (1648). *Breve Relatione del successo della Missione de Frati Minori Cappuccini del Serafico P. S. Francesco al Regno del Congo.* Roma: Sacra Congregatione de Propaganda Fide.

ROMBAUT, M. (1976). *La Parole noire.* Paris: Editions Saint-Germain-des-Prés.

———. (1976). *Nouvelle poésie négro-africaine.* Paris: Editions Saint-Germain-des-Prés.

ROTBERG, R. I. (1970). *Africa and its Explorers: Motives, Method and Impact.* Cambridge: Harvard University Press.

RUCH, E. A. (1974). "Is There an African Philosophy?" *Second Order* 3 (2).

SACHS, I. (1971). *La Découverte du tiers monde.* Paris: Flammarion.

SAGAN, C. (1983). *Broca's Brain: Reflections on the Romance of Science.* New York: Ballantine Books.

SAHLINS, M. (1976). *Culture and Practical Reason.* Chicago: University of Chicago Press.

SAID, E. (1978). *Orientalism.* New York: Pantheon.

SANDERS, E. R. (1969). "The Hamitic Hypothesis: Its Origin and Functions in Time Perspective." *Journal of African History* 10 (4).

SANNEH, L. (1983). *West African Christianity: The Religious Impact.* New York: Orbis.

SARRAUT, A. (1923). *La Mise en valeur des colonies françaises.* Paris: Payot.

SARTRE, J. P. (1943). *L'Etre et le Néant.* Paris: Gallimard. (*Being and Nothingness.* New York: Simon and Schuster, 1956.)

———. (1953). *Qu'est-ce que la littérature?* Paris: Gallimard.

———. (1956). *Situations V.* Paris: Gallimard.

———. (1960). *Critique de la raison dialectique.* Paris: Gallimard.

———. (1976). *Black Orpheus.* Paris: Présence Africaine.

SAUL, J. (1977). *Nationalism, Socialism and Tanzanian history.* In *African Social Studies,* P. C. W. Gutkind and P. Waterman, eds. New York: Monthly Review Press.

SCHEBESTA, P. (1963). *Le Sens religieux des primitifs.* Paris: Mame.

SCHEUB, H. (1971). (1972). *Bibliography of African Oral Narratives.* Madison: University of Wisconsin Press.

———. (1977). *African Oral Narratives, Proverbs, Riddles, Poetry and Song.* Boston: Hall.

———. (1985). "A Review of African Oral Traditions and Literature." *African Studies Review* 26 (2–3):1–72.

SCHILLING, R., ed. (1944). *La Veillée de Vénus. Peruigilium Veneris.* Paris: Collection Budé.

SCHIPPER DE LEEUW, M. (1973). *Le Blanc vu d'Afrique.* Yaoundé: Clé.

SCHMIDT, W. (1931). *The Origin and Growth of Religion.* London: Methuen.

———. (1933–49). *Die Ursprung der Gottesidee.* Munster: Aschendorff.

SCHOLTE, B. (1983). "Cultural Anthropology and the Paradigm Concept: A Brief History of their Recent Convergence." In *Functions and Uses of Disciplinary Histories,* L. Graham, W. Lepenies, and P. Weingart, eds. Dordrecht, Boston: D. Reidel.

SCHUMPETER, J. A. (1951). *Imperialism and Social Classes.* New York: A. M. Kelley.

SCHWARZ, A. (1979). *Colonialistes, africanistes et africains.* Louiseville-Montréal: Nouvelle Optique.

———, ed. (1980). *Les Faux Prophètes de l'Afrique ou l'afr(eu)canisme.* Quebec: Presses de l'Université Laval.

SEBAG, L. (1964). *Marxisme et structuralisme.* Paris: Payot.

SEIDMAN, A. (1985). *The Roots of Crisis in Southern Africa.* Trenton: Africa World Press.

SENE, A. (1966). *Sur le chemin de la négritude.* Cairo: Imprimerie Catholique de Beyrouth.

SENGHOR, L. S. (1961). *Nation et voie africaine du socialisme.* Paris: Présence Africaine.

———. (1962). *Pierre Teilhard de Chardin et la politique africaine.* Paris: Seuil.

———. (1964). *Liberté I: Négritude et humanisme.* Paris: Seuil.

———. (1967a). *Négritude, arabisme, et francité.* Beirut: Dar Al-Kitab Allubnani.

———. (1967b). *Les Fondements de l'africanité ou Négritude et arabité.* Paris: Présence Africaine.

———. (1971). *Liberté II: nation et voie africaine du socialisme.* Paris: Seuil.

———. (1972). "Pourquoi une idéologie négro-africaine?" *Présence Africaine* no. 82:11–38.

———. (1976a). *Pour une relecture africaine de Marx et d'Engels.* Dakar-Abidjan: Nouvelles Editions africaines.

———. (1976b). "Authenticité et négritude." *Zaire-Afrique,* no. 102:81–86.

———. (1977). *Liberté III: négritude et civilisation de l'universel.* Paris: Seuil.

———. (1983). *Liberté IV: socialisme et planification.* Paris: Seuil.

SETILOANE, G. (1976). *Image of God Among the Sotho-Tswana.* Rotterdam: Balkema.

SETILOANE, G. M. (1977). "Where Are We in African Theology?" In *African Theology En Route,* Appiah-Kubi and Torrès eds. New York: Orbis.

SHAW, T. M. (1985). *Towards A Political Economy for Africa: The Dialectics of Dependence*. New York: St. Martin's Press.

SHELTON, A. J. (1963). "Le Principe cyclique de la personnalité africaine." *Présence Africaine* nos. 45–46.

———. (1968). "Causality in African Thought: Igbo and Other." *Practical Anthropology*, 15.

SHEPPERSON, G. (1960). "Notes on Negro-American Influences on the Emergence of African Nationalism." *Journal of African History*, 1, 2.

SHIVJI, I. (1976). *Class Struggles in Tanzania*. London: Heinemann.

SHORTER, A. (1977). *African Christian Theology*. New York: Orbis.

SMET, A. J. (1975a). "Bibliographie sélective des religions traditionnelles de l'Afrique noire" *Cahiers des religions africaines*, 17–18.

———. (1975b). *Philosophie africaine. Textes choisis et bibliographie sélective*. 2 vol. Kinshasa: Presses universitaires du Zaire.

———. (1977a). "Histoire de la philosophie africaine, problèmes et méthodes." *La Philosophie Africaine*, 47–68. Kinshasa: Faculté de Théologie Catholique.

———. (1977b). "Le Père Placide Tempels et son oeuvre publiée." *Revue africaine de théologie* 1, 1.

———. (1977c). "La Jamaa dans l'oeuvre du Père Placide Tempels." *Cahiers des religions africaines*, 11, 21–22, 1.

———. (1977d). "Histoire de la philosophie africaine, problèmes et méthodes." *La Philosophie Africaine*. Kinshasa: Faculté de Théologie Catholique.

———. (1978a). "Le Concept fondamental de l'ontologie bantu." Texte inédit du Père Placide Tempels. *Mélanges de philosophie africaine* 3, 149–80. Kinshasa: Faculté de Théologie Catholique.

———. (1978b). "Bibliographie sélective de la philosophie africaine. Répertoire chronologique." 181–262. *Mélanges de Philosophie Africaine*. op. cit.

———. (1980). *Histoire de la Philosophie Africaine Contemporaine*. Kinshasa: Faculté de Théologie Catholique.

SMITH, P. (1970a) "La Forge de l'intelligence." *L'Homme* 10, 2.

———. (1970b). "La Lance d'une jeune fille." In *Echanges et communications. Mélanges offerts à Cl. Lévi-Strauss*, J. Pouillon et P. Maranda, eds. Paris: La Haye.

———. (1975). *Le Récit Populaire au Rwanda*. Paris: Classiques Africains.

SNOWDEN, F. M. (1970). *Blacks in Antiquity: Ethiopians in the Greco-Roman Experience*. Cambridge: Harvard University Press.

SODIPO, J. O. (1973). "Notes on the concept of Cause and Chance in Yoruba Traditional Thought." *Second Order* 2 (2).

———. (1975). "Philosophy in Africa Today." *Thought and Practice* 2 (2).

———. (1983). "Philosophy, Science, Technology and Traditional African Thought." In *Philosophy and Cultures*, H. O. Oruka, ed. Nairobi: Bookwise Ltd.

SOUSBERGHE, L. DE. (1951). "A propos de 'La Philosophie bantoue'." *Zaire* 5:821–28.

SOUTHALL, A. (1976). "Orientations in Political Anthropology." *Canadian Journal of African Studies* 10 (2).

———. (1983). "The Contribution of Anthropology to African Studies." *African Studies Review* 26, (3/4).

SOUZA, G. DE. (1975). *La Conception de "vie" chez les Fons*. Cotonou: Editions du Bénin.

SOW, I. E. B. (1977). *Psychiatrie dynamique africaine*. Paris: Payot.

———. (1978). *Les Structures anthropologiques de la folie en Afrique noire*. Paris: Payot.

SOYINKA, W. (1976). *Myth, Literature and the African World*. Cambridge: Cambridge University Press.

STAVENHAGEN, R. (1971). "Decolonializing Applied Social Sciences." *Human Organization* 30 (4).

SUMNER, C., ed. (1974–1981). *Ethiopian Philosophy:* I, 1974, *The Book of the Wise Philosophers;* II, 1974, *The Treatise of Zär'a Yacob and of Walda Haywat;* III, 1978, *The Treatise of Zär'a Yacob and of Walda Haywat;* IV, 1981, *The Life and Maxims of Skandas.* Addis-Ababa: Central Printing Press.

———. (1980). *African Philosophy. Philosophie Africaine.* Addis-Ababa: Chamber Printing House.

———. (1983). "An Ethical Study of Ethiopian Philosophy." In *Philosophy and Cultures,* H. O. Oruka, ed. Nairobi: Bookwise Ltd.

SUNDKLER, B. (1964). *Bantu Prophets in South Africa.* London: Oxford University Press.

———. (1976). *Zulu Zion.* Oxford: Oxford University Press.

SURET-CANALE, J. (1958). *Afrique noire occidentale et centrale.* Paris: Editions Sociales.

TAYLOR, J. V. (1963). *The Primal Vision.* London: SCM Press Ltd.

TCHIDIMBO, E. M. (1963). *L'Homme noir dans l'église.* Paris: Présence Africaine.

TEMPELS, P. (1945). *La Philosophie bantoue.* Elisabethville: Lovania. (Paris: Présence Africaine, 1949).

———. (1959). *Bantu Philosophy.* Paris: Présence Africaine.

———. (1962). *Notre rencontre I.* Léopoldville (Kinshasa): Centre d'Etudes Pastorales.

———. (1979). *Philosophie bantu.* Introduction and revision of the Rubbens translation by A. J. Smet. Kinshasa: Faculté de Théologie Catholique.

TERRAY, E. (1969). *Le Marxisme devant les sociétés primitives.* Paris: Maspero.

THEUWS, J. A. T. (1951). "Philosophie bantoue et philosophie occidentale." *Civilisations,* 1.

———. (1954). "Textes luba." *Bulletin trimestriel du Centre d'Etudes des Problèmes Sociaux Indigènes* 27:1–153.

———. (1983). *Word and World. Luba Thought and Literature.* St. Augustin: Verlag des Anthropos-Instituts.

THOMAS, L. V. (1958). "Positivisme et métaphysique. Réflexions à propos de la culture noire." *Aspects de la culture noire.* Paris: Fayard.

———. (1960). "Un système philosophique sénégalais: la cosmologie Diola" *Présence Africaine* nos. 32–33.

———. (1982). *La Mort africaine. Idéologie funéraire en Afrique noire.* Paris: Payot.

THOMAS, L. V.; LUNEAU, R.; and DONEUX, J. L. (1969). *Les Religions d'Afrique noire.* Paris: Fayard/Denoël.

THORNTON, A. P. (1959). *The Imperial Idea and Its Enemies.* London: Macmillan.

THORNTON, R. (1983). "Narrative Ethnography in Africa 1850–1920: The Creation and Capture of an Appropriate Domain for Anthropology." *Man* 18 (3).

TOBNER, O. (1982). "Cheikh Anta Diop, l'hérétique." *Peuples noirs, peuples africains* 30:85–91.

TORT, P., and DESALMAND, P. (1979). *Sciences Humaines et Philosophie en Afrique. La Différence Culturelle.* Paris: Hatier.

TOURE, S. (1959a). *Expérience guinéenne et unité africaine.* Paris: Présence Africaine.

———. (1959b). *Guinée. Prélude à l'indépendance.* Paris: Présence Africaine.

———. (1959c). *République de Guinée.* Conakry: Imprimerie Patrice Lumumba.

TOWA, M. (1971a). *Léopold Sédar Senghor: négritude ou servitude.* Yaoundé: Clé.

———. (1971b). *Essai sur la problématique philosophique dans l'Afrique actuelle.* Yaoundé: Clé.

———. (1979). *L'Idée d'une philosophie africaine.* Yaoundé: Clé.

TRILLES, R. P. (1931). *Les Pygmées de la forêt équatoriale.* Paris: Bloud et Gay.

TSHIAMALENGA, N. (1973). "La Vision ntu de l'homme. Essai de philosophie lin-
    guistique et anthropologique." *Cahiers des religions africaines* 7:176–99.
———. (1974). "La Philosophie de la faute dans la tradition luba." *Cahiers des
    religions africaines* 8:167–86.
———. (1977a). "Qu'est-ce que la 'philosophie africaine." *La Philosophie Africaine*
    I, 33–46. Kinshasa: Faculté de Théologie Catholique.
———. (1977b). "Langues bantu et philosophie. Le cas du ciluba." *La Philosophie
    africaine* I:147–58. Kinshasa: Faculté de Théologie Catholique.
———. (1980). *Denken und Sprechen Ein Beitrag zum Relativitäts Prinzip am
    Beispiel einer Bantusprache (Ciluba)*. Dissertation. Frankfurt/Main.
———. (1981). "La Philosophie dans la situation actuelle de l'Afrique." *Combats
    pour un Christianisme africain*. Kinshasa: Faculté de Théologie Catholique.
TSHIBANGU, T. (1965). *Théologie positive et théologie spéculative. Position tradition-
    nelle et nouvelle problématique*. Louvain-Paris: Béatrice Nauwelaerts.
———. (1974). *Le Propos d'une théologie africaine*. Kinshasa: Presses universitaires
    du Zaire.
———. (1977). "L'Afrique noire et le christianisme." *Cahiers des religions africaines*
    II, 21–22, 1.
———. (1980). *Théologie comme science au XXᵉ siècle*. Kinshasa: Presses univer-
    sitaires du Zaire.
TSHIBANGU, T. and VANNESTE, A. (1960). "Débat sur la théologie africaine." *Revue du
    Clergé Africain* 15.
TSHIBANGU, W. M. (1972). *Science et superstition chez A. Comte*. Ph.D. dissertation.
    Dijon: Faculté des Lettres.
TURGOT, A. R. J. (1913–1923). *Oeuvres de Turgot et documents le concernant, avec
    une bibliographie et notes*. G. Schelle, ed. Paris, 5 vols.
TURNBULL, C. M. (1962). *The Lonely African*. New York: Simon and Schuster.
TURNER, V. W. (1952). *The Lozi Peoples of North-Western Rhodesia*. London:
    International African Institute.
———. (1964) *Schism and Continuity in an African Society*. Manchester: Man-
    chester University Press.
———. (1969). *The Ritual Process*. Chicago: Aldine.
———. (1975). *Revelation and Divination in Ndembu Ritual*. Ithaca: Cornell Uni-
    versity Press.
———. (1981). *The Drums of Affliction: A Study of Religious Processes among the
    Ndembu of Zambia*. Ithaca: Cornell University Press.
TUTU, D. (1984). *Hope and Suffering*. Grand Rapids: W. B. Eerdmans.
UGIRASHEBUJA, O. (1977). *Dialogue entre la poésie et la pensée dans l'oeuvre de
    Heidegger*. Brussels: Lumen Vitae.
VAN CAENEGHAM, R. (1956). *La Notion de Dieu chez les Balubas du Kasai*. Brussels:
    Académie Royale des Sciences Coloniales.
VAN LIERDE, J. (1963). *La Pensée politique de Patrice Lumumba*. Paris: Présence
    Africaine.
VAN OBERBERGH, C. (1913). *Les Nègres de l'Afrique*. Bruxelles: A. de Wit.
VAN PARYS, J. M. (1978). "Philosophie en Afrique. Analyse du séminaire sur la
    philosophie africaine d'Addis-Abeba. 1–3 December 1976." *Mélanges de
    philosophie africaine*. Kinshasa: Faculté de Théologie Catholique.
———. (1981). "Etat actuel de l'activité philosophique en Afrique." *Langage et
    société*. Kinshasa: Faculté de Théologie Catholique.
VANSINA, J. (1961). *De la tradition orale. Essai de méthode historique*. Tervuren:
    Musée Royal de l'Afrique Centrale.
———. (1965). *Les Anciens Royaumes de la savanne*. Kinshasa: Institut de Re-
    cherches Economiques et Sociales.

———. (1972a). *La Légende du passé: traditions orales du Burundi.* Brussels-Tervuren: Musée Royal de l'Afrique Centrale.

———. (1972b). "Once Upon a Time: Oral Traditions as History in Africa." In *Historical Studies Today,* F. Gilbert and S. R. Graubard, eds.

———. (1978). *The Children of Woot: A History of the Kuba Peoples.* Madison: University of Wisconsin Press.

———. (1983). "Is Elegance a Proof? Structuralism and African History." *History in Africa* 10:307–48.

VAN WING, J. (1949). "Humanisme chrétien africain." *Lumen Vitae* 4 (1).

VAUGHAN, A. T. (1982). "From White Man to Redskin: Changing Anglo-American Perception of the American Indian." *The American History Review* 87.

VERGER, P. (1968). *Flux et reflux de la traite des nègres entre le Golf du Bénin et Bahia de Todos os Santos du XVᵉ au XIXᵉ siècle.* Paris: Mouton.

VERHAEGEN, B. (1974). *Introduction à l'histoire immédiate.* Gembloux: Duculot.

———. (1978). *L'Enseignement universitaire au Zaïre.* Paris: L'Harmattan.

———. (1979). "Religion et politique en Afrique noire." *Religions africaines et christianisme* 1, 179–94. Kinshasa: Faculté de Théologie Catholique.

VETO, M. (1962). "Unité et dualité de la conception du mal chez les Bantu orientaux." *Cahiers d'Etudes Africaines* 8.

VEYNE, P. (1984). *Writing History.* Middletown: Wesleyan University Press.

VILASCO, G. (1983). "Philosophie, anthropologie et culture." In *Philosophy and Cultures,* H. O. Oruka ed. Nairobi: Bookwise Ltd.

VINCKE, J. L. (1973). *Le Prix du péché. Essai de psychanalyse existentielle des traditions européenne et Africaine.* Kinshasa-Lubumbashi: Mont Noir.

WAGNER, J. (1962). *Les Poètes noirs des Etats-Unis.* Paris: Istra.

WAGNER, R. (1981). *The Invention of Culture.* Chicago and London: University of Chicago Press.

WALLERSTEIN, I. (1961). *Africa: The Politics of Independence.* New York: Random House.

———. (1967). *Africa: The Politics of Unity.* New York: Random House.

———. (1979). *The Capitalist World Economy.* Cambridge: Cambridge University Press.

———. (1983). "The Evolving Role of the Africa Scholar in African Studies." *African Studies Review* 26 (3–4):155–61.

WAMBA-DIA-WAMBA, E. (1980). "La Philosophie en Afrique ou Les défis de l'Africain philosophe." In *Les Faux Prophètes de l'Afrique ou l'Afr(eu)canisme,* A. Schwarz, ed. Québec: Presses de l'Université Laval.

WASSING, R. S. (1969). *L'Art de l'Afrique noire.* Fribourg: Office du Livre.

WAUTHIER, C. (1964). *L'Afrique des Africains. Inventaire de la négritude.* Paris: Seuil.

WEBER, M. (1978). *Economy and Society.* Berkeley: University of California Press.

WHITE, H. (1979). "Michel Foucault." *Structuralism and Since.* J. Sturrock, ed. Oxford: Oxford University Press.

WILLAME, J. C. (1971). "Recherches sur les modes de production cynégétique et lignager." *L'Homme et la Société* 19:101–20.

———. (1976). "L'Autre Face du royaume ou Le Meurtre du père." *Genève-Afrique* 15 (1).

WILLIAMS, G. (1967). *The Expansion of Europe in the XVIIIth Century. Overseas Rivalry. Discovery and Exploitation.* New York: Walker & Company.

WILSON, B. R., ed. (1970). *Rationality.* Oxford: Basil Blackwell.

WIREDU, J. E. (1973). "Logic and Ontology" *Second Order* 2 (1–2).

———. (1977). "How Not to Compare African Thought with Western Thought." In *African Philosophy: An Introduction,* R. Wright, ed. Washington: University Press of America.

———. (1980). *Philosophy and African Culture.* Cambridge: Cambridge University Press.

WITTE, C. M. DE. (1958). "Les Bulles pontificales et l'expansion portugaise au XVᵉ siècle." *Revue d'histoire ecclésiastique* 53.

WOLPE, H., ed. (1980). *The Articulation of Modes of Production.* London: Routledge & Kegan Paul.

WORLD BANK. (1984). *Toward Sustained Development in Sub-Saharan Africa.* Washington, D.C.: The World Bank.

WRIGHT, R. (1977). *African Philosophy: An Introduction.* Washington: University Press of America.

YAI, O. (1977). "Theory and Practice in African Philosophy: The Poverty of Speculative Philosophy." *Second Order* 6 (2). French version: *Présence Africaine* (1978) no. 108.

YOUNG, M. C. (1965). *Politics in the Congo.* Princeton: Princeton University Press.

———. (1982). *Ideology and Development in Africa.* New Haven: Yale University Press.

ZAHAN, D. (1959). *Sociétés d'initiation bambara.* Paris: Mouton.

———. (1963). *La Dialectique du verbe chez les Bambara.* Paris: Mouton.

———. (1979). *The Religion, Spirituality, and Thought of Traditional Africa.* Chicago: University of Chicago Press.

ZOA, I. (1957). *Pour un nationalisme chrétien au Cameroun.* Yaoundé: Saint Paul.

ZUURE, B. (1932). *L'Ame du Murundi.* Paris: Beauchesne.

INDEX

Abdou, T., 160
Abraham, W. E., 39–41, 79
Acculturation, 20, 68, 191–92
Adaptation, theologies of, 57
Adotévi, S., 36–37, 167
Adventures in a Mud Hut (Barley), 21–22
Afana, Osende, 96
Africa (Schulter), 12
African Allegory (Ripa), 12
Africa and the Africans (Blyden), 99, 100
African Empires and Civilizations (Michelet), 88
African Genesis (Frobenius), 182
African genesis, hypotheses of, 16, 22
Africanism, 9, 166–68, 176, 179; Blyden's attitude toward, 124
Africanity, 37, 79
African languages, 60, 123, 169; missionaries' and anthropologists' knowledge of, 65–66
African nation, concept of, 115–16
African Personality, 38; Blyden as precursor of, 98, 131. *See also* Black personality
African Studies, 9, 36, 44, 169, 183
Afrique ambiguë (Balandier), 38
Aguolo, C., 161
Ahidjo, A., 185–86
Ajayi, J. F. A., 194–95
Akambas (people), 152
Alexander VI (pope), 45
"Alogicality of Immortality, The" (Bodunrin), 162
Alterity. *See* Otherness
Althusser, L., 158, 160, 179
American Colonization Society, 103, 104
Amin, S., 5
Amo, A. G., 162
Anglican Church, 19, 55
Anobo, M.: on Senghor, 94
Anthropological philosophy. *See* Ethnophilosophy *Anthology of New Negro and Malagasy Poetry* (Senghor), 83–84
Anthropology, 16–22, 37, 67–69, 75–78, 184–85; African critique of, 38; and African sociology, 166; Blyden compared to founders of, 119; and Christianity, 56–58; commitment to African values, 60, 88–89; concept of primitive philosophy, 135, 142; on distance from Same to Other, 81; and ethnocentrism, 19; Foucault on, 16, 29; impact on black intelligentsia, 88; Lévi-Strauss on, 28–29; and marginality, 6; mis-

sionaries' information as, 64–67; negritude's influence, 85, 86; and philology, 18; and philosophy, 152, 158, 168; on primitive philosophies, 143–44; relationship to history, 176, 178; structuralist, 198; Tempels' differentiation from, 137
Anyidoho, K., 182
Arabic language: Blyden on, 123, 126
Arendt, Hannah: on racism, 108
Aristotelianism, 146, 147
Arnold, S., 182
Art, African, 9–12
Art, European: depiction of Africans, 6–9, 12
Arusha Declaration, 95
Astronomy, 13–15
Authenticity, 153, 169, 174
Avènement de l'Afrique noire . . . , L' (Brunschwig), 38–39
Awolowo, O., 95
Azikiwe, Nnamdi, 90, 95, 98, 131
Azombo-Menda, S. M.: on Senghor, 94

Ba, A. Hampate, 96
Bachelard, G., 137
Baeta, C. G., 55
Bahoken, J. C.: on Christianity, 56
Baker, Sir Samuel, 118
Balance Sheets of Imperialism (Clark), 3
Balandier, Georges, 80, 88, 89, 166, 177; *Afrique ambiguë*, 38
"Bantou Problematique, Le" (Eboussi-Boulaga), 157–58
Bantu (people), 50, 53–54, 138–39, 169
Bantu languages, 145–46
Bantu philosophy, 58; Crahay's lecture on, 154, 155–56; Kagame on, 145–52; Tempels on, 136–42, 144, 151–52
Bantu Philosophy (Tempels), 50, 67, 136–42, 144, 149, 153, 178; Crahay on, 155; Kagame on, 146
Banyarwanda (people), language of, 162
Barley, N., 21–22
Barthes, R., 129
Basic Ethiopian Philosophical Texts (Sumner, ed.), 202
Baumstark, A., 163
Being, 28, 162; in Bantu philosophy, 138–41, 147–48; in Western philosophy, 140. *See also* Ontology
Being and Nothingness (Sartre), 85
Bellman, B. L., 183
Benedict XV (pope), 53